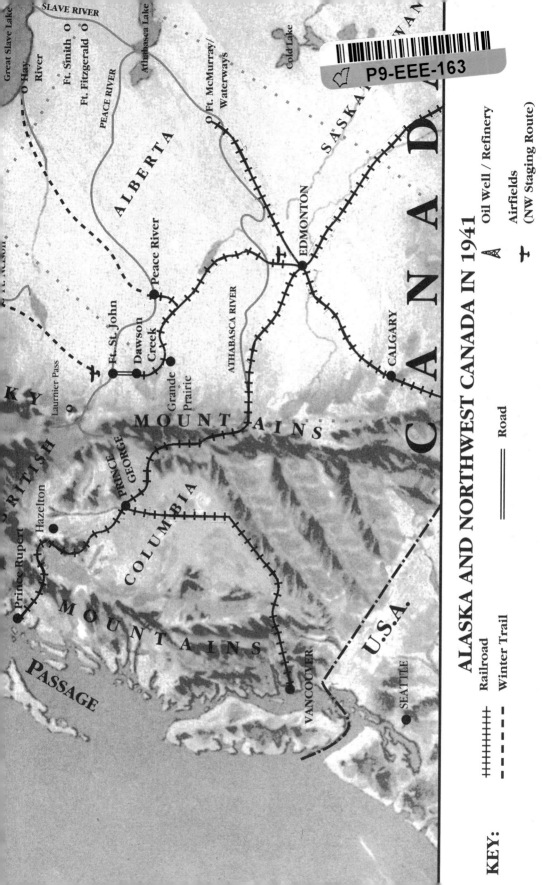

ALASKA AND NORTHWEST CANADA IN 1941

KEY:

+++++++++ Railroad

– – – – – Winter Trail

========= Road

⚑ Oil Well / Refinery

✈ Airfields (NW Staging Route)

GREAT SLAVE LAKE

SLAVE RIVER

Great Slave Lake

O Hay River

Ft. Smith O

Ft. Fitzgerald O

Athabasca Lake

PEACE RIVER

Gold Lake

Ft. McMurray / Waterways O

ALBERTA

SASKATCHEWAN

CANADA

Peace River

Ft. Nelson

Ft. St. John

Dawson Creek

Laurier Pass

Grande Prairie

ROCKY

MOUNTAINS

ATHABASCA RIVER

EDMONTON

CALGARY

BRITISH

COLUMBIA

Hazelton

PRINCE GEORGE

Prince Rupert

PASSAGE

COLUMBIA

MOUNTAINS

VANCOUVER

U.S.A.

SEATTLE

P9-EEE-163

Northwest Epic

S-363

Northwest Epic

The Building of the Alaska Highway

Heath Twichell

ST. MARTIN'S PRESS • NEW YORK

Note to Reader: On all maps, the road connecting Anchorage with Big Delta should instead connect Valdez with Big Delta.

*The photo that appears in the introduction
is reprinted courtesy of the U.S. National Archives.*

NORTHWEST EPIC. Copyright © 1992 by Heath Twichell. All rights reserved. Printed in the United States of America. No part of this book may be used or reproduced in any manner whatsoever without written permission except in the case of brief quotations embodied in critical articles or reviews. For information, address St. Martin's Press, 175 Fifth Avenue, New York, N.Y. 10010.

Design by Ann Gold

Library of Congress Cataloging-in-Publication Data

Twichell, Heath
    Northwest epic : the building of the Alaska Highway / Heath
Twichell.
        p.   cm.
    ISBN 0-312-07754-8
    1. Alaska Highway—History.   I. Title.
F1060.92T85   1992
979.8—dc20   92-941
                                                        CIP

First Edition: July 1992
10 9 8 7 6 5 4 3 2 1

FOR MY FATHER, A BUILDER OF HIGHWAYS AND BRIDGES.
THIS IS THE STORY HE STARTED TO WRITE . . .

CONTENTS

Part One: Route Survey

Early explorers and adventurers; overland routes to Alaska
during the nineteenth century; proposals for a highway to
Alaska prior to WWII.

Pioneers of aviation in Alaska and the Canadian Northwest;
strategic vulnerability of the region at the outbreak of WWII;
construction of the airfields of the Northwest Staging Route
as a defensive measure.

Part Two: Rough Cut for a Road

The decision to build the Alaska Highway after Pearl
Harbor; the Army's plan—first an emergency supply trail
for the airfields and Alaska, and then a finished highway;
gambles and risks involved; opposition to the plan; General
Hoge's hurried reconnaissance; the worsening strategic
situation in the Pacific.

Part Three: Finishing Up

Part Four: Was This Trip Necessary?

Epilogue

LIST OF MAPS AND TABLES

INTRODUCTION

This is a story about 1,500 miles of gravel road. Quickly built by the U.S. Army over an unmapped stretch of the Canadian Rockies in the tense aftermath of Japan's attack on Pearl Harbor, the Alaska Highway was intended to provide an emergency supply line to the airfields of the Northwest Staging Route and to U.S. military bases in Alaska. Initially conceived in simple terms, the wartime highway soon spawned an amazing array of related construction projects across more than 1 million square miles of western Canada and Alaska, an area four times the size of Texas.

In addition to connecting the chain of airfields it was designed to support, by 1944 the Alaska Highway had its own oilfield and a newly built refinery and pipeline system (known as CANOL)—all linked by telephone lines, a network of temporary landing strips, and much, much more. At a time when skilled workmen made $1.50 an hour and oil sold for less than $1 per barrel, the total cost of this enormous enterprise came to $500 million in U.S. and Canadian dollars. No other World War II construction project was more expensive.

Because the Japanese never managed to cut the sea lines of communication to Alaska, neither the Alaska Highway nor CANOL saw heavy military use. But in terms of human effort, resourcefulness, and gritty endurance, they were awesome achievements. Working in a vast, empty land where the temperature could drop 80 degrees overnight and the black flies and mosquitos were almost as formidable as the Japanese, a hastily organized force of 46,000 soldiers and civilian contractors took less than two years to finish what one officer, a West Point–trained Army colonel, called the "biggest and hardest job since the Panama Canal."

That officer was my father, Heath Twichell, Sr. His story is one of many I want to tell. So are the stories of Charlie MacDonald, the native guide who helped his regiment find a pathway through the Rockies, and of Lieutenant General Brehon B. Somervell, the Pentagon's suavely ruthless chief logistician. Most of all, this is a story about people: about individual explorers, adventurers, aviators, soldiers, and construction workers; citizens of the United States and Canada; whites, blacks, and Native Americans. Some were heroes, and a few were less than admirable, but most were simply men and women doing what they had to do under extraordinary circumstances. For many of them, it was the adventure of a lifetime.

Yet both the Alaska Highway and CANOL provoked almost continuous public criticism. Early detractors predicted that neither would have much postwar value. Later critics questioned their military usefulness in comparison to their skyrocketing cost. Most were appalled by the waste and mismanagement revealed during a wartime investigation of CANOL conducted by Senator Harry S. Truman, whose political career was boosted by the attendant publicity.

Fifty years ago most people saw the Northwest Staging Route, CANOL, and the Alaska Highway as three separate projects. Today it is easier to see them as one gigantic military enterprise, a joint U.S.-Canadian attempt to ensure that vital wartime supplies and reinforcements could reach Alaska regardless of whose navy controlled the sea lanes of the North Pacific. I shall try to do justice to both perspectives by developing each major element of the story in one or more chapters and then weaving the various strands together within a rough chronological framework. The Alaska Highway is the central thread of my narrative.

For more than a century before the outbreak of World War II, explorers, adventurers, traders, and settlers had struggled to find the easiest overland route from the south and east into Alaska and the Canadian Yukon. Of the countless pathways they tried, only a few were developed into well-used trails. None was easy or short. The difficult geography, climatic extremes, and sparse population of the northwest corner of the North American continent ensured that a road to Alaska would not just happen. The story of how it finally came to be built thus begins back in 1789 with Alexander Mackenzie, the first European to search for a route through the Rocky Mountains to the Pacific Ocean.

PART ONE

Route Survey

1

"Advise Go by Skagway"

Most roads just happen. Following the easiest contours of the land, a footpath broadens with increasing use into a trail and eventually becomes a thoroughfare. Paving and grading do not make such a highway; they only confirm its existence. But some roads do not follow the dictates of terrain, time, and custom. Instead they are built in response to more urgent imperatives.

When military necessity dictated that the U.S. Army build a highway across Canada to Alaska after the Japanese attack on Pearl Harbor, the highway's inland location immediately provoked strong protests from powerful West Coast political and economic interests. They and others also questioned the military value of this ambitious undertaking, particularly when its scope, complexity, and cost began to mushroom. The Alaska Highway soon became the most controversial construction project of World War II. A discussion of the routes—and the means—most often used to reach the far north in the years before 1942 will help explain what all the fuss was about.

Among the first attempts at overland travel by Westerners in this forbidding region of North America were two remarkable journeys made by a Scottish fur trader named Alexander Mackenzie in the late eighteenth century. Mackenzie's employers in the North West Company were constantly seeking ways to expand their control of the thriving fur trade. Success meant finding profitable new districts and the best routes for taking goods in and furs out. These men knew that a wide river (later named the Yukon) emptied into the Bering Sea from the unexplored interior of Russian Alaska. They also knew that two good-sized streams, the Peace and the Athabasca, joined east of the Rockies to form the Slave River, which in turn drained northward into the stormy waters of Great Slave Lake, the fifth largest lake on the continent.

Although the land that stretched north from Great Slave Lake to the Arctic Ocean and west to the Pacific was terra incognita to Mackenzie and his associates, they were certain of one thing: it had the potential to make them very wealthy. They also suspected that Great Slave Lake held the headwaters of the mighty Alaskan river that flowed down to the Bering Sea, 1,600 miles to the west. If that suspicion proved correct, it could multiply their fortunes many times over. The prospect of a gigantic arc of a river connecting Great Slave Lake with the Pacific Ocean not only opened up incredible possibilities for trade throughout a million square miles of wilderness, it represented a freshwater approximation of the long-sought sea route to Asia, the fabled Northwest Passage.[1]

On June 29, 1789, accompanied by five white companions and several native guides, Alexander Mackenzie set out across Great Slave Lake and into the westward-flowing river it fed, to extend his company's control of the fur trade as far as he and his party could paddle their heavily laden canoes. As the explorers left the lake behind and the river bent northward, Mackenzie's guides grew more fearful, saying that the tribes ahead would kill them all. The persistent Scot, whose foppish good looks masked a fierce will, coaxed them to proceed by alternating threats with cajolery. The scattered native bands they encountered downstream proved more furtive than fearsome.

Mackenzie's summer trip northward down the broad stream that now bears his name was a success in every respect but one. Instead of curving westward toward the Pacific beyond the northern reaches of the Rockies, Mackenzie's great river continued its northerly flow past low hills and ever scrubbier vegetation until it meandered into the Arctic Ocean through a broad delta studded with innumerable muddy hillocks. Maps of North America thenceforth showed the Mackenzie as the continent's second longest river, and the North West Company soon established a string a fortified trading stations at 100-mile intervals along its course and on its northern tributaries.

Three years later, Mackenzie tried again to find an all-water route to the Pacific. This time he followed the Peace River 800 miles west to its headwaters in the Rockies and then, after a series of tortuous portages through the coastal mountains, became the first European to cross the continent north of Mexico. As a reward from the British government for these two great journeys of exploration, Mackenzie was knighted in 1802.

The search for an all-water route through the Rockies continued well into the nineteenth century, although little exploration was undertaken during the "Pemmican War," a bloody fifteen-year struggle for control of the fur trade that ended in 1821 with the absorption of the North West Company by its archrival, the Hudson's Bay Company. Mackenzie and later Hudson's Bay Company explorers never found a Northwest Passage. But they did pioneer most of the portage trails linking the Mackenzie River's western tributaries with various rivers in Alaska and along Canada's Pacific coast, much to the profit of company stockholders and the delight of mapmakers. Mainly used by tough, experienced trappers and traders until the Gold Rush era, these routes could only be traversed by means of an arduous combination of paddling and portage or (during winter) dogsled and snowshoes.[2]

Until the second half of the nineteenth century, most of what is now British Columbia remained a wilderness, penetrated only by an occasional explorer. By 1865, however, after gold was discovered along the Fraser River and in the Cariboo Mountains, settlements began springing up throughout the interior. Five years later, the province entered the Dominion of Canada. The crossing of the Canadian Rockies by the great east-west transcontinental railroads near the turn of the century further accelerated the area's development, although the northern half of the province remained isolated.[3] Before the Gold Rush of 1898, the only serious attempt to cut anything resembling a road northward across the Stikine Plateau was made by the Western Union Telegraph Company (see map B on page 13).

After several unsuccessful attempts by Cyrus W. Field to lay a transatlantic telegraph cable in 1857–1858, Western Union decided in 1865 to back another entrepreneur, Peter M. Collins. He planned to connect Europe and America telegraphically by using a much longer but predominately overland line running through Canada, Alaska, and Russia. The only undersea cable involved would be a 50-mile stretch across the Bering Strait. Collins rapidly obtained the necessary financing and foreign concessions and assembled men and equipment for the job. Line surveys, supervised by the well-known naturalist Robert Kennicott, were begun in Alaska, while similar work was done by a team operating in Siberia. To direct the effort in

Canada, Collins chose Colonel Charles C. Bulkley, a Union veteran of the Civil War.

A fleet of boats carrying 500 men, 1,200 miles of telegraph wire, and several tons of green glass insulators landed at the mouth of the Fraser River in the summer of 1865. The first 200 miles were easy; Bulkley's workmen simply cut poles and strung wire alongside the recently constructed Cariboo Road, which had been built to open up the gold fields. Farther north, Bulkley's crews cleared a swath through forested valleys and over rugged passes. Behind them came the pole setters and the linemen. Despite sub-zero temperatures and fearsome blizzards, the work continued throughout the winter. By New Year's Day, 1866, the Collins Overland Telegraph had reached the banks of the Yukon. Meanwhile, across the Bering Strait, the Siberian team was making equally rapid progress toward St. Petersburg.

Six months later, Collins brought the project to an abrupt halt. Cyrus Field's fifth try at a transatlantic cable in the summer of 1866 was a success. As a result, despite having invested more than $3 million in the overland route, Western Union withdrew its backing of Collins's project. Thousands upon thousands of freshly cut poles festooned with a working telegraph line suddenly became expendable artifacts of the new civilization invading the Pacific Northwest. The native people of the region soon overcame their diffidence toward these strange totems and began to make practical use of them. The shiny glass insulators became a new denomination in the local wampum, while the telegraph wire was used to reinforce many a rope suspension bridge.[4]

After the discovery of gold in the Canadian Yukon in 1897, every existing northbound trail was suddenly crowded with fortune seekers, most of whom were ignorant of the hardships that lay ahead and ill-equipped to survive them. Enough of Colonel Bulkley's telegraph pathway to the Yukon remained intact to serve as a guide for gold seekers unable to afford the price of a steamship ticket. But most prospectors sailed up the Inside Passage from western ports in the United States and Canada, landing at booming Skagway and then struggling north over White Pass or Chilcoot Pass toward the gold fields 600 miles farther inland. As word spread of both the richness of the strike and the rigors of the journey, more than one enterprising individual discovered that easier gold could be mined in the pathetic eagerness of travelers to believe that less difficult routes existed. Many a naive argonaut was fleeced by glib promoters or unscrupulous guides. Among the most outrageous of these fly-by-night operators was the man who sold stock for a glider company that promised to transport would-be prospectors to the Yukon from atop the highest mountain in Montana.[5]

The woeful ignorance of most Americans regarding the conditions of life and travel in the north country was matched by that of their government. By 1897, thirty years had passed since the United States had purchased Alaska from Czarist Russia for $7.2 million, but the farsighted bargain negotiated by Secretary of State William H. Seward continued to be derided as "Seward's Folly." Except as a source of fish and furs, and of ice for thirsty Californians, Alaska was widely considered a barren, inhospitable wasteland, unworthy of any public funding beyond a meager annual sum for minimal government services and a desultory program of exploration and mapping. By contrast, Canada's northwest, just across the border, was far better organized and governed. There never was, for example, an Alaskan equivalent of the Royal Canadian Mounted Police.

An episode from the early months of the gold rush well illustrates the ignorance and misconceptions about the far north that long prevailed in Washington. So rapid was the influx of gold seekers to the new El Dorado along the Yukon that obtaining enough food for them over the winter of 1897–1898 appeared, briefly, to be a serious problem. Alarming rumors of a possible famine began to spread. Not deigning to check with the Canadian government, whose officials on the scene were already dealing with the problem, a well-intentioned Congress passed an emergency appropriation of $200,000 and zealous bureaucrats in the State and War departments hastily organized a relief expedition for the "starving miners."

Some deskbound genius came up with the idea of using reindeer to haul in the supplies—never mind that horses and dogs were the usual means of winter locomotion to and from the gold fields, or that the closest herd of reindeer was in Norway. Nothing would do but to dispatch a delegation to bring back 540 animals from Lappland, along with a corresponding number of Lapp herders and drivers. Across the Atlantic by chartered ship they came, across the continent by special train, and on to Skagway on another chartered vessel, only to find on their arrival that there were no starving miners to be rescued. Sadly, instead, there were a lot of starving reindeer. Nobody had thought to check whether the lichen on which they fed grew in that part of the Yukon. It did not. Before the emaciated beasts could be transported to a more suitable tundra region along Alaska's north coast, all but 160 of them died.[6]

Other less farcical tragedies during the gold rush era are traceable to the U.S. government's neglect of its responsibilities toward Alaska. And although the development of an effective system of administration over the territory certainly dates from the lessons of 1898, more than four decades later powerful men in Washington could still be so ill-informed about conditions there that a modern version of the "great reindeer fiasco" remained a distinct possibility.

Although the vast majority of the estimated 50,000 men and women (three quarters of whom were Americans) who struggled toward the Klondike suffered little more than the usual discomforts of arctic frontier life, some of those who tried less-traveled routes north endured much greater hardships.

Inspector J. D. Moodie, an officer of the Royal Canadian Mounted Police, was instructed by his superiors to find and mark the best trail over the Rockies from Edmonton to the gold fields. He took more than a year to get there. Moodie headed northwest out of Edmonton on September 4, 1897, accompanied by three junior Mounties, a native guide, and thirty horses. Traversing 500 miles of forest, marsh, and prairie, the party got as far as Fort St. John on the Peace River before the approach of winter forced a delay while they sought to obtain horse sleighs and dog teams.

The expedition resumed and on Christmas Day Moodie discovered Laurier Pass over the Rockies' eastern escarpment, from which he began his descent toward Fort Grahame, near the headwaters of the Finlay River in the Rocky Mountain Trench. Snow deeper than the horses' withers forced Moodie to shoot them all for dog meat before he reached Fort Grahame on January 18, 1898. There his party wintered over until they could head north again. Crossing Sifton Pass, the inspector kept on for another 600 miles past McDames, across Francis Lake and down the Pelly River to Fort Selkirk on the Yukon. Having blazed a trail to his assigned destination, he immediately headed for home, this time via Skagway and a steamer south to Victoria. From the first telegraph station on the way, the laconic Scot sent his headquarters a report saying everything necessary: "Advise go by Skagway. Moodie."[7]

Others heading north from Edmonton at the same time as Moodie tried a more circuitous route. Back in 1789 Alexander Mackenzie had passed within a few miles of a small river, later named the Rat, whose significance remained unrecognized for more than eighty years. Emptying into the Arctic Ocean near the Mackenzie's marshy mouth, the Rat River is navigable to within 36 easily portaged miles of another river, the Bell, which leads south and west to the Yukon and the Pacific. Though hardly the fabled Northwest Passage, this pathway through the continent's mountainous western spine never rises more than 1,200 feet above sea level.

With the fur trade already firmly established along a number of more southerly routes, little use was made of the Rat-Bell portage until an unlikely settlement called Destruction City sprang up at the end of the navigable portion of the Rat in 1898. Here the City's transient inhabitants broke up the steamboats and scows that had brought them nearly 2,000 miles down the Athabasca, Slave, and Mackenzie rivers and used the planks and rigging to make smaller craft that could be loaded with supplies and dragged over the portage to the Bell. Faced with tons of cargo to move but with only hand tools and a scanty knowledge of boatbuilding, many of the people who had arrived that summer were still in Destruction City and starting to quarrel and steal from each other when the snows began in September.[8] A survivor of the ensuing winter was Mrs. A. C. Craig of Chicago, whose diary of this and subsequent experiences was published in 1948.

Emily Craig left Chicago for Edmonton and points north in August 1897, with her husband and a party of eleven other men, each of whom had paid $500 to a guide, one Lambertus Warmolts, who claimed to have taken only six weeks to cover the entire route. In fact, Warmolts had never been west of Chicago. These fourteen innocents made it as far as the Hudson's Bay post on Great Slave Lake before the freeze-up came. Wintering over near the trading post, they resumed their voyage north in May of 1898 and stepped ashore amid the bustle of Destruction City in late July.

Within a month, having decided with her husband that they should not attempt the portage until the following spring, Mrs. Craig recorded their preparations to spend a second winter en route to the Klondike. From the stunted native spruce and leftover bits and pieces of their boat they built a small cabin, caulking it with moss and mud. "September 26. My cabin now has a rustic sofa, chair, washstand, a table, a bed with spruce boughs as a mattress in a corner, and some shelves for my dishes," she wrote. "Many called to see us in our new home."

To supplement their stores of dried and canned provisions, she added local fare: fish, caribou, wild currants, and cranberries, smoked or dried and set aside against the coming cold and darkness. Not all of the Craigs' neighbors prepared so well. For eight weeks in the dead of winter the sun never rose above the horizon and the temperature often reached -70° Fahrenheit. Emily Craig stoically recorded the human misery and degradation around her: the loss of hands and feet to frostbite; scurvy and other diseases; hunger; treachery; madness; and death.[9] Strength of character plus the good sense not to scorn the customs of diet, dress, and shelter practiced by the local native people kept the Craigs alive until spring.

Gold fever in the Yukon ended as quickly as it began. Within a few years, the trails leading north carried only trappers and traders again. Relatively few of the thousands who never struck it rich remained, eking out a living by farming or selling furs. Occasionally, vague talk was heard about the desirability of constructing a road to Alaska, but the idea was not seriously considered until the advent of the Automobile Age. Nonetheless, the exploits and writings of a man named Vilhjalmur Stefansson kept the public interested in the subject of arctic travel.

Stefansson was born in 1879 in the Canadian province of Manitoba, the son of Icelandic immigrants who soon afterward moved to North Dakota. His goal upon graduating from the University of Iowa was to become a Unitarian minister. But after a year at Harvard Divinity School, his intense interest in his Norse ancestors and the legacy of their colonization of the New World caused him to take up studies at the Peabody Museum with the anthropologist Frederick Putnam. After accompanying an archeological expedition on a visit to Iceland in 1905, he spent the next year—the first of many—in an area of northern Canada that has ever since been closely associated with his name.

Sponsored by Harvard University and the University of Toronto, whose anthropological interests centered on the Athapascan tribes that lived along the Mackenzie, Stefansson planned to depend for logistical support on the Leffingwell-Mikkelson Expedition, whose focus was the polar region and its indigenous population of Inuits (Eskimos). He was to make his own way northward down the Mackenzie in the summer of 1906 and rendezvous with the expedition's leaders at Herschel Island, just off the coast at the western entrance to Mackenzie Bay. By September it was apparent that Leffingwell and Mikkelson's ship, the *Duchess of Bedford*, had been delayed for some reason and was not likely to put in at Herschel until the following summer. Rather than simply waiting for the *Duchess*, Stefansson decided to spend his time studying at close hand the customs and habits of the nearby coastal Eskimos. For six months he became, in effect, a member of an Inuit family, eating, sleeping, hunting, and traveling with them.[10]

From this experience, and then as the leader of his own expedition east of the lower Mackenzie during the years 1908–1912, Stefansson developed great respect for the Inuits and a profound conviction that white travelers in the Arctic could best survive by adopting their diet, clothing, and methods of hunting. Such ideas were not well received by most of his scientific contemporaries. They remained convinced, despite the disastrous endings of so many well-equipped Arctic expeditions over the previous two centuries, of the superiority of modern ways of coping with the Arctic.

Stefansson, who never found the time to finish his studies at Harvard, raised eyebrows in other disciplines as well. During his four-year exploration of the region between the Mackenzie Delta and Victoria Island, 500 miles farther east, he encountered blond, blue-eyed Inuits—strong evidence to him (if not to historians of the "Columbus-first" persuasion) that Danes and Norsemen had reached the New World long before 1492.[11]

From 1913 to 1918, Stefansson put his theories about arctic travel and survival to the harshest possible test. By boat, by dogsled, and on foot, he and a small group of hardy companions explored and mapped over 100,000 square miles of previously unknown polar territory, traveling light and living in good health for months on end on a diet of raw seal and caribou. World War I began in Europe while Stefansson was in the far north, and almost a year passed before he even knew about it. For him the distant struggle remained irrelevant. He finally returned home a few weeks before the Armistice to face celebrity and controversy.

Honored for his discovery of Brock and Borden islands, at the northeastern edge of the Queen Elizabeth group, and famous for his pioneering use of an ice island as a floating oceanographic research station, Stefansson was also a crowd pleaser on the lecture circuit. Here was a man with the soul of an adventurer, the mind of a scientist, and the flat, deeply lined face of an Eskimo.

Audiences loved the stories he told of incredible sledging journeys across the shifting pack ice of the Beaufort Sea; of finding the sad relics of almost-forgotten earlier expeditions; of several times losing contact with his comrades and being given up for dead.

Despite such acclaim, Stefansson had detractors, especially among officials of the Canadian Geological Survey, who knew that the explorer's own shortcomings as a planner and administrator had frequently put the success of his expeditions at risk. When they pressed him for a full narrative report of his five years in the Arctic, he haughtily submitted a ten-page summary instead.

The scientific and academic communities were equally cool to Stefansson. Raw meat as an antiscorbutic and blond Eskimos were not his only incredible claims. The north polar region, he said, was destined to become the strategic and economic center of the world. Across it lay the shortest line between Europe and Asia, and from North America to both; one day, he asserted, airplanes would make the transit routinely over great circle routes, and giant cargo submarines would move beneath the ice. On his travels down the Mackenzie and along the coast for 1,000 miles both east and west, he had seen enough evidence of vast underground deposits of oil and other minerals to predict a coming boom that would dwarf the Klondike Gold Rush. Wildest of all was his insistence that the Arctic region, properly understood and respected, was not an inhospitable wasteland but a potentially pleasant place for men and women to live and work.

Few knew what to make of this provocative, self-promoting prophet of the Arctic, whose iconoclastic credo combined respect for the ways of the Stone Age with faith in a future worthy of Jules Verne's imagination. With a self-confidence born of facing far greater terrors than being ignored or condescended to, Stefansson continued to speak and write about the things he believed to be true. He could be generous with his time and advice, but his scorn grew for those whose minds were closed to his ideas.[12]

THE ROUTES

Meanwhile, as a result of the great boom in highway construction and tourism brought on by America's increasing infatuation with the automobile, businessmen and politicians began to develop and publicize plans for turning one or another of the various existing trails to Alaska into a safe, practical, all-weather highway. By the end of the 1930s, two such schemes, popularly known as Routes A and B, were generally accepted as the most promising candidates for a commercially viable road. Route A was the favored choice of an advisory body appointed by President Roosevelt, the Alaskan International Highway Commission, and of business associations and automobile clubs throughout the American Northwest and Alaska. Comparable groups in British Columbia and the Yukon preferred Route B. To understand why such a divergence existed and what economic and political issues were at stake, it is necessary to take a closer look at how the rugged topography of British Columbia influenced routes of travel.

On the vastly simplified accompanying map, a ridgeline trace of

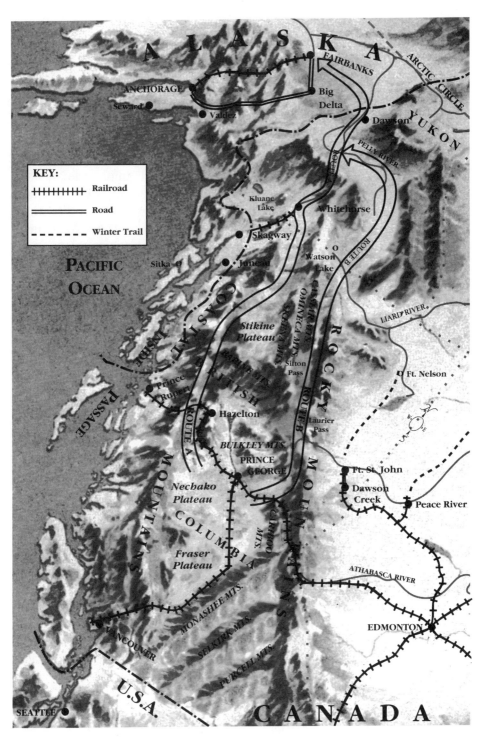

KEY:

+++++++++ Railroad

————— Road

- - - - - - Winter Trail

ROUTES A AND B THROUGH BRITISH COLUMBIA

British Columbia's major mountain ranges appears as an elongated figure H slanting northwest up the Pacific coast from Vancouver for more than 800 miles. The eastern (right) side of the H roughly parallels the Continental Divide along the Canadian Rockies; the western side traces a line along the coast linking the Cascade, Coast, and St. Elias ranges. All of these mountain chains contain peaks that exceed 12,000 feet in height. The wide crossbar of the H corresponds to the Omineca, Skeena, Babine, and Bulkley mountains, ranging in altitude from 6,000 to 11,000 feet. South of the crossbar are the Fraser and Nechako plateaus and to the north is the Stikine Plateau, each with an average elevation of about 4,000 feet. Tucked between the eastern edge of these plateau areas and the Rockies themselves are a jumble of lesser chains: the Cassiar mountains lie north of the crossbar; the Purcell, Selkirk, Monashee, and Cariboo ranges are their counterparts to the south.

Three great elongated depressions follow fault lines paralleling the major mountain chains that form the vertical sides of the figure H. The first of these fault lines runs between the rugged coast and its string of heavily forested offshore islands, forming a natural channel of awesome beauty called the Inside Passage. It offers sailors protection from the North Pacific's gales (though not from its fog) all the way from Vancouver to Skagway. Inland, beyond the Coast Range, is a deep trough known as the Coastal Trench. Its mirror image east of the Continental Divide is the Rocky Mountain Trench, where the headwaters of the Columbia, Fraser, and Peace rivers all lie. Containing numerous cross-compartments connected by steep and difficult passes, neither inland trench offers an unimpeded pathway north. But as Colonel Bulkley, Inspector Moodie, and countless other travelers who headed north through British Columbia to Alaska or the Yukon discovered, there were few other choices. It seemed best to follow either the Coastal Trench (Route A) or the Rocky Mountain Trench (Route B).

In 1929, two International Highway Associations were formed— the American one in Fairbanks, Alaska, and its Canadian twin in Dawson, then the capital of Yukon Territory. Their purpose was to cooperate in arousing public interest in a highway through Canada that would link Alaska with the United States, and to advocate whatever legislation and other measures were necessary to carry out the project. Local chambers of commerce and automobile clubs in Alaska and the northwestern United States enthusiastically endorsed the idea, as did national trade organizations such as the American Road Builders Association.

The response from Ottawa was noticeably less eager, but the provincial government of British Columbia expressed great interest in the plan. Its premier, Simon Fraser Tolmie, authorized a ground and air reconnaissance of possible routes in the northern half of the province in 1930. He also personally led an automobile caravan from Vancouver through Prince George to Hazelton to dramatize the possibilities of highway travel. At Hazelton, midway up the Coastal Trench and as far north as the rough provincial road system then reached, Tolmie was met by George A. Parks, Alaska's governor. Tolmie was accompanied by a representative from the U.S. Department of the Interior but, significantly, no one from Ottawa.

In response to a petition from the Alaska Legislature, Congress passed a bill on May 15, 1930, designating three commissioners to make a study of the proposed road and authorizing $10,000 to pay their expenses. The commission began work on November 7 under its chairman, Herbert H. Rice, Assistant to the President of General Motors. Rice and his fellow commissioners spent the next two years gathering data, refining their estimates, and coordinating with a similar group appointed by the Canadian government. Their final proposal was for a 1,350-mile, 16-foot-wide gravel road along Route A from Prince George via Hazelton, Stikine Crossing, Atlin, Whitehorse, and Dawson to Fairbanks. The American commissioners estimated the total cost of such a road, including all bridges and culverts (except across the Pelly and Yukon rivers, where ferries were envisioned), at $13,960,00. From Ottawa's standpoint this plan had a major drawback: $12 million of the estimated cost was for construction on Canadian soil, presumably to be paid for by Canada.[13]

To drum up support in the United States for the plan, its backers needed a good publicity gimmick. By chance they found one. It all began with a bit of idle bluster.

Alaska has always had more than its share of colorful characters; it is a point of local pride. Slim Williams came to Alaska in 1900 as an eighteen-year-old, looking for gold and adventure. For three decades he found just enough of the former to get by. Though if adventures were gold, he would have been a very wealthy man and not merely "Alaska's most famous sourdough," as the newspapers called him. Buying supplies one day in 1932 at a trading post north of Valdez on the Copper River, the 6-foot-4-inch Williams heard talk around the pot-bellied stove that a man from Nome was planning to drive his dogsled team to represent Alaska at the Century of Progress Fair in Chicago. Contemptuous of the man and his huskies, Williams

claimed that only dogs like his own, which were part wolf, were up
to making such a trip.

"You're so durned good," someone challenged him, "why don't you
just do it then?"

"I'm goin' to," said Williams nonchalantly as he headed for the
door.

Word spreads with surprising speed in the north country. Alaskans
call it the "moccasin telegraph." Having nearly forgotten his boast,
Williams was startled two weeks later to find tacked to the wall of the
trading post a newspaper bearing a big, black headline: SLIM WILLIAMS
TO DRIVE DOGS TO CHICAGO FAIR. Too proud to back out, he began making
preparations for the trip. Newspapers in the forty-eight states picked
up the story, generating sacks of fan mail. To his further surprise,
some influential men quietly offered to help, among them Donald
MacDonald, a senior engineer for the Alaska Road Commission and
the originator of the Route A proposal. MacDonald gave Williams
$300 out of his own pocket, a map with Route A traced on it, and a
letter of introduction to Anthony Dimond, Alaska's non-voting
Congressional delegate in Washington.

Questioning the letter to Dimond, Williams said, "I thought I was
going to Chicago."

"Washington isn't much further," answered MacDonald, "you
go . . . and give him your report of the trip. Maybe you'll even
meet the President."[14]

On the morning of November 21, 1932, Slim Williams left Copper
Center, Alaska, with his prize team of eight dogs pulling a loaded
sled. It was -40° Fahrenheit that day. The first leg of the trip went
well enough, as Williams mushed north over Mentasta Pass and
through Chicken and Fortymile to hit Route A at Dawson. But the
next 800 miles via Whitehorse and Telegraph Creek to Hazelton were
a different story. On the way Williams endured solitary bouts of
illness, a near drowning, and snow blindness. Wolves killed one of
his dogs. On bad days he made only a mile or two through snow so
deep that he had to walk ahead and break trail for his team. Some of
the mountains, he later claimed, were "upendicular."

Finally, on May 15, 1933, almost six months after leaving Copper
Center, Williams broke out of the bush near a Mountie's cabin within
sight of Hazelton. After a bath, a shave, and a few days' rest for
himself and his dogs, Williams headed south once more. But now,
with the snow almost gone and a real road to follow, his animals were
pulling a dogsled on wheels. His Hazelton host, the Mountie, had

helped him find a wrecked Model T Ford and a blacksmith to cut the axles and weld them to the sled frame.

Soon there was a new problem: the dogs were not used to running on gravel or pavement, and their paw pads began to bleed. Although a ladies' sewing club along the way offered to make canvas booties for each dog, the booties had a "tread life" of about 10 miles. Williams quickly figured out that cutting the distance of his daily run in half would make for faster travel than stopping to procure twenty-eight tiny canvas shoes in every town from Hazelton to Chicago.

By the time Williams reached the United States border and began heading east, he was a bona fide celebrity. At every stop along his route a welcome committee saw to it that he and his team were well cared for. His usual campsite was a city park, where he would stake the dogs and cook his supper over an open fire, all the while signing autographs and chatting with passersby. An occasional $50 check from MacDonald helped with his few expenses. As the days grew hotter and harder on his animals he took to traveling only at night. That also meant less traffic to worry about, but more than one approaching motorist panicked at the sight of seven small pairs of bobbing yellow reflectors in his headlights.

On September 16, 1933, accompanied by a police escort down Chicago's Michigan Avenue, Slim Williams arrived at the Century of Progress Fair. There, as part of the Alaskan exhibit for six weeks, he pitched his tent, cooked his meals, and joshed with the crowds. Then it was time to pay a call on Delegate Dimond in Washington. The trip took another thirty days. Making camp in a park near the White House, Williams went straight to see Dimond without bothering to change clothes. The two Alaskans swapped a few yarns and then got down to business. Did Williams think a road could be built over Route A? Yes, came the answer. Leaving Dimond's office, Williams was intercepted by a messenger who presented him with an immediate invitation to the White House. Protesting that he needed to clean up, he was told to go right in and not to worry. Wearing dirty moccasins, faded jeans, and an old shirt, Slim Williams was soon repeating to President Roosevelt what he had said to Dimond about Route A. Invited back for dinner by Mrs. Roosevelt, the lanky sourdough appeared in squeaky new shoes and an ill-fitting store-bought suit.[15]

Dimond persuaded Williams to stay in Washington through the winter of 1934 so that others could hear what he had to say about the proposed highway route, but the nadir of the Great Depression was not the best time to lobby American politicians for a road through

Canada. Williams returned to Copper Center that summer, disappointed at the outcome of his side trip to Washington but with plenty of new stories to tell.

The revival of public interest in constructing a highway to Alaska in the late 1930s was largely due to the continuing efforts of three men: Congressman Warren G. Magnuson of Washington State, Premier Thomas D. Pattullo of British Columbia, and Anthony J. Dimond of Alaska. In the summer of 1938, Congress proposed and the President approved another International Highway Commission, this time with Magnuson as chairman and Donald MacDonald as one of its members. The other three U.S. commissioners were Ernest Gruening, Director of the Interior Department's Division of Territories (and soon to be governor of Alaska); Thomas Riggs, a former governor of Alaska; and James W. Carey, a prominent Seattle civil engineer.[16] The purpose and methods of the new commission were the same as those of its predecessor, and once again the Canadian government's response was ambivalent.

To Premier Pattullo in Victoria, a highway to Alaska through British Columbia meant construction jobs and tourist dollars. As he saw it, since the project obviously required joint U.S.-Canadian funding, why not count the 600 miles of existing highway from Vancouver to Hazelton as British Columbia's contribution toward paying its overall cost and let Washington and Ottawa haggle over who should foot the bill for the rest? Pattullo's proposal seemed both naive and dangerous to Prime Minister Mackenzie King and his cabinet. In a crisis, what was to prevent a takeover by the United States of the right-of-way? It had happened in Panama back in 1903. Although the leaders of Canada and the United States were now on good terms after years of hard feelings over high tariffs, King was wary of any arrangement that might compromise his nation's sovereignty. Some of his advisors also pointed out that the U.S. military would expect to use the road in the event of war with Japan, raising the specter of Canadian citizens being caught in the crossfire while their country tried to remain neutral. King appreciated how closely linked the strategic interests of the United States and Canada had become, but he shuddered at the prospect of a large U.S. military presence on Canadian soil.

To King's mounting exasperation, Pattullo seemed oblivious to such considerations. In February of 1938, he announced that a highway to Alaska would end unemployment in British Columbia and pave the way for economic expansion. When Ottawa did not respond to this opening shot, Pattullo fired his next salvo in April. After meetings with Gruening and Dimond, he released a statement saying that the United States might be willing to loan British Columbia $15 million for the project. That brought an official, if behind-the-scenes, response from the head of Canada's Department of External Affairs, Dr. Oscar D. Skelton. Of Pattullo's highly irregular venture into the federal government's sphere of foreign policy, a flabbergasted Skelton wrote to King: "Surely . . . a high-water mark (or a low-water mark) in provincial diplomacy. [Pattullo's plan] amounts to regarding Canada or British Columbia as a subdivision of the United States."

A series of meetings between King and Pattullo followed, at which the Canadian Prime Minister made it clear to the bumptious Premier that the central government had no money to build the proposed highway and no intention of allowing the Americans to build it on their own. Nevertheless, Canada's constitution made roads a provincial responsibility, and King was sufficiently vague on the subject of funding to give a politician like Pattullo all the leeway he needed. Looking for an acceptable way to obtain financing, Pattullo conferred again with his friends in Washington and came up with a proposal to channel U.S. funds to the project through a dummy corporation. Initially King did not seem averse to this idea, but Skelton's comments about "mortgaging our independence" apparently cooled his interest.

Pushing hard, Pattullo's next tactic was to finesse King into appointing a Canadian version of Magnuson's Alaskan International Highway Commission. Shortly after the Americans met for the first time on August 22, 1938, Pattullo announced that the Canadian government would soon appoint a similar group. The Prime Minister took his time about it. Late in December Ottawa finally created the British Columbia-Yukon-Alaska Highway Commission under the chairmanship of Charles Stewart. Stewart had considerable experience in U.S.-Canadian affairs, but he was also too ill that winter to convene his group.[17]

The two commissions met for the first time in Victoria on July 24, 1939, and then again in Ottawa on January 24–25, 1940, having in the interim reviewed all the data accumulated by their predecessors and made some new ground and aerial reconnaissance surveys. Once again, the U.S. commission came out strongly in favor of following the Coastal Trench, although its recommendations differed in one significant way from the original Route A proposal of 1933. Instead of calling for the road to continue north down the Yukon valley from Whitehorse to Dawson and then swing west to Fairbanks, Magnuson's group preferred a more direct route following an old wagon trail from

Whitehorse west as far as Kluane Lake and thence northwest to Alaska's Tanana River Valley, where it would join the existing Richardson Highway at Big Delta. Besides being slightly shorter than the original version, the revised Route A had the advantage (from the U.S. perspective) of running close enough to the coastline for feeder roads to reach isolated communities in the Alaskan panhandle.

Stewart and his fellow Canadians preferred Route B. This road would also begin at Prince George in British Columbia, but it swung north into the Rocky Mountain Trench, following the trail to the Yukon pioneered by Inspector Moodie in 1898. The advantage of Route B to the Canadians was that it would better serve the needs of northern British Columbia and the Yukon Territory.

Both roads were similar in length: an estimated 1,344 miles for Route A, and 1,306 miles for Route B. As for the possible cost, neither commission felt it had enough information to hazard more than an off-the-record guess. A figure of $25 million, about double the 1933 estimate, seemed the general consensus. The commissions submitted reports to their respective governments, Magnuson's going to President Roosevelt in April 1940, and in due course the War Department got a copy. Later, when Magnuson cited defense considerations in an attempt to parlay his commission's report into a highway appropriations bill, the chairman of the House Committee on Roads sought the opinion of the Secretary of War, Henry L. Stimson. "The value of the highway as a defense measure," said Stimson, "is negligible."[18] There matters stood for sixteen more months. Even another publicity stunt by Slim Williams made no difference. In the summer of 1939, the fifty-seven-year-old Williams rode, pushed, and dragged a 300-pound motorcycle down Route A from Fairbanks to Seattle.[19]

Although Routes A and B had long seemed the most promising candidates for a road to Alaska, two other alternatives surfaced in 1940. The first of these, Route C, appears to have been essentially a "Hey! What about us?" interjection by its Johnny-come-lately backers. If Alaska, Washington State, and Oregon wanted Route A and British Columbia and the Yukon preferred Route B, then Montana, North Dakota, and Alberta might just as well promote a third road to Alaska that served their particular interests.

The problem for advocates of Route C was, almost literally, where on earth to put it. Most of the known east-west passes suitable for a road through the Canadian Rockies were too far south to be of any help. One candidate, a road over Moodie's Laurier Pass northwest of Fort St. John, would simply join Route B near Fort Grahame, making the Laurier Pass connection at best a capillary of the main north-south artery favored by British Columbia. North of this point the Rockies grew increasingly rough and wild. The general contours of the land were known, but thousands of square miles remained unmapped and even unexplored. One attempt to fill in the maps of this area had been made in 1934 by a self-made millionaire turned adventurer, Charles E. Bedaux, who led an expedition from Fort St. John across the Rockies.

Bedaux was born near Paris in 1887 and immigrated to the United States at the age of nineteen. By the late 1920s he was a very wealthy man, having worked his way up the wage scale from bottle washer, sand-hog, and factory hand to efficiency expert and industrial management consultant—with time out along the way for a tour in the French Foreign Legion. A disciple of Frederick W. Taylor, the first guru of scientific management, Bedaux squeezed extra productivity from assembly-line workers, which made him a welcome figure in the boardrooms and estates of the plutocrats of his era. Shrewd investments paid for a hunting lodge in Scotland and a chateau in France where, one day, his good friends the Duke and Duchess of Windsor would spend the first night of their honeymoon.

Bedaux liked to do things other people said could not be done. Not long before his arrival in Fort St. John, for example, he had crossed the roadless Sahara Desert with a fleet of five automobiles, accompanied by his American-born second wife, the former Fern Lombard of Grand Rapids, Michigan. Now Bedaux planned to conquer the Rockies.

The plain folk of Fort St. John had never seen anything like the procession that chugged up the dusty road from the ferry landing in the summer of 1934: two gleaming black limousines, five specially built Citroen half-tracks, three river *bateaux*, dozens of hired cowboys in leather chaps and ten-gallon hats, 130 prairie-bred pack horses, and several trucks loaded with supplies of all kinds, including such necessities as cases of champagne and tins of caviar, pâté de foie gras, and Devonshire cream. Pitching a cluster of fireproof asbestos tents 7 miles north of town near Charlie Lake, where his float-equipped airplane was moored, Bedaux and his wife held court.

Their entourage included Fern's French maid, Josephine; Bedaux's giant of a bodyguard/valet, Bob Chisolm; and a mysterious guest, Madame Alberta Chicsa, whose raison d'être seems to have been solely decorative. There was also a uniformed operator with the latest wireless equipment, a French auto mechanic, a ski-carrying

Swiss Alpine guide, and two Hollywood cameramen. Bedaux showered money on the incredulous locals. Extra packers and guides were hired, and additional horses were purchased at twice the going rate. (Madame Bedaux insisted on using one pack horse just to carry her shoes, and another to tote her collection of French novels.) Discovering that Fort St. John had no water supply system, he donated $40,000 to have water piped in from Charlie Lake.

Despite all this extravagant show, Bedaux clearly had something in mind beyond mere self-dramatization. Some residents of Fort St. John believe to this day that he was a spy for the Germans, sent to appraise the practicability of a highway to Alaska. Given the Germans' interest in geopolitics and Bedaux's subsequent record, this proposition is not altogether implausible. (By 1939, he was summering in Berchtesgaden and had ingratiated himself with several of Hitler's inner circle, including Foreign Minister Joachim von Ribbentrop and Dr. Hjalmar Schacht, the Third Reich's Finance Minister. Captured in North Africa by U.S. forces in late 1942 and placed under arrest as a Nazi collaborator, Bedaux committed suicide in a Miami jail sixteen months later.)

Most likely, his ambition in the summer of 1934 was to set up an enjoyable adventure in an exotic, little-known setting, get some credit for exploring it, and confound scoffers in the process. At any rate, his second in command on the expedition was a reputable geologist named J. B. Bocock, assisted by two local surveyors. One of the surveyors kept a diary:

> July 22. Rain at last ceased. We start at 3 pm but waste another one and a half hours posing in the main street for movie pictures, the pack train being introduced into the scene and then told to unpack, much to the disgust of the packers. Several packs were bucked off during the dress parade . . . entire population lining the mud trench, once the main street. At 7 pm camp chosen eight miles out . . . no water but dig well in a swale. Camp pitched at 9:30 pm[20]

Heading west from Fort St. John, destination Telegraph Creek on the Stikine Plateau, the party managed to travel just 58 miles in the first eleven days. Bedaux had two main problems: his wife's refusal to emerge from her tent until high noon, and the total unsuitability of the Citroen tractors for cross-country travel. Cumbersome machines with the front wheels of a truck and caterpillar treads behind the cab, they often had to be laboriously winched down and up the steep-sided valleys that blocked Bedaux's path. One river, the Cameron, lay in a gorge so deep that it took all day to cross. Add unseasonable cold, incessant rain, and repeated stops for movie stunts, and it is no wonder that Bedaux soon had some very disgruntled companions. Madame Bedaux did her fatuous best for morale by doling out chewing gum from the exquisitely lacquered box she kept in her tent. On August 11, Bedaux decided to abandon the Citroens and proceed on horseback. Before moving on, he staged and filmed the spectacular destruction of all five vehicles. Several were driven off cliffs, the drivers leaping clear at the last moment.

Now able to make better speed, the party skirted the eastern slopes of the Rockies until they reached the Muskwa River, 256 miles northwest of Fort St. John, on September 1. Following the Muskwa to its source high in the snow-covered mountains, they crossed over into the Rocky Mountain Trench about 100 miles north of Laurier Pass, reaching Sifton Pass on a stormy September 29. Faced with a situation very much like Moodie's back in 1898—deepening snows ahead and the exhausted and underfed horses going lame—Bedaux made a similar decision: he shot the horses and wintered over near Fort Grahame. In the spring, the tinhorn adventurer and his bedraggled company drifted on boats down the Finlay and Peace rivers back to Fort St. John. Bedaux's main contribution to the map of British Columbia was the discovery of tiny Fern Lake, near the summit of his route.[21]

After this discouraging sortie, it is somewhat surprising that anyone still thought that a road through the Rockies could be built somewhere northwest of Fort St. John. Nevertheless, in 1940, Governor John Moses of North Dakota succeeded in organizing something called the United States-Canada-Alaska Prairie Highway Association. Heading the Association was the governor's good friend Halvor L. Halvorson, a prominent lawyer in Minot, North Dakota. This group's proposed route ran north from Fort St. John to Fort Nelson and thence northwesterly through Watson Lake, Francis Lake, old Fort Selkirk, Dawson, and on to Fairbanks via Big Delta, a distance of 1,400 miles. Nothing in the way of an actual survey of this route as far as Watson Lake had as yet been attempted; all Halvorson's group had to go on were a handful of published anecdotal accounts by various travelers since 1898. Nevertheless, here was another possibility with organized backing. It quickly became known as Route C.[22]

A fourth possibility was introduced by Vilhjalmur Stefansson, whose interest in a road to Alaska was based more on considerations of strategy than of economics. Although Stefansson had found no comfortable niche in the world of academe, he did serve periodically as a consultant for various U.S. government agencies in the prewar years, drafting a series of Arctic guidebooks for the military and serving as a technical advisor on soil conditions in Alaska.

On August 8, 1940, with France defeated, Great Britain under siege and Japan on the march in Asia, Stefansson met informally with a group of officers in the War Plans Division of the Army's General Staff to discuss prospects for a road to Alaska. He pointed out that the Mackenzie–Yukon river network almost perfectly followed the trace of a great circle leading from the American heartland to the Bering Sea and on to Russia and Japan. By using river barges in the summer and long trains of tractor-drawn sledges when the rivers froze and the ground was firm, Stefansson assured them, the Army could quickly and easily transport large amounts of cargo to build Alaska's defenses. Although the Rat-Bell portage offered the easiest route around the Rockies, Stefansson recommended cutting a more difficult southerly trail through the Mackenzie Range, thereby shortening the overall distance to Fairbanks. His plan was labeled Route D.

Five months later in January 1941, the Army Chief of Staff, General George C. Marshall, asked Stefansson to elaborate on his ideas about a road to Alaska. He did so in a letter to which he appended the draft of an article he had written for publication on Alaskan transportation, along with a scheme for expanding the production of the oil field and small refinery already in operation at Norman Wells, 70 miles below the Arctic Circle on the Mackenzie River. Petroleum could then be delivered to Alaska over Route D by truck or tractor-train, said Stefansson. "While such a road would certainly be of value," responded Marshall, "the War Department does not consider it of sufficient importance to justify its construction at this time on the basis of military necessity."

In July 1941, *Foreign Affairs* published Stefansson's article, entitled "Routes to Alaska." Later that fall, William J. ("Wild Bill") Donovan, Roosevelt's Coordinator of Information, retained Stefansson and his small staff as the nucleus for an Arctic studies center within what soon became the Office of Strategic Services, forerunner of the CIA. Stefansson's first assignment was to work out a plan to free Alaska from dependence on remote sources of petroleum. Three days after the attack on Pearl Harbor, Stefansson sent his boss a copy of the *Foreign Affairs* article and a new version of his scheme for tapping the oil at Norman Wells. Lay a pipeline to Fairbanks along Route D, he suggested.[23]

This idea for making military use of the oil at Norman Wells was

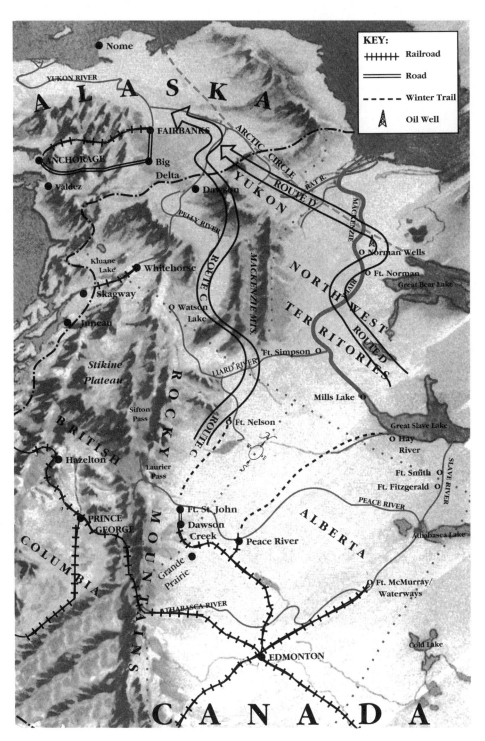

ROUTES C AND D

the seed that eventually grew into CANOL, but the Army remained skeptical about the rest of Stefansson's Route D proposal.

Prior to December 7, 1941, none of these four alternative routes had any immediate likelihood of becoming a concrete reality, although the previous summer, in light of Germany's invasion of Russia and Japan's continued expansion in Asia, the Army's planners finally did conclude that an overland route to Alaska was desirable as a "long-range defensive measure." Even so, neither the United States nor Canada had ever officially expressed more than a mild interest in such a road. The existence of competing schemes, none clearly superior, was one reason why. Mindful of Washington's sometimes cavalier disregard for the sovereignty of its neighbors when U.S. interests were at stake, Ottawa had its own qualms. Yet another factor contributed to the reluctance in both capitals: despite the specific advantages claimed for each proposal by its proponents, nagging doubts persisted as to whether any combination of benefits could possibly outweigh the enormous cost of building and maintaining whichever route was finally selected.

Overlooked in all this talk about an automobile highway to Alaska was the possibility that such a road might also be of great value to air travelers.

2

<u>1920–1941</u>

Bases in the Wilderness

T o the traveler who has wings, snow-capped mountain ranges and turbulent river gorges are not formidable obstacles. Seen from a great height, they shrink to mere jagged folds and creases on the earth's surface. That dramatic perspective, once the exclusive privilege of aviation's pioneers, had become a routine experience for millions of airline passengers by the eve of World War II. Thanks to the achievements of those early aviators, plus a generation of astonishing technological advances, the airplane was changing people's ideas about travel even more profoundly than had the automobile.

Vilhjalmur Stefansson was among the first to appreciate the implications of air travel for exploration and commerce. A frequent theme in his writing was the long, frustrating, and often tragic search of European mariners for a Northwest Passage to the Far East. Although that search finally ended in 1906 with the successful voyage of Roald Amundsen, Stefansson understood that the barrier of the North American continent and the treacherous ice of the polar seas meant that only airplanes could translate the concept of sailing north to reach the Orient into an everyday reality.[1]

One of the first aviators to popularize this idea was Stefansson's good friend Charles Lindbergh. Anne Lindbergh accompanied her husband on their spectacular great circle flight from New York to Shanghai via the Canadian Arctic, Alaska, and Japan in 1931. *North to the Orient*, her memorable account of that adventure, became a bestseller four years later.

If the Lindberghs' ocean-spanning flights symbolized aviation's great potential for shrinking the globe and bringing its people closer together, the exploits of another famous individual from that dynamic era, Brigadier General William L. (Billy) Mitchell, underscored its dangers.

Billy Mitchell quit college in 1898 during the Spanish-American War to join the U.S. Army. Three years later, as part of Washington's effort in the wake of the Klondike Gold Rush to provide basic services to its long-neglected northern possession, Lieutenant Mitchell made a brief visit to Alaska to inspect the government cable and telegraph system that was being built to link the territory's widely scattered military garrisons with the rest of the United States. He soon returned to supervise the construction of additional segments of the telegraph line and grew thoroughly familiar with Alaska's terrain and weather during his eighteen-month assignment. After learning to fly at his own expense prior to World War I, Mitchell became the first American pilot to see service in Europe. He rose under General John J. Pershing to command all U.S. combat aviation units on the Western Front during the final offensives of 1918.

General Mitchell's vision of the future of military air power looked far beyond the limited capabilities of the flimsy fabric-and-wood contraptions he and his men then flew. After the war, as Assistant Chief of the U.S. Army Air Service, he became an outspoken and increasingly controversial advocate for various innovative concepts— long-range strategic bombing, massing tactical fighters to achieve air superiority over the battlefield, using transport planes to drop paratroopers behind enemy lines—all under the command of an air force hierarchy independent of both the Army and the Navy. Such ideas made this cocky boy-general, handsome as a recruiting poster, very unpopular with tradition-minded senior officers.

Mitchell's thinking was also influenced by his knowledge of Alaska. Like Stefansson, with whom he corresponded, he saw the polar region's potential as the "air crossroads of the world," but as a military man Mitchell thought primarily in terms of attack and defense. In the event of a future war with Japan, which he predicted would begin with a surprise attack on one of the United States' Pacific outposts, Alaska-based long-range bombers could retaliate by striking the enemy's homeland. Although the Washington Conference of 1922 bound the United States not to fortify the Aleutian Islands as one inducement to deter Japan from constructing any new heavy warships for ten years, as long as Mitchell remained the nation's leading air power advocate, he did his best to demonstrate to his countrymen that Alaska had indeed become "the most strategic place in the world."[2] First, to prove that the Army's airplanes could safely and reliably be flown that far, he organized the now-legendary flight of the Black Wolf Squadron in 1920.

Under the command of Captain St. Clair Streett, four single-engine DeHavilland biplanes, each with a wolf's head emblazoned on its fuselage, took off from Long Island's Mitchell Field on July 15, 1920, heading for Nome, Alaska. The squadron reached its destination on August 24, having covered 4,500 miles in fifteen short hops totaling less than fifty-five hours of actual flying time. In crossing the Canadian Rockies, Captain Streett and his companions followed the "iron compass," using the railroad from Edmonton to Prince George as their guide. Then it was up the Coastal Trench to Whitehorse and on to Fairbanks and Nome. The return flight went just as smoothly. A jubilant General Mitchell was on hand to greet the four exhausted pilots and their grimy flight mechanics as they touched down on Long Island on October 20.

Having shown that military aircraft could span the continent, Mitchell next set out to prove that they could fly around the world. Once again, Alaska figured in his plans. In 1922 British aviators made the first attempt to circle the globe. They failed, but the next year teams from France, Italy, Portugal, and Argentina joined in preparations for another try. By 1924 the United States was ready for the race as well. On April 6, 1924, four powerful Douglas "World Cruisers," specially built biplanes equipped with both floats and conventional landing wheels, took off from Seattle—destination Japan and points beyond. Their route across the Pacific followed a great land-hugging arc up the Inside Passage to Sitka, across the Gulf of Alaska to Seward, and down the Aleutian chain to Dutch Harbor and Attu.

This time the honor of being flight leader went to Major Frederick L. Martin, but General Mitchell put Captain Streett's expertise from the 1920 New York–Nome expedition to good use. As the World Cruisers' logistical advance man, Streett was responsible (with considerable help from the U.S. Navy) for seeing that Martin and his men were never far from a stockpile of fuel, supplies, and spare parts anywhere along their route. Everything went well until the four planes took off for the Aleutians from Seward's Resurrection Bay on April 15. As they headed southwest down the Alaskan Peninsula, Major Martin's flight mechanic, Sergeant Alva L. Harvey, noticed oil beginning to cover the left side of their engine cowling. Martin made an emergency landing on Portage Bay, where he and Harvey were quickly met by a Navy destroyer and towed to a nearby fishing village for repairs. Meanwhile the three remaining aircraft flew on to Dutch Harbor and waited for their leader.

The installation of a new engine cost Martin and Harvey ten days; bad weather delayed them another five. Finally, on the morning of April 30, they got off again—only to crash into a fog-shrouded mountain near Port Moller a short while later. On May 2, having had no word from the two men in 48 hours and no inkling of whether they were alive or dead, their anxious compatriots at Dutch Harbor received orders from Washington to proceed with the journey. Major Martin's second in command, Lieutenant Lowell H. Smith, became the new flight leader.

Miraculously, Martin and Harvey were uninjured, even though their plane was a crumpled wreck. Exhausted and weak from hunger, they stumbled into Port Moller on May 10, having walked out of the unmapped mountains by following the downward course of snow-fed brooks and streams. Word of their survival reached Lieutenant Smith and the others in Japan, where they had been received with great ceremony and many banquets—interspersed, between polite toasts to Japanese-American friendship, with hints that the Imperial Army and Navy fully understood the strategic threat implied in what the Americans had just accomplished.

While the dejected Martin and Harvey returned home, the remaining three crews flew on from Japan, across southern Asia, into Europe, and back across the North Atlantic, finally returning triumphantly to Seattle on September 28. In 371 flying hours over a period of 175 days, the aptly named World Cruisers had covered a distance of 27,553 miles.[3]

Two sensational long-distance flights in the span of four years were not the only headline-grabbing successes of General Mitchell's tenure as assistant chief of the Army Air Service. Convinced that bomb-carrying aircraft could hit targets at sea as well as on land, Mitchell launched a campaign to convince Congress and the public that the pride of the U.S. Navy, its mighty battleships, were vulnerable to air attack.

In 1921, with the Navy's grudging consent, Congress authorized the use of a number of captured German warships to test Mitchell's claims. Anchored off the Virginia Cape, the flotilla of German vessels included the superdreadnaught *Ostfriesland*, which the British Navy had been unable to sink during the Battle of Jutland five years earlier. To the bottom it went, along with the lesser ships of the formation, under the onslaught of Mitchell's land-based Martin bombers. Still, scoffing persisted in Navy circles about lucky hits on ships already weakened by battle damage. So two years later, Mitchell arranged another demonstration, this time using two obsolete but fully serviceable American battleships, the *Virginia* and the *New Jersey*. His planes took four minutes to sink the former and seven to sink the latter. Embarrassed, but still wedded to its big-gun fleet, the Navy refused to take Mitchell's message seriously until it was restated in Japanese eighteen years later at Pearl Harbor.

General Mitchell did not live to see his ideas about air power vindicated. In 1925 his enemies among the senior generals and admirals managed to get him reassigned, in his permanent rank of colonel, to a dusty Texas army post. Banished but not silenced, Mitchell became ever more strident in his criticism of those who opposed his ideas. In September 1925, following the death of fourteen men in the crash of the Navy dirigible *Shenandoah*, he publicly accused the officials in charge of the dirigible program of "incompetency, criminal negligence, and almost treasonable administration of the national defense." That statement and his refusal to retract it got him court-martialed for insubordination. Found guilty in a highly publicized trial, he resigned within a few months to continue his crusade as a civilian. For ten more years he played the role of prophet-martyr, attracting much attention but little real public support. He died in 1936 at the age of 57.[4]

Despite Mitchell's spectacularly successful demonstrations, the full potential of military air power could not be realized fully until all sorts of practical problems and technical limitations were overcome. Before aircraft range, reliability, and payload were significantly improved and a network of landing fields and navigational aids established, achievements such as the Army Air Service's two long-distance flights could easily be regarded as enormously expensive publicity stunts. After all, future pilots bound for distant points could not expect the luxury of having a traveling ground support team, as Mitchell's men enjoyed in 1920, or relays of well-stocked Navy destroyers deployed around the world, as in 1924.

Billy Mitchell was simply twenty years ahead of his time. It took that long to develop the technological, logistical, and organizational infrastructure that finally turned his vision into reality. The handful of military aviators who shared his dream kept it alive by pushing hard against the technical and budgetary limits they faced. But those limits were kept very narrow by a Congress responsive both to the isolationist mood of the nation and, after 1929, to the more immediate needs of its faltering economy. Thus, in the first decade after Mitchell's court martial, the most dramatic improvements in aviation came not from his disciples in uniform, but from a creative and productive mix of adventurous civilian pilots, risk-taking entrepreneurs, and government-subsidized investors. These were the years when country fairs featured daredevil wing-walkers and barnstorming pilots willing to take anyone aloft for a dollar a minute; when names like Wiley Post, Howard Hughes, and Amelia Earhart joined Lindbergh's in the headlines; when Boeing and Douglas built the first true airliners; and when companies such as United Airlines and Pan American Airways began to serve the hundreds of airports being built around the nation and overseas.

By 1941, commercial airlines in the United States were flying more than 3 million passengers annually—the equivalent of one American in fifty—in cabin-pressurized, multi-engine comfort. In Alaska, where the population was less than 50,000, air travelers were more likely to be sitting with the cargo in some relic of the barnstorming era flown by a bush pilot. Nevertheless, in that same year the sparsely settled territory's hodge-podge fleet of aircraft carried 40,000 passengers.[5] Nowhere was the airplane's wonderful ability to hurdle barriers and telescope distances more appreciated than in the far north.

Many of the difficulties of northern weather and terrain that made overland travel so arduous also made for hair-raising flying conditions. The moisture-laden winds that blew inland off the Gulf of Alaska usually kept the somber crags of the coastal region shrouded in rain, fog, or snow. Violently shifting eddies and downdrafts swirled through the granite-walled valleys. The same winds gave the interior region less precipitation and clearer skies, but equally unpredictable air currents. Moreover, in all this vast area there were few good places to land. Pilots cruising serenely over the "mere folds and creases" far below needed to be constantly on the lookout for a safe place to put down in an emergency. Few and far between were the convenient cow pastures used by barnstormers in the "lower 48."

Until enough airports could be built, the longest and smoothest landing areas were the numerous lakes and rivers, so most planes were equipped with floats in the summer and skis in the winter. With entire mountain ranges and large areas of the interior still unsurveyed and magnetic anomalies not uncommon, flyers soon learned how foolish it was to navigate solely by map and compass. Those who survived to become old-timers also relied heavily on dead reckoning and knowing all the landmarks. Although radio homing beacons were being installed along several of the main Canadian and Alaskan flight routes by the late 1930s, such newfangled devices were of little use to most north country pilots, who made their livelihood by ferrying people and supplies back and forth to settlements deep in the bush. For communication between air and ground, their craft were equipped with nothing more sophisticated than a telegraph key, a headset, and a reel of wire. To send or receive a message in flight, the pilot simply spooled the wire out beneath the plane and then transmitted or received information in Morse code. This was an adequate system for routine situations, but it was not of much help to an aviator frantically fighting a cockpit fire or plummeting earthward with engine trouble.

Considering all these hazards, it is a wonder there weren't more crashes—and more deaths. The slow airspeeds of this era (seldom more than 150 mph) and the crash-wise skill of its pilots were two reasons for the relatively low fatality rate. If your plane was going down, said the old hands, the next best thing to making a pancake landing on a pond or stream was to aim the fuselage between two trees, letting the wings rip off and absorb most of the impact. But surviving a crash more or less in one piece could be the least of a pilot's worries. There might have been no time for an S.O.S.; the nearest settlement might be hundreds of miles away; it might be below zero and snowing; or all of the above. Survivors in such situations could wait for help or they could walk until they found some. Although neither choice guaranteed a happy ending, every airman overdue at his next destination knew that his fellow pilots would soon be up searching for him. The successful outcome of most searches, some of epic scope and danger, was another reason so many people lived to fly again.[6]

Almost exclusively a male fraternity until after World War II, the bush pilots were an unusual breed. A few may have fit the silk-scarved, devil-may-care Hollywood stereotype, but most did not. "There are old pilots and there are bold pilots, but no old, bold pilots" goes a saying in their profession. Among the old, cautious bush pilots were some who had truly amazing careers. If a Bush Pilot Hall of Fame is ever established, two names sure to be enshrined there are Frank Barr and Grant McConachie.

In 1932, twenty-nine-year-old Francis Barr arrived in Juneau, Alaska, looking for work as a commercial pilot. A short, dapper

Midwesterner with a Clark Gable moustache, he had chased bandits on the Mexican border as a cavalry soldier, spent several years as an itinerant sky diver, and held a job as a test pilot for an aircraft firm until it went under during the early years of the Depression. Barr was soon hired by an enterprising trader who owned a World War I–vintage Moth biplane and needed someone to fly supplies out to his customers in the bush. Christening the open-cockpit Moth "La Cucaracha," Barr quickly earned a reputation throughout the north country as a man of invincible calm and resourcefulness.

On the reasonable assumption that an overdue plane might simply be down temporarily while the pilot weathered a passing storm or dealt with an easily remedied engine problem, the usual practice was to wait a day or two before organizing a serious search. Frank Barr's friends eventually learned not to worry about him until he was missing for at least a month.

In November 1932, Barr took off from Atlin in the northwest corner of British Columbia, en route to Sayea Creek on the Liard River with a load of food and fuel for some prospectors. After stopping for gas at Teslin Lake, he headed east over the Rockies but ran out of daylight before reaching his destination. Landing his ski-equipped Moth on the frozen surface of Wolf Lake, he taxied to the lee shore near an unoccupied cabin, tied the plane securely to a stump, folded its wings alongside the fuselage, and retired for the night. Around midnight a storm blew up. From the near-horizontal angle of the spruce trees outside the cabin window, Barr estimated the wind at better than 90 miles per hour and decided it was too dangerous—and too late—to check on his aircraft just then. At dawn, a native came to the cabin door. Wary greetings were exchanged. Barr invited the man in for a cup of coffee and waited for him to state his business. After a while, putting down his empty cup, the visitor said: "Airplane. She upside down."

So it was, lying in a black pool of frozen oil from the crankcase. The damage was sickening: a wing strut had buckled and several ribs were crushed; the plastic windshield was broken, the rudder smashed, and the plane's fabric covering punctured and torn in many places. Most serious of all, one blade of the wooden propeller was now about 6 inches shorter than the other.

With help from several natives, Barr got his stricken craft righted and patiently began the daunting task of making it airworthy again. As they looked on, he straightened the buckled wing strut and splinted it with an axe handle. Next, he flattened a gasoline can, curved it to match the wing's contours, and fitted it over the damaged ribs. The cracked windshield he fixed by drilling holes along the break and lacing it together with strips of moosehide.

Doggedly, Barr kept at it for more than a month, most days in weather so cold he could only work with his mittens off for a few seconds at a time. The slightest moisture on his bare hands caused metal parts to freeze to them; his fingertips grew raw and bled continually. The most critical job came last: rebalancing the broken propeller. After smoothing out the jagged break, he made a paper pattern of the shortened tip and used it as a guide to whittle down the opposite blade. By Christmas Day of 1932, all that remained for Barr to do was to put on his snowshoes and stamp down the snow on the lake for a runway. That accomplished, he prepared the last of his rice and tea for a holiday dinner, ate, and crawled into his sleeping bag.

Taking off the next morning, engine bucking and howling in protest, the battered biplane needed the entire 5-mile width of Wolf Lake to clear the trees on the opposite shore. When Barr landed for fuel at Teslin Lake, the Moth's tank was empty. People there and at Atlin had long since given up looking for him; his obituary had already appeared in the Whitehorse paper. Reading his own death notice was a macabre pleasure he would have more than once. "If you need to get there in the worst way, fly with Barr" became his casual, self-deprecating motto. Yet despite several crashes and countless forced landings (during one "involuntary layover," his plane was literally buried in a snowstorm), neither Frank Barr nor any of his passengers was ever seriously injured.[7]

Frank Barr's hard-won familiarity with flying conditions over the Rockies was matched by that of Grant McConachie. Although the U.S. Army would eventually make good use of his knowledge during World War II, McConachie's most important contribution to the saga of the Alaska Highway was more immediate and more fundamental.

A gangly, freckle-faced youth with a shock of unruly brown hair and an infectious grin, McConachie was determined to become a pilot—an ambition that outweighed his parents' desire to see him finish his engineering studies at the University of Alberta in Edmonton. Strict Calvinists, they feared that Grant would never make something of himself, and this concern seemed well-placed in light of his harum-scarum, high-risk existence during the years of the Great Depression.

With a $2,500 loan from his black-sheep Uncle Harry, McConachie bought a well-used blue Fokker monoplane, and Independent Airways was in business. In December of 1931, only minutes after meeting the final requirements for his commercial license, the young pilot took off with his first paying passengers: Professor Archibald Rowan of the University of Alberta and 200 crows.

The professor had developed a theory that seasonal differences in daylight influenced the migratory habits of birds. The crows, sporting metal leg bands and yellow paint on their tails, were about to test this theory, having had their "midsummer" extended for six months under the artificial lights of Rowan's laboratory. The professor wanted McConachie to fly as far south as his fuel would allow, land, and help him release the birds from their cages. On his return to Edmonton, he planned to publicize the experiment, emphasizing that he would pay $5 for each leg band mailed in with information as to where and when the crow had been shot or captured. (To support his theory he needed data showing the birds had scattered in all directions instead of immediately heading further south.)

The first part of Rowan's plan worked just fine. Having landed and released the crows on a snow-covered wheat field, he and McConachie were invited to warm themselves at a nearby farmhouse before taking off again. The farmer and his large family were naturally curious about the plane and its unusual passengers, so over a mug of hot tea the professor enthusiastically told them all about his experiment, including the cash reward he was offering.

Walking back to the plane, the two men noticed that most of the crows were still nearby, hopping and pecking about in the stubble, apparently in no hurry to try their wings after their caged existence in the laboratory. Gaining altitude, McConachie circled the farmhouse for a friendly wave goodbye. But the man and his sons were too busy to wave back. They were out with their shotguns killing yellow-tailed crows.

The professor eventually got a few leg bands back from western Canada and the United States, but by far the largest number came from one particularly hospitable farmer, along with a claim for $250.[8]

Although McConachie made a profit on his very first commercial charter, the winter of 1931–1932 was not a propitious time for an unknown and underfinanced youngster to start his own airline. The few Edmonton businessmen who had both the need and the cash to hire an airplane preferred to use the services of well-established bush pilots like C. H. "Punch" Dickens and W. R. "Wop" May, who were already famous for their exploits while McConachie was still struggling through high school. He had no better luck trying to get a government airmail contract: "No experience," said the Post Office bureaucrats.

As the monthly bills for hangar rent mounted up, McConachie

finally landed another charter: hauling fish. For the duration of the winter he was to deliver 30,000 pounds of freshly caught whitefish per week from the Cold Lake region on the Alberta-Saskatchewan border to a rail siding northeast of Edmonton, from which point a fast freight rushed them, packed in ice, to the kosher markets of Chicago. After logging flying hours at three times the safe rate in order to meet his contract, an exhausted McConachie was dumbfounded to find himself still in debt to Uncle Harry at the end of the fishing season. In bidding for the job, he had naively calculated only his operating costs and added the slimmest of profit margins, totally forgetting the next major overhaul due on his overworked aircraft. Meanwhile, his competitors made crude jokes about "that Fish Fokker" and held their noses in his presence—though it was a fair question whether a cabinload of fresh fish smelled any worse than a couple of prospectors ripe from six months in the bush. McConachie was painfully learning what it took to survive in his business. He was also building a reputation as a man who would fly anything, anywhere.

Barnstorming, occasional flights with secretive prospectors to remote mountain valleys, and four more winters of hauling fish (at a more profitable rate) kept McConachie out of bankruptcy through the mid-1930s. In fact, he was eventually able to afford several more second-hand planes, even if his small but loyal cadre of pilots and mechanics had to be satisfied with IOUs during slack periods. More than once he had to resort to a kind of aerial shell game, moving his aircraft around from airfield to airfield to keep his creditors from seizing them.[9]

In 1935, McConachie's prospects began to improve. Somehow, for a paltry $2,500, he persuaded an irascible millionaire named Harry Oaks to part with a 1933 Ford Trimotor worth over $50,000. The plane, the largest then flying in Canada, briefly became the mainstay of McConachie's new company, United Air Transport, although he soon sold it (at a huge profit) to buy several smaller but more versatile craft. He had decided that the time was right to begin scheduled flights for passengers and mail between Vancouver, Edmonton, and the Yukon. A similar service, pioneered by the famous duo of Dickens and May, had long existed for those heading "down north" from Edmonton to the trading posts and settlements along the Mackenzie River. That was easy flying compared to the hazards of the high granite country of the Rockies.

McConachie needed two more years to develop the necessary intermediate landing facilities and win government approval for the most dangerous segments of his proposed new airline route. On July

5, 1937, he took off for the first scheduled commercial flight from
Edmonton to Whitehorse, Yukon Territory, 1,200 miles to the
northwest. Flying another Ford Trimotor—this one the very latest
model, with a tastefully decorated cabin and what the newspapers
referred to as "indoor plumbing" (a great advance over the alternatives previously available on UAT)—McConachie's flight plan called
for a fourteen-hour trip with fuel stops at Fort St. John, Fort Nelson,
and Lower Post near Watson Lake. Strong headwinds forced an
unscheduled landing for fuel at Grande Prairie on the flight to Fort
St. John from Edmonton; but the rest of the trip went smoothly, and
the pontoon-equipped Trimotor tied up to the dock at Whitehorse
only three hours behind schedule. The return flight on July 8 was
uneventful and on time.[10] McConachie's goal of regular air service to
the Yukon had become a reality—almost.

All of UAT's planes on the Yukon run were equipped to land on
water, using either skis or floats, depending on the season. To most
north country settlers, accustomed to the difficulties of travel during
the fall freeze-up and the spring thaw, it mattered little that no
airplane could land safely on the region's lakes and rivers during
those transitional periods. To the president and chief pilot of a
cash-poor airline, however, it mattered a lot. With salaries and other
fixed monthly expenses to pay, McConachie risked financial disaster
by having to suspend all flights twice each year for weeks at a time.
But it was equally risky to prolong the flying season. Late one winter,
several of his less-cautious pilots gambled on the ice conditions only
to wreck their planes. Unfortunately, the boss had just canceled most
of UAT's insurance coverage to save money.

There was an obvious solution to the money problems inherent in
a nine-month flying year. All McConachie had to do was put wheels
back on his planes and find good, all-weather airfields for them to
land on. Both Edmonton and Whitehorse already had such fields, in
addition to their float-plane bases; and Grande Prairie and Fort St.
John at least had rudimentary, easily improvable grass strips in
operation. That left only Fort Nelson and Watson Lake. But new
airfields at those tiny, remote settlements were not going to be easy
or cheap to build.

Isolated in the far northeast corner of British Columbia by endless
miles of dense spruce forest and boggy patches of decayed vegetation
called *muskeg*, Fort Nelson consisted of a scruffy collection of frame
houses and log cabins. Its population included the Hudson's Bay
Company's factor, four native families, a variable number of semi-
transient trappers, hunters, and prospectors, and one mixed-race

free trader named Tommy Clark. Clark was famous in those parts for his bizarre collection of glass eyes. On Sundays he wore one emblazoned with a crucifix; on other days the pupil might be yellow and blue, or even brown to match his good eye.

A dozen or so scrawny horses grazed in and around the settlement, which could muster a rusty plow and a wagon or two, but nothing remotely resembling a bulldozer. Had McConachie been able to afford the cost of sending one in, it could only have reached Fort Nelson in one of two ways. During winter months, 300 miles of primitive and lightly traveled sleigh trail wound along frozen rivers and through the muskeg forest to Fort St. John. After the muskeg thawed and the waterways cleared of ice, however, the sleigh trail became impassable. The alternative route involved a circuitous trip of more than 1,000 miles by barge and portage from Edmonton down the Athabasca and Slave rivers, across Great Slave Lake, down the Mackenzie to the confluence of the Liard, and finally up the Liard to the Fort Nelson River. Under the circumstances, the best McConachie could do to get a landing strip started at Fort Nelson was to talk an Edmonton landscape gardener—a rough-looking but college-educated Irishman named Clancy Craig—into accepting the challenge.

Craig flew up to Fort Nelson with a set of plans, some simple tools, and the authority to hire whatever men and horses he could find in the vicinity. Greeting him was Tommy Clark, the trader, whose glass eye that day featured a tiny Union Jack on a field of pink.

McConachie had selected a straight stretch of gravel bank along the Fort Nelson River as the site for his new strip. The first plane rolled to a stop on it one cool September evening in 1940. Having endured months of backbreaking toil, vicious swarms of black flies and mosquitos, and the fickle work habits of his local "helpers"—to whom arduous daily labor with a pick and shovel was a strange and unpleasant new concept—Clancy Craig was glad to return to his gardening business in Edmonton.[11]

For the construction needed at Watson Lake, nestled deep in the Rockies midway between Fort Nelson and Whitehorse, McConachie hired "Tiny" Johnson and Jack Baker. Johnson, an amiable giant of a man—6 feet 6 inches tall and weighing 300 pounds or so—could do amazing things with an axe. He also served as a human crane, single-handedly unloading the heavy drums of aviation gasoline carried aboard almost every inbound cargo flight. But Johnson was better at some things than others. Alone one snowy day in the Watson Lake radio shack with the airfield shut down and Baker, the regular operator, off duty, Johnson was startled to hear McConachie's voice calling urgently through the static. Grabbing the mike, he said, "Hi, Grant. This is Tiny."

"How's the weather down there, Tiny?" asked his boss.

"Not bad for this time of year," came the answer.

". . . Tiny, I'm in trouble. It's snowing like hell up here, and I've got to know what it's like down there where you are before I let down."

"Gosh, Grant, why didn't you say what you wanted to know. It's snowing like hell down here, too."

"No. No. You haven't got the idea, Tiny. Listen. I'm up here on top of the cloud deck. I want to let down through it. What is your ceiling down there?"

Johnson's voice took on new confidence, "Well, I can sure give you the answer to that one. It's beaverboard. I should know. I built this shack myself."

McConachie made it safely through the murk to Watson Lake, but Tiny Johnson's brief career as a radio operator was over.[12]

Slowly, through 1939 and into 1940, the work of improving the airfields along the Edmonton–Whitehorse route continued, helped along by McConachie's uncanny ability to turn every financial crisis to his advantage. Unable to keep up the payments on a $250,000 loan from the Royal Bank of Canada, he persuaded the directors of the Imperial Oil Company to give him $100,000 in temporary credit by reminding them of the business they would lose if the bank foreclosed on him.

With eighteen months of free gas and oil to count on, McConachie then further improved his cash flow by negotiating a deal with a firm that had recently acquired the Canadian sales rights to a new twin-engine monoplane of advanced design, the Barkley-Grow. At an asking price of $70,000 each, none of these sleek, all-aluminum beauties had yet been sold. Eager to have McConachie promote its new aircraft, the company was willing to let him buy three for $10,000 apiece. As broke as ever, McConachie made a counteroffer: he would "demonstrate" the versatility of the Barkley-Grows as his flagships on the Yukon run in exchange for a no-money-down lease-purchase contract with monthly payments of $3,000. It was a deal.[13]

What impressed the directors of these two large corporations was obviously not the current financial status of McConachie's backwoods airline, but his persuasive vision of its potential for future growth. Soon after changing his company's name to Yukon Southern Air Transport in 1939, he instituted through service to Alaska by means of connecting flights at Whitehorse with Pan American Airways. Pan Am's famous Clippership "flying boats" were already a familiar sight along the Inside Passage on the Seattle–Fairbanks run. In the spring of 1940, McConachie announced plans to compete head-to-head with Pan Am for overseas business by extending YSAT's service as far as Vladivostok. Yukon Southern's loyal but long-suffering passengers were less impressed by his ambitious plans than were the business moguls of Toronto and Montreal. The airline's erratic schedule caused north country wags to rechristen it "Yukon Seldom."[14]

Profit-minded businessmen were not the only ones to recognize the growing importance of regular flights to Alaska. In 1935 the Canadian Department of Transportation began a survey of possible airfield sites for a future great-circle route to the Orient. After several years of studies and reports, the bureaucrats in Ottawa reached the obvious conclusion: the route to Alaska and beyond that made the most sense was the one already being pioneered by McConachie.

Thus, in 1939, the Canadian government began its own program to improve the safety and capacity of the chain of landing fields between Edmonton and Whitehorse. Initially, most of its efforts went into installing more and better navigational aids, both radio and visual, but plans were also being drawn up for entirely new airfields at Fort Nelson and Watson Lake to replace McConachie's marginally adequate facilities.[15] Then world events intervened: on September 1, Germany invaded Poland. For Canada, as a member of the British Commonwealth, the Atlantic lines of communication suddenly became all-important.

Since Ottawa found itself preoccupied with the war in Europe, little real progress was made during 1940 on upgrading the Edmonton–Whitehorse flight route. McConachie did what he could at Fort Nelson and Watson Lake, using his own limited resources. He also managed to persuade community-minded civic groups in Grande Prairie and Fort St. John to make some minor improvements on their own fields.

Even as the priorities of war slowed commercial development in the Canadian northwest, the region itself grew in strategic and military importance. The worsening international situation throughout the summer of 1940 compelled both Canadian and American leaders to reexamine their defense plans. The growing threat to both nations—not only from the Atlantic but now from the Pacific as well—meant that a cooperative approach to strategic planning, encompassing the entire North American continent, was becoming daily more necessary.

One result of such new thinking was the Ogdensburg Agreement, announced jointly on August 18, 1940, by President Franklin D. Roosevelt and Prime Minister Mackenzie King after a hastily arranged meeting in that obscure town on the New York-Canada border. Roosevelt had gone there on his private train to inspect seven Regular Army and National Guard divisions that were undergoing training in the vicinity. King drove down from Ottawa for an evening's discussion of "the mutual problems of defense in relation to the safety of Canada and the United States." Their brief declaration announced the immediate establishment of a Permanent Joint Board on Defense (PJBD) consisting of five or six members from each country, mostly military men. The PJBD was to "consider in the broad sense the defense of the north half of the Western Hemisphere" and would "commence immediate studies relating to sea, land and air problems. . . ."[16]

Somewhat surprisingly, Roosevelt's choice for chairman of the American section of the board was New York City's mayor, Fiorello H. LaGuardia. The flamboyant "Little Flower" was both the scourge of the city's political crooks and the public servant who read the funnies over the radio to its children during a newspaper strike. LaGuardia did have some military experience, however. He had commanded an aviation training squadron in Italy during World War I and had flown combat missions as a pilot-bombardier (concurrently retaining his seat in the U.S. Congress), although his brash impatience with red tape and protocol kept him in constant trouble with his superiors. As a U.S. Army major, LaGuardia had blithely addressed Italy's King Victor Emmanuel III as "Manny" during a wartime public relations visit. Such a man was unlikely to abide by the niceties of ceremonial etiquette in his new diplomatic position or be particularly sensitive to Canadian wariness of any martial embrace by the United States. Nevertheless, Roosevelt trusted LaGuardia's political instincts and knew him to be a man of deep integrity and boundless energy.[17]

The senior American military representative on the PJBD was Major General S. D. Embick, a member of the Joint Chiefs of Staff. Assisting him were three field-grade officers, one from each service, including an aviator. The State Department's interests were represented by a Foreign Service officer of middle rank, who also served as the American section's secretary.

The organization of the PJBD's Canadian section mirrored that of its U.S. counterpart. Colonel O. M. Biggar, an eminent Ottawa lawyer who had served as Canada's Judge Advocate General in World War I, was LaGuardia's opposite number. The two chairmen presided jointly over the board's first meeting in Ottawa on August 26, 1940, and the force of the American's personality immediately exerted itself. "In exactly six and one-half minutes all the formalities were cleared and all the courtesies were accomplished," LaGuardia later reported. "The board decided from the outset to use plain, everyday understandable English and to dispense with the complexities involved in diplomatic usage and in legalisms."[18] The Joint Board's periodic meetings, alternating every month or so at sites in the United States and Canada, were noted for their no-nonsense approach to the complex issues of coordinating the continent's defense.

No less than seven formal recommendations went to the leaders of both governments as a result of the Joint Board's first meeting. Most of these dealt with urgent measures to strengthen Canada's defenses in her Maritime Provinces or to establish procedures for exchanging various kinds of military and economic information. Additionally, the board directed its military members to prepare detailed recommendations for improving both nations' coastal defenses. Contained within this comprehensive First Report, submitted to both governments on October 4, 1940, was a recommendation that a chain of landing fields capable of handling military aircraft, including heavy bombers, be established on a route across Canada between the United States and Alaska.[19]

The PJBD's strong interest in building these landing fields was made very clear by its Tenth Recommendation, dated November 14. This called for a series of bases in both Canada and Alaska with cleared approaches, 5,000-foot runways, and facilities for refueling, maintenance, and crew rest. Not surprisingly, all but two of the Canadian bases were to be located along the existing route serviced by Grant McConachie's Yukon Southern. (The exceptions were at Prince George and Smithers, in central British Columbia.) The Joint Board's Tenth Recommendation was quickly approved by both governments. Even if McConachie had been able to afford the construction services of a thousand men like Clancy Craig and Tiny Johnson, he still could never have built his wilderness airfields on the scale Ottawa now envisioned.

The Canadians began work on their portion of what became known as the Northwest Staging Route in early 1941. Top priority was given to carving out an entirely new strip on a hilltop a few miles west of Fort Nelson. All of the necessary men, equipment, and supplies for the job first had to be assembled at Dawson Creek, British Columbia, some 400 miles by rail northwest of Edmonton at the end of the Northern Alberta Railway. Next, everything had to be moved across the ice-covered Peace River to Fort St. John, 50 miles farther north. After that, a team of bulldozers had to widen and improve the 300-mile-long winter sleigh trail to Fort Nelson so that trucks and tractor-drawn cargo sleds could get through. Only then could construction work on the new airfield actually begin. The Western Construction Company of Edmonton had the contract.

On February 9, a crisp, sunny Sunday, the lead train of the company's bulldozers headed north out of Dawson Creek. In front rumbled a heavy, trail-breaking Caterpillar D8 tractor followed by two smaller D4 'dozers, one of which towed a string of six sled-mounted wooden huts. Measuring about 8 by 20 feet each, two of these "cabooses" were bunkhouses, a third contained the kitchen and all its supplies, a fourth housed the foreman, the radio gear, and a first aid station, and the last two carried spare parts, tools, and some sawmill equipment.

A few miles beyond Fort St. John the heavy work of widening and improving the sleigh trail began. It was slow, exhausting work, and dangerous and frustrating as well. Accidents and breakdowns happened often. Clearing 10 miles of new trail was a good day's work; the average came closer to 5 miles. Here is a typical entry from the first aid man's diary:

> March 18th. We have not made very much progress today. Travelled about 4 miles in 24 hours. Hard going through heavy spruce and . . . a nice stand of birch, we are stopped side of another lake. Had supper. . . . Blacksmith doing a little welding. . . . We pulled train again early morning of the 19th about 1½ miles, had breakfast, then went on again . . . heavy willow bush . . . hard work for the bulldozer. . . . Travelled about 3 miles today. . . . The D4 ran a stick through the radiator this morning, took them till noon to get it fixed.[20]

As the trailbreaking party neared Fort Nelson in late March, more bulldozers and a long train of trucks carrying everything from drums of aviation gasoline to flush toilets and office furniture rumbled north through Fort St. John. Any resident old enough to remember Charles Bedaux's ill-fated procession in the summer of 1934 surely must have smiled a little.

Except for a few native and white families who trapped fox and beaver for a living, and the traders who visited their isolated cabins by dogsled or on horseback, the immense region of forest and muskeg beyond Fort St. John had known little human activity in decades. A few oldtimers could no doubt recall (or may even have been among) the eager bands of would-be prospectors who had struggled through the area in 1898 on their way to the gold fields of the Klondike. But nothing in the lifetime of these solitary pioneers had prepared them for the changes World War II was about to bring to their existence. One trader, Slim Byrnes, later recorded his first encounter with mechanized civilization that winter along the trail to Fort Nelson:

> We were taking goods into the north by horse and dog sleighs the way our fathers and grandfathers had done . . . But when we met this cat train pushing its way north [and] . . . a great fleet of trucks as far as the eye could see . . . following up the rear . . . time went ahead more in a few minutes than it had in a whole lifetime. Like the snap of your fingers, we changed from the old to the new.[21]

As the construction work at Fort Nelson continued into mid-1941, the Canadian government turned its attention to upgrading Mc-Conachie's old facilities at Watson Lake. Once again, the first problem was how to bring in the massive amounts of equipment and supplies needed to build a modern airport in the middle of nowhere. The most feasible approach involved shipping everything by coastal steamer up the Inside Passage from Vancouver to the mouth of the Stikine River; from there on smaller boats up to Telegraph Creek; thence by portage to Dease Lake; across the lake and down the Dease River; and finally over yet another portage to the airfield site. Three months and four tedious intermediate transloading operations were required to make this 1,000-mile trip. Boatloads of bulldozers and work crews bound for Watson Lake—as well as more flush toilets and office furniture—began heading north from Vancouver as soon as the ice cleared on the Stikine.[22]

Construction of the two U.S. airfields on the Alaskan end of the Staging Route presented fewer problems. The base at Big Delta was only 100 miles from Fairbanks and was easily accessible via the Richardson Highway, while bulldozers for the work at Northway, near the Canadian border, were driven to within 60 miles of the site over a mining road and then barged the remaining distance down the Nabesna River.

Steadily rising hostility between the United States and Japan was reflected in the PJBD's Joint Basic Defense Plan No. 2, produced in 1941. The plan assigned primary responsibility for protecting shipping in the Northern Pacific to the U.S. Navy, with assistance as necessary from the U.S. Army and all Canadian services. The U.S. Army had the mission of defending military and naval bases in Alaska and the Aleutian Islands, with support from the Royal Canadian Air Force.

The tension that summer also prompted the Joint Board's Nineteenth Recommendation. Dated July 29, 1941, it stated that completion of both the Canadian and the U.S. sections of the Northwest Staging Route was "now of extreme importance." Coupled with the crisis atmosphere, this recommendation eventually led to diversion of a few more resources to speed the project, but both Washington and Ottawa had too many other problems to worry about. In September, the five Canadian and two U.S. airbases of the Staging Route were declared usable under visual flight conditions during daylight. Another year would pass, however, before they became fully operational.[23] The same factors that slowed completion of the Northwest Staging Route—great distances, an antiquated transportation system, and not enough men and equipment for the size of the job—also bedeviled Colonel Simon Bolivar Buckner, the U.S. Army officer responsible for the overall defense of Alaska.

World War II was already ten months old when Buckner arrived in Alaska in July 1940. Dunkerque was history, France had fallen, and the Battle of Britain had begun. In China, three years of undeclared war had left the Japanese in control of most of the coastal provinces and driven the Nationalist armies into the interior, where a trickle of supplies still reached them over the Burma Road. That September, when Japanese armies began to occupy French Indo-China, President Roosevelt responded by imposing an embargo on scrap iron and steel. Simultaneously, Germany, Japan, and Italy concluded a ten-year alliance, the Three-Power Pact. As the British hung on against the aerial blitz into 1941, Lend-Lease and other forms of American aid began to flow across the Atlantic. Similar assistance was extended the Soviet Union after Germany invaded it in June 1941. Russia's desperate all-out effort to halt the German advance eastward left Japan with only one opponent capable of thwarting her plans for military and economic hegemony in the Western Pacific: the United States.

Colonel Buckner's Alaskan command initially consisted of two infantry companies, totaling 276 men, and several construction units on temporary duty that were engaged in erecting new facilities at Anchorage and Fairbanks. The U.S. Army Air Corps maintained small airfields near each of those cities, but no aircraft were permanently stationed at either location. Measuring his miserably inadequate forces against the growing Japanese threat, Buckner sent message after message to the War Department requesting reinforcements. Chief of Staff General George C. Marshall had more nervous commanders than he had resources to satisfy them, but Alaska got what forces he could spare from other priority areas. A squadron of obsolescent B-18 medium bombers and another of P-36 fighters arrived, but Buckner repeatedly asked for more. None would be forthcoming, the War Department kept replying, until the Japanese committed an overt hostile act.

Buckner also asked for Marine detachments to protect the Navy bases at Sitka and Kodiak, for new airfields at Kodiak and Unalaska, and for additional Army troops to guard the latter field and the one at Dutch Harbor. Security forces for most of these bases were eventually approved, as was the airfield at Kodiak, but as late as October 1941 the War Department still refused to authorize the Unalaska facility or any more warplanes.[24] Nevertheless, with the Northwest Staging Route nearing completion and a network of small Civil Aeronautics Administration (CAA) facilities across Alaska under construction, any large formation of aircraft sent north would at least be able to find places to land. By the summer of 1941, Buckner, now a brigadier general, could also draw some satisfaction from the fact that his command had grown to 6,000 men, with 16,000 more promised by the War Department by the end of the year.[25]

General Buckner's anxieties were certainly understandable in view of his orders. In one terse sentence they read: ". . . defend U.S. Military and Naval installations in Alaska . . . against sea, land and air attacks, and against sabotage; deny use by the enemy of the sea and land bases in Alaska and the Aleutian Islands; support the Navy."[26] In September 1941, still worried by the enormous gap between the capabilities of his forces and the requirements of his mission, he wrote his superior:

> There exist alarming deficiencies in both Army and Navy facilities in Alaska. . . . Due to the utter lack of roads and railroads . . . the Army garrison cannot be regarded as anything but local defense forces. There exist no means now of determining when or where the enemy is coming and no means of stopping his approach if we know it. We must have an air striking force now. . . . Additional airfields . . . must be provided. The Navy is . . . wholly unable to perform offshore and inshore patrolling or control harbor entrances.[27]

Three months later, General Buckner's worst fears seemed about to come true. At the time of Japan's attack on Pearl Harbor, the Alaskan Defense Command consisted of 21,945 Army troops stationed in eleven garrisons situated hundreds or even thousands of miles apart. Of the twelve medium bombers and twenty pursuit planes under Buckner's command, perhaps half could have taken off to meet an invader.[28]

PART TWO

Rough Cut for a Road

PREVIOUS SPREAD: Starting west from Fort Nelson, April 1942. Courtesy of Chief of Engineers, Office of History.

3

DECEMBER 1941–MARCH 1942

The Secret Plan

In less than two hours on December 7, 1941, an aerial armada of carrier-based Japanese dive bombers and torpedo planes crippled the U.S. Navy's Pacific Fleet. The surprise attack on Pearl Harbor sank or seriously damaged eight battleships, three cruisers, and dozens of smaller vessels. At Hickam Field and outlying airbases, the remains of nearly 300 aircraft lay amidst the smoldering wreckage of shops and hangars. Casualty lists eventually carried the names of almost 4,500 Americans killed, wounded, or missing that Sunday morning. For those within sight and sound of Hawaii's military bases, the indiscriminate horror and destruction of modern warfare were no longer just grim headlines or flickering newsreel images from places like Shanghai, London, or Leningrad.

Residents of Hawaii felt with special intensity the anger and fear that gripped all Americans. Helen Stermer, a Honolulu woman who managed a small apartment house near Waikiki, recorded in her diary the shock and confusion of the next few weeks. Expecting the Japanese to return at any moment—"which was only natural considering the startling beginning they had made"—she described her activities on that anxious first evening as she waited for her civilian husband to return from his job at the base:

I . . . found some extra rugs and comforters, and nailed them up at our . . . windows, running in and out in the darkness and turning on lights to see how much showed through. . . . I was praying that God would please let us stay in that apartment and let Paul come home to it at night . . .

51

> After I had finished . . . some tenants stumbled in . . . and we
> sat on the floor in our bedroom, because the tiny night light . . .
> gave a nice little glow and seemed cheerful. . . . Then Paul came
> in, dripping wet.

Paul Stermer told the huddled, frightened group of seeing trucks piled high with bodies from the attack; of meeting Navy friends in tears, too stunned to talk; of hearing that sentries were shooting people who failed to halt when challenged; and of walking home the 8 miles from Pearl Harbor in the rain while, high overhead, flashes of anti-aircraft fire lit up the blacked-out streets. "We afterward found out," his wife wrote, "that the 'attack' that night was some of our own planes trying to return. . . . They were all shot down . . . except one."

As the days passed, Helen Stermer grew more philosophical about the continuing need for air-raid alerts, curfews, and blackouts. "When the sun sets we are suddenly prisoners of Japan," she admitted ruefully, "not only because we must stay indoors . . . but because the very darkness has us in its grip." Most of all she was conscious of how much her life and her priorities had changed:

> On the seventh, it was as though a sponge had been wiped across a
> blackboard. Old possessions and ideas to which we have always
> clung . . . were cast aside in one short instant. Time is now the
> precious commodity. . . . The desperate need to make every second
> count . . . in the effort to prepare against the return of our enemies
> gives speed to our every thought and movement.[1]

Helen Stermer was not alone in fearing "the return of our enemies." Nor were such fears without foundation.

Pressing their advantage, the Japanese quickly overwhelmed the defenders of Guam and Wake Island. Although the garrison at Midway withstood the next assault and General Douglas MacArthur continued to hold out in the Philippines, the probability that Japan would soon gain control of the western half of the Pacific was a major concern in Washington by early 1942. Such a circumstance would make Hawaii even more vulnerable to attack and expose the Aleutians and Alaska to invasion.

Not only would a foothold in Alaska put the Japanese in position to mount further attacks on the United States mainland, it might also deny American forces the northern Pacific air and naval bases, which were now seen as essential for final victory. Maintaining military control over Alaska and expanding the bases there were thus considered strategic necessities. But after the U.S. Navy's losses at Pearl Harbor, its ability to protect the sea lines of communication to Alaska was suddenly very much in doubt.

In the first sixty days of the war, intelligence reports regarding Japanese naval activity off the West Coast and in the Gulf of Alaska listed fifty-eight visual sightings or radio fixes on hostile ships or aircraft. Some of these reports were unconfirmed or of doubtful credibility, but others were indisputable. Sixteen actual combat engagements or submarine attacks on merchant shipping occurred in December alone. Six of the freighters and tankers that were torpedoed or shelled managed to make port, but two others went to the bottom. These figures were small in comparison to the worldwide losses of Allied and neutral merchant shipping during the same period, but the cumulative effect of such sinkings, together with the possibility that Japan would intensify its interdiction campaign in U.S. and Canadian coastal waters, cast a pessimistic light on plans to strengthen and supply Alaska by sea. Some protection against submarine attack was gained by routing ships through the Inside Passage to Skagway, but from that point onward they had to travel in escorted convoys. For escort duty, and to scout for submarines throughout the Gulf of Alaska and in Puget Sound, the U.S. Navy could spare only five destroyers.[2]

While the bulk of the cargo bound for Alaska would have to go by sea, weather and enemy permitting, reinforcements were also scheduled to arrive by air—primarily aircraft, crews, and high-priority items. In early January 1942, the first contingent of thirty-eight U.S. warplanes headed out over the Northwest Staging Route. All but eleven crashed along the way, although ten of the downed planes underwent repairs en route and limped into Fairbanks over the next month. Twelve aircraft never made it. Pilot inexperience and severe winter weather contributed to this debacle, as did the distance between airfields and the shortage of navigational aids to mark the unfamiliar and rugged terrain.[3]

Among the subjects discussed at a Cabinet meeting in Washington on January 16, 1942, was the need for a less-risky way to get men and supplies to Alaska. Secretary of the Interior Harold L. Ickes suggested that existing plans for the long-proposed highway to Alaska be reexamined. The President concurred and appointed a committee consisting of Ickes, Secretary of War Henry L. Stimson, and Navy Secretary Frank Knox to study the alternatives and give him a recommendation.[4]

The actual task of analyzing the various possible overland routes to Alaska fell to two Army Engineers assigned to the War Plans Division, Brigadier General Robert W. Crawford and Colonel James K. Tully. The first and easiest question facing Crawford and Tully was whether to build a road or a railroad over whichever route was finally selected. Despite the greater cargo capacity of a rail line, they quickly rejected this option because an equivalent length of two-lane gravel road could be constructed faster and at less expense. Even so, their estimates indicated that such a road would probably take at least two years to complete and cost between $50,000 and $60,000 per mile, depending on the terrain through which it passed.[5]

But how to decide on a route? Despite the optimistic claims of each proponent group, Routes A, B, C, and D all seemed to have more disadvantages than advantages from a military planner's point of view (see maps on p. 13 and 25).

Although Route A was shorter than two of the other proposed alternatives, it was close to the coast and vulnerable to enemy interdiction should the Navy lose control of the Gulf of Alaska. Given the prevailing winds, this proximity to the sea also meant that Route A would be plagued by fog and rain for most of the year and by heavy snows during the remainder. In addition, some very rugged terrain had to be negotiated, including one mountain pass at an elevation of 4,475 feet.

Route B, through the Rocky Mountain Trench, was slightly shorter than Route A and avoided many of the coastal route's disadvantages of terrain and climate. But Route B had its own peculiar problems, not the least of which was the fact that it had no prominent American backers. Although the intervening mountains offered some protection against the foul weather of the coast, snow accumulations and flooding from violent spring runoffs would be major hazards along most of the route for half the year. The greatest disadvantage of Route B, however, from the War Department's standpoint, was that it did not pass through Whitehorse, the terminus of the railroad coming up from Skagway at the northern end of the Inside Passage. The existence of a connecting sea-rail route not only would speed the highway's completion by permitting construction to begin at several points simultaneously, it would also increase the overall capacity and flexibility of the completed supply link between the United States and Alaska.

The main advantage of Route C, the Prairie Route, was the relative lack of fog and snow east of the Rockies, although the sketchy survey data available showed passes nearly as high as those on Route A and at a greater elevation than any on Route B. Route C shared the latter's major disadvantage of not connecting with the railhead at Whitehorse.

Finally, there was Vilhjalmur Stefansson's 1,700-mile-long Inside Prairie Route (Route D), which skirted the Rockies entirely in favor of a westerly crossing through the less-rugged Mackenzie Mountains. In other respects, Stefansson's plan had essentially the same disadvantages as Route C. Balanced against the greater length of Route D was the fact that it would pass near Norman Wells, whose oil could then be more easily developed and exploited in support of the war effort.[6]

Plotting these four alternatives side by side on a map, General Crawford and Colonel Tully undoubtedly noticed that all of them shared another disadvantage that suddenly assumed great importance: none of the proposed routes paralleled the chain of airfields of the Northwest Staging Route. Having recently lost one-third of the first overland flight of military aircraft to Alaska, the War Department recognized the need for both rapid improvements to these airfields and additional navigational aids all along the way. Yet several of the landing strips were hundreds of miles from the nearest railhead or harbor. They had been built in 1941 by equipment laboriously brought over frozen winter trails or by river barge and portage during warmer weather. In the present emergency, such methods were far too slow.

Although the President had not specifically requested that thought be given to building a dual-purpose supply line for Alaska and the airfields along the Staging Route, the idea made such good military sense that the War Plans Division added it as a fifth alternative. All seven airfields of the Staging Route could then be linked by following the southern part of Route C for approximately 630 miles to Watson Lake, crossing over the Rockies to Whitehorse (a distance of about 300 miles), and joining Route A for the last 500 miles to the Richardson Highway at Big Delta. Such a road would combine most of the better features of Routes A and C and eliminate their most serious drawbacks.

Despite the attractiveness of this plan, it too had flaws: a road through the Rockies between Watson Lake and Whitehorse had never been seriously considered before. No one knew for certain whether it could be built, much less what specific route it might follow. Uncertainties also existed regarding the stretch between Fort Nelson and Watson Lake. Available terrain studies of both areas were vague about such matters as elevations, gradients, soil conditions, and hydrography. To be sure, on a large-scale map these particular mountains looked no more difficult to traverse than the roughest sections of the other four routes, but the other proposals all had influential backers eager to vouch for the feasibility of their versions of the highway. Crawford and Tully had no experts to consult and no time for a terrain survey.

Nevertheless, impressed by the overriding military advantage of a road connecting the airfields of the Staging Route, and apparently relying more on faith than on facts that some way through the Rockies could be found, the two officers decided that their own hybrid plan best met the needs of the moment. [7]

The cabinet committee appointed by the President met with General Crawford and Colonel Tully on February 2, 1942. Secretaries Ickes, Knox, and Stimson quickly approved their recommendation and requested that the Army Corps of Engineers submit a preliminary plan for constructing the highway as soon as possible. Within 48 hours it was ready, signed by Brigadier General Clarence L. Sturdevant, Assistant to the Chief of Engineers.

Four 1,300-man Engineer construction regiments, each reinforced with a light pontoon company, were needed to build an initial pioneer trail, said Sturdevant. The 35th and 341st Engineers—the latter a regiment not yet activated—would start work from two different points at the southern end of the route. In the middle, the 18th Engineers and another new regiment, the 340th, would start from Whitehorse and work in opposite directions. Meanwhile, at the Alaskan end, civilian contractors under the supervision of the Public Roads Administration (PRA) would head southeast from Big Delta toward the Canadian border and an eventual linkup with the 18th Engineers. Finally, using the pioneer trail as an access road, other PRA contractors would come along behind the Army Engineers and construct a two-lane gravel-surface highway with permanent bridges and culverts. The first phase of the plan is shown schematically on the accompanying map.

Map coverage of the proposed route from Whitehorse to Big Delta was generally good, said General Sturdevant, so this half of the final survey could be done by the PRA. Southeast of Whitehorse, however, the available maps would have to be supplemented in places— particularly in the Rockies—by aerial photography. Two Army Engineer survey companies would locate this section of the route.

The 35th Engineers would move into position first, taking with them enough supplies to last through the summer and using the existing winter trail from Fort St. John to reach Fort Nelson before the

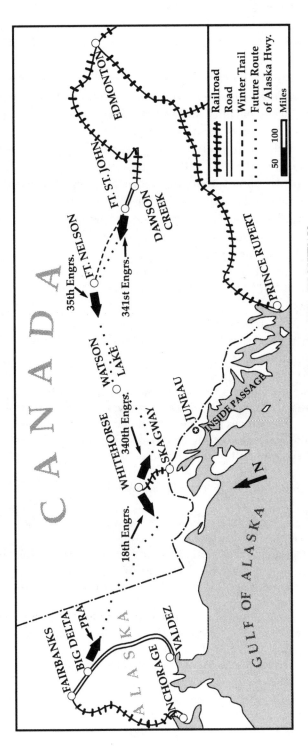

ORIGINAL PLAN FOR THE ALASKA HIGHWAY

spring thaw began in April. In contrast to the 35th's initial isolation at Fort Nelson beyond 250 miles of soggy muskeg, the other three regiments and the PRA contractors would all have the advantage of dependable supply lines, simplifying their logistical problems and allowing them more time to move into position. At any rate, it would be mid-May, at the earliest, before the ground dried enough to permit work to begin anywhere along the route.

Sufficient military and civilian construction equipment was available for the job, Sturdevant concluded; but to meet his troop requirements, he asked that the 340th and 341st Engineer Regiments be immediately activated, along with two pontoon companies. To cover initial expenses, pending the preparation of more detailed cost estimates, he also requested an allotment of $10 million from the President's Emergency Fund.[8]

Although the cabinet committee had already approved the project, Army Chief of Staff General George C. Marshall prudently checked with the Navy's top brass before incorporating General Sturdevant's plan in a final recommendation to the President. Said General Marshall in a February 4, 1942, memorandum to Admiral Ernest J. King, Commander in Chief of the U.S. Fleet:

> I would appreciate a brief statement as to the ability of the Navy, considering all its commitments and probable future requirements, to maintain, under all circumstances, uninterrupted communications for the United States forces in Alaska and to insure the delivery of essential supplies to the civilian population.

An experienced staff officer and a shrewd bureaucrat, Admiral King replied:

> I can make no such categorical commitment.
> In my opinion, the Navy can afford protection to the sea communications between the West Coast and Alaska adequate to ensure the maintenance there of all Army garrisons and the civilian population. It is probable that ships on this run will be lost through enemy action. It seems to me improbable that the enemy can obtain a foothold in Alaska from which he can render our sea communications dangerous. I cannot agree with the thesis that a road to Alaska is necessary because of the reason that the Navy cannot afford adequate protection to the shipping destined for that region.[9]

Though King's response expressly refuted one of the Army's main arguments, the admiral had admitted the possibility of shipping losses and had said nothing about the value of the proposed road as a supply line to the airbases along its route. That was equivocal enough to give General Marshall the leeway he needed to proceed with his recommendation to the President. Roosevelt approved the War Department's plan on February 11, 1942. Two days later, the Canadian War Cabinet gave its consent for survey work to begin and accepted an American request that the Permanent Joint Board on Defense work out a detailed agreement at its next scheduled meeting in late February. On February 14, without waiting for diplomatic confirmation, the War Department directed the Chief of Engineers to begin construction of the highway at once.[10]

Only twenty-six days after Secretary Ickes's suggestion to the President that the various prewar proposals for a highway to Alaska be reexamined, and prior to Canada's having approved anything more than a preliminary survey, the Army had Roosevelt's approval of its own plan and was moving to implement it. But much remained to be done before any actual construction began. Topping the list was the need to select an experienced senior officer to command the project, someone who could be counted on to get the job done despite all obstacles. General Sturdevant had just such a man in mind: Colonel William M. Hoge.

The Hoges were a martially inclined family. Bill Hoge was born in 1894 in Booneville, Missouri, where his father ran a small military school. All three of the Hoge boys graduated from West Point: Benjamin in 1914, Bill in 1916, and Kenneth in 1920. At the Point, the middle Hoge was remembered more for his exploits on the football field than for his achievements in the classroom, but he ranked just high enough in his class academically (twenty-ninth out of 125) to rate a commission in the Corps of Engineers, traditionally the career choice of the Academy's brainiest graduates.

Bill Hoge married his childhood sweetheart, Nettie Fredenhall, three weeks after the United States entered World War I. By the time of the Armistice eighteen months later, he was a highly decorated combat veteran. His courage under fire in command of a river crossing operation won him the Distinguished Service Cross, second only to the Medal of Honor as an award for valor.

Hoge's assignments during the interwar years confirmed his reputation as a comer. In 1921 the Army sent him to MIT for a degree in civil engineering; in 1927 he went to Fort Leavenworth for a year at the Command and General Staff School. One of his instructors at Fort Leavenworth was another bright West Point Engineer, Major Clarence L. Sturdevant, class of 1908. Their paths crossed again seven years later in the Philippines, where Sturdevant's duties as the Department Engineer included supervising Hoge's work as commander of the 14th Engineer Battalion of the Philippine Scouts. From 1935 to 1937, Hoge's battalion built a network of roads and bridges in the jungle of the Bataan Peninsula. Both men left the Philippines in 1937, but for the next five years their careers remained on parallel tracks. Until 1940, Sturdevant served as head of the Missouri River District, where he was responsible for flood-control measures, and Hoge ran one of his field offices in Omaha, Nebraska. Sturdevant's next assignment took him to Washington, D.C., to assist the Chief of Engineers, Major General Eugene Reybold, in all matters relating to the use of Engineer troop units. Soon thereafter, Bill and Nettie Hoge settled comfortably into colonel's quarters at nearby Fort Belvoir, Virginia, the Engineer Training Center.[11]

The two men had much in common. Sturdevant, too, came from the Midwest, was the son of a middle-class professional (a lawyer), and married a hometown girl. Like Hoge, he had been a standout athlete at West Point, holding the cadet records for the hammer throw and rifle marksmanship for many years. He remained a crack shot throughout his Army career, with a roomful of trophies to prove it. Hoge enjoyed shooting as well, but his favorite pastime was quail hunting with his dogs.

Equally revealing of the complex relationship between Hoge and his mentor were their differences. Much to his disappointment, Sturdevant never saw combat during World War I. Despite several successful assignments in command of troops over the years, he seems to have been even better as an instructor, staff officer, and administrator. He was deskbound in a key job in 1942 and looking balder and older than his fifty-seven years; his chances of ever getting close to the front lines were slim. But whatever frustrations and pressures he felt, his wartime photograph shows a kindly face, eyes crinkled with amusement behind rimless glasses.

If Sturdevant looked like Norman Rockwell's ideal grandfather, Hoge could best be described as a warrior. Lean, muscular, and in his prime at forty-eight, Sturdevant's darkly handsome alter ego radiated energy and a gruff competitiveness. It is surely no coincidence that he was stationed nearby and available for reassignment when Sturdevant needed an able commander for a high-priority project. Years later, when asked why he got the Alaska Highway job, Hoge said he thought it had something to do with his work building roads on Bataan.[12] That answer was certainly true, but it left a lot unsaid.

General Sturdevant's preliminary plan for the highway had been written under intense pressure by harried staff officers using only the information already in the War Department's files. Before things went any further, it was absolutely essential that Colonel Hoge make his own reconnaissance of as much of the proposed route as possible. The most pressing question was whether, and for how long, the existing 250 miles of winter trail from Fort St. John to the airfield at Fort Nelson, hastily bulldozed the previous winter, could support the heavy traffic envisioned by Sturdevant's plan.

Hoge also needed to take a look at the terrain between Fort Nelson and Whitehorse, particularly the one area of the Rockies that no one had yet thought to survey for a road—the mountains west of Watson Lake. But a ground-level inspection of that stretch in the dead of winter was out of the question; the best he could hope for was clear enough flying weather to allow him to scout the possibilities by air. Meanwhile, until Hoge was personally confident that a road could be built where the Army wanted it, the very existence of Sturdevant's plan was supposed to remain a military secret.[13]

On February 11, as soon as the President approved the plan, Sturdevant quietly set a lot of wheels in motion. Certain officers got cryptic telegrams assigning them immediately to new but unspecified duties at various locations. Other messages went out to quartermaster depots around the country, alerting them to be prepared to ship massive amounts of construction equipment, arctic clothing, and other supplies on short notice. General Sturdevant then departed for Ottawa to give Canadian officials a personal briefing on the Army's plan and prepare them for the massive incursion of U.S. troops and civilian contractors that was imminent. Simultaneously, Colonel Hoge left Washington by train for Edmonton.

Traveling with Hoge on the train were two other men: Fred Capes, a construction engineer from the Public Roads Administration's Denver office, and Lieutenant Colonel Edward A. Mueller, a Quartermaster Corps expert. Lieutenant Colonel Robert D. Ingalls, commander of the first construction regiment scheduled to begin work on the highway, joined them in Edmonton. Ingalls's unit, the 35th Engineers, was just completing training at Fort Ord, California.[14]

While in Edmonton, Hoge briefed Alberta provincial officials on the reasons for his reconnaissance. He also met with Grant McConachie, both to learn more about flying conditions over the Rockies and to solicit the veteran bush pilot's advice regarding the best path for a highway linking the airfields of the Northwest Staging Route. Hoge also made it clear to McConachie that the Army would soon be needing the services of his company for aerial surveys of portions of the route and for transporting high-priority passengers and cargo to and from the various construction sites.[15]

Despite the secrecy surrounding Hoge's mission, his group's presence in Edmonton did not go unnoticed by reporters, who easily deduced its purpose in being there. After all, how many plausible explanations could there be for the sudden appearance of four high-ranking American officials, three of them road-building experts, in western Canada? Sturdevant's instructions to Hoge evidently included permission to talk noncommittally about the project if cornered by the press. At any rate, a brief account of an interview with him, datelined February 19 from Edmonton, appeared the next day in the *Ottawa Journal.* The gist of the article was that a military highway to Alaska was being considered and that an American "commission" was in Canada to "study the proposed route" and make its recommendations to Washington. Significantly, the route being studied by the Americans was delineated: "Fort St. John, Fort Nelson, Whitehorse and into Alaska."[16] Anyone familiar with the various prewar highway proposals could now see that the U.S. Army had its own ideas about where the road should go.

Leaving Edmonton, the four Americans boarded the twice-weekly train for Dawson Creek, 400 miles to the northwest at the very end of the line for the Northern Alberta Railway. Another question facing Hoge was whether the NAR's lightweight track and rolling stock, adequate for the freight-hauling requirements of a thinly populated agricultural district, could stand up under the heavy loads and urgent timetables his mission entailed.

Long stretches of the roadbed traversed muskeg country, solid enough during the winter but jellylike during the warmer months, when derailments due to shifting or sinking track were so common that every train carried a flatcar-mounted crane and several cars full of gravel ballast for on-the-spot repairs. One prewar traveler on the line claimed to have ridden the cowcatcher to photograph the caribou and moose running alongside. He likened the experience to a roller-coaster ride in which "the mud squirts up in your face when the engine presses down the rails." At an average speed of 11 miles per hour, that midsummer journey between Dawson Creek and Edmonton had lasted a day and a half.[17] But this time, since it was winter, the train took only twenty-four hours to make the trip. On the morning of February 20, 1942, Hoge's group stepped down from their red-painted coach onto the station platform at Dawson Creek, population 600.

Dawson Creek's tallest and most important buildings were the row of five massive wooden grain elevators on a siding beyond the station at the east edge of town. Stretching smoothly to the horizon in all directions, the rich farmland of the Peace River Block—particularly its wheat—was responsible for bringing the railroad this far north and had caused a town to sprout where the tracks ended. From spring planting time until the grain elevators stood empty again in the fall, the frontier-style, false-front stores, hotels, and cafés bustled with activity; but not now. Snow covered the wooden sidewalks and the wide, unpaved streets, where the only traffic was an occasional truck or horse-drawn wagon jouncing over the frozen ruts.[18]

Waiting for Hoge in Dawson Creek was H. P. Keith from the Department of Transport's regional office. He had been assigned by Ottawa to accompany the Americans as chauffeur and guide on their reconnaissance of the winter trail up to Fort Nelson. Leaving Mueller behind in Dawson Creek to work on a plan for the sprawling supply depot that would soon become the southern terminus of the highway, Hoge, Ingalls, and Capes piled into Keith's battered vehicle and headed north.

A 50-mile stretch of rutted provincial road and the 1,500-foot-wide Peace River separated Dawson Creek from Fort St. John. On reaching the river, which was now covered by a thick sheet of ice, Hoge was surprised to learn that there was no bridge—a fact unknown (or overlooked) by the Army's planners in Washington. Keith explained that anyone wishing to cross the river here either did so while it was still frozen solid or waited for several weeks during the spring breakup in April until a ferry could go into operation.

Any chance of opening an emergency supply route to Alaska before the end of 1942 had depended entirely on moving Ingalls's regiment into position at Fort Nelson before warm weather turned the winter trail into a quagmire. Now the strength of the ice on the Peace River was a factor to worry about as well. Once either the river or the trail became impassable, the only way to transport a fully equipped construction regiment to Fort Nelson was to shuttle it by barge and portage down 1,000 miles of the Mackenzie River and its tributaries—a roundabout and tortuous trip that would take all summer.

The provincial road network, such as it was, petered out a few miles north of Fort St. John near Charlie Lake. There the farms ended and the region of unremitting forest and muskeg began. Soon Hoge and his companions were bumping along at 10 miles per hour over a bulldozed swath cut through monotonous miles of pine and spruce, varied every so often by the smoother surface of a frozen marsh or stream. Familiar with the trail and its hazards, Keith pressed on through the night, delivering his cramped and weary passengers to the relative comfort of the operations shack at the Fort Nelson airfield on the morning after their arrival in Dawson Creek.

The three Americans spent the next twenty-four hours at Fort Nelson, Ingalls scouting out a good site on high ground near the airfield for his future basecamp, and Hoge and Capes making several unsuccessful attempts at an aerial reconnaissance westward toward the Rockies through the low overcast.[19]

Having seen as much of the southern half of the proposed route as time and weather permitted, Hoge needed to get back to Washington at once to report to General Sturdevant. The latter was certain to be disappointed that no route through the mountains had yet been located. Otherwise, the reconnaissance had gone well. The cargo capacity of the Northern Alberta Railroad, while limited, seemed adequate for the Army's needs. There was plenty of level ground at Dawson Creek to set up a railhead. And even though the possibility of an early breakup of the ice on the Peace River posed an additional risk, Hoge had taken larger ones. Finally, he was bringing Sturdevant the news that, as long as the ground remained frozen, the trail to Fort Nelson was indeed capable of handling the vehicles and equipment of a reinforced regiment. But with the spring thaw no more than six weeks away, Ingalls and his 35th Engineers had absolutely no time to lose in packing up at Fort Ord and heading north.

Before returning to the States, the Americans checked into the Dawson Hotel for a hot bath and a good night's sleep on Monday, February 23. That evening, a reporter from Dawson Creek's weekly newspaper, the *Peace River Block News*, caught up with Hoge in the hotel lobby. The questions he asked were the obvious ones. Yes, said Hoge, the United States was contemplating construction of a military supply route over the Rockies to Alaska, but how soon the work would start and how long it might take were uncertain. A year might be needed just to complete the survey, he added, admitting that bad weather over the mountains had prevented him from seeing very much of the proposed section between Fort Nelson and Whitehorse. The local reporter asked if the new road would follow the existing winter trail from Fort St. John to Fort Nelson. No, Hoge replied, an all-weather road could not be built over all that muskeg, so a new location for that stretch would have to be surveyed as well.[20]

Here was the second public indication of the U.S. Army's plans for the highway, and of its probable route; but once again Hoge's cautious answers were reflected in the understated tone of the brief article that appeared in the February 26 edition of the *Peace River Block News.*

Considering the other war news in the headlines that week, it is hardly surprising that most newspaper editors overlooked these two low-key reports from the backwaters of western Canada. To many Americans it seemed, for a few days at least, as if the entire Pacific Ocean was about to become a Japanese lake: "SINGAPORE FALLS TO JAPS"; "ANCHORAGE ALASKA HAS AIR RAID ALARM" headlined the *Los Angeles Times* of February 16. Two days later, its banner read: "BOTH COASTS UNDEFENDED, SENATE TOLD." In response to that charge, a pair of stories followed on February 20: "KNOX SAYS NAVY PROTECTING COASTS AS WELL AS POSSIBLE" and (less positively) "STIMSON SAYS RAIDS LIKELY." To Knox's embarrassment, the Japanese quickly corroborated the views of his cabinet colleague. "WEST COAST SHELLED BY ENEMY SUBMARINE" screamed papers nationwide on February 24.

While the sub skipper's aim may have been poor, his timing was perfect. His target, a coastal oil refinery north of Santa Barbara, suffered only minor damage, but the attack took place precisely in the middle of one of President Roosevelt's periodic radio "fireside chats" to the American people on the progress of the war. Despite the President's upbeat tone, his listeners in the vicinity of the California refinery could hear and see for themselves that the war was not going very well just then. The next day's *Los Angeles Times* carried a calming editorial calling the shelling "a nuisance raid, to rattle us."

Although the attack did turn out to be an isolated incident, its immediate effect was to make a lot of coastal residents—including the crews of the U.S. Army anti-aircraft batteries ringing Los Angeles—very nervous. Early on the morning of February 25, an Army searchlight picked out an unidentified aircraft flying over the city. Within moments, a dozen beams frantically swept the sky as more and more ack-ack guns opened fire. Despite the intense barrage, no planes—enemy or otherwise—were shot down that night. Nor, despite much investigation, was the identity (or even the existence) of the mysterious aerial intruder(s) ever conclusively established. An embarrassed silence quickly settled over the entire affair, but not before it widened the evident rift between Navy Secretary Knox and Army Secretary Stimson. Blared the *Los Angeles Times* on February 26: "ARMY SAYS ALARM REAL; KNOX INDICATES RAID JUST JITTERY NERVES." Next day in the same paper: "STIMSON SAYS 15 PLANES OVER CITY; KNOX ASSAILED ON FALSE ALARM."[21]

After such a week, Washington was no doubt glad to be able to announce that it was taking a major step to bolster the strategic security of the Pacific Northwest and Alaska. Early in March, the big-city papers began carrying stories, obviously based on War Department press releases, that a military road to Alaska was being planned. Nevertheless, only after the decision to build the highway had been formally announced by both governments did the story finally become headline news.[22]

In the ten days between Hoge's return to Washington and the official announcement of the highway project, events continued to move very swiftly. Meeting in New York on February 25–26 with special representatives from the U.S. War and Navy departments in attendance, the Permanent Joint Board of Defense adopted a recommendation that the highway be constructed along the route chosen by the U.S. Army. The members of the PJBD accepted without reservation the assumption made both by Hoge and the staff officers who drafted the original plan that the necessary pathway through the mountains west of Fort Nelson would be found once a detailed reconnaissance became possible. Among the justifications the Board gave for its favorable recommendation were these:

> That the effective defense of Alaska is of paramount importance to the defense of the continent against attack from the west since Alaska is most exposed to an attempt by the enemy to establish a foothold in North America.
>
> That sea communications with Alaska in the future may be subject to serious interruption by enemy sea and air action.
>
> That the air route to Alaska and the defense facilities in Alaska cannot be fully utilized without adequate means of supply for the air route. This can best be provided by a highway along this route.[23]

Despite the PJBD's endorsement of the Army's plan, Mayor LaGuardia saw trouble ahead. "We encountered more difficulty in giving 'something to somebody,'" he reported to President Roosevelt on February 27, "than in collecting a war loan from an ally. . . . However . . . there was good cause for the timidity on the part of the Canadians. They fear a terrific political backfire." LaGuardia predicted similar problems for the President: "all hell will break loose when our Washington and Oregon friends learn of the route." Still, he assured Roosevelt that the location of the route adopted was "logical and justifiable" on the basis of military necessity. "It is going to be a blow to the boys of the Northwest," he concluded breezily, "but *c'est la guerre.*"[24]

The Canadians on the PJBD had some additional misgivings about the plan of which LaGuardia seems to have been unaware. On March 3, as the members of the Canadian War Cabinet prepared for a meeting to consider the Board's latest recommendations, the Under Secretary of State for External Affairs N. A. Robertson received a memorandum from Dr. H. L. Keenlyside, Canada's ranking diplomat on the PJBD. Said Keenlyside:

> In my opinion the strategic justifications . . . for the road are of questionable or conditional validity. On the other hand, the United States Government is now so insistent that the road is required that the Canadian Government cannot possibly allow itself to be put in the position of barring the United States from land access to Alaska. . . .

Although it was "extremely unlikely" that, by 1944, Japan would be able to deny the United States access by sea to Alaska, Keenlyside added, "if this should happen and if Canada had prevented the construction of land communications, the Canadian government would be in a completely untenable position." The idea of allowing the Americans to construct a highway on Canadian soil, "thereby acquiring a moral if not legal right to its continued use, at will, in peace or war" was upsetting to him. The alternative, however, was even less palatable: Canada itself putting up the estimated $80 million in construction costs, plus another $1 million annually for maintenance, all for "a road that would be a monument to our friendship for the United States but . . . otherwise pretty much a 'white elephant.'"

Keenlyside ended with a sharply critical analysis of several of the Board's strategic rationalizations for the highway. For example, of the statement that future sea communications with Alaska might be subject to serious interruption by enemy action, he said:

> This is true at present, but, if the United States programme of plane and ship construction is even approximately achieved, it will not be true in 1944. If the road could be built in two weeks instead of two years the argument would be valid.

Robertson, who reported directly to Prime Minister Mackenzie King, jotted his comments on page one of Keenlyside's memorandum: "This is a pretty devastating analysis of the strategic arguments for the highway, but I agree on political grounds we cannot be put in the position of blocking its construction."[25] Two days later, the Canadian War Cabinet formally approved the recommendation of the Permanent Joint Board on Defense for the construction of the Alaska Highway.

On the same day that Keenlyside sent his memorandum to Robertson, Hoge received a letter of instruction from Sturdevant outlining his authority and responsibilities as commander of the Provisional Engineer Brigade. The various units involved would come under his command when they arrived at their destinations in Canada. Left open was the possibility of reinforcements "at a later date." The urgency of Hoge's mission was conveyed in this brief paragraph:

> The pioneer road will be pushed to completion with all speed within the physical capacity of the troops. The objective is to complete the entire route at the earliest practicable date to a standard sufficient only for the supply of the troops engaged in the work. Further refinements will be undertaken only if additional time is available or if all available troops cannot be employed in pushing forward.[26]

"Further refinements" to upgrade the rough pioneer road into a two-lane, all-weather gravel road thus remained the responsibility of the Public Roads Administration and its civilian contractors, under the Army's overall supervision.

On March 5, as soon as word of Canada's approval reached Washington, Secretary Stimson made the first public announcement regarding the highway at a press conference. While indicating that work on the project would soon begin and that the initial contingent of American soldiers assigned to it was already heading north by train, he avoided any mention of the troops' destination or of the route the new highway would follow.[27]

That information was provided the next day in a short statement read to the Canadian Parliament by Prime Minister King. After briefly reviewing the military and diplomatic consultations that had preceded the project's approval by both governments, he described the route in such a way as to undercut the most likely objections from the floor. First, to disarm proponents of the routes not chosen, he emphasized that, even though the selection process had been based on "purely military considerations," the new highway would in fact "connect with the existing road system of Canada and Alaska." Better yet, he declared, "At the conclusion of the war, that part of the highway which is in Canada will become, in all respects, an integral part of the Canadian highway system." Best of all, from the Canadian perspective, was this point:

> The United States Government, appreciating the burden of war expenditure already incurred by Canada since her entry into the war, and particularly on the construction of the air route to Alaska, has offered to undertake the [cost of] building and war time maintenance of the highway.

Concluding, Mr. Mackenzie King said:

> This offer has been accepted and its terms will be set forth in an exchange of notes which will be signed and made public in the near future. Canada will, of course, provide all necessary facilities. Meanwhile, American Engineers . . . have been authorized to commence work without . . . delay.[28]

The "American Engineers" to whom the Canadian leader's words most immediately applied were Colonel Robert D. Ingalls and his 35th Engineer Regiment. The Army's entire plan depended on their getting to Fort Nelson on schedule.

4

AUGUST 1941–APRIL 1942

Of Mighty Midgets and Galloping Canaries

For Lieutenant Colonel Robert Ingalls and his 35th Engineers, the last seven months had been a tumultuous time of preparation. The newly activated regiment had established its headquarters in August 1941 at Camp Robinson, Arkansas, just outside Little Rock. With a cadre of Regular Army officers and noncoms (noncommissioned officers) plus the leavening of a few experienced reservists recently called into full-time service, Ingalls quickly began the process of converting 1,000 draftees fresh from basic training into proficient combat engineers. The new officers who accompanied these men were mostly recent college graduates with engineering degrees of one sort or another, serving out their ROTC commitments.

Because the Army tried to screen and assign each inductee who possessed technical skills to a military job that bore, whenever possible, some resemblance to his previous occupation, a few of the new soldiers had actually been carpenters, welders, or truck drivers in civilian life. But the draft could not possibly provide a unit like the 35th Engineers with all the trained specialists and technicians specified in its Table of Organization. Ingalls and his staff would have to build a unit from scratch out of this cross-section of the nation's draftable manpower, many more of whom were shoe clerks, soda jerks, or farm boys than bulldozer operators.

The process had barely begun at Camp Robinson when the regiment received orders to participate in the Louisiana Maneuvers, the largest peacetime training exercise ever staged up to that time by the U.S. Army. From bases throughout the central United States, more than 400,000 soldiers, organized as two contending armies, were to converge on the maneuver area.[1]

On September 9, 1941, just five days after the last shipment of 319 recruits stepped off the train at Camp Robinson, the lead elements of the 35th began their march southward toward the Texas-Louisiana border, 300 hot and dusty miles away. Not one to waste any opportunity, Ingalls used the march for all sorts of extra training. Airplanes passing overhead called for taking cover from an "air attack"; pup tents pitched among the scrubby pines at the end of a day's march had to be camouflaged; medics checked to see that latrines and mess hall sumps were properly dug and screened; noncoms checked their men's feet for blisters before darkness fell; blackout and noise discipline was enforced after that. Because most of the regiment's trucks were loaded with equipment and supplies, only a fraction of the troops could ride at any one time.

Notwithstanding Ingalls's attempts to inject some combat realism along the way, and despite their heavy packs and sore feet, most of the 35th's civilian-soldiers must have felt that the entire trip had a certain amusing unreality about it. While the regiment was playing at war, they were marching through peaceful southern towns where folks cheered and clapped and offered them lemonade and cookies. Lake Village, Arkansas, not only turned out its high-school band to lead the troops through town, but later that evening put on a street dance for the entire regiment when it bivouacked nearby.[2]

The War Department planned the Louisiana Maneuvers as both a test and a demonstration of the growing strength and capabilities of the U.S. Army, which had increased from under 200,000 men to over 1.6 million in the two years since Germany's invasion of Poland had touched off World War II. Nevertheless, disillusioned by the failure of World War I to settle Europe's problems, many Americans, especially Midwesterners, remained strongly isolationist. Some even suspected that President Roosevelt and his chief military advisors, as they sought to bolster the country's long-neglected defenses, were secretly plotting to involve the United States in Europe's latest war. General Marshall, two years on the job as Army Chief of Staff and widely respected for his integrity and professionalism, repeatedly faced a hostile or indifferent Congress as he tried to justify the Army's needs and pleaded for the resources and legal authority to proceed with the buildup.

On August 12, 1941, for example, the House of Representatives approved by one vote (203–202) an eighteen-month extension of the one-year-old Selective Service Act, due to expire in October. General Marshall's eloquence, prestige, and moral authority on Capitol Hill were generally credited with saving the day on this crucial vote. Had the extension failed to pass, many of the Louisiana Maneuver's participants would have been mustered out prior to Pearl Harbor.

The U.S. Army's eightfold increase in manpower in two years was incontrovertible evidence of Marshall's effectiveness as an advocate of military preparedness, but Congress rarely gave the War Department everything it asked for. Moreover, so enormous were the demands—not only of the military, but also for Lend-Lease shipments to the beleaguered British, Russians, and Chinese—that American factories could barely keep up with the levels of production Congress grudgingly authorized.

The uneven results of this rapid buildup were obvious to any observer of the Louisiana Maneuvers, including the farmers and villagers through whose fields and hamlets the two opposing armies "fought" in late September. Although the operation was conceived on a grand scale, with the first American use of airborne troops and an entire armored corps and more than 1,000 military aircraft in action, many details showed just how unprepared for a real war the U.S. Army still was. Communication and coordination between ground and air forces was almost totally lacking. Unaccustomed to the intense pressures and special demands created by a military operation of this magnitude, many commanders and staff officers made mistakes that would have been costly in battle.[3]

The official records of the 35th Engineers credit it with "blowing up" 108 bridges in support of its side's general withdrawal during the course of the exercise. Placing simulated explosive charges made of wood blocks and string under bridge abutments may have been good training for the regiment's few demolition specialists, but nobody else in the unit got much out of it. During withdrawal operations, engineer troops usually build roadblocks and lay mine fields; but given the need to keep the public highways open, little realistic training would have resulted from simulating such activities. However, Ingalls's Executive Officer later recalled with pride his outfit's support of an infantry unit's river crossing, "carrying the pontoon boats from the rear down to the river . . . so carefully . . . silently and swiftly that the . . . crossing was a great success."[4] Overall, this early chapter of the regiment's history suggests a green and untested outfit assigned mainly trivial missions during the maneuvers. For the average soldier in the 35th Engineers, it amounted to a chance to practice the very basics of his calling: marching, keeping his equipment clean—and waiting.

Nevertheless, the Louisiana Maneuvers were a valuable experience for all concerned. Even the mistakes made by commanders and their staffs pointed the way to new and better tactical principles and improved planning techniques. When some of their more egregious blunders aroused public criticism, General Marshall responded calmly:

> The present maneuvers are the closest peacetime approximation to actual fighting conditions that has ever been undertaken in this country. But what is of the greatest importance, the mistakes and failures will not imperil the nation or cost the lives of men.[5]

What Marshall did not say, but what every senior officer in the Army was discovering, was that the Chief of Staff had very little tolerance for officers who adjusted slowly to expanded responsibility and none whatsoever for those who failed to learn from their mistakes. The former found themselves sidetracked into dead-end jobs, while the latter were peremptorily retired.

Conversely, officers who demonstrated initiative and ability were rapidly promoted. To keep track of those who showed promise and those who did not, the Chief of Staff kept a little black book. By the fall of 1941, that book already contained numerous favorable entries beside the names of two rising stars in the firmament of the U.S. Army: George S. Patton and Dwight D. Eisenhower. After their outstanding performances in Louisiana—Patton as the aggressive commander of the 2nd Armored Division and Eisenhower as the Third Army's resourceful Chief of Staff—both men were definitely marked for greatness.[6]

The performance of Lieutenant Colonel Ingalls as commander of the newly activated 35th Engineer Regiment may have been eclipsed by such brilliance, but it did not go unnoticed. A Cornell ROTC graduate who had served in the trenches during the last months of World War I, Ingalls had been promoted slowly thereafter despite his solid peacetime record in a series of assignments of increasing responsibility. Command of a regiment was a rare opportunity. He was determined to make the 35th Engineers the talk of the Army.

Returning to its olive-drab tent city at Camp Robinson in mid-October, the regiment plunged into the hectic sixteen-hours-a-day, six-days-a-week garrison routine established by Ingalls. Given the military buildup then underway, such hours and living conditions were not unusual, but the same could not be said about Ingalls's ideas about training soldiers. Although his perfectionism and occasionally unorthodox approach to matters involving discipline and morale later embroiled him in controversy, the effectiveness of his methods was already becoming apparent at Camp Robinson. The process had begun back in August, when the first batch of new men arrived.

Ingalls had decreed that each arriving trainload of soldiers be lined up and arranged according to height. Those 6 feet tall and over were to be assigned to "A" Company; those a few inches shorter to "B" Company; and so on down to "F" Company, whose members barely met the Army's minimum standards of 5 feet ½ inch. (At the regiment's nerve center, Headquarters and Service Company, what counted was not a man's height, but whether he already had the special skills needed to be a typist, supply clerk, or mechanic.) Such sizing of military units was customary at West Point because it reinforced the impression of precision and uniformity during parades, but it was not standard procedure in the Army. Many of Ingalls's contemporaries thought him a bit old-fashioned—if not downright odd—for insisting on it.

Nevertheless, the practice seemed to have a positive effect on morale in the 35th. Every good commander tries to foster a spirit of friendly competition among units in his outfit, whether on the rifle range or the volleyball court, but Ingalls's system lent an additional intensity to this rivalry. "F" Company's "Mighty Midgets," as they soon dubbed themselves, were unwilling to concede that they couldn't do everything as well as, if not better than, the "flankers" of "A" Company, despite spotting them almost a foot in height per man. Conversely, it was a matter of pride for the members of "A" Company never to let themselves be outdone by the "runts"—a category that included not only "F" Company, but everyone else in the regiment. As the 35th's training progressed, this friendly intercompany jousting was always a factor, whether the issue was which company had the most expert riflemen, the most solidly constructed timber trestle bridge, or the fewest deficiencies at Saturday inspection.

Another morale builder was Ingalls's practice of assigning each company the task of becoming proficient enough at some particular job to be able to teach the rest of the regiment how to do it. The men of "F" Company, for example, eventually became the 35th's experts on preparing and loading heavy equipment for movement by rail. Swarming like worker bees under, over, and around each dump truck and bulldozer as they chained it securely to a flatcar, the "Mighty

Midgets" put on such an impressive show that Corps Headquarters was soon exhorting other units in the command to emulate the 35th's example.

Among the duties crowding the regiment's schedule were such assignments as repairing flood-control levees along the Arkansas River and upgrading Camp Robinson's network of gravel roads and temporary bridges. These jobs were above and beyond the training officially prescribed by the War Department, but Ingalls eagerly sought them out. It occasionally meant working on Sunday, but it also gave his men more practice.

Ingalls's determination to have his unit stand out went even further. Although the regiment was not authorized to have its own band, a search for musicians among the ranks turned up a handful of "volunteers" who had their own instruments. This group was soon banging and tootling away in rehearsals, practicing several marching tunes that Ingalls himself taught them on his ocarina. Not yet content, he wrote several new verses to one of the tunes, renamed it "Hail to the Engineers," and let it be known that every last soldier was expected to learn the regiment's new marching song in time for an impending inspection visit by the Division's Commanding General.

At last came the day, November 18, climaxed by a spit and polish parade. Ingalls joined the general on the reviewing stand overlooking the regiment's newly leveled and graded parade ground. As his 1,300 troops marched past in a solid rectangular mass (sized by height, of course, from front to rear), the effect was indeed impressive. Ingalls's boss told him so.

Ingalls replied, "Just wait a minute, general; they're coming around again."

And so they did, this time marching at double time and lustily singing "Hail to the Engineers":

> *Hail to the Engineers*
> *On Land or Sea*
> *Hail to the Engineers*
> *Where 'er they be*
>
> *The Army all rolled in one*
> *None are their peers*
> *In Peace or War*
> *Who goes before?*
>
> *It's the Army*
> *Engineers!*

Doubly impressed, the general was soon telling his staff that he would like to see other units try something similar at future parades. Whether the commanders of these units took him at his word is not recorded, but how well the suggestion sat with them can be judged from the regiment's new nickname. For a long time thereafter, the 35th Engineer Regiment was known throughout the Army as the "Galloping Canaries."

Less than three weeks after the parade, just as the line companies of the regiment were completing another of Ingalls's weekend projects, repairing a road on the rifle range, word came of the Japanese attack on Pearl Harbor. Weeks of frenzied activity ensued. All furloughs were canceled; Corps Headquarters waived the 35th's required Mobilization Training Test; and orders came to prepare for movement to the West Coast. Rumor had it that the regiment was headed to the Southwest Pacific, perhaps to reinforce General Douglas MacArthur's forces in the Philippines, already in danger of being cut off by the Japanese. On December 20, with all its equipment on board, the regiment left Camp Robinson in three long trains, arriving at Fort Ord, California, on Christmas Day. Home, for the holidays, was a bleak and rain-swept tent camp.

Overlooking Monterey Bay, 150 miles south of San Francisco, Fort Ord was already overcrowded with newly arrived units awaiting further deployment as soon as a clearer indication of Japan's next move emerged. Given the rash of submarine attacks on coastal shipping, including two on Christmas Eve, the Army's movement of reinforcements to the Pacific Coast may not have calmed the local population's fears that the U.S. mainland itself was in danger.

Despite frequent disruptive alerts, the 35th's daily routine at Fort Ord soon resembled what it had been at Camp Robinson. But whether they were returning from a day spent in regular training or on one of the innumerable extra projects quickly lined up by Ingalls, at least the men now slept in heated wooden barracks, out of the rain and fog. For the officers and senior noncoms, however, the first two months of 1942 were filled with more turbulence and uncertainty than ever. Each week, a few more of them got orders to report to Camp X or Unit Y, there to become cadre for one of the many new Engineer outfits being organized around the country. In addition, several hundred of the better-educated men from the lower ranks were pulled out to go to Officer Candidate School.

The first hint of the regiment's new assignment came on February 11, when Ingalls received a War Department telegram placing him on "detached service" for a secret mission. Similarly worded orders came for Captain Alvin C. Welling, commanding officer of the 35th's 1st Battalion and one of the regiment's few remaining officers above the rank of lieutenant besides Ingalls and his Executive Officer, Major Heath Twichell.[7]

Ingalls and Welling left Fort Ord the next day, the former to join Colonel Hoge in Edmonton, the latter to go to the Engineer Training Center at Fort Belvoir, Virginia, to assist staff planners as they prepared requisitions for the enormous quantity of supplies and equipment the Alaska Highway project would need.

Ingalls's departure left Major Twichell temporarily in command of the regiment. Twichell was a West Point graduate who had spent the interwar years on a succession of Corps of Engineers civil works projects and training assignments. An intense, wiry, graying man of 46, he had joined the 35th in Arkansas the previous August, leaving his family behind in State College, Pennsylvania, where he had spent a pleasant two years as an assistant ROTC professor.

When Ingalls returned to Fort Ord with the regiment's new assignment, Twichell learned that both he and Ingalls had been promoted one rank in the intervening two weeks. He reported the good news to his wife, Frances, in a letter written on Wednesday, March 4, and told her of the regiment's new assignment:

> Bob returned from Canada last Friday. He was up there . . . with Col. Hoge . . . making a preliminary reconnaissance for the new road to Alaska that you have probably been reading about in the papers. We all had a sneaking idea that's what he was doing, but it was only a guess.
>
> The regiment is going up there soon to construct some four hundred miles of new road through a trackless wilderness. . . . It is going to be a huge job, with many hardships and adventures no doubt, but probably the chance of a lifetime.[8]

Then Twichell described the brand new bulldozers and other road-building machinery that had just arrived, as well as the eleven vanloads of arctic clothing—enough to issue each man a sheepskin-lined trench coat, a reversible parka, a fur helmet, a sweater, a scarf, gloves, wool pants, wool socks and underwear, two pairs of heavy shoes, goggles, and a sleeping bag. "We certainly will be warm enough," he said.

Two days before the regiment's advance party was due to leave, "F" Company put on a farewell dinner in its mess hall. The humorous menu Colonel Ingalls found at his place at the head table indicated the prevailing mood. A cartoon drawing showed a neat row of igloos, in front of which stood a very short man in a very long and bulky overcoat, beady eyes barely visible behind goggles and an oversized fur hood. Beneath the sketch were typed these words:

VITTLES FOR VICTORY
Prepared and proffered
for your gustatory delight by the cooks of the
Mighty Midgets
at their usual place of business
March 3, 1942——7:00 p.m.
just to help upholster your epidermis
as a protection from future cold
and to help fill up your overcoats[9]

Company "B," with five officers and 160 men, was the first to leave, taking five days to make the 2,000-mile trip. As their comfortable railroad coaches rolled up the coast into Canada and east over the Rockies, the men had little to do for the moment but enjoy the spectacular scenery, relax, "shoot the bull," play cards, or sleep. Early each morning the train paused at some whistlestop long enough for everyone to line up outside for mass calisthenics in the chill mountain air. This novel sight always drew crowds of townspeople, who brought gifts of cigarettes or candy and stayed to cheer and wave as the train moved on. Delayed for several hours in Calgary, the men were even treated to a hearty potluck buffet hastily organized by local volunteers.[10]

Next stop: Edmonton, 200 miles due north. Then on to the northwest, across 400 miles of snow-covered prairie, to the "end of steel" at Dawson Creek. The company arrived just before dawn on March 10. Waiting to greet them on the dimly lit station platform, wearing brand new major's leaves on his decidedly nonregulation parka, was the familiar angular figure of Alvin Welling.

No longer assigned to the 35th, but working as Colonel Hoge's executive officer/advance man in Canada, the thirty-one-year-old Welling had spent a busy month since leaving Fort Ord. Based on experience gained from previous duty in Alaska, he had done his best to convince the supply experts in Washington that their estimate of the logistical needs of Hoge's new command was pitifully unrealistic.

"My contribution," he recalled years later, "was merely to double or triple or, in the case of such items as welding rods and bar steel, to double-triple the quantities." Arriving alone in Dawson Creek less than a week before the onslaught of men and supplies was scheduled to begin, Welling faced a challenge that might have daunted a less self-assured officer. "From the outset it was for me an eight-day week, thirty-two hours per day," he said. "I do not have the slightest recollection of having any quarters in those early days—no tent, no room, nothing do I remember but my sleeping bag, my field kit, my caribou socks, reindeer parka, and sealskin mucklucks. . . ."

Priority number one for Welling was community relations, "in the Corps of Engineers' tradition," as he drily put it. He began by meeting with town officials, businessmen, and landowners in both Dawson Creek and Fort St. John to explain what the U.S. Army was immediately going to need: additional sidings for unloading and storage at the railhead, every available square foot of nearby warehouse and other covered storage space, several large tracts of land for bivouac areas, and buildings suitable for headquarters in each town. The Canadians were eager to help, but the job of reconnoitering the sites they suggested was Welling's alone. Given the short days at that latitude in early March, he spent many hours stumbling around with a flashlight through snowdrift-covered fields and vacant lots, aided by the headlight beams of his waiting automobile.[11]

Much to Welling's relief, some badly needed assistance arrived the day before the first wave from the 35th was due. At 1:30 A.M. on March 9, a Quartermaster detachment consisting of five officers and 125 men sleepily disembarked at the station. Their responsibility was to set up and operate the Army railhead and supply depot that would quickly transform the quiet village of 600 inhabitants into a military boomtown. Arriving that evening was Lieutenant Colonel Edward A. Mueller, the quartermaster expert who had been in Dawson Creek with Hoge the previous month and was now assigned as the railhead commander.

As Mueller set up his headquarters in the local "Five Cents to a Dollar" store, the Quartermaster soldiers tried to make camp near the railroad station. The frozen ground made tent pegs useless, so they secured their tents with ropes tied to trees and logs, scooped out the snow and installed a stove in each one. Expecting to spend a warm and dry first night in Dawson Creek, but lacking any cold-weather experience, the men awoke at dawn lying in slushy mud, each heated tent having quickly become a canvas-enclosed steam bath. They soon moved their camp to higher, drier ground on the western edge of town.[12]

Meanwhile, Company "B" of the 35th Engineers arrived, bringing with them an unseasonable warm spell. An early thaw meant serious trouble. If the ice gave way on the Peace River before the entire regiment could get across, all hope of getting to Fort Nelson and pushing a road across the Rockies before the end of 1942 would disappear. Although Welling could do nothing about the warming weather, he could at least do something about the softening river ice.

Scouring the local sawmills, he obtained enough sawdust to provide a one-lane blanket from bank to bank, and sufficient heavy planks to lay a makeshift deck on top of that. The purpose of this combination was to insulate the ice and spread the weight of the Engineers' heavy equipment as it rumbled across the river. Putting down the sawdust and laying the planks became the advance party's first job after reaching Dawson Creek.[13] That done, along with minor repairs to several small bridges south of the river, the men got a well-deserved evening off. Most spent it crowded three-deep around one or another of the town's few bars.[14]

With the buildup barely begun, American soldiers already out-numbered Dawson Creek's male population. Ingalls's men were on their best behavior, but how the townspeople felt about their presence is hinted in the headline of that week's *Peace River Block News*: "UNITED STATES TROOPS INVADE DAWSON CREEK TO BUILD ALASKA ROAD."

Next morning at reveille, despite a few hangovers, all members of Company "B" were present and accounted for. By late afternoon, after some tense moments during the crossing, the company's heavily loaded trucks and bulldozers had arrived safely on the north bank of the Peace. Reaching Fort St. John by nightfall of March 11, the men hastily pitched their pup tents in a wheat field and made final preparations for the 250-mile trek up the winter trail to Fort Nelson.

As the advance party, Company "B" was under orders to make quick repairs to the rougher stretches of the trail, and then, at Fort Nelson, not only to clear and lay out an area for the 35th's base camp, but also to construct storage facilities for the enormous quantities of fuel and other supplies that would be coming up with the main body of the regiment. As "B" Company headed north on March 12, the temperature rose above freezing for yet another day.[15] By then, the rest of the regiment was already on its way.

Traveling on four separate trains, each consisting of about thirty-five Pullman, coach, and flat cars, the 35th's main body left Fort Ord on March 10 and followed the same general route as the advance party, except that Calgary was bypassed in favor of a more northerly crossing of the Rockies via Jasper. Converging on the same destination from camps elsewhere in the United States were two more trains similarly loaded. Each carried special-purpose Engineer troops being attached to the 35th to increase its versatility. Due to arrive two days ahead of the regiment was a survey unit, Company "A" of the 648th Topographic Battalion, with five officers and 160 men. Right behind it came the 74th Light Pontoon Company, six officers and 101 men trained and equipped for river-crossing operations. Bringing up the rear was one more train, made up entirely of freight cars and carrying enough gasoline, oil, rations, tentage, replacement parts, and other things to last the force at Fort Nelson for the next five months.[16]

Since word of the highway had appeared meanwhile in the newspapers, the crowds along the route were even more numerous and friendly than those encountered by Company "B." A troop movement of this size was an irresistible attraction to citizens on both sides of the border eager for some sign that the tide of war might be turning. Despite being cooped up in crowded coaches for a week with only one short break outside each day, Ingalls's men were in high spirits when they reached Dawson Creek. By late afternoon on March 16, as the regiment's last trainload of men, equipment, and supplies pulled in, the earlier arrivals had already reached Fort St. John or were on their way.

The ice on the Peace River still held firm, but as the thaw continued the risk increased of losing one of the Engineers' large new road-building machines, some of which weighed more than 20 tons. The solution, much to the annoyance of the news photographers on hand to cover the story, was to cross all the heaviest (and most photogenic) equipment late at night, when the air was coldest. Even then, the ice visibly sagged and rippled under the passing weight of each vehicle.[17]

By this time, with the 35th Engineers about to begin the last and most crucial leg of their journey, Colonel Hoge had flown in to Fort St. John from Washington. Setting up temporary headquarters in a log cabin, he met with Ingalls and his staff to assess the regiment's prospects for reaching Fort Nelson before the balmy air turned the winter trail into an impassable quagmire. Welling's recent reconnaissance confirmed that much of the surface of the trail had already thawed. Beneath that layer of slush and mud, however, the ground was still frozen solid to a depth of several feet. What to do if the melting continued? The possibility of the regiment getting stranded in a morass of muskeg halfway to Fort Nelson had unimaginable consequences.

Hoge already had a reputation for audacity and courage, but he was not reckless. Hedging his bets, he ordered Ingalls to split the 35th into two balanced forces. One was to start immediately for Fort Nelson; the other would hold back at Fort St. John. When the first half was certain of reaching its destination, a decision would be made about whether or not to send on the rest of the regiment. Hoge was certain that if the trail held up for at least two more weeks, Ingalls would be able to get his entire unit to Fort Nelson. If the trail dissolved sooner, Hoge's contingency plan ensured that at least half the unit would still be positioned where it could do useful work.[18]

This scheme went into effect even before the last trainload of men and equipment made it across the Peace River and into camp at Fort St. John, not to mention the hundred or so freight cars of the 35th's supplies still enroute to Dawson Creek. To move all this extra cargo, Ingalls planned to use the regiment's trucks like buckets in a giant conveyor belt. After making an initial run from Fort St. John to Fort Nelson, each truck would return to Dawson Creek to be reloaded and sent back north. With three or four round trips per vehicle (assuming that the trail, drivers, and trucks all held up), everything would finally get to Fort Nelson.

Complicating the situation further, a civilian contractor hired by the Canadian government now arrived with 100 trucks loaded with drums of aviation gasoline for the Fort Nelson airfield. To accommodate the Canadians, Ingalls made yet another revision to an already complex movement schedule. The first half of the regiment began moving up the trail on March 16. By that time the temperature had been above freezing for over a week, going well above 50°F on several days.[19]

According to the plan worked out by Ingalls and Twichell, the 250 miles of trail between Fort St. John and Fort Nelson were divided into three sectors, each with an officer in charge and a roving tow truck operating out of a temporary base camp. Each camp had stockpiles of fuel and oil; a chow line ready to serve meals around the clock; and heated tents with cots, where rested drivers could change places with exhausted ones coming in off the trail. The key to keeping the column moving constantly forward was having enough extra drivers. That meant using nearly every man in the regiment who could handle a truck, regardless of his normal duties. For several days this arrangement worked well, although the deep gumbo of the trail and the inexperience of most of the drivers began to take its toll. Accidents and breakdowns became increasingly common.[20] A driver left behind with his immobile vehicle by an advancing convoy knew that the nearest sector base camp could be as far as 40 miles away. All he could do until help arrived was to wait in the stillness and try to keep warm.

Day and night the march continued, as the stockpiles at Fort Nelson steadily grew and empty trucks headed back down the mushy trail for another load. Then, suddenly, winter returned. Overnight the temperature dropped almost 80 degrees. With the trail again frozen solid, Ingalls immediately ordered a speedup. All remaining units were to leave Fort St. John as quickly as possible; even a few hours' delay could make a crucial difference at the other end. April, with its warm chinook winds, was just nine days away.[21]

The numbing cold may have been a lucky break for the overall success of the regiment's mission, but for Ingalls's men, trained for the Pacific, not the Arctic, it meant hardship beyond anything they had yet endured. Driving in the open cab of a bulldozer or road grader was the most terrible job of all, but even the canvas tops and side curtains of the trucks barely protected their drivers from the wind. Nor were their passengers to be envied, bouncing along in the back atop piles of cargo or jammed together on hard wooden benches. Every soldier wore the winter clothing that had been issued back in the States. As protection from the bitter temperature, most of this new gear was adequate—but just barely. One complaint was that it was so bulky that the wearer had the mobility and appearance of a well-stuffed duffle bag. More serious were problems with the insulated boot, called a shoe-pac. Ingalls began to receive reports of frostbitten toes and feet.[22]

Another report, written by Welling for Hoge's eyes, mentioned finding drivers so cold that they had parked their vehicles and were sitting beside them "crying violently."[23] Hoge needed little reminding how bitterly cold it was. Having arrived from Washington with only his short garrison overcoat for an outer garment, he had been grateful to a sympathetic junior officer at Fort St. John for the loan of warmer clothes.[24]

The cold was so intense that engines had to be kept running continuously. At -30°F, the only way to restart a stalled vehicle was to build a fire under its oil pan, a procedure emphatically not recommended by the Army's drivers' manuals. Fire posed other risks as well. Cold, exhausted men became drowsy and disoriented when exposed to sudden warmth. Although drivers stopping for a bite to eat after many hours behind the wheel did no real damage to themselves when they literally fell asleep in their plates, several soldiers found themselves with scorched clothing and minor burns after having toppled dizzily into a campfire while warming their hands.

The round-the-clock pace increased the toll. With reflexes and judgment dulled from lack of sleep, men began to take more chances and make more mistakes. Wrecked and broken-down vehicles accumulated along the trail faster than they could be towed to the nearest base camp and repaired. The regiment quickly exhausted its on-hand supply of spare parts, necessitating another violation of Army regulations: cannibalizing some vehicles to keep others running. Before long, each temporary base camp began to resemble a military junkyard.[25]

Toward the end of March came another sudden weather change. This time winter seemed gone for good. As the mud season arrived in earnest, the last convoy of trucks and machinery started up the trail. Preparing to head north himself, Ingalls had one more problem dumped in his lap. The civilian contractor hired to haul the aviation gasoline to Fort Nelson had been using vehicles without four-wheel drive and the draft horses he had brought along to help pull his overloaded trucks through the softest spots were no match for the axle-deep mire. Finally, the contractor gave up and pulled his equipment off the job. Many hundreds of 55-gallon fuel drums now lay abandoned along the route, well short of their destination. Concerned, the Canadian government asked if the U.S. Army would mind carrying them the rest of the way. Ingalls agreed, having planned all along to send a salvage crew with a wrecker and flatbed to sweep down the trail from Fort Nelson at the last possible moment and bring back every broken-down vehicle that had been left behind.[26]

The sweating, cursing, bone-tired soldiers who had to push and tug and winch this collection of wrecks to the regiment's new base camp no doubt had a few choice epithets for their accommodating commander. Now they had to finish the contractor's work as well. But as Ingalls and his adjutant slogged their way north, the colonel's pride in what the regiment had just accomplished was increased by his satisfaction in finding no abandoned equipment along the way. His men had left nothing in their wake but 250 miles of rutted mud.[27]

Ingalls had intended to be the last man over the trail before it became impassable, but matters did not quite work out that way. Having waited at Fort St. John as long as he dared for the arrival of six command cars equipped with two-way radios, he finally left without them. The missing vehicles belonged to a Signal Corps detachment commanded by Lieutenant W. R. Schwarte. Ingalls instructed Schwarte not to risk the trail when his equipment arrived; instead, he was to remove the radios and bring them up on the next cargo flight, leaving the command cars behind.

Arriving exhausted but triumphant at Fort Nelson, the mud-spattered colonel was informed that the lieutenant had disobeyed his instructions. The regiment's radios were on their way, somewhere in the morass north of Fort St. John. An apoplectic Ingalls ordered the salvage crews on the northern end of the trail to be on the lookout for Schwarte and his vehicles. Hours passed with no sign of the lieutenant; then his party was spotted halfway to Fort Nelson, crossing the Sikanni Chief River on ice so rotten that a foot of rushing water already covered it. On April 9 the detachment crossed the Muskwa River, just south of Fort Nelson. With the help of the hydraulic winch on one of the vehicles and the muscle power of his men, Schwarte had managed to pull through.

Reporting to a relieved but still angry Ingalls, the lieutenant justified his rashness by explaining the dilemma he had found himself in. His orders from the War Department, said Schwarte, specified that he was to report to Colonel Ingalls with his detachment "and all its equipment." To Schwarte, "all" meant all. Having to choose between disregarding Ingalls's wishes or those of the War Department, he had taken what he considered to be the smaller risk of heading north during one last, brief cold snap. Less than completely satisfied by this explanation but impressed by Schwarte's obvious courage, Ingalls let the matter drop.[28]

A demanding taskmaster but no petty martinet, Ingalls had earned this command through his proven ability as a trainer of soldiers. The trying experience his men had just come through and their disciplined, professional response to it were no doubt very much on his mind when he eventually wrote down his philosophy of training men for combat:

> You cannot press too hard. Put the pressure on hard as you may, yet you still will not approach the conditions of fatigue and hardship your units will soon face. An attitude of tolerance, pity or sympathy for your unit during the rigors of training will be reflected in poor preparation and consequent suffering or disaster when in an active theater. Every training task must be approached as though it were a battle mission. There must be no "breaks." No rest should be prescribed, except that due to physical exhaustion.[29]

For Ingall's "Galloping Canaries," the overland march to Fort Nelson had been just the opening skirmish in the overall battle to build their section of the Alaska Highway. But Ingalls could see that his men now needed a break. Until the ground dried sufficiently to permit construction to begin, he let up on the pressure, if only a little. After all, the battered collection of vehicles and heavy equipment parked in the motor pool still needed lots of maintenance work.

Lined up in neat rows on the damp, raw earth stood ninety-three half-ton dump trucks, forty-four heavy and medium bulldozers, twenty-five jeeps, sixteen heavy and medium cargo trucks, twelve three-quarter-yard pick-up trucks, ten command cars, nine road graders, six twelve-yard carrying scrapers, six rooter plows, two half-yard power shovels, several pile drivers, a truck-mounted crane, a six-ton flatbed, a concrete mixer—and one sedan. Off to one side were stacked enough pontoon boats and decking timbers to cross a good-sized river. Canvas tents protected the more portable items: electric generators, air compressors, welding machines, and gasoline-powered chainsaws.[30] Ingalls soon set up a training school to teach his heavy-equipment operators how to do more than start, steer, and stop their powerful new machines—all there had been time for in Fort St. John.

With the work came adequate sleep and three square meals a day, plus time for letters home and even an occasional nap in the mild afternoon sun. The next courier flight out of Fort Nelson carried news to many waiting families that the regiment had made it through.

"Now we are safely encamped on top of a hill . . . overlooking the river, in a clearing carved out of the woods," wrote Lieutenant Colonel Twichell, describing the regiment's adventure in his first letter to Frances in a month. "My part in all this was to organize and direct the movement, and to keep things moving generally. I traveled over 3,000 miles in two weeks, with only a few hours' sleep each night." He continued:

> There is a mountain of supplies and gasoline, every ton of which represents a struggle to get it here. We are housed in pyramidal tents, heated by a new type of army stove, which is wonderful. We sleep on cots in sleeping bags, and eat the best of chow. . . . We have 80 tons of fresh meat (steaks and chops) . . . in an ice house that we built. The quartermaster has set up a field bakery, and we will have fresh bread, rolls and pastry. Some of the other items of the ration include powdered milk and eggs, dehydrated potatoes, all kinds of canned fruits, meats and vegetables, etc. We have a post exchange that sells most of the necessities, including candy and cigarettes.

Twichell ended this cheerful litany on a cautious note: "We are going to live the life of Riley until our supplies run out some time this summer," he said, "by which time it is contemplated that the road connecting us . . . to Fort St. John will be completed."[31]

By reaching Fort Nelson, the 35th Engineers had eliminated only the first uncertainty in the complex plan devised by Hoge and Sturdevant for building the highway. Whether the inexperienced 341st Engineers, cloned from a small cadre of the 35th back at Fort Ord and soon to arrive in Dawson Creek, could ever construct a dry, all-weather route through the gelatinous expanse of muskeg between Fort St. John and Fort Nelson was very much an open question. Plenty of experts familiar with the territory said it couldn't be done. Even greater unknowns now faced Colonel Ingalls. Was there really a buildable route through the poorly mapped and incompletely explored area of the Rockies that stretched west of Fort Nelson? Were there passes through the mountains low enough to remain free of impassable snowfalls? Until an airplane could be made available for reconnaissance, nobody—certainly neither the War Department's planners in Washington nor Ingalls and his staff at Fort Nelson—knew the answers.

On April 9, Bataan fell. With the withdrawal of General Jonathan Wainwright's forces to the tiny island of Corregidor in Manila Bay, Japan's military control of the western Pacific was nearly complete.

Ingalls knew that this was the psychological moment to start work. Although the predicted rains of the next six weeks would not permit much real progress, why not have the bulldozer crews complete their training by beginning a trail over the 50 or so miles of rolling foothills that lay between Fort Nelson and the eastern slopes of the Rockies? Surely, long before his men reached those first, mile-high ramparts, a way through them would be found.

On April 11, 1942, following open-air religious services, the 35th Engineer Regiment began its work on the Alaska Highway. The casual instructions given to Lieutenant Mike Miletich, who was in charge of the 'dozers that day, belied the drama of the moment: "Colonel Ingalls and [Lieutenant] Colonel Twichell called me into the tent," recalled Miletich, "and they said, 'This morning we are going to start the Alcan Highway. . . . Take a starting point . . . just west of the Fort Nelson air strip and . . . head west on an azimuth."[32]

5

Senator Langer
Raises Cain

As the backers of the other routes to Alaska got wind of the Army's plans for the highway, various high-level officials in the federal government began receiving emphatic warnings that a "tragic mistake" was about to be made. Quick to sound off, as predicted by Mayor LaGuardia, were "the boys of the Northwest"— the proponents of Routes A and B from Oregon, Washington, and British Columbia (see map on p. 13). Surprisingly, however, it was freshman Senator William Langer of North Dakota who eventually gave the Army the most hell for its decision. Considering the now-urgent need for a dependable overland supply line to Alaska, these critics all said, the Army's version of the highway would take too long to construct—if it could be built at all. How, they asked, were the Army Engineers planning to get around the terrible muskeg bogs that lay north of Fort St. John? Where did they intend to cross the Continental Divide through the jumble of rugged peaks west of Watson Lake? Neither stretch of land, they pointed out, had even been surveyed.

By contrast, of course, surveys for Routes A and B already existed. These long-standing proposals not only avoided the difficult terrain of the Inland Route, but were slightly shorter as well. As for the concurrent need to have a supply line for the airfields of the Northwest Staging Route, said opponents of the Army's plan, that was a secondary issue. It was far more important to ensure that Alaska itself could be supplied by road if Japan gained control of the North

Pacific. That ominous prospect seemed very real in the early months of 1942.

Charles Stewart, the Canadian chairman of the British Columbia-Yukon-Alaska Highway Commission, was first to raise the alarm. On February 20, 1942, having learned of General Sturdevant's recent visit to Ottawa, Stewart dispatched a worried letter to Thomas Riggs, a former governor of Alaska and the acting U.S. chairman of the Alaskan International Highway Commission (AIHC). Riggs was in Washington, D.C., substituting for Congressman Warren Magnuson, who was then on active duty in the Pacific as a Navy Lieutenant Commander. "From what I can gather," wrote Stewart, "[the U.S. Army is] determined, if agreeable to the Canadian authorities, to construct a road through the same territory in which the airline is located." After listing all the reasons why this route was unsuitable, he concluded, "it will be a serious blunder and will cost a great deal of money which might be saved by following either the A or B route outlined in our report."[1]

Acting quickly, Riggs forwarded Stewart's warning to Secretary of War Stimson on February 24. A strongly worded cover letter advised Stimson that, in the opinion of the AIHC, a highway paralleling the airfields "would be a most serious mistake, a feeling concurred in by all who know anything about the country." Riggs then complained, "As a Commission appointed by the President for the purpose of securing information and for making arrangements for construction with the Canadian Government, we have naturally thought that we would be consulted. . . ." In closing, Riggs reminded Stimson that Route A offered the shortest route to Alaska; he apologized for making a direct appeal, "but the situation is one which should not be haphazardly determined."[2]

Next to join the chorus was Ernest Gruening, Governor of the Territory of Alaska and a longtime member of the AIHC. Gruening opened a blistering memorandum to Secretary of the Interior Harold Ickes by saying: "I wish to go on record most emphatically in stating that the route to Alaska now proposed by the Army *will not get us the highway in any reasonable period of time.*"

The Army's plan was a "hodge-podge," said Gruening. He had no quarrel with the portion of the route between Whitehorse and Fairbanks, which followed the same line he and his fellow commissioners had long recommended. But he hammered away at the "folly" of ignoring the southern half of Route A in favor of "crossing the Continental Divide through some highly rugged and difficult terrain. . . ." A road to service the airports at Fort St. John, Fort

Nelson, and Watson Lake was "no doubt a desirable objective," he added, "and may be entitled to a special highway for that purpose. . . ." However the objective of the highway to Alaska, he insisted, should be "to convey men, munitions, food and other supplies at the earliest moment . . . because we no longer have . . . the complete control of our coastal sea lanes, which, prior to December 7, the Army and Navy took for granted."[3]

At Gruening's request, Ickes immediately sent copies of this memorandum to the Secretary of War and the Secretary of the Navy. Secretary Stimson responded in a "Dear Harold" note dated March 4. He reported that he had just had an angry visit from Gruening and Alaska's Congressional Delegate, Tony Dimond. In response, Stimson continued:

> I called in General Crawford of the War Plans Division . . . and he explained the advantages of the route chosen by us . . . so clearly and thoroughly that I think Governor Gruening was much impressed, if not converted. At any rate he was silenced. . . .[4]

The next day, March 5, Stimson publicly announced the decision to build the Alaska Highway. Chairman Riggs of the AIHC, having had no reply to his appeal of February 24, now went over Stimson's head. On March 6, he angrily dispatched a long telegram to the President. "The Alaskan International Highway Commission," Riggs said acidly, "is delighted to hear through the press that the road to Alaska is to become a reality and that the Army has belatedly accepted the [necessity for such a road] which your commission has been urging upon it for several years." He then restated the charges and complaints about the Army's chosen route that he had earlier made to Stimson. Moreover, he added, the Chairman of the Canadian Commission had recently dropped his advocacy of Route B, and now, "for defense purposes," totally agreed that Route A "should be constructed immediately" and that going ahead with the "route near the Canadian airfields would be a grave mistake."[5]

But the worsening situation in the Pacific left no time for the President to second-guess his military advisors. Thomas Riggs was wasting his breath. "JAPANESE INVADE NEW GUINEA AT TWO POINTS; CLAIM RANGOON, AND PUSH WEST IN BURMA" headlined *The New York Times* on March 9, 1942. A subheading made the approaching danger even clearer: "Menace of the Invader Draws Closer to Australia."[6] That same day, the first contingent of American soldiers pitched their tents at Dawson Creek. Also on March 9, Chief of Staff General

Marshall paused from considering more urgent matters to initial a one-page memorandum that responded, point by point, to Riggs's case against the Army's plan for the highway. Although the risks being taken were acknowledged, they were balanced against the military disadvantages of Route A. Attached to the memo was the draft of a polite letter for Stimson's signature. "Dear Governor Riggs," it began, "In reply to your letter of February 24 . . . I beg to advise you as follows":

> In its study of possible alternative routes . . . to Alaska the War Department gave full consideration to the reports of the International Highway Commission. . . .
> The recommendation of the War Department . . . was based purely on military considerations. The chain of airways to Alaska now under construction can be used to . . . its potential capacity only if linked by a highway which will permit it to be serviced adequately. It will also provide a route for the supply of Alaska in the event of the interruption of sea communications.[7]

The officer responsible for guiding this document through the labyrinth of the General Staff was a new Assistant Chief of Staff, Brigadier General Dwight D. Eisenhower, handpicked for the job by General Marshall. Eisenhower's qualifications included good political instincts in difficult situations like this one. Stimson signed the letter on March 14.

Significantly, the War Department now appeared to be changing its rationale for the highway. Originally, the route's purpose was to provide an emergency supply line to Alaska; service to the Northwest Staging Route had been cited simply as an added benefit. But Stimson's letter to Riggs reversed those priorities. The question of which purpose was, in fact, more important soon became the focus of a public debate.

The backers of Routes A and B were deeply concerned that the Army's highway would not serve the future needs of their constituents, most of whom lived in the coastal region of the U.S. and Canadian Northwest. By using "purely military considerations" to justify its decision, the Army had neatly avoided the issue of the highway's peacetime value; but it also outraged the politicians and planners who saw a decade's worth of advocacy coming to naught. Refusing to accept the Army's plan as a fait accompli, they took their campaign against "the Inland Route," as it came to be known, to the press.

As early as March 7, newspapers in Washington State, Oregon, and California began running stories on the emerging controversy. These usually quoted some member of the AIHC lamenting the mistake the War Department was about to commit and reiterating the advantages of Route A.[8] Although most national wire service and big-city reporters who actually covered the arrival of U.S. troops in northwest Canada during the next few weeks filed upbeat news articles about the rapid buildup of men and supplies, a few pieces focused on the "tragic blunder" charges.

"SWAMP DISEASE FACES ENGINEERS" cried a page-one story in the March 12 *Boston Globe*. Sounding as if he might have found his sources in an Edmonton bar, the reporter colorfully detailed the problems and dangers awaiting the American Engineers.[9] Not everything in this article was exaggerated, as the builders of the highway could soon attest. The muskeg was indeed miles across in places, and bulldozers could sink into it without leaving a trace. Nor did anyone contest the article's claim that the local black flies and mosquitos were among the world's fiercest. But at least they transmitted no yellow fever or other epidemic diseases. The Yankee reporter's northwoods "experts" may simply have been pulling his leg with their dark allusions to a supposedly deadly "swamp disease."

Within a week, the War Department called in reporters to explain its reasons for choosing the inland route and to rebut the growing criticism. On March 14, the fruits of this effort appeared in most major newspapers in the form of an Associated Press dispatch. The copy editor for *The New York Times* deftly summarized the AP's 500-word article in a series of column headings. "INSIST INLAND ROAD IS ALASKA'S NEED/Army Officials Declare This Route Essential for Supplying Chain of Air Bases/DENY A 'TRAGIC BLUNDER'/And Rule Out Argument for Coastal System – Hoge, Decorated in '18, Heads Work." A confidence-inspiring photograph of Colonel Hoge—level gaze, strong mouth and chin—accompanied the piece.[10]

This public relations counterattack was psychologically well-timed. Even before it was launched, newspaper editorials around the country began saying, in effect, "Let's get the road built and stop the squabbling."[11] But opponents of the Inland Route soon resumed their offensive.

Premier John Hart of British Columbia was among the first to propose a compromise solution: construction of an additional 250 miles of highway across the Rockies between Prince George and Dawson Creek, thereby linking the cities of the coastal region with the southern end of the Inland Route. To the question of where the laborers would come from to build another 250 miles of road, two-thirds of it over terrain as rugged as any in British Columbia, Hart had a ready answer: use the thousands of American and Canadian citizens of Japanese ancestry, who had recently been arbitrarily characterized as "potentially dangerous," stripped of their civil rights, and interned in concentration camps on both sides of the border. For this purpose, Hart estimated, the Canadian camps alone could provide at least 5,000 able-bodied men. [12] Despite the prevailing intense prejudice against these citizens, Hart's idea got little support in either Washington or Ottawa.

Meanwhile, some opponents, suspicious of the U.S. Army's vaguely defined "military considerations," began looking for a more sinister explanation for the chosen route. They soon found one. On April 10, 1942, the tabloid *Alaska Weekly* carried this breathless headline: "REVEAL PRESSURE FORCED THE UNITED STATES TO ADOPT INLAND ROUTE." Paragraph one read:

> Inside story of a gigantic "squeeze play" whereby the United States was pressured into financing, building, and maintaining for the duration a network of roads linking Canadian airports under the label of an Alaskan Highway for the post-war private profit of Canadian air lines came to light this week. [13]

What political or economic leverage the Canadians could have used to "pressure" the far more powerful United States into this decision the article did not say. Nor did it explain why Ottawa would even attempt such a tactic after resisting U.S. plans for a highway to Alaska for more than a decade. No doubt most senior Canadian officials found the *Alaska Weekly*'s headline laughably mistaken. The pressure had all been the other way.

And yet there was no denying that a U.S.-built network of roads linking Canadian airports in the far Northwest would indeed be a great postwar boon to the airline franchised to use those particular facilities. That lucky company was none other than Grant McConachie's Yukon Southern Air Transport. Although the *Alaska Weekly* failed to mention YSAT, which had recently been bought up by the Canadian Pacific Railroad (CP Rail), it was no secret that CP Rail, Canada's most powerful privately owned corporation, was a major beneficiary of the U.S.–Canadian agreement to build the Alaska Highway. Populist opponents of big business and fanciers of conspiracy theories (among them North Dakota's Senator Langer) soon made much of the implications of that fact.

Meanwhile, the United States members of the AIHC kept up the pressure on Washington. On April 16, Interior Secretary Ickes received another blast from Alaska's Governor Gruening. Even angrier than his first memo, it began by summarizing that earlier document. Speed now being the *"summum desideratum,"* he repeated, it was "folly" to delay construction while surveyors looked for possible routes through mountains and muskeg when a well-surveyed alternative already existed. Turning to the alleged need for a highway to keep the airfields supplied, he reminded Ickes that "this could be done at far less cost and effort by sending trucks equipped with caterpillar treads over the frozen ground to take in a six-months' fuel supply." The proponents of the Inland Route, he continued, had tried to finesse this argument by stating that it was also "necessary to have a road along which . . . pilots could fly in order not to be lost," and next to which additional landing strips would be constructed "should the flyers get into trouble." Gruening would have none of it. "This state of mind was undoubtedly induced," he said, ". . . by the crashing of over half a dozen bombers on their way to Alaska in the preceding weeks . . . what appears to be sought by the Army is not a highway at all but a kind of leading string for the young flyers." Gruening then made a prediction:

> It is my reasoned judgement that the [Inland] Route will require at least an additional year to build; that it will be a highly unsatisfactory road when "completed"; that its theoretical completion will precede its actual serviceability by many years; and that what will be called "maintenance" for several years thereafter will in effect be continuous construction and reconstruction.

Finally, Gruening presented a "constructive proposal": "Assuming that the commitment to build the [Inland] Route is definite and irrevocable," he said, "all desired objectives will be attained" if 400 additional miles of highway were built from the vicinity of Prince George northward to the point near Whitehorse where the Army's road joined Route A. In that event, he explained, "the Army will have . . . [its road] and Alaska and the United States will also be connected by a legitimate and serviceable highway." Governor Gruening's proposed source of the manpower to construct those extra 400 miles of road echoed Premier Hart's: the interned Japanese-Americans.[14]

Few men in the Roosevelt Administration were as secure in their position as the recipient of this memorandum. At the age of sixty-eight, the crusty, bespectacled Secretary of the Interior, Harold L. Ickes, had the absolute confidence of FDR and the well-deserved nickname "Honest Harold." He was also a tough and resilient politician: a lifelong champion of not-yet-popular causes (land conservation; the rights of blacks and Native Americans), a survivor of nine years of political infighting within the New Deal, and a sharp-tongued, self-described curmudgeon. Yet the drumfire of criticism aimed at the Army's plan for the Alaska Highway had clearly begun to rattle him. After stewing over Gruening's latest missive for several days, he sent a copy to Stimson.

"My Dear Henry," Ickes said in his covering note, "Governor Gruening . . . argues so vigorously . . . against the route we have decided upon . . . that I do not . . . want to have the responsibility of putting it into my own files and forgetting about it." Then he went on:

> After all, we have had to make a snap judgement, and I recall that at our last meeting the Engineers were frank enough to say that the route selected did present some very great difficulties. Upon you and Frank [Knox] and me rests a very great responsibility. If it should turn out . . . that we have not selected the best route, it would not be much of a defense to say that we approved one selected by the Army Engineers, especially if it could be shown by the records that [they] were not only guessing but told us they were guessing.[15]

Such unvarnished frankness in a formal letter from a cabinet colleague may have given Stimson momentary pause; but if anything he was even more secure in his position than Ickes was in his. Both men had been successful lawyers, but otherwise they had little in common. Still vigorous at 74, the austere, patrician Stimson had attended Yale and Harvard Law School, served in combat as a field artillery officer in World War I, and held cabinet posts in two previous administrations. He had been William Howard Taft's Secretary of War from 1911 to 1913 and Herbert Hoover's Secretary of State from 1929 to 1932. In 1940, Stimson had been read out of the Republican Party for agreeing to serve in Roosevelt's cabinet (as had his fellow Republican, Frank Knox, who came aboard as Navy Secretary at the same time).[16]

Stimson had one characteristic that did not always serve him well: he trusted what his generals told him. His readiness to accept the near-hysterical assessment of the Japanese threat made by General DeWitt, the Army's commander of the West Coast, helps explain both

Stimson's willingness to believe the mid-February reports of an "air raid" over Los Angeles and his subsequent decision to order the internment of more than 100,000 Japanese-Americans. It also makes his unwavering support of the Army's plan for the Alaska Highway more understandable. But Stimson's confidence in the advice and common sense of calm, experienced officers such as George Marshall and Dwight Eisenhower was not misplaced. And they, in turn, had a well-founded faith in Clarence Sturdevant and Bill Hoge.

On May 12, six days after Corregidor fell, Stimson signed another reassuring letter to "My Dear Harold." Pointing out that not only the Corps of Engineers but also the General Staff and the Air Staff had been consulted, he said:

> This country has unhesitatingly made graver decisions based on advice from the same sources, and while this advice is, of course, not infallible, it is undoubtedly better . . . than could be obtained from any other single source.
>
> Personally, I concur in . . . the supply route along the airline, as we could not rely on winter tractor road supply of these vital staging fields. Furthermore, I do not believe that military necessity exists for . . . constructing another road . . . paralleling this [Inland] Route.

"Perhaps I am unduly optimistic," he concluded, "but I do not share Governor Gruening's apprehensions."[17]

Stimson's serene confidence regarding the wisdom of the route chosen was reflected in every briefing, press conference, and public statement on the subject made by his busy subordinates in the desperate spring of 1942. At the expense of more pressing military matters, the General Staff's original experts on the road, General Crawford and Colonel Tully, spent many hours drafting letters, memoranda, and staff studies for the higher-ups to use in defending their plan. When the chairman of the House Committee on Roads wanted a briefing on the reasons for the controversy, Crawford and Tully gave it. General Sturdevant, representing the Chief of Engineers, often found himself on the Alaska Highway "hot seat" as well. Eventually, when opponents of the Inland Route found an ally in Senator Langer, these officers were also called to testify on Capitol Hill.

Despite the confident statements emanating from the War Department, many officials there from Stimson down knew as well as Ickes did that the Army Engineers really were guessing about the feasibility of the Inland Route. But in view of the still-deteriorating military situation in the Pacific and the bureaucratic momentum already behind their plan, belated adoption of the recommendations of Route A's proponents was not a palatable option.

In the meantime, what could be done to speed the highway's construction, reduce the risk of ultimate failure, and lower the volume of criticism? The question practically answered itself: give Hoge more troops to work with. The next question was more difficult: where would they come from? Every Engineer regiment on the Army's pre–Pearl Harbor troop list already had an assignment. Most were now either in the South Pacific or on their way. And as General Sturdevant well knew, the number of Engineer units activated since December 7 fell short of the Army's ever-growing requirements. It had taken some juggling just to get Hoge's new command up to its present total of four regiments. Nevertheless, the question of finding reinforcements for Hoge had an answer that also helped solve another vexing problem. Hoge's additional construction regiments could be made up of black troops.

Mirroring the society they defended, the nation's armed services were still racially segregated in 1942. Although the peacetime Army had long had a small number of "colored" units on its rolls, this military tokenism was swept away by the Selective Service Act of 1940. Blacks were thenceforth to be examined, classified, and drafted under the same rules and standards as Caucasians.

In 1942, still heavily concentrated in the poorest parts of the rural South, blacks made up about 10 percent of the United States' population. As it began training millions of draftees for military service under the constraints of institutional policies and societal norms firmly committed to racial segregation, the Army was faced with the problem of where to assign hundreds of thousands of black soldiers. Segregation's legacy of bigotry and prejudice severely limited the possibilities. Despite evidence to the contrary drawn from every conflict since the Revolutionary War, many white officers and administrators still believed that blacks would prove unreliable in front-line combat. As a result, relatively few black infantry, armor, or artillery units were organized during World War II. In addition, the supposedly objective (but culturally biased) results of the Army's tests measuring educational level and mechanical aptitude were used as an excuse to exclude all but a token number of blacks from highly technical branches like the Air Corps and Signal Corps.

In the end, black soldiers were assigned to more than their share of units engaged in low-tech, high-sweat duties in the Engineers and

Quartermaster Corps. Black soldiers in Ammunition Handling companies and Port Clearance battalions contributed significantly to the war effort—by doing demanding and often dangerous stevedore work. Although the Corps of Engineers put most of its new black soldiers into general-purpose construction battalions and regiments, shortages of heavy equipment sometimes resulted in the black units' being issued fewer bulldozers and more shovels and wheelbarrows than the white units got. When this happened, the effect on the units' morale was devastating.

Another touchy issue was where to station the new black units. In the United States, military leaders felt they had to worry about the impact of large numbers of young black soldiers on nearby civilian communities. This was true whether (as in the South) the rules of segregation were well-understood and enforced or (as elsewhere in the country) the rules were vague or nonexistent. In one extreme case, a Texas mayor sent word to the President that he would personally shoot the first black who came into town. [18]

Overseas, in countries where racial harmony was the norm, fewer problems were expected, but several United States' allies, including China, Australia, and even Liberia, made it clear that they preferred not to play host to black American troops. In addition, at the outset of the war, in the erroneous belief that blacks would be unable to perform satisfactorily under Arctic conditions, Secretary Stimson had insisted that no black units be sent to the far north. [19]

As Hoge's need for additional troops became more apparent, so did the fact that the bulk of these reinforcements would have to be black. Hoge's Provisional Engineer Brigade had originally consisted of four construction regiments with a combined strength of 190 officers and 5,095 enlisted men, plus more than a dozen smaller specialized units, for an overall total of more than 220 officers and 6,400 men. In late March and April, after Stimson reversed his policy on sending black units to cold climates, the War Department assigned the 93rd, 95th, and 97th Engineer Regiments to Hoge's Brigade, swelling his force to over 10,000 men and markedly improving his chances of accomplishing his mission. [20] Hoge's promotion to Brigadier General was announced on March 27.

Personally confident, Hoge was well aware that many others had serious misgivings about the Army's choice of the Inland Route. On an early April stopover in Anchorage, Alaska, he outlined his plans for the highway to a group of local businessmen and civic leaders, most of whom favored Route A. To a skeptical question as to just how he expected to get through the muskeg swamps and unmapped mountains that blocked his way, Hoge shot back: "With six machines of one thousand men each."[21] While these six regiments might have been described more prosaically as "heavily mechanized," Hoge's retort captured both the essence of his planned method of operation and his knack for deflecting questions he preferred not to answer. (The seventh regiment, the 95th Engineers, had not yet been assigned when Hoge spoke.)

General Hoge's gruff public manner could not entirely conceal his own reservations and concerns. On April 12, when asked by a reporter whether a suitable pathway through the Rockies between Watson Lake and Whitehorse had been located yet, Hoge would only say that he was "strongly encouraged to believe that a favorable route exists through this section." Nonetheless, he added, "the drainage and soil conditions cannot of course be determined until later in spring." Governor Gruening took Hoge's words as a clear admission that he still had no idea of how to get across the Rockies. Meanwhile, Gruening fumed, "precious weeks are flitting by."[22]

As Gruening, Dimond, Riggs, and their allies gathered under the banner of Route A for a frontal assault on the Army's Inland Route, Vilhjalmur Stefansson adopted more subtle tactics on behalf of his own cause, Route D. While sharing the conviction of Gruening and the others that the Army's plan would soon fail, Stefansson felt equally certain that military necessity and the logic of geography would then favor Route D over Route A. In the meantime, he quietly gathered more information and recruited allies of his own to bolster Route D's chances.

Stefansson liked to point out that he had no constituents to please or investments to protect by his advocating Route D. No doubt he sincerely believed that the quickest, cheapest, and safest way to move wartime supplies and equipment overland to Alaska was by transporting them north from Edmonton down the Mackenzie River to the vicinity of Norman Wells and then west across the Mackenzie Range to Fairbanks. That there was oil at Norman Wells to fuel this entire network made Route D, in Stefansson's mind at least, far superior to all others. A proud and stubborn man, he was well accustomed to having his knowledge ignored and his ideas scoffed at. Conveniently, his new position as the chief Arctic expert for Colonel Bill Donovan's emerging Office of Strategic Studies (OSS) gave him an opportunity to demonstrate both his correctness and his patriotism as the main proponent of Route D. One of his first assignments for Donovan was to come up with a way to reduce Alaska's dependence on sea-going oil tankers.

By both temperament and training, Stefansson was an industrious gatherer of information about the far north. Long before making his talents available to Donovan in the fall of 1941, he had begun maintaining a file of information related to various possible overland routes to Alaska. In it, for example, was a note from Slim Williams on the superiority of Route A over Route B: "A is 50 percent better for military purposes," said the famous sourdough, "10 percent cheaper to build—25 percent to keep open and 75 percent more scenic." The file also contained a series of letters between Stefansson and his fellow North Dakotan, Halvor Halvorson, head of the group sponsoring Route C. Beyond mentioning the oil at Norman Wells, Stefansson did not attempt to change Halvorson's mind about which route was preferable, but he reminded his friend that they had a strong mutual interest in opposing any planned highway to Alaska that began west of the Rockies instead of serving the needs of the U.S.-Canadian heartland.[23]

After the attack on Pearl Harbor, Stefansson's file on routes to Alaska rapidly grew thicker. Most of all, he needed better information on the best path through the mountains immediately west of Norman Wells. (A key part of his plan, like Hoge's, depended on nonexistent data.) Stefansson turned for help to Richard Finnie, the son of an old friend and fellow explorer of the Canadian north. Young Finnie, a writer and photographer, was something of an expert on the region himself and regarded his father's friend with a mixture of awe and affection. Well connected politically and living near Ottawa, he found it easy to gather whatever information Stefansson wanted.

It did not take Finnie long to obtain and forward the reports of several men who had crossed the Mackenzie Range by air or on foot. He also sent along tidbits of information about which, if any, routes to Alaska were favored by various Canadian government ministers and Members of Parliament. On February 13, 1942, three days before General Sturdevant's visit to Ottawa, Finnie wrote to Stefansson:

> I believe that you can do a great deal toward bringing the highway plan to fruition. In Canada, we are bogged down in red tape and ignorance. . . . If this road is to be put through, pressure from Washington will have to be brought to bear.[24]

Finnie was a busy man in the week after Sturdevant's arrival. As the Permanent Joint Board on Defense prepared to consider the U.S. Army's plan for the Alaska Highway, Finnie sought out influential friends in the ministries of Transport and Defense to "get in a lick for Route D," as he put it to Stefansson, and to keep him posted on the latest developments. Pushing hard for Stefansson's plan, Finnie began to encounter resistance and suspicion among his contacts. The questionable propriety of helping Stefansson promote a scheme that had no official backing in either capital suddenly dawned on him. "I cannot urge too strongly that you . . . gain proper recognition for yourself," he wrote Stefansson, "and for me as your representative." He then went on:

> So long as I was doing research involving little or no confidential information I could . . . enjoy the confidence of these men; but if I am to continue as your representative in the interests of U.S.-Canadian defense, it is imperative that this recognition be secured. Once that has been done, all doors will be open. But if it is not done . . . we will both be discredited. . . .[25]

Despite repeated pleas that he obtain some sort of official status for Finnie, Stefansson never did so. Consequently, after both governments had agreed on the U.S. Army's plan for the Alaska Highway, Finnie went back to sending nonclassified data on the Mackenzie region, along with hearsay reports on the Army's problems along the Inland Route.[26] Stefansson no longer seemed to need his young Canadian friend to help him campaign for Route D. In Frederick A. Delano, Chairman of the National Resources Planning Board—and an uncle of President Roosevelt—he believed he had found a much more powerful ally.

Delano appears to have loved grandiose schemes and having people believe in the efficacy of his connections. At any rate, a meeting in Delano's Washington office in early April 1942 put Stefansson in an optimistic mood. "In the years since I began to advocate a survey of Route D," he wrote to Delano in a letter dated April 8, "my most encouraging experience was in your office last Friday. . . ." He continued:

> It was especially heartening when you said that even if three millions have already been spent on the airports that are to be serviced by [the Inland Route], it was still an open question whether it might not be better to drop [that route] and to construct another series of air bases along Highway D. . . .
>
>   But it is my view that we ought to refrain from discouraging [the Inland Route] as a road servicing the air bases . . . the thing to do, in my opinion, is to push a survey of Highway D. If that proves

favorable, then we push the use of Highway D as a real supply route, as opposed to a mere airplane servicing road like [the Inland Route].[27]

Enclosed with this letter was a sixteen-page memorandum elaborating the advantages of Route D.

Stefansson had met his match as a manipulator. Roosevelt's uncle was indeed interested in any argument that undermined the Army's rationale for the Inland Route, but only to further his own pet project, not Stefansson's. A former railroad executive, Delano believed that a railroad to Alaska via Route B and the Rocky Mountain Trench would cost less and carry more freight than any road could. On April 13, he sent his nephew a memorandum to that effect.[28]

During the next month, as Delano busied himself behind the scenes on behalf of his own railroad scheme, the backers of Route A found a partisan spokesman of their own on Capitol Hill. He was Senator William Langer, Republican of North Dakota. In his campaign to discredit the Inland Route and embarrass everyone connected with it, Langer put on quite a show of disinterested patriotism. Why else, he asked his colleagues, would he be against a highway that linked his home state with the riches of Alaska? What Langer was really doing, however, was exploiting the issue to settle political scores.

The rangy, rumpled, God-fearing son of a prosperous German homesteader, Langer's on-again, off-again political career had been punctuated by a number of confrontations as nasty as any Saturday night brawl in a Fargo saloon. He collected enemies almost gleefully and ensured himself a plentiful supply of them by adopting uncompromising stands against the evils of alcohol, big business, the Roosevelt New Deal, and American involvement in Europe's wars. A graduate of Columbia University (valedictorian of the class of 1910), Langer was soon in the thick of state politics. In 1916, with the support of temperance organizations and the neo-populist Nonpartisan League, he was elected State Attorney General on the Republican ticket. His idea of enforcing North Dakota's laws included holding one town's telephone exchange at gunpoint to prevent suspects from learning of an impending vice raid. During the 1930s, Langer's efforts on behalf of the state's hard-pressed wheat farmers won him two terms as governor, interrupted by his conviction and impeachment (followed by a retrial and reversal on appeal) on a charge of unlawfully soliciting funds from federal employees.

In 1940, after a close and dirty campaign, he was elected to the

U.S. Senate. Incensed, Langer's North Dakota foes petitioned the Senate's Committee on Elections and Privileges to investigate allegations that he was guilty of vote fraud, corruption, income-tax evasion, soliciting false endorsements, and making a crooked deal with the Northern Pacific Railroad. The committee's hearings filled 4,000 pages of testimony. A majority of its members concluded that Langer had shown "continuous, contemptuous and shameful disregard of public duty" and recommended his expulsion; a minority said the evidence was inconclusive. The question of Langer's expulsion went to the full Senate for a vote. Back home, his enemies, led by Governor Moses, already had a replacement picked out to fill Langer's unexpired term: Stefansson's friend, Halvor Halvorson, the Minot attorney. But then, in the spring of 1942, after a long and bitter debate, the Senate voted 52 to 30 not to expel one of its own.[29] His seat (if not his reputation) secure, Langer was ready to get even. The controversy over the routing of the Alaska Highway gave him just the right opportunity.

On May 21, Langer sought the floor of the U.S. Senate "to discuss a matter," he told his colleagues, "which gravely concerns the defense of the United States . . . [and] demands the immediate attention of the Senate." Having made a study of the new military highway to Alaska and found so many "odd coincidences," "decidedly curious" methods, and "inexplicable" decisions concerning its route, he had begun "to have disquieting doubts about the road," he said. With the down-home rhetoric of a former "crossroads attorney," he built his case for a Senate investigation of the Alaska Highway.

First and foremost, he said, the Army's plan was opposed by every single American member of the Alaskan International Highway Commission and by many Canadian experts as well—not only because it failed "in its military purpose of safeguarding Alaska" but because it was, "in fact, . . . a colossal engineering blunder."

That Alaska should be so exposed to attack at this late date was "an incredible state of affairs," he added, quoting "no less an authority than the late General Billy Mitchell" on the subject of the Territory's great strategic importance. Mitchell's name evoked memories of military shortsightedness and stupidity and gave Langer a wonderful club with which to beat the current military establishment without seeming unpatriotic:

> Within the past year the Senate sought to make amends for the treatment Billy Mitchell received by posthumously raising his rank. It was a deserved gesture, but we build a more enduring monument . . .

by . . . making sure that the Alaska Mitchell envisioned as the
ranking military base in the Northern Hemisphere is properly
protected. . . .

Langer next trained his fire on a man whose cosmopolitan
background, beliefs, and activities he loathed: New York's Mayor
LaGuardia, co-chairman of the Permanent Joint Board on Defense.
LaGuardia had been rudely inaccessible when various members of
the AIHC attempted to get a hearing with him prior to the Joint
Board's February 26 decision to recommend the Inland Route, said
Langer. Far worse, in reaching that decision, LaGuardia and his
cohorts had been "wittingly or unwittingly victimized" into selecting
a route that enormously benefited the Canadian Pacific Railroad.
Calling CP Rail "the stormy petrel of Canadian politics," Langer
reminded his listeners that the giant conglomerate owned not only
Yukon Southern Airlines but also a coastal steamship line that stood
to lose business if Route A were adopted.

Who else besides CP Rail was going to benefit from the present
location of the road, asked Langer? Why, none other than a certain
prominent North Dakota lawyer and spokesman for Route C named
Halvor Halvorson. (Route C and the Army's Inland Route were
identical as far north as Watson Lake.) "I know Mr. Halvorson," said
Langer, "and feel that the Senate should find out if he was also the
attorney for powerful railroad and corporate interests. . . ."

Langer went on in this portentous vein for over an hour. Summing
up, he presented a resolution for an investigation of the Alaska
Highway. Its key clauses read:

Whereas . . . the leading construction engineers of the Alaska
Territory characterize the route selected as (1) an engineering
monstrosity because of the muskeg swamp along a major portion of the
route; (2) an economic absurdity because it is hundreds of miles from
Alaska's supply bases in the United States; (3) militarily insignificant
because it fails to fulfill its function as a military route of speedy
ground supply for Alaska; . . .
  Resolved by the Senate of the United States, that a committee be
named from among its members to inquire into the location of the
Alaska Highway on the so-called [Inland Route].[30]

A three-man subcommittee of the Senate Foreign Relations
Committee met on the morning of June 1, 1942, to consider Langer's
charges. From the start, he had an uphill battle. Given only a few
minutes' notice before the hearing, he had no time to call any

witnesses from the Highway Commission. Angry and flustered, he arrived in the committee room accompanied only by an old college chum, John M. Holzworth, a lawyer and writer with considerable first-hand knowledge of Alaska and the Canadian northwest. When the committee chairman, Senator Bennett Champ Clark of Missouri, made his opening remarks, Langer got another unpleasant surprise. "This is not an investigation . . . of the location of the route," said Senator Clark, "but simply a preliminary proceeding for the purpose of making a report to the full Committee. . . ."

Langer sputtered a protest. Clark, as skilled a parliamentarian as his legendary father, House Speaker Champ Clark, continued firmly, "The subcommittee has no authority to do what you are calling for in your resolution . . . and this is more or less . . . to see whether the subcommittee thinks an investigation is justified. . . ." With that, General Sturdevant took the stand.

The burden of Sturdevant's testimony was that the route in question had been selected by the War Department because the short-range, high-speed fighter planes needed for Alaska's defense could be flown more safely over the Inland Route with its already operational airfields than up the Coastal or Rocky Mountain trenches (Routes A and B). As for the muskeg north of Fort St. John, said Sturdevant, General Hoge and his men planned to bypass most of it by swinging the road farther west toward the Rockies. Good-naturedly, the chairman dominated the questioning:

> SENATOR CLARK: "You do not mean to say that the engineers are actually building roads, do you? When I was in the Army the infantry always built the roads and the engineers just stood around to supervise."
>
> GENERAL STURDEVANT: "Yes, sir . . . we have about ten thousand of them in there now."
>
> SENATOR CLARK: "As an old infantryman, I am encouraged to hear that."

When Langer asked whether his friend Holzworth could ask Sturdevant some questions, Clark responded curtly, "I'm sorry, it is not permitted to outsiders to ask questions."

Following Sturdevant on the stand were the War Department's Colonel Tully and Lieutenant Colonel George F. Brewer of the Army Air Force Ferry Command. About all the panel got from Tully was a reiteration of the need for a road to service the Northwest Staging Route and his assurance that both he and General Crawford had consulted the members of the AIHC prior to recommending the Inland Route. Brewer's main contribution was to describe the seven large new airfields under construction along the route and to point out, quoting General Mitchell, that flyers headed north to Alaska were well advised to stay in the clear skies east of the Rockies as long as possible.

Beaten by the Army with his own "Billy" club, Langer struck back with another weapon. "How many planes have been wrecked on this . . . route?" he asked Brewer, and why was the press "already calling it the million-dollar graveyard?" Brewer ducked. He did not know how many aircraft had been lost, he said blandly, and he had never heard of any such "graveyard." Stymied, Langer asked permission for Holzworth to testify.

Holzworth began by claiming no greater personal interest in the outcome of the hearing than any patriotic citizen might have. He happened to be working, he said, on a book about Alaska's strategic role in the war. His research that winter had raised the question of the best overland route, and so he had sought more information from an expert: "Stefansson, the Arctic Explorer, whom you all know. . . ." Convinced both by Stefansson and by his own "intimate familiarity" with the area that the worst possible place for a road was the muskeg country north of Fort St. John, Holzworth was now coming forward at the request of Senator Langer to help rectify the situation before it was too late.

From five years of collecting big game specimens in the Canadian Northwest for the U.S. Biological Survey, Holzworth was exceptionally knowledgeable about the terrain in question. Eventually, however, the senators began to lose patience, more befuddled than enlightened by Holzworth's torrent of facts, figures, and anecdotes about muskeg and the soil and climate conditions that perpetuate it. Senator Clark gently tried to dismiss the witness: "Thank you, Mr. Holzworth."

But Langer's old friend was not through yet. "I was wondering if there was something else here," he said.

The "something else" Holzworth had in mind was the question of the Canadian Pacific Railroad's involvement in the decision to select the Inland Route. Circuitously, he led up to his point: how had it happened that a powerful Canadian company would be the chief postwar beneficiary of a project funded by American taxpayers? Senator Clark reminded the witness that the road's immediate purpose was to help win the war. Besides, he added, "we have to go through a foreign country, and . . . take into consideration that they will necessarily get some advantage out of it as well as ourselves." Holzworth hinted that he still suspected skullduggery.

That was enough for Senator Clark. "You do not mean to suggest that the General Staff of the United States Army knows anything about the Canadian Pacific Railroad?" he asked.

"Oh no," said Holzworth.

"Or is interested in anything else than determining which is the best road for military purposes?"

"No," Holzworth plunged on. "But sometimes the wool is pulled over our eyes and the Canadians and the English sometimes get the better of us, diplomatically. . . . So I am telling you what I have heard, and it can be entirely disregarded if it is not supported."

Holzworth did not know when to stop. Next, he asserted that fighter planes based along the Northwest Staging Route lacked the range to defend the coastal region against attack, prompting Clark to ask: "Do you think that is a matter on which the General Staff of the Army is competent to pass, rather than basing it on your opinion . . . ?"

Unfazed, Holzworth then repeatedly challenged Sturdevant's assertion that areas of muskeg could be located and avoided based on aerial surveys. To which the general kept interjecting: "It can be done."

The gavel pounded at noon. "Senator Langer," said Clark, "if you will have your [other] witnesses here when we reconvene we shall be glad to hear them."[31] Whether any new witnesses could repair the damage done Langer's cause by his pompous friend was questionable. Nevertheless, two weeks later, the three senators patiently heard Donald MacDonald, the longest-serving member of the Highway Commission, give his expert testimony in favor of Route A. The Roosevelt Administration countered by producing Thomas H. McDonald, head of the Public Roads Administration, who conceded the difficulties of the Inland Route but stoutly maintained that they could be overcome.

Meanwhile, events in Alaska's Aleutian Islands made the outcome of the hearing a foregone conclusion. On June 4, 1942, Japanese forces bombed Dutch Harbor. The following week, they occupied the island of Attu. On June 17, Senator Clark's subcommittee released its report, which said, in part:

> Inasmuch . . . as the road to Alaska . . . is already under construction, and a large number of men and . . . machinery are already engaged . . . an investigation by the Senate . . . would

be futile, a waste of vitally necessary time and an unwarrantable interference with the strategic efforts of the Army.

While avoiding direct comment on the charges contained in Langer's resolution to investigate the highway, the report said this about the testimony of his first witness:

The insinuation of the witness Holzworth that the General Staff of the United States Army or other high government officials were moved by a desire to favor the Canadian Pacific Railroad, the subcommittee dismisses as beneath contempt.

As a sop to the influential losers in all this, the report concluded:

. . . your subcommittee does feel that the so-called A Route is for normal peacetime a feasible and desirable route to Alaska . . . [and] should be constructed if, as, and when it can be done without interference with the other war efforts of the United States.[32]

Thus ended, for the moment, a concerted political effort to block the Army's plan. Had Langer and his friends been able to ascertain how little headway had actually been made on the Inland Route, they might have presented a more convincing case against it. But the disturbing truth about General Hoge's lack of progress was a well-kept military secret. Although by early June one of Hoge's major problems had at last been solved, his men had only 95 miles of rough pioneer trail to show for their two months of work. With less than five months remaining in the 1942 construction season, they still had more than 1,400 miles to go.[33]

6

APRIL–JUNE 1942

"Nobody Ever Go That Way"

Awaiting the 35th Engineers in the dense stand of spruce, aspen, and birch stretching westward beyond the Fort Nelson airstrip was a familiar enemy: mud. On April 11, as the first wave of 20-ton bulldozers tore into the woodline, pushing the mangled trees aside into giant windrows, the machines quickly churned the damp clay silt of the forest floor into an oozing, rutted bog. A bespattered Lieutenant Miletich could report only a few hundred yards of progress to Colonel Ingalls that evening. "Press on tomorrow," said Ingalls, confident that, stripped of its shady cover and exposed to the mild spring sunshine, the soggy swath behind the bulldozers would soon firm up again.

Just the opposite happened. Melting snow and April showers more than offset the drying effects of sun and wind, and the daily truck and 'dozer traffic down the slowly lengthening corridor merely kept the muck well homogenized. For the moment, such refinements as culverts, drainage ditches, and gravel topping were not only pointless but impossible. They would come later, perhaps in June or July, at which time the problem would no longer be mud, but dust. The local soil was going to make a lousy road.

Day after day of straining through the gooey yellow clay wore down men and machinery. The number of vehicles out of commission with damaged transmissions and broken axles began to mount. At one point, until an emergency shipment of spare parts arrived by air, only four trucks were still running. Morale, so high in early April, began to slump. On April 30, when the time came to make the first official progress report, Ingalls's surveyors told him that the regiment could only claim 8 miles of cleared right-of-way, not the 13 that registered on the odometer of his jeep. The spinning of its tires in the axle-deep mud accounted for the difference.[1]

Perhaps Ingalls should have taken the advice of the Fort Nelson locals and waited another month before starting work on the road, but a delay would have been even worse for morale. What his men were doing could at least be justified in the name of training, if not of efficiency. Besides, like General Hoge, he was acutely aware of pressure from the War Department to "get on with it."

Hoge had flown in from Washington at the beginning of April to congratulate the 35th on its successful dash up the winter trail. After a short planning conference with Ingalls and a collective pat-on-the-back for the regiment's assembled officers and men, he took off for his northern sector headquarters in Whitehorse. With the 35th safely in position at Fort Nelson and his executive officer, Major Welling, capably in charge at Fort St. John, Hoge's next priority was to get the 18th Engineers started on their segment of the highway north of Whitehorse. Within a few weeks the other three regiments assigned to the northern sector would also be arriving.

In the meantime, however, a serious problem remained unsolved: finding the best pathway through the Rockies from Fort Nelson to Whitehorse. Hoge planned to reconnoiter the stretch between Whitehorse and Watson Lake himself. The task of determining the final route between Fort Nelson and Watson Lake he now delegated to Ingalls and Welling, promising them his personal airplane when he could spare it.[2]

As far as anyone knew, the only reasonably direct and practical way to travel from Fort Nelson to Watson Lake in summer was over the often steeply winding McCusker Trail, pioneered back in 1898. Another route, seldom used, followed the first 40 miles of the McCusker Trail and then slanted off to the northwest, traversing 50 miles of marshy upland valley before reaching the Liard River. This trail then followed the Liard upstream another 150 miles to Watson Lake, passing through a narrow gorge between the Sentinel and Barricade ranges along the way. The mountainous McCusker Trail was impassable in winter; the muskeg on the early part of the Liard route blocked all travel across it in the summer.

Faced with this Hobson's choice during his reconnaissance that winter, and prevented by the persistent cloud cover from inspecting the higher reaches of the McCusker Trail, Hoge had provisionally settled on the Liard route as the more promising of the two. If necessary, patches of muskeg could always be crossed after being covered with a thick layer of brush and logs, called corduroy; but as with the marshy area between Fort St. John and Fort Nelson, Hoge was betting that his men could bypass most of the muskeg leading to the Liard.

On April 16, with only Welling and the pilot aboard, Hoge's twin-engine Beechcraft touched down briefly at Fort Nelson to pick up three more passengers. Getting their first close look at what lay ahead were Ingalls, Lieutenant Colonel Twichell, and an officer from the regimental operations section. Ten minutes west of Fort Nelson, Ingalls told the pilot to bank right and head for the Liard. As they flew low over the broad uplands leading to the river, the view beneath the Beechcraft's wings was not encouraging. As Twichell later wrote:

> The route lay over a flat plain featureless except for numerous lakes and swamps. The country was covered with small spruce, the unfailing sign of muskeg underneath. Larger trees, the usual sign of good ground, were noticeably lacking in this section, and no continuous firm route through it could be [seen anywhere].[3]

The valley of the Liard itself, though free of muskeg, presented more problems. Silty clay, similar to that causing Lieutenant Miletich such trouble back at Fort Nelson, lined both banks for many miles. At one point where a crossing was required, the river was too wide and swift to be easily bridged. (A ferry for this spot had already been ordered by Hoge.) After flying the entire route several times in a futile search for a better alternative, Ingalls and Twichell found themselves in agreement. With heroic effort, they concluded, a road of sorts could eventually be built by way of the Liard to Watson Lake. But not by one regiment in one construction season.

"It was all too obvious now what the newspapers had been talking about," Twichell recalled. "We had a chilling vision of the 35th laboring in this morass . . . with the press jeering from a distance." The two senior officers decided to keep looking. They hid their rising pessimism, "not wishing to dampen the high spirits of the 35th," Twichell admitted, "or to have General Hoge think us chicken-hearted."[4]

One afternoon, as Ingalls and Twichell alighted glumly from the Beechcraft after yet another fruitless aerial search, a scruffy-looking stranger approached them from his tent at the edge of the airstrip. His name was Curwen, he said, and he worked for the Public Roads

Administration as a highway-locating engineer. He had recently returned from a month's trip by dogsled to scout the McCusker Trail and wanted them to know what he had seen. He had only gone as far as Summit Lake, 90 miles out, Curwen acknowledged, before the approaching thaw had forced him to turn back. But, he insisted, nothing along the trail to that point presented any great challenge to modern road-building equipment. He had a strong feeling that the same was true for the rest of the trail, all the way to Watson Lake. Could he persuade the colonel to take him along on the next flight to check out his hunch? Ingalls agreed readily. In fact, he said, since more immediate problems demanded his personal attention on the ground just then, Curwen could have his own seat.

Airborne again a day or so later, Twichell, Welling, and Curwen were soon cruising at 200 mph through a maze of narrow, steep-walled valleys shadowed by towering white peaks. The faint thread of the McCusker Trail was intermittently visible through the tall lodgepole pines below. For the first 65 miles beyond Summit Lake, Curwen's hunch proved entirely correct. "A road builder's paradise," said Twichell of the rock-strewn valley floors. But then the trail disappeared into a cloud-shrouded pass beyond Muncho Lake. Hoge had encountered exactly the same problem two months earlier. Unless they knew for sure what lay beneath those clouds, the Liard route—muskeg and all—was a safer bet.

Undaunted, Curwen suggested that they try flying the trail eastward from the Watson Lake end. But the pass was socked-in from that direction as well. The PRA engineer would not give up. Perhaps they could find a native at Watson Lake who knew another route, he said. Twichell and Welling agreed, having nothing more to lose at this point than another day's flying time.

Landing at Watson Lake, Curwen had no trouble finding a man who claimed to know the country. Sounding like a character in a Hollywood western, Curwen asked, "How you go Watson Lake to Fort Nelson?"

"By McCusker Trail," came the answer.

"Suppose no McCusker Trail," said Curwen.

The man smiled and shook his head. "McCusker Trail the only way to Fort Nelson."

Curwen persisted. "Suppose man go on foot with very sharp ax?"

After a long silence, the native answered. "Maybe you go down the Liard River and up the Trout River to Muncho Lake. Not sure though. Nobody ever go that way."[5]

Back in the air, the white men jubilantly discovered that the native's suggested alternative was indeed a good route for a road. Only one big obstacle remained. A sheer limestone cliff blocked the path along the eastern shore of Muncho Lake. Circling above the lake, still ice-bound in late April, the three engineers conferred. Could the problem be solved by using dynamite to blast out a ledge for a roadway? Yes, they decided, although the job might take more than 50 tons of explosives. Nevertheless, that much dynamite was a bargain compared with the cost of an extra year's work on the other route.

Back to Fort Nelson they flew with the good news. A much-relieved Ingalls asked Welling to see to it that higher headquarters knew and approved of the Muncho Lake alternative. By then, the 35th's "higher headquarters" no longer meant General Hoge. While Hoge still commanded the northern sector, Colonel James A. O'Connor was taking over at Fort St. John. After a quick flight out over the mountains with Welling to see for himself, O'Connor approved the 35th's new route in early May.[6]

The reason for the organizational change was that the two halves of Hoge's command could not communicate with each other. Fort St. John had a telephone line back to Washington and reasonably reliable radio contact with the 35th Engineers at Fort Nelson, but no direct communications at all with Whitehorse. Designed for temperate-zone combat situations, the Army Engineers' radios simply could not reach across the Rockies; when the northern lights played, static blocked even local message traffic.

Of course, reports and other documents could always be forwarded on one of Yukon Southern's mail and passenger runs, scheduled out of Edmonton three times per week, but Welling soon understood why Grant McConachie's countrymen called his airline "Yukon Seldom." Bad weather and equipment problems combined to cancel more than half the civilian flights to and from Whitehorse. The only way for Welling, left in charge at Fort St. John, to send information quickly to his boss in Whitehorse was to relay messages through Sturdevant's office in Washington. This awkward and inefficient arrangement especially annoyed Hoge, who did not like to be the last person in the chain of command to know what his own subordinates were doing. In addition, Sturdevant sometimes exercised his prerogative of acting on Welling's reports before they even reached Whitehorse. With plenty of headaches to confront in the northern sector, Hoge did not object to letting O'Connor have the ones in the southern sector.[7]

The decision to split Hoge's command was a logical quick fix to the existing communications problem. The long-term solution seemed

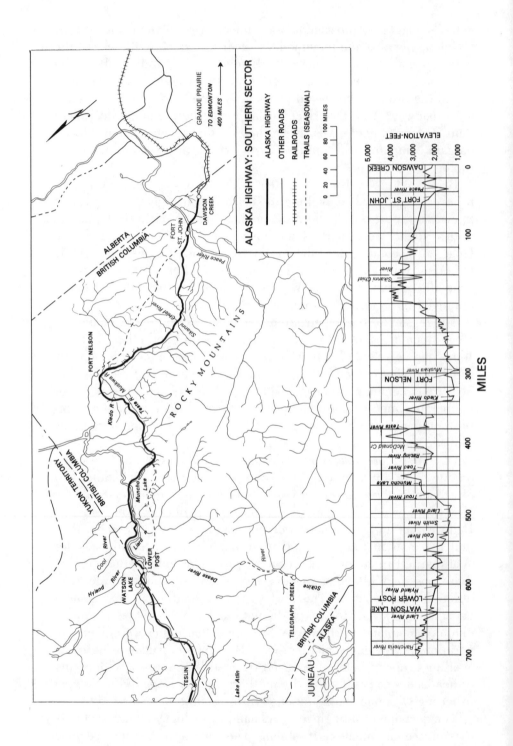

ALASKA HIGHWAY: SOUTHERN SECTOR

ALASKA HIGHWAY
OTHER ROADS
RAILROADS
TRAILS (SEASONAL)

0 20 40 60 80 100 MILES

equally logical: give the finished highway (and the Northwest Staging Route) its own modern telephone and teletype system. When the War Department authorized the construction of such a system in the summer of 1942, it became another of the highway's many add-ons.[8]

The new command arrangement eliminated one source of annoyance for Hoge, but it did nothing to allay a more serious problem. Within a few days of his arrival in Whitehorse, he found himself being second-guessed by the higher-ups in not one but two powerful Washington fiefdoms: the Public Roads Administration and the U.S. Army Corps of Engineers. Although the agreement worked out by General Sturdevant with the PRA gave the Army the final say on the road's location and specifications, the PRA's engineers in the field took their instructions from PRA Commissioner Thomas MacDonald, not from Hoge. Nor did MacDonald take orders from Sturdevant; the two men had merely agreed "to cooperate."[9] This arrangement practically guaranteed serious misunderstandings and confusion among their subordinates.

Early in April, Hoge learned from Frank Andrews, MacDonald's man in Whitehorse, that Sturdevant had given the PRA and its civilian contractors primary responsibility for constructing several additional segments of the highway in the northern sector. Not only that, but Sturdevant and MacDonald had also made some significant changes in the location of the route without consulting Hoge. A letter soon arrived from Sturdevant explaining his actions, but the damage had already been done. On April 11, feeling undercut and humiliated by his old comrade, Hoge fired off an angry reply:

> I have made every effort to carry out this project as outlined in [my] instructions . . . [and am] making reconnaissances with the limited means at my disposal. . . . Plans have been formulated for the carrying out of the work. . . . These . . . are rendered more or less futile when changes . . . are made . . . without my being informed. It is also embarrassing to receive notification of such changes through the [PRA].[10]

The unwieldy relationship between the Army and the PRA had other unfortunate consequences. MacDonald's people were accustomed to laying out first-class scenic highways in national parks; Sturdevant's men had been told to push through a no-frills supply road as quickly as possible. Differences of opinion over what path the road should follow or how safe to make it often escalated into bureaucratic battles. It took until July, for example, to resolve the dispute over the northern sector routing changes that had so infuriated Hoge in April.[11]

Besieged by such problems, Hoge jumped at any chance to get away from his makeshift Whitehorse headquarters, an old barracks leased from the local Mounties. As often as possible, he went flying. When Ingalls and Welling were using his Army Beechcraft, he hitched rides in a high-wing Norseman flown by Les Cook, a local bush pilot, often sitting on an oil drum or a crate of pork and beans destined for some trapper or prospector up in the mountains.

"For bush flying you couldn't beat him," said Norm Harlin, a trapper who often flew with Cook. "He'd go anyplace. Within reason." Cook's passengers learned to trust his sense of where and when it was safe to fly. "My neck's just as important to me as yours is to you," he'd tell them.[12]

"Les Cook was the great one," Hoge remembered. "Les took me everyplace. He went between the mountains. We went down at elevations. We got lost, but I got to know the country pretty well, and the streams by the flying back and forth. . . ."[13]

Les Cook showed Hoge a way over the Continental Divide between Whitehorse and Watson Lake that never rose above an elevation of 3,200 feet. It ran through an unexplored and unmapped network of valleys beginning 80 miles east of Lake Teslin and emerging into the upper Liard Valley about the same distance west of Watson Lake. Although two months passed before a ground reconnaissance confirmed the feasibility of this route (and of Curwen's Muncho Lake alternative as well), Hoge no longer worried much about the mountainous middle third of the Alaska Highway after April 1942. Transportation snarl-ups were to become his next big problem.[14]

On April 1, a small advance party from the 18th Engineers had arrived in Whitehorse and begun laying out a base camp on a bluff at the western edge of town. Over the next several weeks, all 2,000 officers and men of the regiment (including its attached survey, bridging, and medical companies, plus a quartermaster detachment) made the trip up into Canada from Skagway on the rickety, narrow-gauge White Pass and Yukon Railroad. Lacking any room on the jam-packed troopships for its trucks, graders, and bulldozers, the regiment had left these behind on the docks in Seattle. Besides their rifles and duffle bags, the troops brought with them only their portable power equipment and enough canned "B" rations—Vienna sausages, chile con carne, corned beef hash, and dehydrated vegetables—to last several months.

Despite Seattle's repeated assurances to the 18th's Commanding

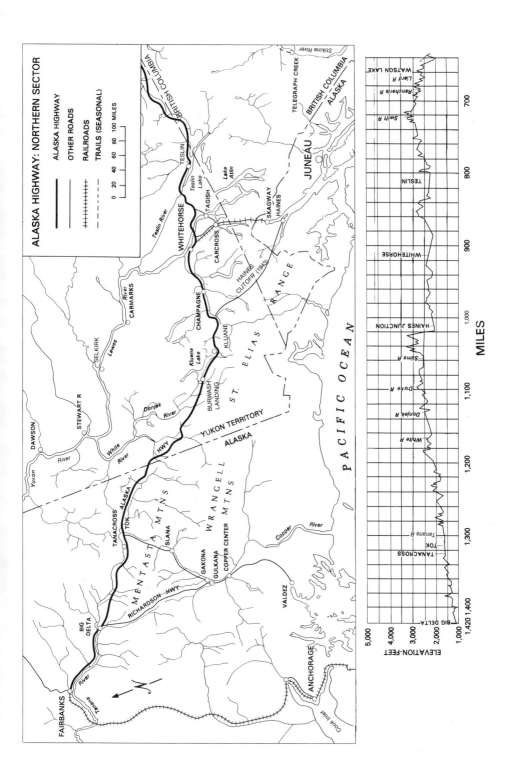

ALASKA HIGHWAY: NORTHERN SECTOR

ALASKA HIGHWAY
OTHER ROADS
RAILROADS
TRAILS (SEASONAL)

0 20 40 60 80 100 MILES

Officer, Colonel Earl G. Paules, that the regiment's heavy construction machinery would be coming up the Inside Passage on the next available boat, April stretched into May before any of it reached Whitehorse. In the interim, while his operators took turns practicing on several borrowed civilian 'dozers, Colonel Paules kept the majority of his men busy and warm clearing the first few miles of right-of-way by hand. He also sent a twelve-man party led by his executive officer, Lieutenant Colonel Walter W. Hodge, on a horseback reconnaissance to the far end of the regiment's sector, 300 miles to the northwest near the Canada-Alaska border. [15]

While the 18th Engineers waited in Whitehorse for their heavy equipment, the next two construction regiments began arriving at Skagway—the first two companies of the 93rd Engineers docking in the narrow, crowded harbor on April 16, and the last units of the 340th Engineers debarking nine days later. Again, as with the 18th Engineers, there had been no room on the troopships for road-building equipment. Until their machines could be shipped north, Hoge decided that the 93rd and 340th should remain in Skagway.

A lawless, brawling boomtown at the height of the Gold Rush, Skagway's population had shrunk from 20,000 to less than 300 in the span of forty years. Now it was virtually deserted. Most of the remaining inhabitants had moved elsewhere after the Pearl Harbor debacle, out of fear of a Japanese attack or simply because no more summer tour boats would be docking for the duration. The arriving troops whistled and cheered as they marched off the dock and up Broadway Street past such emporiums as the Pack Train Inn, the Silver Bar, and Soapy Smith's Parlor, only to realize that no sleeve-gartered bartenders or tightly-corseted dancehall girls waited within. There was only dusty, piled-up furniture beyond the swinging doors. [16] At the nearby grass airstrip—the only large patch of level ground for miles around—2,500 soldiers, half of them blacks, pitched their tents, lit their stoves, and settled in for an indefinite wait.

The few civilians left in Skagway worked for the White Pass and Yukon Railroad, the town's other longtime source of employment. Begun in the feverish summer of 1898 and finished by 2,000 laborers just two years later, the railroad was a monument to human audacity and greed. It is a wonder that it was ever finished. Accidents and labor violence took a heavy toll, but many more workmen simply "borrowed" the company's picks and shovels and departed for the gold fields in the middle of the night. In the first 20 miles out of Skagway the single narrow track rose from sea level to an elevation of 2,900 feet, snaking up and over White Pass on some of the world's steepest grades, around heart-stopping curves, across numerous spindly trestle bridges, and through a dozen tunnels and avalanche-proof wooden snowsheds. Once past the Canadian border at the summit, however, the line ran almost straight and level for another 90 miles along Lake Bennett, through Carcross, and on into Whitehorse.

Although the lure of gold was already fading by 1900, the railroad survived because its monopoly on year-round surface transportation into the Whitehorse region allowed it to charge exorbitant rates. An average of 25,000 tons of freight moved over White Pass each year. By 1942, the line's rolling stock, much of it forty years old, consisted of 10 locomotives, 18 passenger cars, and 173 freight cars. It took three engines just to pull a 10-car mixed train to the top of the pass.[17]

In Hoge's latest plan, the newly activated 340th Engineers had responsibility for building approximately 200 miles of highway eastward from the village of Teslin on Morley Bay (known today as Nisutlin Bay). Following the pathway through the Rockies that Hoge and Les Cook had located, the regiment was supposed to link up by late summer with the 35th Engineers in the vicinity of Watson Lake. But moving the 340th into position at Teslin was not going to be easy. Once the regiment's 'dozers and other equipment finally got to Skagway, they would have to be hauled over the mountains to Whitehorse. There, men and machinery would transfer to shallow-draft steamers and barges for a roundabout 200-mile voyage via the Lewes (now Yukon) and Teslin rivers to Morley Bay on the eastern shore of Teslin Lake. Since these waterways were unlikely to be ice-free until late May, the 340th would not be able to start work until mid-June, at the earliest.

Hoge needed a faster way to move at least part of the regiment to Morley Bay. His best bet, he decided, was to cut a 70-mile access trail from Carcross eastward to the Teslin River. From the river, boats could easily ferry the troops to Morley Bay. Constructing such a trail for the 340th's use became the priority mission of the 93rd Engineers as soon as the War Department added them to Hoge's command. But both regiments continued to mark time in Skagway while their equipment sat on docks far to the south.[18]

Finally, a supply ship arrived. Its cargo: 90 tons of Coca-Cola and beer, plus several hundred tons of almost useless slab wood and coal. (The troops had oil-burning stoves.) His patience exhausted, Hoge flew to Seattle to see for himself what the problem was. The chaotic situation he found there was typical of every port on the Pacific coast in the spring of 1942. With the United States' military buildup in

Hawaii and the South Pacific creating a demand for shipping far in excess of supply, the needs of Hoge's small command were not high among the priorities of Seattle's overworked port officials. Nor, he discovered to his horror, did they seem to care much that, as the backlog on the docks grew ever larger, equipment tagged for Skagway was being sent instead to Honolulu or Sydney.

In desperation, Hoge turned for help to E. W. Elliot, whose Seattle construction firm had recently put its three tugs and handful of barges under contract to the PRA to ship civilian highway workers and equipment north. An Annapolis graduate, Elliot was glad to give Hoge a hand.

Scouring Puget Sound for vessels to purchase or lease, Elliot quickly assembled a motley fleet that included three small freighters, ten tugs, a number of barges and scows, and at least five large pleasure yachts (which had their elegant teak and mahogany accommodations ripped out by Elliot's carpenters to make room for rows of triple bunks and extra cooking and toilet facilities). Satisfied with the promising results of his trip, Hoge flew back to Whitehorse, leaving behind a staff officer to coordinate future shipments with both Elliot and the authorities in Seattle. Above all, Hoge told the officer, the Army did not need any more coal or slab wood in Skagway.[19]

By this time, most of the soldiers in Skagway had been sitting around for nearly three weeks. Their commanders kept thinking up useful projects—building a rifle range at the airfield, filling potholes in the town's streets, patching up the wooden sidewalks, making repairs on the Dyea road and around the railroad station—but nobody pretended that such jobs were anything but make-work.

Cheers went up when the next ship docked; its cargo included the 18th Engineers' bulldozers, graders, and dump trucks. Several trains of heavily loaded flatcars were soon inching their way over White Pass and rolling on to Whitehorse. Although Colonel Paules and his men had only a few miles of completed pioneer road behind them by the end of May, with all of their machinery finally present and accounted for, the 18th was poised to make good progress toward Kluane Lake during the summer.

Confident that Elliot's ragtag collection of barges and scows had broken the shipping bottleneck, Hoge ordered the 93rd Engineers to begin work on the access trail to the Teslin River without waiting for their heavy equipment. Carrying only hand tools, the black Engineers arrived in Carcross on May 5. Although the regiment's commanding officer, Colonel Frank M. S. Johnson, managed to borrow two bulldozers from Whitehorse temporarily, his men made little headway against the frozen hardpan for the next few days. By June 4, however, Johnson had moved his headquarters from Carcross to Tagish, 22 miles farther east, while the regiment's own 'dozers pushed on toward the river, another 48 miles ahead.

On May 22, still stuck in Skagway, the 340th Engineers got word that the ice on both the Lewes and the Teslin was at last breaking up. More men and machinery headed north over the pass during the next three weeks, their movement interrupted by a tense alert following Japan's strike in the Aleutians. At Carcross, Colonel F. Russell Lyons split his regiment. According to the plan worked out earlier by Hoge, the 2nd battalion of the 340th, along with most of the regiment's vehicles and machinery, continued on to Whitehorse. From there, relays of riverboats loaded to the gunwales began the roundabout trip to Morley Bay. Meanwhile, Lyons's 1st battalion, traveling light, headed east from Carcross over the freshly cut trail. When the 93rd's clearing crews broke through to the banks of the Teslin on June 17, Lyons's men were right behind them. Mud-caked, mosquito-bitten and footsore after 70 miles of hiking, they clambered wearily aboard waiting barges for the last part of their journey, a short ride upriver and down Teslin Lake to Morley Bay.

On June 18, nearly one month after the first elements of the 340th had left Skagway for their new base camp, the regiment was at last in position and starting work on the trail toward Watson Lake. Up ahead, accompanied by native guides and pack dogs (the going was too rough for horses), a reconnaissance party led by Lyons's executive officer, Lieutenant Colonel Reinder F. Schilsky, struggled to find and mark the best route over the Continental Divide.[20]

Although Hoge focused much of his attention during May and June on the transportation problems of his troops in the Skagway-Whitehorse area, he had similar concerns about his fourth regiment, the 97th Engineers, camped near Valdez, 400 miles west of Skagway on the Gulf of Alaska. On April 29, when the 97th landed, several feet of snow covered the ground, a strange new sight for most of the regiment's 1,100 enlisted men, recently drafted blacks from Florida, Georgia, and Alabama. Adding to their woes was the 97th's battered fleet of dump trucks, which had been classified as unserviceable and turned in for salvage at the port of embarkation in Seattle. The 97th's commander, Colonel Stephen C. Whipple, had hoped to obtain brand-new replacements on the next transport sailing north, but when it docked in Valdez a month later, off rolled the same old wrecks.

A tiny fishing village at the southern end of the 350-mile

Richardson Highway to Fairbanks, Valdez was the main entry port for the Army units and PRA civilian contractors scheduled to build the northernmost segment of the Alaska Highway. The road north out of Valdez would later be jammed with civilian rigs headed for the PRA's assigned sector southeast of Big Delta, but snowdrifts as high as 13 feet made it impassable at the moment.

Hoge had given the 97th the preliminary mission of opening an access road from Slana, 200 miles north of Valdez, over a pass in the Mentasta Mountains and down to the vicinity of Tok, a village in the upper Tanana Valley. (By coincidence, this was also the first leg of Slim Williams's famous dog sled trip in the winter of 1932.) After crossing the Tanana, the 97th would be in position to start on its assigned sector of the highway, moving southeast up the valley towards the Canada-Alaska border and an eventual linkup with the 18th Engineers. With the initial wait for trucks and bulldozers and subsequent delays due to washouts, flooding, and mudslides along the Richardson Highway, it was June 7 before Colonel Whipple could report that his men had begun work on the trail over the pass from Slana.[21] It would be July before they even reached the top.

If Hoge thought that the worst of his transportation and supply problems would be over once his four construction regiments had been reunited with their gear, he was wrong. Earlier that spring he had asked the War Department to augment his command with three truck companies, one of which (a dump truck unit) was to haul gravel. The other two were slated to deliver supplies. The first of these companies landed in Skagway in early June, without trucks, arctic clothing, kitchen equipment, tents, or bedding. Not to worry, the company commander had been told in Seattle: his men could draw everything they needed from the stockpiles in Skagway. But no such stockpiles existed. Hoge's command was living hand-to-mouth.

While 120 Quartermaster soldiers found spartan accommodations in Skagway's airfield hangar, Hoge sent an urgent message back to Seattle not to let the next truck company sail until it was completely outfitted. To no avail. The unit arrived in mid-June, similarly ill-equipped. Despite the hard edge on Hoge's next message, the same thing happened a third time. By the end of June, the hangar housed over 300 hapless drivers and mechanics. It was midsummer before the last of them moved out and went to work.[22] The acronym SNAFU, "Situation Normal—All Fucked Up," originated in World War II. The long-suffering GIs stranded in Skagway that spring could well have coined the term.

General Hoge had plenty of snafus to deal with in the Whitehorse area; and his counterpart at Fort St. John had his share, too. On April 30, 1942, shortly before Colonel O'Connor took over the southern sector, trains began unloading the 341st Engineers at Dawson Creek. While Company "A" remained at the railhead to build warehouses, the bulk of the regiment moved north of Fort St. John to set up a base camp near Charlie Lake. The 341st was a brand-new outfit. Commanded by Lieutenant Colonel Albert L. Lane, it had been organized at Fort Ord on March 6 around a small cadre of one officer and 96 men from the departing 35th Engineers. In contrast to the well-equipped 35th, the 341st arrived in Canada with some serious equipment shortages. For example, the gremlins infesting the Army's logistical system had somehow misplaced the regiment's entire consignment of twenty D-8 bulldozers, as well as eighteen of its twenty-four much less powerful D-4 models.[23] Lane's inexperienced operators quickly discovered that the D-4 was a fine machine for clearing underbrush but not very good at knocking down trees. During the next several weeks, just as in the northern sector, miserable, sweating men armed with axes and shovels tried to do the work of 20-ton 'dozers. Their bright green headnets and leather work gloves kept the mosquitos at bay—except during smoke breaks and chow time. There was no escape at all from the ever-present mud.

Although Colonel O'Connor kept finding jobs for the 341st to do around Fort St. John, such as repairing the existing roads and expanding "Fort Alcan," his elaborate new headquarters, Colonel Lane managed to move Company "E" north of Charlie Lake and get it started on the regiment's primary mission. On May 15, as an outboard-powered pontoon raft ferried additional men and equipment down the 9-mile length of the lake, disaster struck. A sudden squall blew up, capsizing the raft half a mile from shore. Five soldiers clung to the wreckage, but twelve others quickly drowned in the frigid, choppy water. All on board would likely have perished had it not been for a trapper named Gus Hedin, who happened to see the accident from his cabin. As the storm intensified, Hedin rowed out to rescue the survivors, making three round trips in his tiny homemade boat. An hour later, launches dragging grappling hooks began crisscrossing the lake. In the long evening twilight, their wakes glinted green and yellow under the pale, shimmering fire of the northern lights. The last body was not recovered until June 9.[24]

Farther north, just as the 35th Engineers began making better progress, an outbreak of jaundice threatened their momentum. Later traced to yellow fever shots from several spoiled batches of serum, the disease struck selectively. Less than half of Colonel Ingalls's regiment came down with it, but Company "A" of the 648th Engineers was not so lucky. Trained as surveyors and route reconnaissance specialists at Camp Claibourne, Louisiana, almost every member of the 648th spent several feverish weeks on light duty that spring.

A detachment from the 648th had remained at Fort St. John to work with the 341st Engineers, but the Company Commander, Captain A. M. Eschbach, along with ninety of his men, had made the trek to Fort Nelson back in March. With no similarly trained specialists of his own, Ingalls depended heavily on Eschbach's unit for thorough, ground-level reconnaissance and precise surveying to give the 35th's bulldozers a well-marked pathway to follow. Fortunately for Ingalls, laying out the first 40 miles of new road turned out to be relatively easy. Eschbach's understrength pathfinders simply stayed on the bluffs north of the Muskwa River and followed the general trace of the McCusker Trail. After the trail left these forested uplands and climbed the first outriders of the Rockies, however, pinpointing the exact location of a buildable route was not so easy. Here, Ingalls was thankful that Eschbach himself had escaped the jaundice that spring.

Some 45 miles west of Fort Nelson, rising more than 3,000 feet above the surrounding river valleys, Steamboat Mountain looms over the McCusker Trail. Viewed from a distance, the mountain's tree-covered slopes and gently undulating profile made it seem no great obstacle, but on the basis of Curwen's preliminary reconnaissance and their own observations from Hoge's Beechcraft, the 35th's leaders knew otherwise. Finding the best way over or around Steamboat Mountain became Captain Eschbach's first challenge. (See map on p. 114.)

The map Eschbach carried with him gave no hint that Steamboat Mountain even existed. Hastily compiled in Washington from a series of high-altitude photographs taken by Army photo-reconnaissance planes returning from a mapping mission in Alaska the previous summer, this map depicted, on a scale of 8 miles to the inch, nothing but the local lakes, streams, and rivers. No other clues to the region's complex topography had been plotted—no contour lines, no spot elevations, no trails, no settlements, nothing.[25]

Accompanied by a lieutenant and several enlisted men, Eschbach stumbled around for a week near the summit of Steamboat Mountain looking for a pass that would lead farther west into the Tetsa River valley. Every promising possibility led either to a dead-end canyon or a precipice. Regrouping near the foot of the mountain, the party met a trapper who claimed he knew the way. Leaving his exhausted companions to set up a base camp, and carrying only his pack and sleeping bag, Eschbach followed the trapper back up the mountain. Five days later the two men were standing on the banks of the Tetsa. Next, to find out if a water-level route around Steamboat Mountain was preferable, Eschbach decided to follow the Tetsa downstream to the Muskwa. From there it would be a fairly short hike around the foot of the mountain back to his base camp. The trapper took him as far as the confluence of the two rivers. There they made camp for the night on a low hummock overlooking the Tetsa's shallow, rocky canyon, and dozed off to the sound of gently burbling water.

After midnight a violent downpour began. Before dawn, the burble had grown to a steady roar. Still huddled in their soggy sleeping bags, the two men suddenly became aware of a more ominous sound: a deep, booming rumble. They barely had time to escape to higher ground before a churning wall of water, boulders, trees, and jagged chunks of ice swept over their campsite and on into the swollen Muskwa. Within an hour the flash flood was over and the Tetsa subsided again, but nothing remained of their gear. Even their boots were gone. The trapper allowed as how he had better return to his cabin and check his lines, leaving Eschbach on his own to find his companions. "It took me a very long day to get back," he recalled:

> I had no bearings or markings to follow other than just an instinctive sense of the direction I was to go. I shall never forget late that evening, after being on the trail since early dawn, smelling fried potatoes! I . . . followed my nose. Over a hill I came into Lt. Stewart's camp and they were actually frying potatoes . . . mixed with powdered eggs, powdered milk and lard into potato patties. This was the second best meal of my life! [The best was "hot oatmeal cooked in powdered milk with lots of sugar," eaten at −30°F on arriving at Fort St. John back in March.][26]

Wearing new boots, Eschbach reported to Ingalls at Fort Nelson. The canyon of the lower Tetsa was no place for a road around Steamboat Mountain, he said. But at least he had found a way to get over it.

If Ingalls had any lingering doubts about the awesome power of storm-fed mountain streams, they were soon dispelled by the experience of his own men on the Kledo River. The Kledo, another tributary of the Muskwa, flowed through a huge burned-out area and crossed the McCusker Trail about 35 miles west of Fort Nelson. On

June 7, after the 35th's clearing crew had forded the river and moved on, the regiment's attached Pontoon Company put in a 150-foot floating bridge until a more permanent timber structure could be erected. On June 9 another downpour began. Twenty-four hours later, the Kledo had risen 6 feet, and pieces of the bridge lined the downstream banks for half a mile. Doggedly, the pontoon specialists put their bridge back together as soon as the Kledo subsided.

The receding river left behind a new problem: the trail west across its charred and poorly drained floodplain had turned into 3 miles of impassable swamp. Up ahead, cut off from their supply of fuel, the clearing crew's bulldozers soon sputtered to a stop. The only quick way to get things moving again was to cover the trail with a matting of branches and logs, but laying 3 miles of corduroy meant cutting and trimming thousands upon thousands of trees. To fight "the battle of the swamp," as it came to be known, Ingalls turned out every man in the regiment—cooks and clerks included. Sooty, callused, and hollow-eyed from exhaustion, they won the battle in a week.

Despite such setbacks and the continuing miseries inflicted by mosquitos and "no-see-ums," most problems also had a lighter side. After a bulldozer crew under Lieutenant Mason left their machine at the bottom of a deep cut during the same storm that sent the Kledo on a rampage, all that could be seen of the submerged vehicle the next day was the tip of its vertical exhaust pipe. Although Ingalls could chuckle over a radio message that said, "Send help. Enemy submarine sighted in Lake Mason," his appreciation of the joke may not have been apparent to the chagrined lieutenant. Nor was it in Ingalls's makeup or his mission to ease the pressure on his men as the days grew longer, warmer, and drier. Long before June 21, when a real enemy submarine shelled the Oregon coast, the regiment had begun working two ten-hour shifts each day, seven days a week.[27]

Constantly on the go and keeping crazy hours, Ingalls and Twichell decided they needed an orderly to fix their meals and take care of the tent they shared. The British call such a man a "striker"; American GI's use a less elegant term: "dog robber." When no volunteers came forth, Ingalls asked that the regimental roster be screened for the best-qualified soldier. Private First Class Francis F. Beckman— civilian occupation, manservant—was soon back at his former trade.

Born and raised in Germany, Beckman proved to be a jewel. No matter when the two officers needed a fresh mug of coffee, a bite to eat, or hot water for a washup, it was always ready. Beckman could turn Spam, powdered eggs, and dehydrated potatoes into a gourmet breakfast, and he worked even greater wonders with fresh trout or partridge. Pressed about his former employers, Beckman maintained a dignified reticence. Eventually, he let slip the names of Walter Teagle, Chairman of the Board at Standard Oil, and Myron Taylor, a former Chairman at U.S. Steel. "Since then," said Twichell, "I have tried not to act cowed in Beckman's presence, and feel mightily the strain of deserving his approbation."

Moving the Commanding Officer's tent to keep up with the road-building crews was among Beckman's many duties. As the 35th Engineers finally began to make steady progress toward the mountains, he moved it every day, carefully noting the distance covered. Ingalls no longer needed to ask his surveyors how far the regiment had come from Fort Nelson. Beckman could tell him, to the tenth of a mile.[28]

In late June, Ingalls decided to send out two new ground reconnaissance parties. One, led by Eschbach, was to pick up the McCusker Trail beyond Steamboat Mountain and this time follow it all the way to Watson Lake. The other, led by Lieutenant Stewart, was to travel with Eschbach as far west as Muncho Lake and then split off and head north to confirm the feasibility of Curwen's alternate route to Watson Lake. Although the regiment had recently received a long-awaited set of low-altitude stereographic photographs covering both possibilities, these had been taken on a day when the high trail west of Muncho Lake was, as usual, covered by clouds. Before committing himself irrevocably to Curwen's route, Ingalls was determined to find out whether a better path lay beneath those clouds. A wrangler with a team of pack horses would soon be coming up from Fort St. John, Eschbach was told. These animals were for his use, now that they could find firm footing and plenty of forage along the trail. Eschbach could include as many of his own men in the party as he wished, Ingalls continued, but a native who knew every inch of the McCusker Trail had already agreed to be their guide. His name was Charlie MacDonald.[29]

MacDonald lived in a small cabin midway along the McCusker Trail, in the high valley where MacDonald Creek joins the Toad River. A man of perhaps fifty summers, he trapped animals to support his wife, Nellie, eight or nine children (MacDonald was hazy about numbers), and his aged father, the patriarch of the family. It was not an easy, carefree life. That winter, when the dried fish and game ran out, Nellie had had to stretch their dwindling supplies of trading post canned goods with concoctions of boiled bark and herbs. MacDonald's bad teeth, short stature, and gaunt, deeply lined brown face told of enduring many such winters. His eyes, black and alert, also bespoke a persistent curiosity. Numbers may have flummoxed him, but maps did not—although, on the trail, MacDonald had no real need of maps. Eschbach would soon be glad of that.

The 35th Engineers first made Charlie MacDonald's acquaintance in mid-June, when he passed eastward through their forward base near the Kledo River on his way to Fort Nelson with a load of furs. Within a few days, his pack horses heavily laden with food and other supplies, he was back at the forward camp. In no apparent hurry to return home to his family, he hung around for several days, cadging free meals and quietly watching the goings-on. What fascinated him so much was not the noisy bulldozers; those he'd already grown used to at Fort Nelson. Rather, it was the white men's odd habits and endless hustle and bustle. Before long he was asking questions: "What this?" and "Why you do that?" At first Ingalls thought this inquisitive native a pest, but eventually he recognized the quick intelligence behind his broken English. Moreover, the man claimed to know a pass through the mountains west of Muncho Lake where a road might be built. So Charlie MacDonald was hired as Eschbach's guide.

One day, while Eschbach was still waiting for the pack horses from Fort St. John, MacDonald wandered into the regimental operations tent. There, Lieutenant Colonel Twichell was bent over a large table spread with dozens of aerial photographs, peering intently down at one pair of them through a binocular device mounted on short metal legs. Looking over Twichell's shoulder for several minutes, MacDonald finally asked, "Why you do that?"

Twichell tried his best to explain how the stereoscopic viewer worked, and that it made pictures of things seem real. It helped him figure out the best pathway for the new road, he said.

"Me look?" asked MacDonald.

Twichell sorted through the photos, found the pair showing MacDonald Creek, adjusted everything, and let MacDonald take his place at the viewer. There was no immediate reaction. Then, as his eyes adjusted to the stereoscope, a three-dimensional image suddenly came into focus. The startled native jumped about 3 feet.

"Me cabin! Me cabin!" he shouted, pointing at the table top in surprise and delight.[30]

Although Twichell obviously felt both affection and sympathy for Charlie MacDonald in recounting this tale, the white man's assumption of cultural and racial superiority is uncomfortably clear. It would be interesting to hear MacDonald's version of the same episode, but his is not recorded.

Twichell's patronizing attitude toward native people was hardly unique. Most of his contemporaries among the white, middle-class U.S. Army officers who worked on the Alaska Highway had similar stories to tell. Some of the earlier, nonmilitary sources on which the first part of this book is based are even more biased. Mackenzie's native guides, and later Moodie's, though entrusted with their white employers' very lives, exist in these sources only as inscrutable, nameless ciphers. Similarly the natives who helped Frank Barr rebuild his airplane and those who worked for Clancy Craig on the Fort Nelson airstrip come across as comic stereotypes—monosyllabic and smelly, or shiftless and lazy. How these people felt about the jobs they performed was of little or no concern to a busy supervisor like Moodie, Craig, or Twichell. What the native men and women of northwest Canada and Alaska did think of all this hustle and bustle—and how it changed their lives—is told in a later chapter.

Next to be considered are the experiences of the black American soldiers who constituted 40 percent of the military workforce on the Alaska Highway. Without their efforts, the highway would have taken at least another year to construct and might never have been finished at all. Besides being treated with condescension or downright contempt by most of their commanders, they, too, were either ignored by contemporaneous chroniclers or portrayed in grossly stereotypical terms: "Light-hearted lads, heavy logs on their shoulders . . . shuffling out of the brush to a red-hot vocalization of the 'Chattanooga Choo-Choo.'"[31]

They deserved better.

7

Welcome at the Party?

The 95th Engineers, the last of the three black construction regiments assigned to work on the Alaska Highway, arrived in Dawson Creek over a four-day period, beginning on May 29, 1942. Cooped up in stale coaches with only brief stops for trainside calisthenics during the week-long trip from the East Coast, the troops were glad to stretch their cramped muscles and breathe fresh air again without having to climb right back aboard. Their high spirits showed as they slung their rifles, shouldered their duffle bags, and marched away toward the railhead bivouac area, chanting cadence as they went.

Their white commander, Colonel David L. Neuman, headed for the Southern Sector headquarters to pay his respects to Colonel O'Connor and to report that his men were ready to begin work just as soon as their bulldozers, trucks, and other equipment could be unloaded. Neuman was in for a nasty surprise. To make up the equipment shortages in Colonel Lane's white 341st Engineers, Neuman's outfit was about to be stripped of most of its heavy machinery.[1]

The decision to beef up the 341st at the expense of the 95th was defensible, given the assignments of the two regiments. Colonel Lane's men were under orders to push a rough pioneer road through to Fort Nelson and link up with the 35th Engineers before their supplies ran out that summer. Colonel Neuman's regiment was simply to come along behind the 341st and improve the road's durability and safety. Although O'Connor could have given primary responsibility for the trail to Fort Nelson to the better-equipped 95th Engineers and let the 341st bring up the rear, such a switch might have delayed the linkup. After having worked for the past month in the area north of Fort St. John, Lane's men were acclimated and rapidly learning the techniques of road building in muskeg country. Neuman's troops would need an equivalent shakedown period before hitting their stride. The morale of the 341st was another factor O'Connor might have considered. How would this white regiment have reacted to the humiliation of being taken out of the lead and given a supporting role behind a black outfit?

But a good case could also have been made for letting the more experienced 95th Engineers keep their equipment and take over the mission of the 341st. The latter had existed as a full-strength unit for less than two months; more than 90 percent of its present total of 45 officers and 1,250 enlisted men had been added during March and April to the original small cadre that came from the 35th Engineers at Fort Ord. Most of the training Colonel Lane had been able to give his men was accomplished after their arrival in Canada.

By contrast, the 95th Engineers were old-timers. Organized as a separate battalion at the Engineer Training Center at Fort Belvoir, Virginia, in April 1941, the original members of the 95th had gone through thirteen weeks of training at Fort Belvoir, participated in the Carolina Maneuvers during the fall of 1941, and worked on various construction projects at Virginia's Camp A. P. Hill before ending up at Fort Bragg, North Carolina, in early 1942. There, the 95th was joined by enough new men to fill out a second battalion and expanded to become a regiment. Ten more weeks of training followed before the reorganized unit shipped out for Canada, eager to show what it could do.[2]

Thus, O'Connor might have contemplated another question: how would Neuman's men be affected by the decision to take away most of their heavy equipment, leaving them to perform their supporting mission with little more than shovels and wheelbarrows?

The morale of one or the other regiment was bound to suffer, whatever Colonel O'Connor decided to do about the 341st's missing bulldozers. His primary concern, however, was to get the road to Fort Nelson built as quickly as possible. As an abstract, race-neutral exercise back at the Command and General Staff School, where O'Connor had served as an instructor, this would have been an easy call. All else being equal, logic dictated that the more difficult of the two assignments should go to the regiment with more training and better equipment. Even taking into account the fact that the 341st had a month's head start on the 95th in on-the-job experience, the balance still weighed in favor of putting the 95th in the lead, assuming that its potentially greater road-building efficiency would compensate for any work days lost during its shakedown period. But since Colonel Neuman's regiment was not yet in action, Colonel O'Connor's assessment of the relative strengths and weaknesses of these two units necessarily relied on several other assumptions— including, almost certainly, some extremely derogatory ideas about blacks that were prevalent in the command hierarchy of the U.S. Army.

The following compendium of those ideas comes from a 1936 Army War College study by a group of white majors and colonels, most of whom went on to higher rank in World War II.

> As an individual the negro is docile, tractable, lighthearted, carefree and good natured. If unjustly treated he is likely to become surly and stubborn, though this is usually a temporary phase. . . . He is careless, shiftless, irresponsible and secretive. He resents censure and is best handled by praise and with ridicule. He is unmoral and untruthful and his sense of right doing is relatively inferior . . .
>
> On the other hand the negro is cheerful, loyal and usually uncomplaining if well fed. He has a musical nature and a marked sense of rhythm. His art is primitive. He is religious. With proper direction in mass, negroes are industrious. They are emotional and can be stirred to a high state of enthusiasm. Their emotions are unstable and their reactions uncertain. Bad leadership in particular is easily communicated to them.[3]

Colonel O'Connor had never worked with a black Engineer regiment before, but the conventional wisdom in the U.S. Army of his day was that most blacks made poor soldiers and that black units tended to fall apart under stress.[4] His decision to favor the 341st at the expense of the 95th suggests that he subscribed to that "wisdom." Most likely O'Connor based his decision on a careful estimate of the relative efficiency of the two regiments, with no conscious intent to keep blacks "in their place." Nevertheless, his decision conveyed a blatantly familiar message to the soldiers of the 95th: we don't think you are as good as whites.

Black Americans had been hearing that message all their lives. Yet what happened to the 95th Engineers at Dawson Creek in 1942 reflected not only the racial attitudes held by most white Americans of that era, but also what the U.S. Army had chosen to learn from its experiences with black soldiers in World War I.

Following policies that dated back to the Civil War, the mass army raised by the United States in 1917 was a segregated force. Of Americans drafted for service in World War I, 13 percent were blacks—some 368,000 in all. Of these, the vast majority were relegated to the role of uniformed laborers in Engineer or Quartermaster battalions, two-thirds of which never left the United States.[5] This systematic denigration of their loyalty, bravery, and capacity to handle difficult assignments embittered many black Americans. Having already proved themselves as Indian-fighting "Buffalo soldiers" on the western plains and as volunteer militiamen in the Spanish-American War, they not unreasonably expected that something closer to equality might result from their wholehearted participation in a war supposedly intended "to make the world safe for democracy." They saw instead the terrible irony of a Jim Crow Army fighting such a war.

Only two black fighting units, with a combined strength of about 40,000 men, saw front-line action in France. One, the 93rd Infantry Division, was the only large U.S. unit to serve under the control of the French army. Although the combat effectiveness of the 93rd gradually deteriorated as ill-trained replacements were brought in to fill vacancies created by casualties, the French high command remained generally satisfied with its battlefield performance.

The other black division, the 92nd, quickly developed a reputation for cowardice and inefficiency. Kept under General Pershing's control in the American Expeditionary Force, the 92nd's high AWOL, equipment-loss, and sick-call rates were clear indicators of bad morale, weak discipline, and poor leadership.[6]

Of the leadership problems within the 92nd Division, its white wartime commander, Major General C. C. Ballou, wrote in 1920: "all experience indicates that, in their present state of education and development, colored troops to compare favorably with white troops must have an even better leadership than the whites." But then he added, "For the parts of a machine requiring the finest steel, pot metal was provided."

The Army's policy of relaxing the commissioning requirements for black junior officers, said Ballou, was "the first fault in the making of the 92nd Division." He elaborated:

> To officer a division in which the best possible leadership was required, only one-half as many students were summoned to the training camp as were summoned . . . to select the officers of a white division. And, whereas [white] candidates for commissions . . .

were required to be college graduates, only high school educations were required [of black officer candidates]. And in many cases these high school educations would have been a disgrace to any grammar school.

As for the Army's insistence on restricting blacks to the lower rungs of the promotion ladder and reserving the higher ranks for whites, Ballou said, "The colored officers never could understand this, and . . . it made no end of trouble. . . ."

Ballou was careful to point out, however, that frustrated black junior officers were by no means the only sources of friction:

It was my misfortune to be handicapped by many white officers who were rabidly hostile to the idea of a colored officer, and who continually conveyed misinformation to [higher headquarters]. . . . Such men will never give the Negro the square deal that is his just due.

Ballou's conclusion was emphatically stated:

"The colored man is entitled to *equality of opportunity*—nothing more and nothing less. A dual code of opportunity based upon color is iniquitous . . . [and has no] proper place in a civilized country. . . ."[7]

Such ideas were too far ahead of their time to be widely accepted by Ballou's contemporaries. What stuck in the minds of most white officers who had served in France were the bad things they had seen or (more often) heard about the 92nd Division. Few bothered to ask why the performance of some black units on the Western Front was plainly inadequate while other black units had fought bravely and well. It was convenient to attribute the below-average performance of some blacks in World War I to supposedly inherent racial characteristics, rather than to look for explanations within the structure of the military itself. Army studies and plans of the interwar period that prescribed how to use black manpower in any future mobilization rarely suggested that black soldiers should be treated with the same decency and respect as whites and should be given adequate training, meaningful assignments, and competent leadership—not to mention some reasonable expectation of individual and group advancement as a result of meritorious service.[8]

But even as the Army gradually came to recognize the connection between denial of such rights to black soldiers and widespread lack of motivation among them, its continuing commitment to the principle of segregation undercut its attempts to prohibit other forms of discrimination. The military leaders who did not actually favor segregation accepted it as a societal "given," beyond their capacity or responsibility to change. Thus, whenever possible, the two races were still to be kept separate on every military base, both on duty and off. World War II was over before the U.S. Army fully understood the logical inconsistency, practical impossibility, and wasteful inefficiency of the notion of "separate but equal."[9]

Another "given" confronting planners of the military mobilization was the disparity in "ability to learn" or "trainability" between draft-age blacks and Caucasians, as measured by standardized tests. Seeking a reliable way to sort large numbers of men according to their aptitude for learning the elements of soldiering, the War Department adopted the Army General Classification Test (AGCT) in March 1941. The AGCT was designed so that scores would follow a normal distribution curve, with 100 considered Average/Grade III. Extra-fast learners (130 and above) were classified Superior/Grade I, and the slowest men (69 and below) were classified as Inferior/Grade V. The results of the test did not flatter blacks.[10]

AGCT RESULTS, BY RACE (THROUGH DECEMBER 1942)

	WHITES		BLACKS	
Grade	No.	%	No.	%
I	273,626	6.6	1,580	0.4
II	1,154,700	28.0	14,891	3.4
III	1,327,164	32.1	54,302	12.3
IV	1,021,818	24.8	152,725	34.7
V	351,951	8.5	216,664	49.2
TOTAL	4,129,259	100.0	440,162	100.0

Although the Army's psychologists stoutly maintained that the AGCT was not an intelligence test per se, it struck most laymen—both civilian and military—that the difference between "intelligence" and "ability to learn" was largely a matter of semantics. At any rate, for whites convinced of their inherent racial superiority, these were comforting statistics. Believers in racial equality, on the other hand, challenged the test on the grounds that its questions reflected a built-in cultural bias and pointed out that blacks and whites with similar backgrounds tended to have similar scores. What the test really measured, they said, was the shameful cumulative effect of generations of educational and socioeconomic deprivation of black Americans as a group.[11]

Whether heredity or environment was the source of the disparity identified by the test was of no immediate interest to the Army's manpower experts. Of far greater concern were its implications about the quality and effectiveness of the new black troop units called for by the mobilization plan. It did not take a statistical genius to conclude that the learning ability of 83.9 percent of the men in the typical black company, battalion, or regiment would be classified as below average or inferior (Grade IV or V), while the corresponding figure for soldiers in white units would be only 33.3 percent.

Equally distressing was the disparity between the races in the number of men available in Grades I and II. From this pool of "fast learners," the Army intended to select and train the large numbers of new NCOs and junior officers it was going to need. That 34.6 percent of all whites being inducted were rated as having the mental qualifications to be eligible for leadership training meant that only the very best need be chosen; that only 3.8 percent of black inductees were rated as having the same qualifications was cause for alarm.[12]

Nor was there much of a foundation to build on from the ranks of black officers already in the Regular Army, National Guard, and Reserves. When the mobilization began in 1940, just five black Regular Army officers were on active duty, and three of them were chaplains. The three existing black National Guard regiments were staffed by 150 black officers, but these individuals were supposed to remain with their units when they were called up. As for the Army Reserve Corps, only 353 of its officers were black, and 298 of these were First and Second Lieutenants. Although somewhat higher percentages of experienced black noncommissioned officers existed among the Regulars, the Guard, and the Reserves, the numbers here, too, yielded a pitifully small cadre compared to the thousands that would soon be needed.[13]

Clearly, the conditions underlying the problems that had beset General Ballou in World War I had not been significantly reformed in the ensuing two decades. The midrank and senior positions would again be monopolized by white officers, many of whom were likely to be unhappy with their assignments, while an inexperienced and uneasy mixture of similarly disgruntled whites and educationally less-qualified blacks would fill the junior officer positions.

Remembering their frustrated hopes for improved economic and social status during World War I, and well aware of the Army's continuing adherence to Jim Crow practices, leaders of an increasingly articulate black citizenry resolved to use these longstanding grievances as a lever to effect change as World War II approached. To wage such a campaign, however, they first needed to learn the Army's mobilization plans for the nation's black manpower.

The War Department long resisted making an official statement on the matter, both to avoid the public criticism it knew would follow from blacks and their supporters and to keep a lid on the very real differences that existed among its various staff divisions as to what the policy should be. But passage of the Selective Service Act in the summer of 1940—which made it certain that blacks were going to be drafted in proportion to their numbers in the population—increased the public pressure on the War Department to say just how it planned to use these men.[14]

With an election year at hand and war impending, President Roosevelt did not wish to alienate black voters—even though their electoral clout, in those days of widespread poll taxes, literacy tests, and outright intimidation, was far less than it has since become. Accordingly, on September 27, 1940, Roosevelt met with a group of prominent black leaders, including A. Philip Randolph, head of the Brotherhood of Sleeping Car Porters, Walter White, executive secretary of the NAACP, and Mary McLeod Bethune, president of a black women's college, to hear their concerns regarding black participation in the war effort. Also present were Navy Secretary Frank Knox and Under Secretary of War Robert P. Patterson.

The black leaders' agenda was dominated by their desire to see military segregation ended—an idea that apparently had never before been seriously considered by any of the white officials in the room. Secretary Knox flatly rejected the possibility of mixing blacks and whites within the tight confines of a ship—although the Navy had done precisely that for forty years after the Civil War. Less dogmatically, Under Secretary Patterson said that he personally thought the Army might be willing to experiment with integrated units. The meeting closed with assurances from the administration that it intended to end discrimination in the military and that it would work on the problems of segregation as well.[15]

Twelve days later, on October 9, 1940, the White House released the War Department's "Policy in Regard to Negroes." This document outlined the Army's plan to draft blacks in accordance with the provisions of the Selective Service Act, to establish "Negro organizations . . . in each major branch of the service, combatant as well as noncombatant," and to afford the "opportunity . . . to Negroes to qualify for reserve commissions . . . when officer candidate schools are established." On the other hand, the last paragraph of the statement read:

> 7. The policy of the War Department is not to intermingle colored and white enlisted personnel in the same regimental organization. This policy has proven satisfactory over a long period of years and to make changes would produce situations destructive to morale and detrimental to the preparations for national defense. . . . These regular units are going concerns, accustomed through many years to the present system. Their morale is splendid . . . and their field training is well advanced. It is the opinion of the War Department that no experiments should be tried with the organizational setup of these units at this critical time.[16]

Black outrage at this blunt reaffirmation of military segregation on the heels of the September 27 meeting was intensified by a simultaneous White House press release implying that White and his colleagues had condoned the policy. Denouncing this "trick," the NAACP immediately released the text of a telegram to Mr. Roosevelt, which said, in part:

> We are inexpressibly shocked that a president of the United States at a time of national peril should surrender so completely to enemies of democracy who would destroy national unity by advocating segregation. Official approval by the commander in chief . . . of such discrimination is a stab in the back of democracy . . . [and a] blow at the patriotism of twelve million Negro citizens.[17]

But despite such protests, the Army's policy of October 9 stood. Personally "ok'd" by FDR, it remained essentially unchanged throughout World War II.

Roosevelt did what he could to repair the immediate damage to his standing among black voters by making several highly visible and symbolic appointments. On October 25, Secretary Stimson announced that a distinguished black jurist and legal scholar, William Hastie, the first black member of the federal judiciary prior to becoming Dean of the Howard University Law School, would become his Civilian Aide on Negro Affairs. On the same day, the president nominated Colonel Benjamin O. Davis, the senior black Regular Army officer, for promotion to brigadier general.[18]

General Davis, born in 1877, began his Army service in 1898 as a lieutenant in the 8th U.S. Volunteer Infantry in the Spanish-American War. In his early career he had fought *banditos* on the

Mexican border, only to be shunted off to the Philippines during World War I. As he rose in rank thereafter, most of his assignments were as an instructor for black National Guard and ROTC units. Capable, thick-skinned, and patient, he had waited forty-two years for this recognition.[19] It was grudgingly given.

Of the political circumstances surrounding both Hastie's appointment and Davis's promotion, Stimson said this in his diary:

> [T]here is a tremendous drive going on by the Negroes, taking advantage of the last weeks of the campaign in order to force the Army and Navy into doing things for their race which would not otherwise be done and which are certainly not in the interest of sound national defense.

He added sarcastically:

> I had a good deal of fun with Knox over the necessity he was facing of appointing a colored Admiral and a battle fleet full of colored sailors according to a resolution passed by the Colored Federal Employees Association and I told him that when I called next time at the Navy Department with my colored Brigadier General I expected to be met with the colored Admiral.[20]

In the wake of Roosevelt's third-term victory, activist leaders in the black community pressed for and won additional reforms. To avoid a mass civil rights demonstration in the nation's capital, which had been scheduled for the summer of 1941, the administration agreed to create a new federal agency to oversee the imposition of nondiscriminatory hiring practices in defense industries.[21]

But this gesture only highlighted the hypocrisy of the government's position on military segregation. If it could contemplate integrating the civilian workplace without fear of social chaos in a time of impending crisis, why not do the same with respect to the military workplace? Otherwise, what sense did it make to expect black soldiers to protect freedoms overseas that were denied them at home? Black community newspapers around the country asked these two questions with increasing stridency during the fall of 1941. Finally, Chief of Staff General Marshall decided to set up a conference with leading black editors and publishers to discuss the reasons for the Army's racial policies and to ask for their forbearance, if not their support. The meeting was scheduled for December 8, 1941.

General Marshall's presence at this meeting only hours after Japan's attack on Pearl Harbor was a measure of the importance he attached to it. In his opening remarks he asserted that he was dissatisfied with the War Department's progress in its treatment of black soldiers, and he promised further changes. Despite Marshall's conciliatory tone, the dominant chord was struck by the day's final speaker, a colonel from the Adjutant General's office, who said:

> The Army is made up of individual citizens of the United States who have pronounced views with respect to the Negro. . . . . Military orders, fiat, or dicta, will not change their viewpoints. The Army then cannot be made the means of engendering conflict among the mass of people because of a stand with respect to Negroes which is not compatible with the position attained by the Negro in civil life. . . . The Army is not a sociological laboratory; to be effective it must be organized and trained according to the principles which will ensure success. Experiments to meet the wishes and demands of the champions of every race and creed . . . are a danger to efficiency, discipline and morale and would result in ultimate defeat.[22]

Secretary Stimson's Aide on Negro Affairs, Judge Hastie, was one of many black leaders who refused to concede that the matter was now closed, but his continual efforts on behalf of the rights of black soldiers only brought questions about the patriotism of black protesters from many white officials, who seldom failed to remind him how much worse blacks would have it if the United States lost the war. What blacks should do, Hastie was told, was support the war effort now and ask for concrete benefits later. Hastie had a powerful ally in Eleanor Roosevelt, but even she was no match for the War Department's bureaucrats. At odds with his superiors on too many basic issues, Hastie eventually resigned his position.[23]

Meanwhile, in the twenty-seven months between the outbreak of the war in Europe and the attack on Pearl Harbor, black enlisted strength in the U.S. Army increased almost twenty-seven-fold: from 3,640 men on August 31, 1939, to 97,725 on November 30, 1941. The latter figure would increase by a factor of five (to 467,883) by the end of 1942.[24]

The 93rd, 95th, and 97th Engineers—the three black units destined to work on the Alaska Highway—were all initially activated as separate battalions during the last hectic months of the peacetime buildup and were expanded into regiments in early 1942. In many respects their training camp experiences and problems were similar to those of the white 35th and 18th Engineers. The chief question for all five regiments was how to conduct effective training in the face of equipment shortages, disruptive moves and changes, and the re-peated loss of experienced men to provide cadres for newer units. Several months before shipping out for Skagway, for example, the 93rd Engineers had to give up several dozen officers and NCOs to help form the 388th battalion. (The 388th soon followed the 93rd to northwest Canada, not to work on the Alaska Highway, but to participate in the closely related CANOL Project.) But while race had nothing to do with this sort of training camp frustration, most black units experienced additional aggravations no white outfit ever had to confront.

In addition to having a disproportionate number of its men labeled "slow learners," the average black unit contained relatively few men who had entered military service already possessing a technical skill. Among the many specialist positions listed on the organizational chart of an Engineer regiment were such key jobs as construction supervisor, general surveyor, electrical designer, road construction designer, structural designer, machine shop foreman, and mechan-ical draftsman. The planners who drew up these charts assumed that, among the stream of inductees, enough men could be found with job backgrounds that would enable them to fill such positions quickly after a brief period of training. But in most black Engineer battalions and regiments, according to one white training officer:

> The specialists required may be named, may be rated, and may draw the pay of specialists, but the real specialist is not there. Who does the technical work of these so-called specialists? It is probable that the white officer does . . . thus being forced to neglect his own work.[25]

On the other hand, a discerning officer could find young black soldiers like Charles Gardner of Savannah, Georgia, whose eagerness to learn a technical skill overcame their lack of training. Raised an orphan but now equipped with a year of college, Gardner happened to be doing some free-hand sketching between guard-duty shifts late one night at the battalion headquarters. His work caught the eye of the operations officer, and Private Gardner soon found himself assigned to the 93rd Engineers' headquarters detachment as a draftsman.

Gardner's recollection of how he spent his off-duty time illustrates another problem familiar to most black soldiers, particularly those stationed in the South. The 93rd Engineers were based at Camp Livingston, Louisiana. To go out the camp's gate on pass was to risk harassment, humiliation, and even physical harm in the nearby towns; individual blacks were not much safer wandering through Camp Livingston's white cantonment areas. Most of the time, Gardner stayed in the remote part of the base reserved for his unit—"way back of the beyond"—and went to the segregated movie theater and service club. Despite wearing the uniform of his country, he was still virtually a prisoner within it.[26]

But the biggest problem black units faced was the same one that had beset them in World War I: the lack of black leadership and the bigotry of white leaders. Most white officers, especially careerists conscious of the risks to their professional reputation, looked upon duty with black troops as an experience to be avoided if at all possible. Indeed, many officers given such assignments devoted considerable time and energy trying to get reassigned—an effort not lost on the men they were supposed to be leading. A white officer in one of the black combat divisions wrote this:

> It was bad enough training these colored, but no one had the idea we'd go overseas with them. That would be sheer suicide. These troops are not ready and never will be ready for or capable of combat. . . . I have to get out of this outfit, but can't unless someone asks for me. . . . Every white officer here is writing, phoning, and sending wires to everyone he knows. We are all trying to get out.[27]

Not every white officer serving with black troops had such negative feelings, however. From overseas, the commander of a black anti-aircraft regiment wrote this to a friend in the War Department:

> I am sincere in my admiration for these troops and I say that with full knowledge, that if I get a chance to take them into battle my own life . . . will depend on them. I am supremely confident of their ability. . . . My God, these men are human and only waiting to be led. They are actually eager to do what is right. That sounds as though I am a negrophile whereas I am not. I am only a realist wanting to see the army make full use of this vast reservoir of manpower. It must be used.[28]

Although the shortage of black officers continued throughout the war, it was especially acute during the most rapid phase of the Army's buildup. While in training during 1941 and 1942, Engineer units such as the 93rd, 95th, 97th, and 388th could expect to receive only a handful of black officers—most likely a chaplain and a doctor hastily commissioned direct from civilian life, and perhaps an infantry lieutenant or two from the Reserve Corps. Officer Candidate Schools (OCS) began accepting qualified black volunteers in the summer of 1941, but four months later less than 1 percent of those enrolled were black.

One obvious reason for this low turnout was the scarcity of black GIs with high enough AGCT scores, but other factors explain the lack of interest in OCS among blacks who *were* qualified. Why should they volunteer to become officers when doing so just exposed them to even more hostility from reactionary whites who were determined to keep "uppity niggers" in their place? Consider the pain in this letter of resignation submitted by a young black officer:

> I am unable to adjust myself to the handicap of being a Negro Officer in the United States Army. Realizing that minorities are always at odds for consideration commensurate with the privileges enjoyed by the greater number, I have tried earnestly to find this . . . and nothing more, in the relationships and situations around me here. Prolonged observation reveals that inconsistencies . . . are rampant. Sins of omission, sins of commission, humiliations, insults—injustices, all, are mounted one upon another until one's zest is chilled and spirit broken.[29]

In addition, in a rapidly expanding army, many young blacks of ambition and ability soon realized that becoming an NCO offered a less confrontational way to improve their status. Wansley W. Hill's experience was not unusual.

Having enlisted after one year at Mississippi's Alcorn A&M College, Hill went through basic training at Camp Livingston and was then assigned to the 93rd Engineers in June 1941. It did not take Hill's company commander long to recognize his potential; within two months he was wearing sergeant's stripes and working in the supply room. Five months later, in early 1942, he was transferred as a cadre member to the newly formed 388th Engineers and promoted to the position of company first sergeant.

As a noncommissioned officer, Hill recalled, he was not the object of particular hostility from the white officers at Camp Livingston. It was the old-time black NCOs with less education and many more years of service in the Regular Army who resented his quick promotion.[30]

Despite the greater risk of harassment and humiliation at OCS, however, more and more black soldiers decided to try for an officer's commission as the war progressed. An inspection visit to Camp Livingston by General Davis motivated several members of the 93rd

Engineers to apply for OCS, including Charles Gardner and his good friend, Master Sergeant George A. Owens, the ranking NCO in the 93rd's Operations Section. A sharecropper's son with a B.A. degree in economics from Tougaloo College, Owens said of General Davis's visit, "we felt proud that one of us was being saluted first."

Owens has described what he and Gardner went through just to get the necessary application forms for OCS. Although there was no official announcement in the 93rd that blacks could now apply, the two men heard about it through the grapevine and quietly researched the regulations to find out if they were eligible. They were. But Regimental Headquarters had no forms and couldn't seem to locate any. Owens finally asked a buddy in the supply room to pick up the applications at a neighboring post. Forms in hand, they made another discovery:

> [T]he recommendation of a commissioned officer was required with the completed application. There were no Negro . . . officers in our regiment and we were apprehensive about asking the white officers to recommend us because most of them were from the South . . . [so] we finally decided to ask an officer who was a graduate engineer from the Colorado School of Mines. He obligingly provided us with recommendations. . . .[31]

Owens and Gardner shipped out for Skagway with the 93rd in April 1942 and spent six months working on the Alaska Highway before their OCS applications were finally approved in Washington. By contrast, Owens's friend Wansley Hill served in the rank of master sergeant for the remainder of World War II. Long after Owens and Gardner left the 93rd for OCS, Hill remained with the 388th Engineers on the CANOL Project in Canada's Northwest Territories.

While news that the 93rd would soon be leaving Camp Livingston was welcomed by the men of the regiment, the impending arrival of black troops in the Alaskan Defense Command did not overjoy its commander, General Simon B. Buckner. As the War Department moved to augment General Hoge's Provisional Engineer Brigade with three black regiments, General Sturdevant asked General Buckner for his reaction to the plan. The son of a Confederate general, Buckner replied in a "Dear Sturdy" letter:

> I appreciate your consideration of my views concerning negro troops in Alaska. The thing which I have opposed . . . has been their establishment as port troops for the unloading of transports at our docks. The very high wages offered to unskilled labor here would

Alexander Mackenzie. Courtesy
of National Archives of Canada.

Vilhjalmur Stefansson.
Courtesy of Baker Library,
Dartmouth College.

ABOVE: Fort Nelson, British Columbia, 1942. Courtesy of U.S. National Archives.
BELOW: Welcome to Dawson Creek, British Columbia. Courtesy of Yukon Archives, U.S. Army Collection.

LEFT: Brigadier General Clarence L. Sturdevant. Courtesy of Chief of Engineers, Office of History.
RIGHT: Colonel William M. Hoge. Courtesy of Chief of Engineers, Office of History.

Colonel Robert D. Ingalls.
Courtesy of Thomas P. Ingalls.

ABOVE: Loaded flatcars of the White Pass and Yukon Railroad, Skagway, spring 1942. Courtesy of Chief of Engineers, Office of History.
RIGHT, TOP: Plank and sawdust road across ice on the Peace River, March 1942. Courtesy of Chief of Engineers, Office of History.
BOTTOM: Fort St. John, British Columbia, spring 1942. Courtesy of Chief of Engineers, Office of History.

ABOVE: The winter march to Fort Nelson, March 1942. Temperature: −30°F. Courtesy of U.S. National Archives.

BELOW: Base camp, 35th Engineers, Fort Nelson, March 1942. Courtesy of Chief of Engineers, Office of History.

RIGHT: Jeep on the winter trail to Fort Nelson. Author's collection.
BELOW: The 35th Engineers laying corduroy, May 1942. Courtesy of Chief of Engineers, Office of History.

Lieutenant Mike Miletich (as a colonel). Courtesy of Chief of Engineers, Office of History.

ABOVE: Chow time, 18th Engineers, May 1942. Courtesy of Yukon Archives, Robert Hays Collection.
LEFT: Brigadier General James A. O'Connor. Courtesy of Chief of Engineers, Office of History.
BELOW: The 341st Engineers arriving in Dawson Creek, spring 1942. Author's collection.

ABOVE: Port of Skagway, 1942. Courtesy of Chief of Engineers, Office of History.
BELOW: The 18th Engineers camp at Whitehorse, spring 1942. Courtesy of Yukon Archives, Robert Hays Collection.

LEFT: Captain Alfred M. Eschbach. Courtesy of U.S. National Archives. BELOW: Supply warehouses going up at Dawson Creek, summer 1942. Courtesy of Chief of Engineers, Office of History.

ABOVE: The 35th Engineers in the "Battle of the Swamp," June 1942. Courtesy of Chief of Engineers, Office of History.
LEFT: General Brehon Burke Somervell. Courtesy of Chief of Engineers, Office of History.

BELOW: Movable sawmill (35th Engineers). Courtesy of Chief of Engineers, Office of History.
BOTTOM: Log culvert (35th Engineers). Courtesy of Chief of Engineers, Office of History.

ABOVE: "To our eyes, it is a very good road." Courtesy of Yukon Archives, U.S. Army Collection.

RIGHT: A sign of desperation. Courtesy of Chief of Engineers, Office of History.

LEFT: Old and new Sikanni Chief River bridges, April 1943. Courtesy of Chief of Engineers, Office of History. BELOW: The 95th Engineers starting work on the Sikanni Chief River Bridge, July 1942. Courtesy of Chief of Engineers, Office of History.

ABOVE: Band concert, 18th Engineers, summer 1942. Courtesy of Yukon Archives, MacBride Museum Collection. RIGHT: Colonel Heath Twichell with *Saturday Evening Post* writer William H. Upson. Author's collection.

ABOVE: The finished road at Muncho Lake, 1943. Courtesy of U.S. National Archives.
RIGHT: Blasting down by Lieutenant Miletich at Muncho Lake, August 1942. Courtesy of Chief of Engineers, Office of History.
BELOW: Building winter quarters, October 1942. Courtesy of Chief of Engineers, Office of History.

attract a large number of them and cause them to . . . settle after the war, with the natural result that they would interbreed with the Indians and Eskimos and produce an astonishingly objectionable race of mongrels which would be a problem here from now on. . . . I have no objection whatever to your employing them on the roads if they are kept far enough from the settlements and kept busy and then sent home as soon as possible.[32]

Hoge's reaction to the plan to augment his brigade is not recorded, although he had been pressing for all the help he could get. Nevertheless, like Buckner, he seems to have had a low opinion of blacks in general and of black Engineer troops in particular. "They could do pick and shovel work and that was about all," he recalled almost thirty-two years later; then he continued:

> I remember up there when we got that regiment [the 97th] . . . in at Valdez. Those niggers just looked at all that snow—it was all white . . . they had to go across the mountains up through that pass and get over into the valley beyond . . . they got worried about whether they were going to get out of there and . . . I told them . . . the only way you're going to get home—back to Alabama or Georgia—is to work down south. Head south and keep working . . . . because they took all the ships out behind them. [The 97th] were just left there. They were practically useless.[33]

In view of these statements by Generals Buckner and Hoge, it is instructive to compare the missions of the four white regiments initially assigned to build the Alaska Highway with those subsequently given to the three black regiments.

As originally laid out by General Sturdevant, the first phase of the Army's plan divided the 1,500 miles of forest, mountain, and muskeg between Big Delta and Fort St. John into five approximately equal segments. Responsibility for constructing each segment of the pioneer road was assigned as shown in the accompanying table.

INITIAL PIONEER ROAD CONSTRUCTION ASSIGNMENTS

Origin	Destination	Responsibility (CO)
Ft. St. John	Ft. Nelson	341st Engineers (Lane)
Ft. Nelson	vicinity Watson Lake	35th Engineers (Ingalls)
Whitehorse	vicinity Watson Lake	340th Engineers (Lyons)
Whitehorse	vicinity Alaska border	18th Engineers (Paules)
Big Delta	vicinity Alaska border	Civilian contractors (PRA)

After General Hoge's February 1942 reconnaissance, as the immensity of the difficulties ahead began to sink in and the military situation in the Pacific worsened, the Army modified this original plan in several significant ways. To ease some of the pressure on the 340th Engineers, the Public Roads Administration picked up responsibility for half of the 100-mile stretch between Whitehorse and Teslin. (At about the same time, the PRA got orders not only to widen and improve the existing provincial road between Dawson Creek and Fort St. John, but also, during the 1943 construction season, to span the Peace River with a 2,130-foot steel suspension bridge.)[34] The most important change to the plan for 1942, however, involved the addition of the three black regiments to General Hoge's command.

Further study had shown where at least two of the black units could be employed to good advantage while keeping them away from populated areas. Accordingly, after cutting an access road over Mentasta Pass from Slana to Tok, Colonel Whipple's 97th Engineers would be used to speed the opening of the northernmost third of the Alaska Highway by helping the PRA and the 18th Engineers close the gap between Whitehorse and Big Delta. Similarly, after opening a trail from Carcross to help the 340th Engineers reach Teslin, one battalion of Colonel Johnson's 93rd Engineers would start work on the pioneer road from that point back toward Whitehorse, while the other began improving the 340th's newly cut trail to Watson Lake. As for Colonel Neuman's 95th Engineers, neither Hoge nor (subsequently) O'Connor could find anything more worthwhile for them to do than to upgrade the pioneer road to Fort Nelson behind the 341st.[35]

The addition of these three black regiments greatly improved the chances of opening an overland supply line to Alaska during 1942; nonetheless, Hoge's low opinion of their reliability and technical competence is revealed by the failsafe missions he gave them. No matter how poor their performance turned out to be, the highway was still sure to be completed eventually. In the worst case, the four white regiments and the PRA's contractors could simply reassume their duties under the original plan.

In the eyes of Hoge and O'Connor, the urgency of building the Alaska Highway was paramount. Having deep-seated doubts about the efficiency of Engineer units largely manned by unskilled blacks, particularly under arctic conditions, both generals chose not to take what they considered unnecessary risks. They had no more interest in experimenting with equal opportunity in the middle of a war than did Secretary Stimson and General Marshall.

To serve their country, blacks in uniform had to endure the Army's discriminatory racial policies. The frequent expressions of hostility and contempt they encountered from individual whites only made that experience all the more painful. It is small wonder that many black units had serious morale and discipline problems.

Against this stark backdrop of white discrimination and black resentment how well black units such as the 93rd, 95th, 97th, and 388th Engineers would actually do on the job was very much an open question. The low expectations of the generals might well constitute a self-fulfilling prophecy, although other, more positive outcomes were also possible. Much depended on whether the men of these regiments were given the opportunity and the means to accomplish something worthwhile. Equally important, given the shortage of black officers in 1942, were the leadership qualities of their white lieutenants, captains, and colonels. General Ballou had said as much after World War I. But ultimately the outcome would depend on the qualities of the soldiers themselves—on their own black spirit.

An attempt to define that spirit with such terms as "self-acceptance," "pride," and "courage" only sets up another stereotype. It is better just to say that men like Charles Gardner, George Owens, and Wansley Hill had it. So did the nameless black GI whose mutual first encounter with a brown-skinned native along the Alaskan Highway was recorded by a Canadian bystander.

Exclaimed the startled native, perhaps with a tinge of awe: "*Tipiskow inninew* . . . You are Midnight man!"

Chuckled the soldier: "Then, I guess you must be 'bout quarter to twelve yourself!"[36]

8

APRIL–JUNE 1942

"Dynamite in a Tiffany Box"

When the 388th Engineer Battalion went off to war, Master Sergeant Wansley Hill almost missed the train. Away on a pass to visit his fiancée, Hill returned to Camp Livingston to find his unit area half-deserted, a bare field where the tents of Company "B" had stood, the men of the remaining companies hastily loading a waiting line of trucks. Hill caught up with his outfit at the railroad siding. None of his buddies knew where the battalion was headed, but the higher-ups obviously wanted them there in a hurry.[1]

On June 7, 1942, the first of the 388th's three trains arrived at a dismal railhead hamlet called Waterways, 220 miles north of Edmonton near Fort McMurray on the Clearwater River. By now, Hill and his company-mates had begun to get an inkling of what lay ahead for them. Together with the 89th and 90th Heavy Pontoon Battalions, whose trains had been disgorging men, supplies, and equipment into the rain-soaked fields adjacent to the siding for the past six days, the 388th Engineers were going to set up and operate a waterborne transportation system between Waterways and Norman Wells, almost 1,200 miles farther north on the Mackenzie River.

Designated as Task Force 2600, the three battalions were there to support a much larger force of civilian contractors about to embark on a big new undertaking—a hush-hush operation called Project CANOL. The all-white 89th and 90th Engineers were to construct the necessary docks and cargo-handling facilities and man the power-boats, barges, and pontoon rafts ferrying supplies for CANOL. The black 388th Engineers, whose 26 officers and 1,218 enlisted men constituted half the total strength of the task force, were to work as stevedores.[2]

CANOL, begun in haste in the spring of 1942 and continually expanded in scope and complexity over the next six months, was built to supply gasoline and other petroleum products for the Alaska Highway and Northwest Staging Route. In its final form, the project had four main components: a producing oilfield at Norman Wells, 70 miles south of the Arctic Circle on the Mackenzie River; a 4-inch-diameter pipeline to carry the crude oil 577 miles over the Mackenzie and Pelly mountains to Whitehorse (Task Force 2600 was organized to support these two parts of CANOL); a newly built refinery at Whitehorse; and another 1,000-mile system of pipelines to deliver refined gasoline from Whitehorse to vehicular refueling points and airfields along the highway, as far north as Fairbanks and as far south as Skagway and Watson Lake.[3]

Nothing of this far-flung network existed when Wansley Hill and his 388th Engineer comrades first pitched their pup tents in the driving rain near Waterways. A dozen or so tiny communities, most of them built around a Hudson's Bay Company trading post and inhabited by a few native families, dotted the banks of the 2,000-mile watercourse that led north from Waterways to the Mackenzie River and thence to the Arctic Ocean.

Fuel for the more northerly of these settlements, as well as for the riverboats and float planes that provided their only connection to the outside world, came from Norman Wells. Following the discovery of oil there in 1921, the Imperial Oil Company, a Canadian subsidiary of Standard Oil of New Jersey, sank a few wells and built a small refinery, pumping and refining just enough oil each summer to meet the limited local demand. At the end of the 1941 production season the Norman Wells field had three operating wells with a maximum total capacity of 850 barrels per day, which the adjacent refinery could turn into low-octane gasoline or fuel oil. Thus the potential annual production of the Norman Wells facility was approximately 300,000 barrels. U.S. and Canadian petroleum experts disagreed about the extent of the field's total recoverable reserves, but the figure most often cited by its owners was 2.5 to 3 million barrels.[4]

Alaska was already known to possess far greater oil reserves, but there was no operating oilfield or refinery within the territory when World War II began. Although the February 1942 decision to build the Alaska Highway had initially seemed to answer the question of how to keep Alaska supplied if the Japanese Navy cut the sea lines

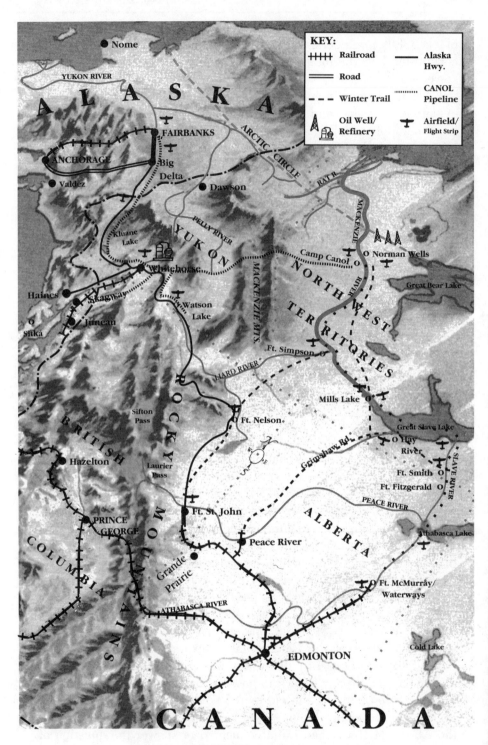

PROJECT CANOL

of communication from the United States, it soon became obvious that the highway alone would not solve this problem. If the Japanese could prevent U.S. oil tankers from reaching the ports of Skagway, Valdez, and Anchorage, then the trucks and aircraft bringing supplies and reinforcements north via the Alaska Highway and the Northwest Staging Route would be starved for fuel—as would Alaska's beleaguered defenders.

Calculations showed that hauling fuel up the highway in tank trucks, though feasible, was going to be horrendously inefficient. On a 3,000-mile round trip through some of the roughest terrain and harshest climate in North America, each Army tank truck would consume an estimated 3 gallons of gasoline for every 4 it delivered.[5]

What the Army urgently needed was a source of fuel not exposed to Japanese attack and closer to Alaska and its overland supply lines than were the U.S. refineries and shipping terminals on the West Coast. Norman Wells fit that description, as Vilhjalmur Stefansson had been saying for several years.

Stefansson had first called attention to the strategic implications of Norman Wells's location in an April 1939 article in *Foreign Affairs* entitled "The American Far North." Next, as described in Chapter 1, came his August 1940 discussion with members of the Army General Staff regarding the best overland route to Alaska and his subsequent correspondence on the same subject in January 1941 with General Marshall. Stefansson's purpose on both occasions was to convince the Army's high command of the superiority of Route D (the Mackenzie River/Mackenzie Mountain pathway to the Yukon and Fairbanks) over Routes A, B, and C. But Route D's best selling point as a transportation network was that it had its own source of fuel, which might also supply most of Alaska's needs.

Regardless of Route D's merits, the War Department saw no urgent military necessity for any overland supply route to Alaska until after the attack on Pearl Harbor. Nevertheless, the possibilities involving Norman Wells were sufficiently intriguing that two key officers on General Marshall's staff kept copies of Stefansson's January 1941 memorandum. They were Major Generals Henry (Hap) Arnold, Chief of the U.S. Army Air Corps, and Brehon B. Somervell, the Army's G-4 or chief logistician.[6]

Two more articles touting the military potential of Norman Wells appeared during this period. The October 1940 issue of *World Petroleum* carried a piece entitled "Norman Wells: Sub-Arctic Refining" by Stefansson's young protegé, Richard Finnie. The following July, *Foreign Affairs* printed Stefansson's "Routes to

Alaska." Neither article had any discernible impact on the War Department's thinking.

In the fall of 1941, however, as the Arctic expert for Colonel William Donovan's new intelligence organization, Stefansson was told to develop a plan to free Alaska from dependence on imported oil. This gave him a splendid opportunity to campaign for Route D and Norman Wells from within the administration, as detailed in Chapter 5.

In early February 1942, Donovan sent President Roosevelt a memorandum summarizing the arguments in favor of the "Stefansson Route" and recommending its construction. Of the oil field at Norman Wells, Donovan's memo said:

> Drilling is very easy and can be done all year round, and the wells will flow in winter as well as summer. Indeed, the crude oil has a pour point of minus 90 degrees Fahrenheit. . . . Even more important than the present ability of this field to service the proposed highway are its possibilities. Standard Oil of New Jersey has not thoroughly investigated the potentialities of this field but based on what they have done, their feeling is that there is a lot of oil at Norman Wells. They do not deem it impossible that production there could be expanded to 5000 barrels per day. If such is the case, the Army and Navy establishments in Alaska have near at hand a source capable of supplementing their needs for aviation and other types of gasoline and oil.[7]

Coincidentally (or not), Roosevelt also received telegrams that week from two old friends of Stefansson, the governors of North Dakota and Montana. Both men urged the selection of Route D and mentioned the advantages of Norman Wells. Unfortunately for Stefansson's scheme, the President decided to approve his cabinet committee's recommendation to build the Army's Inland Route. On February 12, however, he sent Donovan's Route D/Norman Wells proposal to the War Department with a request that it be "carefully studied." Copies went to the Plans Division, the Chief of Engineers, and the G-4, General Somervell.[8]

Alaska's need for a secure source of oil was brought up at a cabinet meeting on April 2, 1942. Harold Ickes, in his dual role as Secretary of Interior and Petroleum Administrator for War, urged that a vigorous program of oil exploration within Alaska be undertaken at once. The President agreed that military necessity justified such exploration, but the meeting adjourned without a formal decision on the matter. The implication of the discussion was that Ickes and

Secretary of War Henry Stimson should examine the possibilities and work out the details. As this process began within the War Department, various officials began to see Norman Wells in a new and more favorable light.[9] Vilhjalmur Stefansson was glad to provide supporting details.

On April 15, after further consultations with officials of Imperial Oil and its parent company, as well as with representatives of Canada's Department of Mines and Resources and the Canadian Geological Survey, Stefansson submitted a lengthy memorandum directly to General Somervell, entitled "Local Oil Supply – Yukon, Alaska and Bering Sea." This paper once again summarized all the facts and arguments in support of developing Norman Wells to meet Alaska's wartime need for oil. Stefansson's plan envisaged a 300-mile pipeline west across the Mackenzie Mountains from Norman Wells to Mayo, near the headwaters of the Yukon River. From Mayo, the crude oil would be barged or hauled by tractor train downstream to a refinery "somewhere on the Yukon." The refinery's products could then be distributed throughout Alaska over existing roads and railroads and the territory's extensive river network. Stefansson quoted statements by several Standard and Imperial Oil "officers and technicians" to reinforce his assertion that the Norman field had the potential to expand its production to 5,000 barrels per day.[10]

General Somervell was too busy to give Stefansson's memorandum much attention, so it went to his special assistant for transportation problems, James H. Graham. In wartime Washington as a part-time, dollar-a-year consultant, Graham's credentials were excellent. He had risen to the rank of colonel as a logistics expert in World War I and had subsequently become a successful businessman, serving for a time as an oil company executive before becoming dean of the University of Kentucky School of Engineering.

Helping Dean Graham with the Norman Wells study was another newcomer to the War Department—its liaison representative with the petroleum industry, Brigadier General Walter B. Pyron. Pyron owed his rank not to his military experience, which was nil, but to his civilian expertise. A Texas oil executive prior to the war, he had been a vice president in charge of production and transportation at Gulf Oil.[11]

While Graham and Pyron did their homework on Stefansson's most recent memorandum, Norman Wells drew increasing attention elsewhere in the War Department. It came up, for example, at an April 21 conference called by Brigadier General A. H. Carter, the Army's Budget Officer, to review the combined plans for the Alaska Highway and Northwest Staging Route. Present that day were senior officers from the U.S. Army Air Force, the Chief of Engineers, and the Plans Division. General Somervell was represented by Dean Graham. Harold Bixby, Chief of Alaskan Services for Pan American Airways, also attended. The only other man in the room with sub-arctic flying experience was Brigadier General St. Clair Streett of the Plans Division, who as a captain had led the Black Wolf Squadron on its famous round-trip flight between New York and Nome for Billy Mitchell back in 1920. To learn more about how the oil field at Norman Wells might "fit into the national defense effort," the conferees decided they needed to talk to its owners.[12]

Stefansson's proposal was now on the fast track. At General Carter's request, the president of Standard Oil of New Jersey agreed on April 25 to arrange for several experts from Imperial Oil to attend a meeting in Washington on April 29, and to send one of his top executives as well. Also on April 25, Stefansson spent an hour with General Pyron, discussing the details of his plan once again. Afterwards, Pyron seemed confident that production at Norman Wells could be expanded to the hoped-for 5,000 barrels per day.

As Pyron advised Somervell's Director of Materiel, Major General Lucius D. Clay, however, "The principal problem is transportation of the crude oil. . . . I have discussed this matter also with Mr. [Eugene] Holman, Vice President of Standard Oil of New Jersey, who is not too optimistic about the whole proposition." Pyron then informed Clay of the scheduled April 29 meeting with representatives of Standard and Imperial Oil, "at which time we will definitely develop the amount of materials required, the time required, whether or not it is feasible, and if the whole program can be completed in time to be of value to the war effort."[13]

The conference took place in General Carter's office on the morning of April 29. In addition to oil company officials and representatives of several federal agencies that were responsible for resource planning and allocation, most of the planners who had attended General Carter's April 21 meeting were present. This time, however, no one spoke for the Chief of Engineers. Nor was Stefansson invited.

General Carter began by stating the Army's requirement for 3,000 to 5,000 additional barrels of crude oil per day from northwest Canada to help meet the anticipated fuel needs of the Alaska Highway and the airfields of the Staging Route. In view of the existing strategic situation and future war plans, the Army was willing to take risks "not justified by ordinary commercial standards" to develop this supply. More cautious than their subordinates had earlier been when queried by Stefansson, the oil company executives suggested that by drilling nine more wells, Norman Wells's current daily production of 450 barrels could probably be increased about threefold by the end of 1942. As for the explorers' 5,000-barrel-per-day claim, they were highly skeptical that such a level could be reached. To achieve even 3,000 barrels per day, they said, at least forty-five wells would be needed. Moreover, until the actual drilling occurred, they could not be sure of achieving any increase at all in production—not even to 1,500 barrels per day.

When the discussion turned to locating a site for the refinery, it became evident that the Army had settled on Whitehorse, the midpoint of both the Alaska Highway and the Northwest Staging Route.[14] Although a refinery at Whitehorse was logical from a military standpoint, it meant that almost 600 miles of pipeline from Norman Wells were needed—not the 300 called for in Stefansson's plan. No trail suitable for a pipeline over the mountainous terrain between Norman Wells and Whitehorse had yet been explored, but the conferees agreed that such a pathway could probably be found by an aerial survey. A similar gamble was simultaneously being made with regard to finding a route for the Alaska Highway.

Other topics included the size of the pipeline, the design of the refinery, and the source of materials for building both. Dean Graham suggested that second-hand, 4-inch-diameter pipe be used because large quantities of it were already available. Anything bigger, he said, would have to be manufactured to order, consuming both time and resources. Brought to the meeting by Graham, General Pyron assured the group that up to 5,000 barrels per day could be pumped through a 4-inch pipe. Graham's make-do logic also guided the discussion of the refinery: the conferees agreed that, among the many outdated, small-capacity refineries scattered around the United States, one could be found that could be dismantled and shipped to Whitehorse.

After all this blithe optimism from the military side of the table, the businessmen brought the discussion back to more practical considerations. Assuming that the Canadian government approved this project, they said, and that the United States was willing to pay for it, the Imperial Oil Company would be happy to try to expand production at Norman Wells to the agreed-upon goal of 3,000 bpd. But neither Imperial nor its parent company had any interest in building the pipeline or the refinery; the Army would have to find someone else to handle those tasks.

The oilmen also pointed out that the existing barge and riverboat system serving Norman Wells was woefully inadequate to deliver the thousands of tons of pipe, drilling equipment, and other supplies that the project would need in the coming months. On average, they said, the Mackenzie River and its tributaries were ice-free and safely navigable only four months each year.[15]

Immediately after this meeting, Dean Graham prepared a two-page memorandum for General Somervell recommending that he authorize the Chief of Engineers to do the following:

(a) Contract with Imperial for the drilling of nine or more additional oil wells by September 1942 to increase production at Norman Wells.

(b) Build or acquire by 15 June 1942 necessary river shipping to transport the required quantity of freight from railhead down the Mackenzie River to Norman Wells.

(c) Survey by air or ground the most feasible route for a pipeline from Norman Wells to Whitehorse and to construct a four-inch pipeline over this route by 15 September 1942.

(d) Obtain a second-hand refinery in the U.S., obsolete because of size but in good operating condition . . . and to transport this refinery to Whitehorse and there erect it and have it in readiness for operation by 1 October 1942.[16]

At first glance, considering the enormous difficulties and risks involved in this scheme and the decidedly cool reaction of the oil companies to it, these recommendations would seem to be the brainchild of a very naive or foolish man. But Dean Graham was neither; he simply knew what his boss wanted.

General Somervell approved Graham's memorandum on the same day, April 29, 1942. It was forwarded on April 30 to General Reybold, the Chief of Engineers, with a cover letter directing him to "take the necessary steps to carry out these recommendations at the earliest practicable date."[17] Reybold immediately turned this directive over to his deputy, Major General Thomas M. Robins, who had prudently scheduled a meeting for April 30 with General Pyron and the oil company executives. During this meeting, Robins made no secret of his opposition to the plan, expressing "the opinion that it would be more expeditious and economical to deliver petroleum products by barges already available on U.S. rivers than to construct the project as proposed." But he also stated that he was prepared to carry out Somervell's order.

General Robins was not the only senior Engineer officer with serious misgivings about CANOL. Major General Lucius D. Clay, Somervell's Director of Materiel (and Pyron's boss) felt strongly that the proliferation of military construction projects in northwest Canada was "utter foolishness" and a waste of resources, and he sent Somervell a memorandum telling him so.[18]

Despite these warning signals, Project CANOL now took shape with stunning speed. On May 1, 1942, the War Department issued a letter of intent to Imperial Oil, detailing the agreed-upon obligations of both parties. Simultaneously, General Robins informed the State Department of the need to obtain Canada's immediate permission to proceed with the project. On May 4, another letter of intent, this one to cover construction of the pipeline and the refinery, went to a newly formed consortium of three large West Coast contractors, Bechtel-Price-Callahan (BPC). Then, on May 5, the Chief of Engineers designated Colonel Theodore Wyman as officer-in-charge of the project, gave him a "start-up" allocation of $200,000, and vested him with the powers of a district engineer so that he reported directly to the Chief himself. Finally, on May 6, capping a busy week, a third letter of intent was issued. Its recipient was another newly formed partnership: the firm of J. Gordon Turnbull and Sverdrup and Parcel (TS&P), who were to act as architect-engineers to design the pipeline and the refinery.

This rapid and detailed sequence of events strongly suggests that Dean Graham's memorandum and recommendations of April 29 were merely a paperwork cover for a decision that had already been made.

All three letters of intent were subsequently replaced, with minor changes, by formal contracts. Imperial's contract protected the company from financial loss should the new wells prove nonproductive. It also set the price of whatever oil Imperial did deliver to the U.S. Army in such a way that the company would recover its entire wartime investment before having to remit a portion of its profits to the U.S. Treasury. The other two firms got cost-plus-fixed-fee contracts, BPC's fee being $1.5 million and TS&P's $285,000.[19]

To save time, the arrangements made with BPC and TS&P circumvented the government's usual process of soliciting competitive sealed bids. Instead, the selection of these firms was the result of simultaneous negotiations with a number of construction companies that had previously done good work for the Corps of Engineers. From his most recent assignment as district engineer in Hawaii, Colonel Wyman was already familiar with the capabilities of the

Callahan Company and Sverdrup and Parcel—a connection that undoubtedly speeded the selection process.[20]

Lieutenant General Brehon Burke Somervell was the man making things happen so fast. Few men in the inner circle of Roosevelt's wartime administration had more power—and less hesitancy to use it—than this remarkable West Pointer from the Class of 1914.

Like Generals Hoge, Sturdevant, and O'Connor, Somervell had spent years in the Corps of Engineers' highly politicized civil works program, but in the wider world of national and international politics they could not match his experience—or his connections. As the G-4 of U.S. Forces in Germany after World War I, Somervell was given a leave of absence to assist Walker D. Hines, a prominent American lawyer and railroad executive, who had been asked by the League of Nations to undertake a study of navigation problems on the Rhine and Danube rivers. Then, in 1934, when the Turkish government retained Hines to do an economic modernization survey, Somervell again took a leave of absence to help him. Hines died before the survey was completed; Somervell stayed in Ankara and worked sixteen-hour days to finish it. In the decade between these two "high visibility" jobs, Somervell's career progressed well along more conventional lines: prestigious assignments to the Command and General Staff School and the Army War College came his way, interspersed with more prosaic duties on various flood control projects along the Mississippi River. Twenty years out of West Point, Somervell had earned an Army-wide reputation as a tirelessly efficient and politically savvy administrator. But his sleek good looks, elegant tailoring, and courtly, soft-spoken manner concealed gnawing ambition, a violent temper, and a mean streak. "Dynamite in a Tiffany box," his friends called him.[21]

In 1935, Harry Hopkins, President Roosevelt's adviser and confidant, borrowed Somervell and several other of the Army's most capable mid-rank officers to help supervise the burgeoning activities of the Work Projects Administration (WPA). A New Deal program designed to ease unemployment by funding socially needed projects during the Depression, the WPA was fast becoming a kind of economic never-neverland in which little distinction was made between the worthwhile and the worthless. Hopkins was so impressed by Somervell's tough-minded administration of the WPA's southeast regional office that in 1936, he transferred him to the agency's number-one trouble spot: New York City. The WPA's byzantine maze of power alliances and coalitions of convenience had ruined the health and/or careers of several of Somervell's predecessors in New

York, but he survived there for four years, earning a national reputation as a brilliant manager while seldom raising his velvety Southern drawl except to engage in shouting matches with Mayor LaGuardia.

Somervell also clashed with Stefansson, who was preparing an extensive Arctic bibliography with WPA funding. Concluding that this was only a make-work project for a few underemployed academics, Somervell tried to get the funds diverted to something more useful—perhaps (as Stefansson later sarcastically suggested in his memoirs) a suburban golf course. Stefansson went over Somervell's head to Washington and won.[22]

In November 1940, when Chief of Staff General Marshall needed a hard-driving officer to ramrod the Army's lagging camp construction program, Hopkins had just the man for him. Somervell got the job and the rapidly expanding army soon had the barracks and other facilities it needed—eventually including the Pentagon, his most enduring monument. Although Somervell later admitted that his crash building program probably cost the taxpayers $100 million over the budgeted amount, time was shorter than money just then. Marshall promoted Somervell to major general in 1941 and made him his chief assistant for logistics.

Three months after the attack on Pearl Harbor, the War Department underwent a much-needed organizational streamlining. In the shakeup, many bureaucratic fiefdoms, particularly those controlled by the chiefs of the various service branches (such as the Corps of Engineers), lost their time-honored semiautonomous status. As of March 9, 1942, the chain of command ran straight from the President, as commander-in-chief, through Secretary of War Stimson to General Marshall. Beneath Marshall on the revised organizational chart, three officers gained new prominence: Lieutenant Generals Leslie J. McNair, Henry H. Arnold, and Brehon B. Somervell. With the exception of overseas commands and theaters, every unit, bureau, and activity in the U.S. Army was now controlled by one of these three men—McNair as head of Army Ground Forces (Infantry, Artillery, Armor, and so on), Arnold as head of Army Air Forces, and Somervell in charge of everything else. Somervell's empire was initially known as the Services of Supply (SOS), but its name was quickly changed to Army Service Forces (ASF).[23]

The list of Somervell's responsibilities was impressive. As chief buyer and production boss for the Army, he exercised great power over the civilian economy of the United States, often clashing in the process with its nominal wartime czar, Donald Nelson of the War

Production Board. On the military side, the organization Somervell commanded was likened by a *Life* magazine journalist to a "super-holding company":

> It receives raw recruits (Service Commands), feeds, houses and clothes the Army (Quartermaster), builds the camps and roads and bridges (Construction and Engineers), pays off the troops (Finance Division), acts as policeman and judge (Provost Marshal and Judge Advocate), provides the weapons for killing the enemy and services them under fire (Ordnance), runs the communications (Signal Corps), moves the troops and supplies (Transportation), cares for the wounded (Surgeon General) and ministers to the soul (Corps of Chaplains). [Army Service Forces] employs more than a million civilians, and in the 8,200,000-man Army to be built in 1943, one man out of four will belong to [ASF].[24]

General Marshall's selection of the relatively junior Somervell for this powerful position raised a lot of eyebrows in Washington—and not only because of his lack of seniority. "I'll say this for General Somervell," said Senator Harry S. Truman, who had watched him revive the lagging camp construction program, "he will get the stuff, but it is going to be hell on the taxpayer. He has a WPA attitude on the expenditure of money."[25]

Although the campaigns in North Africa, Italy, France, and the Pacific were still months or years away, and nobody could yet say precisely what the logistical requirements of each theater of operations would be, it was now Somervell's responsibility to make the estimates, place the orders, and see to it that enough beans and bullets were delivered whenever and wherever they might be needed. As the military buildup moved into high gear, Somervell appeared on the cover of *Time* as the War Department's "man of the hour." His elevation was a clear sign that he enjoyed the complete confidence of President Roosevelt and General Marshall. Given Somervell's temperament, such backing made him a truly formidable player in the Washington game of bureaucratic poker.

Impatient with paperwork in general and buck-passing memoranda in particular, he took pride in his ability to make quick decisions and cut through red tape and routine procedures. Like Marshall, Somervell gave trusted subordinates all the authority and support they needed to do their jobs, and he was just as ruthless in the face of incompetence and sloth. Unlike Marshall, though, he was not above humiliating his victims. Typical was Somervell's treatment of Major

General Dawson Olmstead, whose performance as Chief Signal Officer displeased him. Olmstead was summarily forced to retire in 1943 despite his pleas to be allowed a face-saving transition assignment prior to taking off his uniform. As the stories of Somervell's temper and vindictiveness spread, so did the number of his enemies.[26]

The Chief of Engineers, Major General Reybold, could not have been happy about losing his direct access to General Marshall in the March 9 reorganization—or about being placed under an officer eight years his junior with the management style of a buzzsaw. The imperatives of Somervell's responsibilities soon made themselves felt within Reybold's domain.

As G-4, Somervell had played only a supporting role in the decision to build the Alaska Highway. His new mandate gave him the power and authority to expand the project in ways the highway's original proponents had never intended or imagined. When Somervell looked at how many tons of supplies General Buckner's forces in Alaska could expect to receive over the completed road and compared that figure with Buckner's needs if the Japanese managed to cut him off and then attacked in force, he quickly concluded that a single emergency overland supply line to Alaska would not be enough.

Accordingly, in late March, he reversed a recent Reybold decision and ordered an immediate study of the feasibility of building a railroad to Fairbanks via the Rocky Mountain Trench (Route B) by 1944.[27] Then, in April 1942, came the series of meetings and decisions leading to Project CANOL. That operation was Somervell's show from the start; no heckling or interference was tolerated.

Among themselves, many officials in Ottawa were as skeptical of CANOL's military value as they were of the need for the Alaska Highway, and for the same reason: they doubted that Japan would still be a threat in the northwest Pacific by the time either project was finished. On the other hand, why risk the wrath of a powerful neighbor, especially when its strategic concerns largely matched those of Canada and might also be made to serve certain more purely domestic political interests? The PJBD was never even asked for a recommendation on CANOL.

And so, on May 16, pending a formal exchange of notes, the Canadian War Cabinet approved Project CANOL. At the same time, Ottawa signaled its doubts and ambivalence by warning Washington that the goal of 3,000 barrels per day from Norman Wells was probably unrealistic.[28] The War Department brushed this cautionary information aside as nothing new. It was prepared to take the risk, so Colonel Wyman was ordered to proceed to Canada with his advance party. He arrived in Edmonton on May 18 and set up an office there the next day. Three days later, with two of his staff, Wyman headed north to Waterways for his first look at the tiny railhead settlement that was soon to be inundated by 2,500 American soldiers and train after train of supplies and equipment. The order to begin the troop movement to Waterways went out from the Adjutant General's office in Washington on May 26.[29]

Meanwhile, Secretary of the Interior Harold Ickes got wind of all this through the Washington grapevine. Irascible as ever, he began raising holy hell about Project CANOL. First, the prospect of finding more oil at Norman Wells was "unpromising," he said, and the pipeline and refinery scheme were "decidedly impractical." Second, he insisted that such projects properly belonged under his jurisdiction as Petroleum Administrator for War, whereas the War Department had not even had the courtesy to inform him of CANOL's existence.

Ickes's protests to War Secretary Stimson were politely but firmly rebuffed. It was left to Stimson's underlings to remind the Petroleum Administrator that his jurisdiction stopped at the United States border. On May 29, in frustration and outrage, Ickes wrote President Roosevelt of his grievances against CANOL and the War Department. Two weeks later came the President's response—a restatement of the Army's justification for the project. The last sentence read: "Of course, there is no positive assurance that [CANOL will succeed], but we are daily taking greater chances and, in view of the military needs of Alaska, the project has my full approval."[30] It did not strengthen Ickes's case against CANOL (nor Senator Langer's concurrent campaign against the Alaska Highway) that Japan had just that week invaded the Aleutian Islands.

No doubt anticipating what Roosevelt would say, Ickes tried another approach with Stimson on June 3. "As an alternative to this project," he wrote, "I would suggest consideration of transporting the desired petroleum products from California via the Inland Passage to Skagway, and thence to protected storage at Whitehorse and other strategic points by tank car or . . . pipeline." Ickes repeated this suggestion in another letter to Stimson on June 22, adding pointedly that "these facilities could be provided within a short time, whereas the crude oil pipeline and refinery could not possibly be completed prior to April or May, 1943."[31]

Ickes's suggestion was not a new idea. General Robins, the Deputy

Chief of Engineers, had proposed it when he first read General Somervell's CANOL directive on April 30. On June 4, a similar plan landed on Stimson's desk from another source, Standard Oil of California, which suggested a pipeline following the old Route A from Prince Rupert to Whitehorse in lieu of barge and rail shipments over the same territory.[32]

Originally, the only U.S. oil company associated with Project CANOL was Standard Oil of New Jersey, whose Canadian subsidiary was developing the Norman Wells oil field. How the New Jersey corporation's West Coast competitor got aboard the CANOL band-wagon is part of the story of the project's evolution from a simple, if risky, scheme to what its critics called "a Rube Goldberg gadget on a colossal scale," and one historian has characterized as a "hydra-headed monster."[33]

Standard Oil of California (SOCAL) was invited to participate in Project CANOL by way of two letters Secretary Stimson sent the company on May 23, 1942. Both letters were written because the Bechtel Corporation wanted the technical expertise of a major oil company available to it during its work on the crude-oil pipeline and refinery. Bechtel specifically requested help from Standard Oil of California, having worked with the corporation before. Stimson's first letter asked if SOCAL would act as a consultant during the construction phase. His second letter asked if the company would be willing to operate the facilities upon their completion. J. L. Hanna, vice-president of SOCAL, accepted both requests on May 28. Hanna's next letter to Stimson was the one of June 4, mentioned earlier. It contained, in support of the proposal to build the Prince Rupert–Whitehorse pipeline, Hanna's professional opinion that the pipeline from Norman Wells and the refinery in Whitehorse not only would take far longer to construct than originally planned, but might never deliver the desired quantities of fuel.[34]

With the situation in the Aleutians adding new urgency to the question of Alaska's fuel supply, the upshot of this flurry of activity was a memorandum from the Chief of Engineers to General Somervell on June 25. It contained the following recommendations, which he approved the same day:

a. That, pending the successful outcome of new drilling at Norman Wells, the completion date for the crude oil pipeline and refinery [henceforth known as CANOL 1] be deferred until not later than December 1, 1943 [a delay of up to 14 months].

b. That petroleum storage and loading facilities be immediately constructed at the railhead and harbor of Prince Rupert, British Columbia.

   c. That an oil barge line be immediately established between Prince Rupert and Skagway.

   d. That 110 miles of four-inch pipeline be immediately laid from Skagway to Whitehorse, the mid-point of the staging route and highway.[35]

Collectively, the facilities listed in recommendations b, c, and d became known as CANOL 2, for which the appropriate cost-plus-fixed-fee contracts were soon let. On the recommendation of SOCAL, the 110 miles of pipe for the Skagway-Whitehorse pipeline were obtained by diverting a shipment destined for the Norman Wells–Whitehorse line.[36]

Whether intended by anyone in the War Department or not, these various moves had the effect of ensuring that the war in Alaska would be fought using SOCAL's petroleum products—and not its East Coast competitor's—for some time to come.

But the main reason CANOL 1 suddenly took a back seat to CANOL 2 had nothing to do with corporate gamesmanship or the Army's desire to placate Harold Ickes. Contrary to Vilhjalmur Stefansson's repeated assertion that the river system stretching north from Waterways offered easy access to the riches of Norman Wells, the troops of Task Force 2600 had quickly discovered otherwise. Despite his familiarity with the geography of the region, Stefansson seems to have both overestimated the capacity of the existing transportation system and underestimated the demands CANOL would place on it.

By the end of June 1942, it was painfully obvious both at Waterways and in Washington how unrealistic Dean Graham's original five-month timetable for CANOL 1 had been. To begin with, the 1,171-mile trip downstream to Norman Wells could not be made in one uninterrupted voyage. Between Fort Fitzgerald, 287 miles north of Waterways, and Fort Smith, 16 miles closer to Norman Wells, the Slave River dropped 120 feet, creating a long stretch of unnavigable rapids. Prior to the war, two wood-burning, 1918-vintage, paddle-wheel river steamers carried passengers and cargo between Waterways and Fort Fitzgerald. At the Fort Smith end of the 16-mile portage, two similar vessels picked up everything headed "down north." While the competing Hudson's Bay and North West Trading companies owned the river steamers, control of the portage was divided between two other firms, Ryan Brothers Transportation and Corser and Duncan. Two separate dirt roads—sandy in some places, swampy in others—thus connected Fort Fitzgerald with Fort Smith.

But the portage was the least of the obstacles on the way to Norman Wells. Although the Clearwater, Athabasca, and Slave rivers south of Fort Fitzgerald were ice-free from June through October, their shifting, unmarked channels challenged the skill of even the most experienced river boat captains. In addition, when the wind blew from the north (which was often), 3-foot waves rolled across shallow Lake Athabasca. Then, 200 miles beyond Fort Smith, connecting the Slave and Mackenzie rivers, lay Great Slave Lake, a body of water the size of Lake Erie and ten times deeper. Seldom ice-free until mid-July, Great Slave Lake in the middle of a summer storm could resemble the North Atlantic at its worst. And once safely at the lake's western end, cargo and passengers still faced a 600-mile run down the Mackenzie to reach Norman Wells.

During any given summer prior to 1942, no more than 5,000 tons of cargo moved north over this primitive transportation system, about one ton for every person—white and native—who lived in the 527,490 square miles of the Mackenzie District of Canada's Northwest Territories between Fort Smith and the Arctic Ocean. The plans for CANOL 1 called for more than 55,000 tons of cargo to be shipped to Norman Wells. To achieve this goal, the U.S. Army intended to operate a fleet of heavy barges on the waterways both north and south of the Fort Fitzgerald–Fort Smith portage. Previously, the largest vessel ever moved over either 16-mile stretch of unimproved road was a pusher boat, approximately 50 feet long and weighing 75 tons. By midsummer, however, loads twice that size were to become routine over the portage.

At first, all the men of the 89th and 90th Engineer battalions had to work with were the standard 6x33-foot Army pontoons and outboard-powered utility boats they had brought with them. Eight pontoons lashed together, two units wide by four units long, made a raft. Two utility boats could tow one such raft; the paddlewheel steamers could tow a whole string of them. On June 6, the first raft, heavily laden with a crane, a bulldozer, fuel, rations, and several tons of 4-inch pipe, left Waterways. Aboard one of the tow boats was a native guide. Two days later, after a passing storm, only the arm of the crane and the cab of the bulldozer showed above the surface of Lake Athabasca. Raft number two met the same fate the following day. Raft number three, more lightly loaded and with its pontoons decked over, made it across the 18-mile width of the lake and arrived at Fort Fitzgerald late on June 12. Thereafter, for the next several weeks, one or more rafts each day reached Fort Fitzgerald and headed back upstream for another trip. The cargo at the bottom of Lake Athabasca was eventually salvaged.

By the end of June 1942, 8,000 tons of supplies and equipment had already been shipped north from Waterways, and the Army had a camp, docks, and storage facilities in operation there, as well as at Fort Fitzgerald and Fort Smith. It was a start, but nothing had yet reached Norman Wells except some drilling equipment and a few technicians sent in ahead of the Army by Imperial Oil.

As supplies for CANOL 1 continued to arrive from the United States at a rate of 300 tons per day, the black soldiers of the 388th Engineers were deployed to unload and reload all this cargo—not just at Waterways, but again at every transfer point on the way to Norman Wells. Any black Engineers not working as stevedores were engaged in cutting firewood—2,000 cords in all—to heat the antiquated boilers of the paddle-wheel river steamers.[37]

Thus far, only a handful of CANOL's civilian workers had arrived in Canada. But thousands more were coming. On June 15, this challenge was posted in the employment offices of Bechtel-Price-Callahan around the United States:

THIS IS NO PICNIC

WORKING AND LIVING CONDITIONS ON THIS JOB ARE AS DIFFICULT AS THOSE ENCOUNTERED ON ANY CONSTRUCTION JOB EVER DONE IN THE UNITED STATES OR FOREIGN TERRITORY. MEN HIRED FOR THIS JOB WILL BE REQUIRED TO WORK AND LIVE UNDER THE MOST EXTREME CONDITIONS IMAGINABLE. TEMPERATURES WILL RANGE FROM 90 DEGREES ABOVE ZERO TO 70 DEGREES BELOW ZERO. MEN WILL HAVE TO FIGHT SWAMPS, RIVERS, ICE AND COLD. MOSQUITOS, FLIES AND GNATS WILL NOT ONLY BE ANNOYING BUT WILL CAUSE BODILY HARM. IF YOU ARE NOT PREPARED TO WORK UNDER THESE AND SIMILAR CONDITIONS

DO NOT APPLY[38]

Wansley Hill and his company-mates already knew they weren't on a picnic—as did all the other Engineer soldiers working on CANOL and the Alaska Highway. Unlike their civilian counterparts, however, they couldn't just call it quits and demand their final paycheck when the mosquitos got too bad.

9

"Miles and Miles of Miles and Miles"

B y July 1942, the work of constructing the Alaska Highway had settled into a well-organized routine. Although each Engineer regiment developed its own solutions to the problems it encountered, the pattern of activity along the 35th Engineers' section of the pioneer trail was typical of what was happening all up and down the route's 1,500-mile length.

After the general trace of the future highway had been established by aerial observation and photography, the next step was to send out fast-moving ground reconnaissance teams to locate, mark, and report back on the most buildable pathway along the proposed route.

Faced with two possible ways to reach Watson Lake from the midpoint of the McCusker Trail, Colonel Robert Ingalls sent out two such teams under the overall command of Captain Alfred Eschbach. Accompanied by a long column of heavily laden pack animals and extra saddle horses, they headed west from the 35th's advance base near Steamboat Mountain on July 11.[1] Eschbach's native guide, Charlie MacDonald, had ridden ahead with his family's supplies for the coming winter. He was to join the captain's party when they reached his cabin.

Guided only by a crude map of the region's watercourses, the Engineer soldiers carefully logged a variety of additional topographical data as they went. Averaging about 10 miles per day up the Tetsa Canyon, past Summit Lake, and down MacDonald Creek, it took them a week to reach MacDonald's cabin. Then, with MacDonald leading, they headed farther west along the Toad River. The narrow trail was littered with rock debris from the slopes above. Eschbach described what happened next:

Two horses, one of them MacDonald's great black stallion, slipped off the trail and fell into the swift-flowing river, floundering out on the opposite bank. MacDonald, helped by one of the wranglers, quickly chopped down several trees and calmly lashed together a raft. Poling across to the frightened animals, he loaded their packs on the raft and chased them back into the river. As they struggled across, one horse kicked the other in the head, knocking it senseless. Eschbach recalled the scene:

> The horse actually began to roll . . . head over heels down the river—first feet up, then head up and then feet. [We] . . . raced down to the edge . . . and were able to grab hold of the halter. . . . It came to almost immediately and seemed to have no . . . ill effects. . . .

"If Charlie had lost his horse," concluded Eschbach, "we would have been left to our own devices for the rest of the trip."[2]

On July 22, eleven days out from Steamboat Mountain, the party made camp near the south end of Muncho Lake. The next morning, as planned, Eschbach and MacDonald continued west up the McCusker Trail into the mountains. That left Lieutenant Stewart to check out the alternate route to Watson Lake first proposed by Curwen, Welling, and Twichell: past the cliffs on Muncho's eastern shore, north down the canyon of the Trout, and then west again up the wide valley of the Liard River. The two teams planned to meet again along the Liard in several weeks.

Meanwhile, in Peterson Pass, only one day west of Muncho Lake, Captain Eschbach finally had a definitive answer to the question that had been tormenting Colonel Ingalls since April. Charlie MacDonald was right: a road could be built over this least accessible stretch of the McCusker Trail—but it would be very hard going. Eschbach sent two men hurrying back to Ingalls with this information, while he and MacDonald continued on.

On July 30, coming down into the Rocky Mountain Trench about 50 miles south of Watson Lake, Eschbach met a survey party from the District Engineer's Office in Portland, Oregon. The group was just one of many, he learned, that were looking for the best route for a north–south railroad to Fairbanks. Cost was no object, they said; somebody in Washington wanted their report in a hurry.

Late on August 2, their reconnaissance complete, Eschbach and MacDonald stood on the south bank of the Liard River opposite the native settlement known as Lower Post. Following local custom, they fired two shots in rapid succession as a signal for the settlement's priest to come ferry them across in his rowboat. A gracious man, he urged them to stay for dinner and spend the night before continuing on to Watson Lake. Eschbach never forgot Father Pierre Poullet, O.M.I.:

> That evening we had moose meat, sauerkraut and potatoes . . . and wild berries for dessert. He then showed me around the little [chapel] he had built. The altar was made of plank he had whip-sawed himself. . . . The next morning he held his usual 5:30 mass and several Indians came. . . . [He told me] his cycle of existence consisted of fishing in the summer, drying . . . and trading them to the Indians for furs, . . . [selling] the furs . . . to Hudson's Bay Company for medicine—and then giving the medicine back to the Indians. . . . He was confident this was what God intended him to do, and I left Lower Post feeling I had met and known a man who truly knew why he had been born.[3]

Even before Eschbach reached Lower Post, the 35th Engineers were gaining rapidly on him. By July 31, guided by the data he sent back, surveyors had finished laying out the exact route all the way to Muncho Lake, and Ingalls's bulldozers were already clearing a pathway near Charlie MacDonald's cabin.[4] Having watched with curiosity as the surveyors came and went with their compasses and plotting boards, Nellie MacDonald and her children now had a ringside seat at an amazing show.

First, under the command of Captain McGaughey and Lieutenant Miletich, came the 35th's "Advance Clearing Detachment"—ten heavy D-8 bulldozers that were kept running twenty hours a day by two shifts of operators and mechanics from Companies "A" and "B." Four or five abreast, the lead 'dozers advanced along the trail, knocking down and uprooting all trees and other vegetation in a swath 100 feet wide. In their wake, the second wave of machines simply pushed all this verdant debris to the sides of the cut. The powerful D-8 was capable of toppling a shallow-rooted tree 12 inches in diameter without even losing momentum; those with trunks in the 20-inch range needed an extra nudge or two. When one of McGaughey's operators encountered a truly giant tree, he simply used his blade to build an earthen ramp against its trunk, chugged up the incline to gain extra leverage, and battered away until both tree and 'dozer came crashing down together. The operator's only protection against falling limbs was a stout iron bar welded to the frame above his seat; hard hats were not a government-issue item. But fifteen weeks, 135 miles, and more than 2 million trees west of Fort Nelson, nobody had yet been seriously injured. The men stored their rations and their sleeping bags on two huge wooden sleds, which were dragged forward when the shifts changed. In rough or soggy going, the sleds advanced only a mile or so each day. But here, in Charlie MacDonald's neighborhood, the clearing detachment was moving six times faster than that.

Next, struggling to keep pace, came a second work party whose responsibility was to ensure that fuel and rations could always be trucked forward to McGaughey, Miletich, and their men. Using local materials to make the roughest sort of road, this group hastily corduroyed soft spots with brush and logs and built crude temporary bridges and culverts of hand-hewn timbers. A pair of bulldozers made up the rearguard of this contingent, moving just enough earth to cover the culverts and stabilize the corduroy matting.

Another team of surveyors trudged a few miles in back of all this bustling activity. Their job was first to locate, plot, and stake out the centerline of the finished road, and then to delineate its final contours by placing additional stakes at regular intervals along the shoulders. These would show the grading crews where to add or remove soil.

Guided by this endless line of surveyor's stakes, Captain Paul Symbol's "Rough Grading Detachment" (Companies "C" and "D") spent twenty hours each day cutting down small hills, filling in low spots, and carving out drainage ditches. Equipped with the remainder of the regiment's heavy D-8 bulldozers, plus most of its carryalls, dump trucks, and power shovels, Symbol's men had become expert at this work. "It is a pleasure," said Lieutenant Colonel Twichell, "to see a half dozen of these machines, each plowing along with a huge scoopful of fresh earth ahead of it."

Mixed in with and trailing behind the rough grading crews, clusters of men worked to replace the temporary bridges and culverts with more permanent wooden structures. These were constructed from green timber that had been cut to standard dimensions by the 35th's own sawmill and delivered by truck to each job site, along with all the necessary steel joining plates, bolts, spikes, and other hardware. Certain bridge and culvert sections came prefabricated from the sawmill and could be dropped into place by a roving crane, but most of the posts, planks, and beams in every structure had to be lifted and fastened laboriously by hand. Like everything else, the sawmill moved periodically to keep up with the clearing and grading work.

As the bridge and culvert construction teams finished their work at each site, Captain James A. McCarty's "Final Grading Detachment" (Company "E" and the Mighty Midgets of Company "F") moved in behind them. Using all twenty of the regiment's smaller D-4 tractors and an assortment of scrapers, dump trucks, and rollers, McCarty's men had the satisfying job of putting the finishing touches on the road: shaping and compacting its crown, adding more earth to any remaining weak spots, and truing up the drainage ditches. When time allowed, stretches that lay near easily accessible gravel deposits even got a topping of stones. More often, however, this was a refinement McCarty left to the Public Roads Administration.

"Now our job [on a particular stretch] is completed," concluded Twichell in describing the foregoing sequence, "and we are able to speed along at 40 miles per hour or more."

> To our eyes it is a very good road, although the critical might find fault with it. It is narrow and winding and has piles of trash . . . along the way . . . [and other] minor irregularities that our rough and ready methods result in. We will have to leave the correction of these defects to those who follow us, content to have opened up the way.[5]

The Army Engineers called this method of road building the "train system"—all units moving forward in a column, each one doing its particular part of the job over and over again. This approach permitted efficient specialization, but it also limited the overall rate of advance to the speed of the slowest unit. Conditions along the highway in mid-1942 were such, however, that commanders had little choice but to employ the train system. One exception was Colonel Earl Paules of the 18th Engineers, who had the great advantage of being able to move supplies and equipment along a rough but usable wagon trail that ran parallel to the first 150 miles of his route, from Whitehorse west to Kluane Lake.

When his regiment's heavy equipment finally arrived from Seattle in May, Paules divided it as equally as possible among his six companies, enabling each one to build a 5-to-10-mile stretch of road entirely on its own. Using the wagon trail for access to their assigned sections, the companies went to work. As soon as a company finished one stretch, Paules would leapfrog it to the head of the column to start on the next unclaimed section. An intense intercompany rivalry soon emerged over which unit was going to build the most miles of road that summer.

By the end of June, Paules could report that the 18th Engineers had already located and surveyed 170 miles of road, with 112 miles of that total actually completed and 43 more under construction. The 18th's closest competitors for the month of June were the 35th Engineers, but the raw numbers for Ingalls's outfit were not even half as impressive: 62 miles located, 48 miles completed, and 8 miles under construction.[6]

How "rough and ready" the pioneer trail was intended to be can be seen by comparing its specifications as established by General Sturdevant in February 1942 with those issued to the PRA for the 1943 construction season:[7]

ALASKA HIGHWAY SPECIFICATIONS

Highway Feature	Army Pioneer Trail (1942)	PRA Finished Road (1943)
Roadbed width	12 feet (min.)	24 feet
Shoulders	3 feet (min.)	6 feet (max.)
Grades	10% (max.)	7% (max.)
		5% (avg.)
Curves	50-foot radius	717-foot radius
Surface	compacted earth	2 feet crushed stone/gravel
Bridges	one-way, H-15 (15-ton limit/axle)	two-way, H-20 (20-ton limit/axle

The initial (1942) specifications given to the PRA were even more ample than these (a 36-foot road width, for example), but exigencies of cost and speed resulted in several downward revisions later on. The first of these came after a July inspection visit to the project by General Sturdevant. His original plan had envisioned that the PRA would use the Army's rough pioneer trail as a temporary access road to facilitate construction of the finished highway—in much the same way as Colonel Paules's regiment was then using the old wagon path to speed its work toward Kluane Lake. Most of the pioneer trail, however, was already a far better road than the general had intended.

Each regiment had quickly found that a trail built to Sturdevant's minimum specifications did not hold up very well under sub-arctic weather and soil conditions. Consequently, to keep themselves supplied and to ensure their continued forward progress, they had to build a much more substantial road. Seeing this, Sturdevant realized that both time and money could be saved if the PRA simply upgraded the Army's road instead of building a new one beside it. Accordingly, on August 7, the Chief of Engineers declared that creating two separate roads would constitute a "duplication of effort" and issued new instructions "that the pioneer road be incorporated in the permanent road . . . insofar as practicable."[8]

That same week, the Army Signal Corps got the go-ahead from General Somervell to begin work on the 2,000-mile Edmonton-to-Fairbanks telephone circuit. Hoge and O'Connor received concurrent instructions to set up rest camps and emergency shelters at regular intervals along completed sections of the highway.[9]

With some drivable stretches of road to show off at last, the Army began to allow visits to the various regimental work zones by newspaper and magazine reporters. As the public relations officers had hoped, most of the resulting pieces emphasized—in flag-waving prose—the strategic value of the new supply line ("Our Glory Road to Tokyo"), or the triumphs and travails of its builders ("Alaskan Highway an Engineering Epic: Mosquitoes, Mud and Muskeg Minor Obstacles . . ."). Nevertheless, a few publications still voiced the complaints and warnings first heard from the backers of routes A and B. For instance, the headline "Fiasco to Alaska: Mysterious Selection of the Worst Route for the Military Highway to Alaska" introduced a shrill attack on Mayor LaGuardia and the Joint Defense Board in the August 18, 1942, edition of *Pic* magazine. Illustrating the "stupidity" of the Army's chosen route with a photo of the 35th's plank roadway across the frozen Peace River and another of a truck axle-deep in mud, the article echoed the tenor of Senator Langer's speeches on the subject.[10]

No reporter, even *Pic*'s, had anything but praise for the Engineer soldiers who were doing the actual work. In the summer of 1942, with little war news to cheer about other than the recent naval victory at Midway, the progress being made along the Alaska Highway made Americans feel very good. Combining two archetypal motifs (conquering the wilderness to help defeat an evil enemy), the story was a natural for superlatives and patriotic hyperbole. Here were weary, dust-covered GI's manning giant machines, two races working together to build a lifeline to Alaska's beleaguered defenders amidst the most spectacularly rugged terrain and horrendous weather conditions imaginable. Only the gory excitement of actual combat was missing. But, although no "Japs" lurked in ambush along the way, that threat now seemed less far-fetched in light of Japan's seizure of the islands of Attu and Kiska in the western Aleutians and the propaganda broadcasts from Tokyo thanking the builders of the Alaska Highway for preparing a high-speed invasion route for Hirohito's armies.

Adding to the public's anxiety were persistent rumors that fighters and bombers emblazoned with the Rising Sun of Japan had been spotted over the highway. Actually, these were Lend-Lease aircraft, freshly painted with the Red Star of the Soviet Union, the first of thousands flown up the Northwest Staging Route during the war by the Army Air Force Ferry Command. From Fairbanks, Soviet pilots flew these planes on to Russia over the Bering Strait. When the true identity of the mysterious airships was officially revealed in 1944, home-front readers enjoyed another upbeat war story. [11]

What editors seemed to want most in the dispatches their reporters filed from along the highway was human interest. From the August 31, 1942, issue of *Time*, for example, Americans got lots of homey details about General Hoge:

> In a 26-foot-square house at Whitehorse lives the boss of the road, quiet, firm William Morris Hoge. . . . [E]very mucker and cat driver knew the general was on the job. "A tough guy, but square," they said. "A regular guy, too. . . ."
>
> In his little green-painted house, Hoge likes to slump his square shoulders in a chair and sit with the wife he met in a Lexington, MO, kindergarten—planning the week ahead. Pretty, brown-eyed Mrs. Hoge knows how to live the frontier life. As the general's lady she still does her cooking and washing. When the general is in town they take a short evening stroll on the board sidewalk with their fox terrier— Hoge puffing a favorite pipe. [12]

Few of Hoge's men begrudged him the pleasure of his wife's company, but Nettie Hoge's presence in Whitehorse, followed by the arrival of several American military wives in Edmonton, soon raised eyebrows in Washington. Although these women had a legal right to visit Canada, General Somervell, as head of Army Service Forces, eventually decided that such cozy domestic arrangements for a few senior officers could hurt both the morale of their less fortunate subordinates and the Army's image back home. [13]

Somervell had a point. Out in the boondocks, most soldiers rarely saw any females except for an occasional native woman. Since they were seldom in one place long enough to put up a tent, few even bothered to collect the usual bevy of pinups. "But," laughed a colonel quoted by *Time*, "I'm sorry for the first town they hit when they get away from here." The colonel was no doubt thinking of larger, more cosmopolitan places than Whitehorse, Dawson Creek, and Fort St. John. Few unattached women, respectable or otherwise, lived in any of these settlements, despite their boom-town appearance. Most tended to be frightened off by the appalling living conditions and utter lack of privacy created by the sudden influx of military and civilian construction workers. Obvious prostitutes were quickly arrested as "vagrants" by the Canadian authorities or simply told to move on by the U.S. Military Police. Any GI looking for wine, women, and song along the Alaska Highway usually had to settle for a disappointing two out of three: a couple of overpriced beers in some dingy, jam-packed bar and boozy, all-male harmony around a badly tuned piano.[14]

Although even these tame pleasures were out of reach for most soldiers, an exhausting work week and a variety of home-grown recreation programs left them little time to feel restless or bored. While the work went on twenty hours a day, seven days a week, commanders took care to stagger the shifts and give everyone a day off now and then. Next to catching up on sleep, card playing and reading were the favorite off-duty pastimes. Every unit maintained a "lending library"—a large box containing hundreds of dog-eared dime novels, magazines, and comic books.

Also widely popular were hunting and fishing, for which no American soldier needed the usual Canadian permits. Thanks to these recreational pursuits, mess sergeants were able to vary their monotonous offerings of canned meats and dehydrated vegetables with moose and bear steaks, venison, spruce grouse ("Yukon chicken"), ptarmigan, and lake trout. Nobody needed a fishing rod and fancy lures; a length of telephone wire and a hook attached to a bent tin can lid worked just fine. Charles Gardner and his friends in the 93rd Engineers went "fishing" for salmon in the shallows of the Teslin River with their rifles. Bagging a bear was almost as easy. Hungry and inquisitive, most were shot trying to break into kitchen supplies or rooting around in nearby garbage dumps. Although adult bears rarely attacked humans, they became such a nuisance in the 35th's area that camp sentries had standing orders to open fire after shouting "Halt! Who goes there?" three times.[15]

Animal mascots were another popular diversion. Nearly every unit adopted a pet of some kind—most often a mongrel dog or stray cat from a settlement along the way, but sometimes an orphaned bear cub or baby moose. Wild creatures rarely lasted long as pets. The 341st Engineers tried to raise Eleanor and Franklin D. Moosevelt, but both animals died in captivity, Franklin from overindulging in powdered eggs. Although bear cubs had stronger digestive systems, they quickly outgrew being cute and cuddly and had to be set free.[16]

The unit chaplain usually served as his outfit's "Morale and Recreation Officer" in addition to conducting weekly religious services and offering all-purpose spiritual counseling. The chaplain for the 93rd Engineers also ran the PX, selling smokes and chocolate bars at cost from the back of his tent. Among the miracles routinely performed by the 35th Engineers' popular and resourceful chaplain was obtaining a steady supply of films for the regiment's generator-powered 16mm movie projector. Playing that summer at Fort Nelson and points west: *Meet Boston Blackie*, featuring Chester Morris; *The Great McGinty*, with Brian Donlevy; *Honeymoon in Bali*, with Fred MacMurray; and *One Hundred Men and a Girl*, starring Deanna Durbin, Leopold Stokowski, and Adolphe Menjou. At Colonel Ingalls's suggestion, the 35th's chaplain even organized a soldier variety show around the regimental band, but he gave up on the music after one rehearsal. The trumpet, trombone, and tuba players couldn't play with their mosquito headnets on; and with them off, their mouthpieces soon clogged with inhaled insects.[17]

On payday, after pocketing the few dollars needed for PX incidentals, the average soldier could really do only two things with the rest of his $50 monthly salary: send it home in a money order or gamble with it. Uncle Sam didn't approve of gambling, but he also couldn't stop it. The normally low-stakes games of poker and dice became serious business for a few days, until all but the most skillful players in each platoon were broke again. Then it was the turn of the card sharps and craps "scientists" to send home *their* money orders, often totaling thousands of dollars. In the absence of women and hard liquor, however, the usual disciplinary infractions commanders had to deal with after stateside paydays were not much of a problem. Their men were simply too busy, too tired, or too far out in the bush to get into very much trouble.[18]

All in all, General Hoge and Colonel O'Connor had good reason to be pleased with the situation in their respective sectors as the summer of 1942 drew to an end. The entire route had finally been surveyed, and the prospect of its being open all the way to Fairbanks by early winter improved with each regiment's weekly construction report. During the month of July alone, the total mileage completed had more than doubled, from 360 to 794; another 392 miles of road were opened in August.[19]

After a discouraging initial month of incessant rain and miscellaneous snafus, the ultimate success of the project was no longer in doubt. No one understood this better than the troops themselves, who knew first-hand the incredible obstacles they had already overcome and the rapid progress they were now making. No visitor could fail to be impressed by their high morale and esprit de corps.

Conditions in the 95th Engineers' sector at the southern end of the highway were a glaring exception. Starting with Colonel O'Connor's decision to appropriate most of the 95th's heavy equipment and transfer it to the 341st Engineers, June had been a bad month for Colonel Neuman's black soldiers. Although the same cold, torrential rains that deluged the 35th Engineers also drenched the men of the 341st and 95th, Neuman's men did not have enough work to keep their minds off their misery—nor enough equipment to make meaningful progress. Left with only two 'dozers, one grader, a carryall, and less than twenty small dump trucks, they were supposed to be improving the rough trail pioneered by the 341st. But all through June, even though Colonel Lane's clearing crews were avoiding the worst of the muskeg by hugging the foothills of the Rockies, the slowly lengthening trail behind the 341st Engineers remained barely passable.

Neuman's men could no more shape a finished road by hand out of this rutted, rain-soaked bog than they could make one out of chocolate pudding. Until the rain let up, they spent most days either hauling supplies for the 341st or huddling in their soggy encampment near Charlie Lake, wishing for warmer, drier climes. An archeologist named Froelich Rainey, who was writing an article on the highway for *National Geographic*, hitched a ride north from Charlie Lake with one of the 95th's supply trucks. "This awful country," bemoaned the driver, "nothing but cold rain, mud and trees!"[20]

The black enlisted men of the 95th Engineers had other complaints as well, but not ones they chose to reveal to hitchiking strangers or their own white officers. Instead, they let off steam in letters to relatives or friends back home, to black editors and civil rights leaders, and sometimes even to President or Mrs. Roosevelt. A collection of such letters, compiled by Phillip McGuire, has been published. Entitled *Taps for a Jim Crow Army*, it documents the mistreatment of black soldiers in many different units and theaters of

World War II. One of these letters, from Corporal Jonathan Welch of the 95th Engineers—although written after his unit left Canada—describes practices that clearly had been going on a long time:

> That old Southern principle of keeping Negroes as slaves is still being practiced. . . . Some of the men have the benefit of the doubt providing that they are good Rats. Those who run to the white officer and repeat all of the conversation that they have heard, are promised ratings as it appears to be the best way of getting advancement. The First Sergeant is . . . incapable of his position, repeating every incident to the Commanding Officer.[21]

Such complaints seldom made it past the unit censor, whose thankless job it was to read all outgoing personal mail, delete any information of possible use to the enemy, and report the offending author (whether officer or enlisted man) in case of a serious violation. This passage was clipped from a letter by Corporal H. C. Roberts of the 95th Engineers on July 14, 1942:

> In this unit we have a new major, from Texas. . . . The boys really hate him and he knows it. When the major was at Belvoir he was a Lt. Col. One day Gen. Davis visited the post and the major wouldn't salute him. Because of this incident he was reduced to major and he has hated colored every sence.
>
> Then, we have a captain just the same. One day he told a boy if he didn't be quite [quiet], he make him. The boy told him that the first time he tryed to close his mouth he would cut his throat. The boy really meant it.

The gripes from within the 95th came not only from black enlisted men. On July 15, the censor deleted this part of a letter from a white officer, Lieutenant Joseph J. Sincavage, to his wife:

> [T]he Army certainly has a lot of ornamentation that's getting money under false pretenses. We have a few officers in our company that are a disgrace to the service. As a result of higher education, they were given commissions without any trial.
>
> . . . I saw in my own tent an officer lying in bed and giving his platoon sergeant orders for the day while the lazy scum loffed in bed.
>
> They won't eat the same food that is dished out to the men. . . . The cooks prepare what they demand, and if their pork chop is cold, they won't eat it. . . .
>
> Strange as it seems, these dastardly punks are southerners. The

Army works for them, and the colored man is still his slave. I'd like to line them against a stone wall and then convert them into fertilizer. . . . If this despicable corruption was in the enlisted ranks, they'd spend their life on the "bull gang."[22]

Mrs. Sincavage never saw these words from her husband, but General Sturdevant did. Several weeks before he received the censor's report, however, the general had already seen for himself the problems besetting the 95th Engineers. They began with Colonel Neuman, who could no longer properly exercise command due to a recent leg injury. He was also drinking too much. Out of a meeting between General Sturdevant and Colonel O'Connor came the decision to relieve Neuman and send him home. Sturdevant also approved O'Connor's recommendation for Neuman's replacement: the 35th Engineers' second-in-command. On July 19, 1942, Lieutenant Colonel Heath Twichell took command of the 95th Engineer Regiment.

If Twichell needed confirmation of the 95th's lax discipline, he got it during his first day on the job. That morning, six soldiers at a forward camp on the Beatton River, about 100 miles north of Fort St. John, wandered off and disappeared into the woods. Twenty-four hours later, hungry and tired, four of the men were safely back in camp. Their story was that they had decided to explore west up the river valley in the direction of Pink Mountain, about 20 miles distant. Without a map or compass, the group argued and split up after becoming disoriented. Search parties and native trackers eventually picked up the trail of the two missing men, only to lose it again.

Thirty-five days later, one of the men stumbled into a PRA camp just north of Fort St. John. Though exhausted, he was able to give a coherent account of his ordeal. He and his companion had wandered for weeks through the forest without finding so much as a cabin, surviving on berries and small game. Eventually, they parted company after another argument over which way to proceed. With fresh clues to go on, the search parties redoubled their efforts, but the last missing man was never found. Twichell had to declare him "missing in action."[23]

It was a week before Twichell had time to write home about his new assignment. Perhaps mindful of the ever-watchful censor, he was guarded in his comments about the 95th's problems. But Frances Twichell could read her husband's mixed feelings easily enough:

Naturally, I am gratified to have a regiment of my own at last. I come to it with the prestige of having made good on a difficult assignment. . . . The difficulties here seem to be very small ones, after those encountered and conquered in the 35th, so that, while I miss the excitement and thrills that used to be our daily fare there, it is very satisfying to have an outfit of my own. Service with the Negro troops is very pleasant. They are so polite and so pathetically eager not to be found wanting, that it is really a splendid opportunity.

Up to now, most of the work has been somewhat unglamorous. . . . A lot of pick and shovel work, which tends to become monotonous.[24]

In his first meeting with Major Owain J. Hughes, the most senior of the regiment's three majors and its capable but overburdened Executive Officer, Twichell discussed what could be done to boost the 95th's sagging morale. The outfit was still essentially sound, said Hughes; all that it needed was some hard task that it could do well and get credit for. "It occurred to me," wrote Twichell, "that building a timber bridge across the Sikanni Chief River might be a job of this description and Hughes enthusiastically agreed. . . ." O'Connor, who had planned to have Colonel Lane's outfit build this bridge, was only too glad to turn the job over to the 95th, thereby freeing up the 341st to press on toward Fort Nelson. O'Connor told Twichell he wanted the bridge finished in a week.

Snow-fed, swift-flowing, and nearly 300 feet wide at the designated crossing point, the Sikanni Chief swept through a gorge whose steep banks supported a lush growth of giant spruce. Assembling the 95th's best axmen and carpenters on the near bank, Twichell gave them their orders. He later recalled what the regiment accomplished "in seventy-two hours of ceaseless effort":

Quickly they felled a number of these forest giants, and from them squared timbers out of which bridge trestles of the proper width and height were framed.

Waiting crews then waded chest-deep into the icy stream with these trestles, using long ropes tied to the bank to keep from being swept down by the current. Floating the trestles into position, they lowered them into place and weighted them with rocks. . . .

Substantial beams of squared logs were then placed from trestle to trestle, and on top of these a decking of smaller logs cut to form a roadway. A layer of earth on top of this provided a surface on which the heaviest loads could travel easily.

To protect the bridge from ice or driftwood, heavy timber cribs were then built upstream, and these were also filled with rocks. . . .

[All this] time the woods rang with the sound of axes and were lit up by headlights of vehicles used to illuminate the work. There are some Negro work chants. . . . The woods resounded with these songs as the work progressed, and when it was finished, all the regiment's troubles had been washed away in the bracing waters of the Sikanni Chief.[25]

A photograph of this bridge, giving credit to the black soldiers who built it, illustrated *Time*'s August 31 article about the Alaska Highway and General Hoge. It was, said Twichell proudly,

one of the few bridges of its description on the road that was never destroyed by nature. Long after it had been rendered unnecessary by the construction of a permanent structure nearby, it remained a monument to the hardihood and skill of the men who built it.[26]

With the 95th's reputation for excellence in this line of work now solidly established in Colonel O'Connor's eyes, the regiment took over responsibility for constructing several more bridges from the 341st. None was anywhere near as large as the Sikanni Chief structure, but all were very sturdily built. In fact, after encountering a freshly painted sign on one massive new span just north of the Sikanni Chief that read "Built by Company A, 95th Engineers; Capacity 60 tons," Twichell had to rein in his troops, reminding them that a bridge capacity of 15 tons was all the Army needed.

Major Miles H. Thompson, one of Twichell's battalion commanders, came up with another way to raise morale. Sick of disparaging comments made about the rough condition of the 95th's sector of the route by visitors unaware of the regiment's dearth of heavy equipment, Thompson started concentrating his few machines every so often to upgrade a short stretch of the trail to PRA standards. His signs then proudly proclaimed: "Model Road: Built by 2d Bn, 95th Engineers"—as if to say, "This is what we could do if we had enough time and equipment."[27]

Among the factors that probably contributed to O'Connor's decision to strip the 95th of most of its bulldozers and graders was the prevailing opinion in Army circles that black troops were less competent than whites to operate and maintain such equipment. Twichell set out to disprove this idea by providing extra instruction for all drivers and mechanics and then holding them strictly responsible for the condition of their machines. "We have had their names painted in neat letters on their assigned vehicles," he wrote, adding:

This is a great help to the men's self-esteem, particularly the heavy cat drivers, who, with the power of 100 horses at their disposal, are little kings in the eyes of their fellows. Consequently there is keen competition for such jobs and it is becoming a disgrace to be put back on hand labor for neglect to make necessary repairs, for overspeeding, or overloading. . . .

"Our mechanical performance is fast approaching in excellence that of the best outfits on the road," he concluded, "and we hear less and less of the supposed deficiencies of Negro troops in this connection."[28]
These attempts at morale building, however successful, did nothing to change the underlying reality of the 95th Engineers' situation. The harsh truth was that at least 80 percent of Twichell's men were still doing backbreaking pick-and-shovel work. Here is an extract from the regiment's Operation Report for the week of July 26 to August 1, 1942:

Weather: Four days of intermittent rain; fog. Two days fair.
Work accomplished: Road maintenance: with hand labor, cut drainage ditches on both sides of road between [mile] 132 and . . . 145. Opened and drained culverts; drained road bed; kept right of way clear; built up road at 133.5. Operated one D-7 and one D-8 Caterpillar, leaning-wheel grader . . . and Carry-All between [mile] 130 and 138. Completed refinements on Sikanni River bridge. . . . Searching party was sent out for lost men. . . .[29]

Nevertheless, Twichell sensed that the sullen resentment and passive resistance from the enlisted ranks which had so undone his predecessor had begun to subside. His main source of information on the troops' morale was his driver and orderly, Corporal Little, who was never reluctant to tell the colonel "what the menses say." According to Little, what they were saying now was that it looked like a sure thing that the regiment would finish its section of the road and be sent back to the States long before winter came. Traveling up and down the road to inspect work and visit his men, Twichell confidently reinforced the talk that the 95th would soon reach Fort Nelson. As for everyone going home after that, all he could say was that higher headquarters hadn't yet decided.
Little drove Twichell on his daily rounds to the various work sites. The two men got on well together, especially after an incident in which the corporal made his preferences clear to the colonel. It was one of Twichell's favorite stories:

A fixture in the regiment, Little was a man of many parts. Well over six feet in height, he had a magnificent physique and keenly developed senses. He had been by turn a farmer in Georgia, a factory worker in the North and a taxicab driver in Washington, D.C. Judging him capable of much better things than he was doing, I offered him a chance to earn promotion as a duty sergeant. Little was so hurt by this offer that I never repeated it. To him, driving for and taking care of "The Colonel" was by far the best job that a man could have, and as he really felt that way about it, I was content to have it so.[30]

Called south to a conference at Sector Headquarters, Twichell struck off one morning for Fort St. John with Little at the wheel. After cruising down the dusty, tree-lined corridor for several hours, Little broke the companionable silence. "Colonel," he said, "this road ain't nothing but miles and miles of miles and miles."

The conference at Fort St. John lasted well into the evening. Twichell had scheduled a meeting at his own headquarters for early the next morning, so he had no choice but to head back north over the unlit and deserted road immediately after the headquarters meeting ended. Confident of Little's skill as a driver, he curled up in the back of the command car and went to sleep, only to be awakened around 1:00 A.M. by the back and forth rocking motion of the car and the sound of its tires spinning in the mud. They were stuck in a soft spot about 10 miles short of camp. With scant hope that help would arrive until the traffic picked up after dawn, Twichell climbed out and pushed while Little worked the gears. The car just settled deeper in the muck. Then the two men switched places and tried again. That only resulted in Little's getting as muddy as his boss was. "So I started off afoot for headquarters," Twichell recalled, "and left Little to guard the car, promising to send a truck back for him . . . and urging him to get some sleep in the meantime."

I had only gone a short distance . . . when I saw the lights of a vehicle approaching from the rear. . . . Expecting to see an ambulance or some other emergency vehicle, I was amazed when Little himself drove up. I never was able to discover how he found strength to . . . extricate the car. . . . Perhaps it was his chagrin at having failed in getting me back to camp. Or perhaps it was as he confessed: "Wasn't going to get left behind to get bitten by no bears."[31]

Within a month of his taking command of the 95th, Twichell had almost as many good stories to tell about his new outfit as about his old one. Although he admitted in his letters home that he missed the easy camaraderie among the officers and men of the 35th, it was also quite clear that he was losing many of his preconceived notions about the inherent limitations of blacks.

He was especially pleased when *Time* acknowledged their work on the Sikanni Chief River bridge. There was even a good chance that a fictionalized version of that exploit might appear in the *Saturday Evening Post*. William Hazlett Upson, author of the *Post*'s humorous "Alexander Botts" stories, spent several days with Twichell and his men and was present for the dedication of the bridge, before moving on to visit the 35th Engineers. When the next story about the "Earthworm Tractor Company's" peripatetic sales manager appeared in the *Post*, however, its heroes—besides Botts himself—were a thinly disguised "Colonel Ingham" (Ingalls) and "Captain McGehee" (McGaughey). In Upson's merry tale, entitled "Give Us More Rope," Captain Botts acts as a "Construction Equipment Expediter" who worries whether Ingham's bulldozers will run out of wire cable before the nincompoops in the Earthworm Company's home office realize how dire the shortage is. Botts of course saves the day, and in gratitude Ingham names a mountain after him.

Twenty-five years later, when Twichell's youngest daughter, Ruth Twichell Cochrane, was helping him complete his memoir of the highway, she wrote to William Upson, asking him whether he had based any of his characters on her father. No, Upson replied, "He was a little too sane to introduce into any of my improbable yarns."[32]

Toward the end of August 1942, Twichell had an unexpected chance to see for himself what Ingalls and his "Galloping Canaries" had recently been up to. A commanders' meeting was to be held on the banks of the Liard River, which the 35th's clearing crews had just reached in their race to beat the 340th Engineers to Watson Lake. Twichell, Colonel Lane, and Colonel John W. Wheeler, an officer from Sector Headquarters, traveled to the meeting together—most of the way in a sedan thoughtfully provided by Ingalls.

En route, they camped overnight at Summit Lake, which at 4,250 feet was the highest point on the highway. As they neared the lake, 90 miles west of Fort Nelson, Twichell recalled, "it was the first time I had viewed much of the country except from the air, so that it was a great satisfaction to me to see something that was once only a line on a map, now a completed road. . . ." But when they reached the lake itself, he was angered by an all-too-familiar sight along the highway that summer: "All of the country around, as far as the eye could see, had been burned and blackened, the result of someone's carelessness with matches or a cigarette."[33]

The next morning, heading west again, Twichell's mood improved. He wrote:

I was not disappointed in the country, which is indescribably beautiful. . . . For many hours we traveled smoothly past towering peaks, now beginning to be capped with new fallen snow. . . . It will be, I think, one of the scenic highways of the world. . . .[34]

The road took them past Charlie MacDonald's cabin, along the shore of Muncho Lake, and down the Trout River to the Liard—Ingalls having finally opted for Curwen's route, not Eschbach and MacDonald's. Ingalls greeted his three visitors at his headquarters overlooking the riverbank. A ferry crossing had already been established there, and work on driving the pilings for a 1,200-foot timber span was to begin soon.

Colonel Wheeler conducted the meeting. In view of the approach of winter, plus the imminent completion of the 341st Engineers' section south of Fort Nelson and the 35th's impending linkup with the 340th, Sector Headquarters felt it was time for some adjustments. First, to speed Ingalls's progress over the only uncleared stretch remaining between Dawson Creek and Whitehorse, the 35th Engineers were relieved of all responsibility for the road south and east of the Liard River. The job of upgrading and maintaining the roughest 70 miles of that stretch—back past Muncho Lake to the Toad River—went to Colonel Lane and the 341st. That left Twichell's lightly equipped men with the daunting task of keeping 250 miles of road open, all the way from the Toad River back to their present position south of Fort Nelson. Not to worry, Wheeler told him, the PRA would eventually take over much of that responsibility.[35]

The four officers then drove back to Muncho Lake, where Ingalls led his visitors to a neat cluster of large tents that offered a breathtaking lakeside view of the surrounding peaks. There, attended by enlisted waiters, they sat down at a linen-covered table set with real china and dined on freshly caught lake trout. All this had been recently set up to entertain some junketing congressmen, Ingalls explained, but they had canceled their visit, and it seemed a shame to waste so much effort.

After supper, supplied with ample whiskey and cigars, the commanders swapped yarns around a crackling fire on the beach. As usual, Ingalls had the best stories to tell. Recently, he said, one of his men had been attacked by a bear while bathing in a stream and had escaped by punching the giant beast on the snout and swimming away under water. The conversation soon turned to the problems their units were having with forest fires, which prompted Ingalls to tell of the 35th's efforts to span the Toad River with a 165-foot pontoon bridge while both banks were ablaze. Flying sparks sent two pontoons filled with oil-soaked beams up in flames. A far worse disaster was narrowly averted by throwing several dozen gasoline drums into the river. He also told of the 35th's first serious accident. One of Miletich's bulldozer operators had finally run out of luck when a falling tree fractured his skull. With no anesthetics available, the regimental surgeon, Captain Stotts, had performed an on-the-spot emergency operation, using only sterilized carpentry tools to remove the largest bone fragments. The man had just been flown back to a U.S. hospital, Ingalls added, and he hoped he would survive. (He did not.)[36]

Ingalls saved his best story for last. It featured none other than Lieutenant Mike Miletich and his conquest of the shale and limestone cliffs at the southern end of Muncho Lake. As Twichell, Welling, and Curwen had hoped during their aerial reconnaissance back in April, all that was needed to convert the vertical cliff into a horizontal roadbed was a little ingenuity and a lot of explosives. This was Twichell's version of Ingalls's account:

> The cliff ran sheer down to the water line, but below this the action of the waves and ice had cut holes, some of a size to hold a box of TNT. . . . Miletich sent a man up the cliff to fasten a long rope to a projecting rock. . . . After taking off his clothes, Miletich tied a noose in the other end of the rope, and slipped it under his arms. Then he dived into . . . the icy lake, using the rope for support while he explored the face of the cliff to locate a hole of the right size below the water. When he [found a hole, he then] removed the wooden cover from a box of TNT, . . . took out one block and laid it aside. Placing the box under his arm, he swam with it back to . . . the hole, into which he placed the box . . . opened side out.
>
> [Then] he took the spare stick of explosive and placed a blasting cap in it, to which a [waterproof] fuse . . . had been attached. Placing the device in his teeth, he lighted it, and with the fuse spluttering and set to go off at the proper time, he swam back to the box. Into this he placed the charge and then swam out of danger.[37]

After a good many repetitions of this process, the 35th Engineers had the beginnings of a rough but serviceable road along the edge of Muncho Lake. (It would take more than 100 tons of explosives and the combined efforts of Colonel Lane's 341st Engineers and the PRA's contractors to finish the job.)[38]

As the bonfire burned low, Ingalls showed his guests to their sleeping tent. Inside, the cots all had blankets and sheets instead of sleeping bags; a pot-bellied stove warded off the midnight chill. At dawn, Ingalls had one last surprise arranged: as the last notes of a reveille bugle drifted over the misty lake, the regimental band swung into a medley of marches. The band's final number took Twichell all the way back to his prewar days at Camp Robinson, Arkansas. It was Ingalls's version of "To the Engineers."

Twichell's return to his own outfit could well have been a letdown after such a visit, but it was not. As he wrote to Frances at the end of a memorable week, "upon my arrival, I was informed that my promotion to the grade of Colonel has been announced, effective as of August 24." Referring to the new silver eagle on his collar, he continued:

> So now I am a "Chicken Colonel," as the colored boys say, and you may address me accordingly. Was somewhat taken by surprise, for although I had hoped for something of the sort I did not expect it quite so soon after assuming command of the regiment.

At the end of his letter, quite causally, came the bad news: he and his men would not be coming home that winter.

> We are getting ready for the colder weather that lies ahead, issuing warm clothing, etc. . . . Having been through the tail end of last winter, I do not dread the prospect as much as some of the others. Our colored boys especially are allergic to cold weather, and it is going to be a problem to keep them well and happy I fear. That will be my big problem in the months to come.[39]

The 95th Engineers were not the only ones dismayed by this news. Every soldier along the highway had heard the same talk all summer: except for small caretaker detachments left to guard their equipment, they were all going back to the States when the blizzards began; then they would return to finish the job during the 1943 construction season. Indeed, that was the Army's original plan, which assumed that an emergency supply line all the way to Fairbanks probably could not be opened any sooner. But now, with the goal in sight almost a year ahead of schedule, it was going to take a lot of plowing and sanding by Army road graders and dump trucks to keep the convoys moving all winter.

10

"This Is No Picnic"

The work of CANOL's Task Force 2600 had barely begun in June 1942 when it became obvious that only a fraction of the 55,000 tons of supplies and equipment needed at Norman Wells could be barged downriver before the October freezeup. General Somervell's subsequent decision to allow another fourteen months for completion of the Norman Wells–Whitehorse pipeline and refinery (CANOL 1) was thus a tacit admission of how unrealistic his original timetable had been. Although Somervell also authorized an interim barge/pipeline system between Prince Rupert and Whitehorse (CANOL 2), he remained convinced that oil from Norman Wells for the Alaska Highway and Northwest Staging Route was a military necessity. He therefore decreed that Task Force 2600 would stay on in northwest Canada until all cargo for the Norman Wells end of CANOL 1 had been delivered.

The news that they were not going home in the fall as previously planned came as a shock to CANOL's three Engineer battalions—just as it did to the seven Engineer regiments on the Alaska Highway. Reflecting the prevailing stereotype, an additional worry for the commanders of black units on both projects was whether their troops could endure as well as whites the hardships of an Arctic winter. The settlers at Fort Smith and elsewhere along the Mackenzie route were especially blunt, telling the black soldiers of the 388th Engineers over and over again that they would never make it through the winter. Although Master Sergeant Wansley Hill and his friends tried to laugh off that unsettling prediction, nobody in Company "B" was smiling on the morning of August 1. Overnight, ice had formed in their washbuckets.[1]

While CANOL's higher-ups tried desperately to figure out ways to increase the flow of supplies to Norman Wells before winter arrived, each battalion in Task Force 2600 did the best it could with the limited means at hand.

For the 388th Engineers, the "means at hand" was their own muscle power. What they moved was mostly 4-inch-diameter metal pipe—337 miles of it, weighing nearly 9,000 tons. Each 22-foot, 230-pound length of pipe had to be handled at least six times on its 1,171-mile trip north: from railroad car to truck to barge at Waterways; from barge to truck to barge over the 16-mile portage between Fort Fitzgerald and Fort Smith; and from barge to truck to stockpile at Camp CANOL, on the west bank of the Mackenzie across from Norman Wells. In addition, bargeloads of pipe frequently went aground on one of the ever-shifting sandbars along the route, requiring more unloading and reloading to refloat and refill the barge.

The official history of Task Force 2600 conceded that the 388th Engineers were doing backbreaking stevedore work, but summoned up a plantation image of them as carefree, singing "darkeys" who enjoyed their constant toil:

> The Negro soldiers had devised numerous songs to fit the job. One refrain went "crackers in the morning, crackers at night, here comes the *Athabasca* with mo' damn pipe." Another version was "the night is light, mosquitos sho' do bite, look up the river and see mo' damn pipe."[2]

As a break from the monotony of handling pipe, a soldier in the 388th could look forward to cutting firewood to keep the paddle wheels turning on the *Athabasca* and its three sister ships working on Project CANOL. With luck, he might be sent to one of the sawmills downriver or out on the islands of Great Slave Lake, where the spruce grew tall enough to make good timbers for docks, decking, and storage sheds. While the isolation of sawmill duty could get on a man's nerves, at least there were fewer officers around to yell at him.[3]

There were also forest fires to fight, although no one bothered unless they threatened a Canadian settlement or a U.S. facility. Whether ignited by lightning or someone's carelessly thrown cigarette, most fires were left to burn themselves out, often consuming thousands of square miles of scrubby muskeg forest before they did so. The smoky haze over the Mackenzie valley grew so thick in July and August that aircraft headed for Norman Wells frequently had to turn back because their pilots could not see well enough to navigate.[4]

Official histories rarely mention how seldom the troops got time off. The experience of Company "A" of the 388th was typical. Between unloading thousands of tons of pipe, cutting and stacking hundreds of cords of firewood, putting out several forest fires, and building their own camp at Fort Fitzgerald, the company worked sixty-nine straight days, from June 14 to August 22, without a break.[5]

Not that there was much to do when time off was given. The only recreational equipment available at first were several pairs of boxing gloves and a couple of baseballs and bats, although the Army's wondrous supply system later coughed up surf-casting rods, ice skates, and skis. Wansley Hill taught himself how to skate that winter. Usually, he and the others filled their few free hours the same way soldiers everywhere did: by playing cards, reading, writing letters home, and talking about what they would do when they got there.[6]

Other simple pleasures helped relieve the tedium. Army mess sergeants had a standard recipe for ice cream made from powdered milk, powdered eggs, and sugar that was much in demand. Sometimes, when the Hudson's Bay Company could squeeze a load of its own supplies on the *Athabasca*, the trading posts downriver from Waterways got fresh candy and cigarettes—and even such luxuries as tinned sardines and beer. (The HBC also sold hard liquor, but not to enlisted men or natives.) Although the candy, beer, and sardines always sold out quickly, some soldiers found ways to ensure their own supply.

In the 388th, for example, one of "B" Company's lieutenants had an agreement with the manager of the Fort Smith trading post: in exchange for a couple of free bottles of booze for himself, the officer would have a GI detail standing by whenever a shipment of HBC supplies came in. Hill's friend Sergeant George Young was a regular on this detail and remembers how it worked. The lieutenant would ask for volunteers, who pretended not to know about his crooked little deal. The lieutenant, in turn, never seemed to notice that his men were helping themselves to all the goodies they could carry.[7] Presumably, the trading post manager felt this arrangement cost him less than hiring locals to do the unloading. Perhaps he carried the loss from such petty pilfering as "labor expense" in his ledger book.

Laughter, especially at the foibles of their officers, also helped. The 388th's Commanding Officer, Lieutenant Colonel Thomas Adcock, a stickler for military courtesy, was not a man to be openly ridiculed, but his troops found a subtle way to mock their pompous commander. Adcock's headquarters, located in a decrepit building near the swampy riverbank at Fort Smith, quickly became known as "Sunken Heights."

Then there was Bridges the bugler. The way Wansley Hill remembers it, more and more soldiers in Company "B" had begun sleeping through reveille formation—a minor infraction for which Captain Gouldin, the company commander, imposed extra KP or latrine-cleaning duty. As First Sergeant, Hill took it upon himself to investigate what was going on. The answer was simple. Most of the men around the edge of the encampment couldn't hear the bugle because Bridges had taken to blowing it from inside his tent while snug in his sleeping bag. Bridges found himself cleaning latrines for a while after that.[8]

Almost everyone's favorite story (it is even in the official Task Force history) involved Company "D"'s encounter with a native band while en route to Norman Wells to begin work on Camp CANOL. On July 4, 1942, soon after Great Slave Lake was reported free of ice, most of the company headed north from Fort Smith aboard the paddle-wheel steamer *Distributor*, with two heavily loaded barges in tow. During the company's 100-mile trip across the lake, a vicious gale blew up, forcing the *Distributor* to run for the harbor at Hay River, a settlement with the usual HBC trading post and more than a dozen native and mixed-race families living nearby. Storm-bound in the harbor for several days, the troops grew so restless that the company commander ordered everyone ashore for a dose of the Army's all-purpose remedy for tension and boredom: a vigorous session of calisthenics.

No one at Hay River had ever seen black men before, let alone 160 of them in formation doing push-ups, jumping jacks and knee bends in singsong unison. Interpreting this strange activity as some sort of ceremonial war dance for the benefit of his people, the native leader asked the company commander if they could return this honor with a performance of their own. And so the black soldiers came ashore once more before the *Distributor* got underway, this time to enjoy the ceremonial songs and dances of their native hosts.[9]

On July 13, the troops of "D" Company reached the site of Camp CANOL, 70 miles below the Arctic Circle, and began unloading supplies and equipment from the *Distributor* and its barges. Their own canvas-covered huts were considerably more austere than the prefabricated structures they had been sent to erect for the civilian workers coming to drill the oil wells, weld the storage tanks, and lay the pipeline for the northern half of CANOL 1. Within a year Camp CANOL would become a self-contained "city" with enough well-insulated barracks to house more than 1,000 men (plus separate quarters for several dozen female staff members), a mess hall capable of feeding 500 at one sitting, recreational facilities, repair shops of all descriptions, and row upon row of well-stocked warehouses.[10]

Although General Somervell's recent order delaying the completion date for CANOL 1 had made construction of the camp's full complement of buildings contingent on finding enough oil at Norman Wells to justify laying the pipeline and setting up the refinery, Somervell was still betting heavily on his original plan. Trainloads of materiel earmarked for CANOL 1 kept arriving at Waterways all summer, including steel plates for three oil storage tanks with a combined capacity of 220,000 barrels taken from a dismantled Texas refinery and enough boats and barges to constitute a small navy: five radio-equipped cabin cruisers, thirty-two 100-hp diesel towboats, eleven steel self-propelled barges (cut into sections for rail travel), and sixty large prefabricated wooden barges—fifty of 100 tons displacement and ten of 300 tons.[11]

The cabin cruisers and towboats were easily launched and put into service, but the barges took time to assemble in the Army's makeshift shipyard on the banks of the Clearwater River. By early July, only five new barges had come off the ways there; it was July 11 before the first of these made it downriver and over the portage to Fort Smith.

Transporting barges that were 15 to 20 feet wide, 60 to 120 feet long, and up to 160 tons in weight over the sandy portage road was no small undertaking. Moving each one required positioning a heavy dockside crane at both ends of the road; placing the barge on an enormous, tractor-drawn multi-wheeled flatbed trailer; and deploying a fleet of sprinkler trucks to soak and compact the sandiest spots continuously to keep the loaded rig from bogging down. The 16-mile trip took up to eight hours. Nonetheless, by the end of the summer, the two wood-burning stern-wheelers on the 800-mile run from Fort Smith to Norman Wells had been augmented by about thirty new barges and half of the new diesel towboats. The remaining towboats and the other two stern-wheelers continued to shuttle between Waterways and Fort Fitzgerald, while the makeshift pontoon rafts still being used on that stretch were replaced as fast as more barges could be launched at Waterways.[12]

Colonel Theodore Wyman controlled the diverse operations of Task Force 2600 through four zone commanders, each of whom was responsible for a specific geographical sector. The Base Zone, extending from Edmonton to Fort Fitzgerald, was run by the 90th Engineers' Commanding Officer, Lieutenant Colonel J. N. Krueger, who shared his headquarters at Waterways with Colonel Wyman. The other three commanders were Lieutenant Colonel Adcock, Commanding Officer of the 388th Engineers/Portage Zone at Fort Smith; Lieutenant Colonel L. E. Laurion, Commanding Officer of the 89th Engineers/Mackenzie River Zone at Fort Simpson; and Lieutenant Colonel L. G. Lyman, Commanding Officer of the Norman Wells Zone.

Each zone except Laurion's had its own fully staffed field hospital, and all four included smaller detachments from the Quartermaster, Finance, and Signal Corps. Over the summer, the signal technicians set up a series of radio relay stations linking every U.S. Army installation between Edmonton and Camp CANOL. This freed Wyman from having to make an endless round of inspection visits up and down the route in a chartered float plane, allowing him instead to keep up-to-date by reading the summary of radio messages in his in-basket each morning.[13]

All too often, the messages Wyman received contained depressing news of bottlenecks, delays, and accidents. In the Base Zone, the violent summer winds that periodically swept down the Slave River and across Lake Athabasca were as likely as ever to capsize the 90th Engineers' remaining pontoon rafts—sometimes in water too deep to allow for easy salvage operations. On the other hand, while the battalion's large new barges easily rode out such squalls, they were far more likely to run aground on sandbars and hidden snags because of their deeper draft; this problem only grew worse in July and August as the river levels fell for lack of rain.

In the Portage Zone, on July 10, 1942, Task Force 2600 had its first fatality, when a member of the 90th Engineers fell off a barge at Fort Fitzgerald and drowned. Swept downstream into the rapids, his body was never recovered.

Next, the Army discovered that even its largest barges were no match for the powerful storms on Great Slave Lake. These often lasted a week or more, during which no towboat skipper dared attempt the 100-mile crossing. If caught out on the lake when a major storm blew up, a pilot's choice was either to cut the tow lines or to founder with his cargo. During one such gale in late July, two bargeloads of trucks, bulldozers, and pipe bound for Camp CANOL went down in 60 feet of water. The return of foul weather in September and October caused more losses and delays on the lake.[14]

Even before the full extent of the transportation problems on the Mackenzie River route was known in Washington, General Sturdevant had prudently tried to obtain at least fifteen amphibious cargo planes to haul high-priority passengers and cargo for CANOL. In a June 9 memorandum, he requested General Somervell's assistance in obtaining such planes. But at that time the Air Force had a more urgent need for its few flying boats in the South Pacific, so Colonel Wyman got permission to hire some local bush pilots. The faces and legends of Grant McConachie and "Punch" Dickens were soon as familiar to the American soldiers and civilians working along the Mackenzie as they were to the region's Canadian settlers. No longer competing against each other, McConachie and Dickens had been bought out in late 1941 by Canadian Pacific Airlines, which now paid them to manage the companies they had struggled so long to build up. With the arrival of the U.S. Army in northwest Canada, their lean years were finally over.[15]

Although the float-equipped, single-engine, high-wing Norseman favored by most Canadian pilots on the Mackenzie run was ideal for ferrying military and civilian VIPs from place to place, it was not designed to haul anything much larger and heavier than a few drums of fuel or a diesel generator or a truck engine. Without a large fleet of heavy-duty cargo aircraft, Colonel Wyman faced the certainty that much of the priority cargo due at Waterways that summer would not make it all the way downriver before the freezeup.

One possible source of help was Bechtel-Price-Callahan, the civilian contracting firm hired for CANOL 1, which had applied for a permit to buy several twin-engine Lockheed "Lodestars." (Meanwhile, BPC officials in northwest Canada were getting around in a scrounged-up collection of relics from the barnstorming era— including a biplane that had been used in filming *Hell's Angels*, Howard Hughes's 1930 epic about the flying aces of World War 1.) In addition, the Army's Air Transport Command was willing to put some of its workhorse Douglas DC-3 "Skymasters" at Wyman's disposal. Unfortunately, none of these large aircraft could land on water and, as of July 1942, not a single airfield existed north of Edmonton along the 1,500-mile route down the Mackenzie to Norman Wells. Grant McConachie had faced a similar problem three years earlier in setting up Yukon Southern's year-round air service between Edmonton and Whitehorse. Like McConachie, Wyman was going to have to build his own bases in the wilderness. Unlike him, Wyman did not have to worry about money or manpower.

Wyman's hastily made plans called for his men to build a fully equipped, well-lighted airfield near the headquarters of each of the four zones—at Fort McMurray, Fort Smith, Fort Simpson, and Camp CANOL—plus six more emergency landing strips with minimal facilities at various other points along the way.

Although the troops of Task Force 2600 had neither the equipment nor the training for such work, they began construction on all but four of these fields in the summer of 1942, gradually turned them over in various stages of completion to BPC's civilian crews during the next twelve months. The remaining fields were built entirely by civilians. All ten sites required work crews to clear, grade, and gravel a swath of forest at least 500 feet wide and 1 mile long. Nobody in Washington or at Wyman's headquarters thought it necessary to obtain Canada's prior permission for this work. Indeed, only after Ottawa made a polite inquiry about the "rumored airfields" was the Canadian government officially informed that Project CANOL had expanded again.[16]

As a matter of fact, the expansion had barely begun. CANOL 3, 4, 5, 6, and more were still to come.

General Somervell visited both the CANOL and Alaska Highway projects during a week-long swing through northwest Canada during the summer of 1942. With General Reybold, the Chief of Engineers, in tow, he met with Colonel Wyman and several BPC officials in Edmonton and Waterways on August 17 and 18. Despite all of his problems, Wyman had some good news to report: the Imperial Oil Company had already sunk several successful new wells and was now confidently predicting that the Army's production goal of 3,000 barrels per day at Norman Wells would soon be reached.[17]

Hearing this, Somervell swiftly reaffirmed several of his earlier decisions. Work on CANOL 1, he said, would continue as planned, with no letup over the winter. Meanwhile, CANOL 2 (the barge/pipeline system between Prince Rupert and Whitehorse) was still to be completed "at the earliest practicable date." Then, to enhance CANOL's strategic value further, Somervell instructed Wyman "to develop a plan for distribution of petroleum products from Whitehorse to Fairbanks, Nome and Anchorage, Alaska, and points in the Aleutian Islands."[18]

Within weeks, Wyman's plan for such a distribution system was making its way back up the chain of command. Soon thereafter Somervell ordered contracts to be let and work to begin on a

600-mile, 3-inch pipeline capable of delivering 3,000 barrels of gasoline per day along the Alaska Highway from the refinery at Whitehorse north to Fairbanks (CANOL 3); and on a 270-mile, 2-inch pipeline to deliver 800 barrels of gasoline per day from Whitehorse back down the highway to Watson Lake (CANOL 4). (CANOL 5, a short extension of the pipeline beyond Fairbanks to the rail connection with Anchorage at Nenana, was the one part of Wyman's plan not approved by Somervell.)[19]

Word that more oil had been found at Norman Wells also came as good news to Major General C. P. Gross, the Army's Chief of Transportation, whose staff was then preparing a study of the military's transportation and shipping needs in the Alaskan theater of operations in the event Japan entered the war against Russia. In August 1942, the Axis powers' expansion was at its zenith. With the opening of a major German offensive to capture Stalingrad and cut off the Soviet Union's vital Caspian Sea oil supply, a Japanese stab at the Soviet Union's Siberian "back" would obviously have grave repercussions for the Allies. If such an attack did occur, a large-scale counteroffensive by the United States against Japan by way of Alaska might become necessary to keep the beleaguered Russians in the war. But, in 1942, all of Alaska's oil had to be imported.

Against this background, and in view of the continuing threat to U.S. oil tankers from German U-boats in the Caribbean and Japanese submarines in the North Pacific, General Gross's staff reached the following conclusions:

1. Alaska with an ample supply of oil becomes the key to the Pacific and the base for an offensive against Japan.
2. There is every evidence of an oil province in Northwestern Canada capable of sustaining a major war effort.
3. To attempt to [supply Alaska] from oil supplies in the United States would bog down transportation and limit possible action to indecisive proportions.
4. The whole character of the war effort from Alaska is therefore founded on the extent of the local oil supply.[20]

The study specified a production level of 20,000 barrels of crude oil per day as an "ample supply of oil" to enable Alaska to become "the base for an offensive against Japan." It also pointed to the Mackenzie River basin as "the most geologically promising area for further oil discoveries in the Pacific Northwest."

On September 4, 1942, General Gross submitted this document to

General Somervell, who immediately forwarded it to Colonel Wyman "for study and necessary action."

Wyman's swift response was to recommend a "comprehensive 'wildcat drilling' program in the Mackenzie basin . . . and . . . geophysical explorations in other areas both north and south of the proven oil field at Norman Wells." On September 25, with Somervell's verbal blessing, Wyman negotiated a contract with the Noble Drilling Corporation to undertake just such a program of new drilling and exploration within a 500,000-square-mile area of the Yukon and Northwest Territories. This document called for drilling 100 wildcat wells at sites to be chosen by the Imperial Oil Company over a vast expanse bounded on the east by the 112th meridian, on the south by the 60th parallel (these two lines intersected at Fort Smith), on the north by the Arctic Ocean, and on the west by the Continental Divide. The crude-oil production goal from these new wells was 15,000 to 20,000 barrels per day. This time, the Americans remembered to go through the formality of asking for Canada's permission—although not until the ink was already dry on Noble's drilling contract.[21]

With the October freezeup only weeks away, the Americans also informed Ottawa of their intent to build a series of winter trails over which to continue hauling supplies and equipment. More than 19,000 tons of cargo for CANOL 1 remained undelivered, the bulk of it piling up at Waterways. At least half of this total, including the Noble Corporation's seven portable drilling rigs, was needed in the Norman Wells area as quickly as possible that winter.[22]

The question of how best to solve the problem of winter transportation had been anticipated by Colonel Wyman within a few weeks of his arrival in Canada. Initially, he and his staff had favored the deceptively simple solution that formed the basis of Stefansson's original Route D proposal: using the region's solidly frozen lakes and rivers as a "highway" for long trains of tractor-drawn cargo sledges. As with almost everything else about his Route D scheme, however, theory and reality were two different things. The old explorer had last driven a dog sled over the icy surface of the Mackenzie in the winter of 1912. A team of dogs can pull about 1,000 pounds on a sled, but the Army was thinking in terms of putting thirty times that weight on a single sledge—and then towing a dozen or more of these at a time with a 20-ton bulldozer.

It so happened that Stefansson's Canadian protegé, Richard Finnie, who knew the Mackenzie's winter moods as well as any man, had recently been hired by the U.S. Army as a combination consultant/photographer/historian for Project CANOL. Finnie's advice to Wyman was to use the Mackenzie as a winter highway only at points where it had to be crossed. He listed the reasons for avoiding the river under three headings: rough ice, treacherous ice, and open water—and discussed them as follows:

> Conditions of rough ice on the Mackenzie are caused by thaws and jams which often fill long stretches of the river with chaotic masses of ice, the huge pieces tilted and jammed askew in such fashion as to make even walking . . . a difficult and tortuous process. . . .
>
> Treacherous ice . . . is caused by . . . the underlying currents, which in many places undermine the ice or prevent it from freezing solidly enough to support tractor trains. Such ice may, however, appear perfectly safe on the surface.
>
> Stretches of open water occur at points of swift current . . . and even short periods of comparatively mild weather will widen these . . . stretches. . . .[23]

Stefansson, for his part, had never abandoned his behind-the-scenes campaign to convince the War Department of the superiority of Route D as Alaska's main supply line, and he was still using Finnie to keep him apprised of everything the U.S. Army was doing in northwest Canada. Finnie's wife Alyce, who had moved with him to Edmonton that summer and taken a job there with BPC, was now equally valuable to Stefansson as a source of information. On September 4, 1942, he wrote this to her:

> Please keep writing on our principle that if you should happen on a secret you must not pass it along. [But] You put us continually in your debt if you do pass along things that are subjects of discussion sufficiently common so that they are beyond the secret stage. Such things can be of value and can have their bearing on developments in the Northwest. For I am being called on now a good deal more than before, and my facts, opinions and advice now go more directly to where they may possibly have an influence.[24]

But Stefansson was only kidding himself about how much influence he had left in Washington. Rather than directly challenging his mentor on the subject of winter travel on the Mackenzie, Finnie found a gentler way to tell him he was full of horsefeathers: "Dear Stef," he wrote on September 29:

> I have found only two men in the North who support you on the use of the river as a winter road. One of them is a cat skinner with a

reputation for bombast, and he hasn't seen the Mackenzie in winter; the other is a man you must know by reputation—Bill Boland—and he supports you with reservations. Boland has spent many years in the Mackenzie District. . . . His idea is that the river *can* be used, but only as an emergency measure, and that an overland road is far preferable.[25]

In this same letter, as if to remind Stefansson that a summer trip down the Mackenzie could also be difficult, Finnie casually mentioned that it had just taken him almost two months to reach Norman Wells on the *Distributor*. He then described Colonel Wyman's plans to build CANOL 6, a 1,000-mile overland winter supply road linking "the Wells" with the closest railhead, the town of Peace River, Alberta.[26]

Located due west of Waterways, about two-thirds of the 360-mile distance to Fort St. John, the town of Peace River had one advantage that was suddenly of great importance to the U.S. Army. A rudimentary winter trail, known as the Grimshaw Road, already ran straight north from the Peace River railhead to Hay River on Great Slave Lake—almost half the distance to Norman Wells.

The basic concept for CANOL 6 was simple enough: three companies of the 90th Engineers, assisted by one from the 388th, would improve the Grimshaw Road a bit; then BPC's civilian construction crews would take over to blaze a new winter trail from the vicinity of Hay River to Norman Wells. Only one crossing of the Mackenzie, at a place called Mills Lake, would be necessary. Meanwhile, all cargo still at Waterways after the freezeup would be sent 600 miles by rail via Edmonton to Peace River. From there it would head north on tractor-drawn sledge trains close behind BPC's trailblazers. As is usual with simple concepts, the headaches came in the details, which in this case included building a new camp for 800 troops at Peace River and attempting to move 19,000 tons of cargo more than 1,600 miles by rail and tractor train in subzero weather.[27]

The laborious relocation of CANOL 1's undelivered cargo began in early October. Arriving with the first trainload from Waterways on October 11, Company "C" of the 388th Engineers immediately started laying out "Camp Pioneer," Colonel Wyman's new logistical base at the Peace River railhead. The 90th Engineers pulled in three days later to lend a hand in constructing a headquarters, prefabricated barracks, and temporary warehouses. On October 23, with a few essential buildings already up and the rest underway, the first work party of Engineer soldiers was dispatched northward to begin upgrading the 400-mile Grimshaw Road to Hay River.[28]

Meanwhile, because Colonel Wyman had anticipated that the freezeup would also strand nearly 1,000 tons of supplies destined for Camp CANOL at Fort Smith, another winter trail toward Hay River had already been started by a detachment from Wansley Hill's outfit, Company "B" of the 388th. Once hauled 200 miles cross-country to Hay River, these supplies could be put on the tractor trains moving north to Norman Wells from Camp Pioneer. A winter trail linking Fort Smith to the Grimshaw Road would serve another purpose as well. From October through May, the only other way to resupply Fort Smith's 500-man garrison was by air.

On August 29, leaving the bulk of "B" company to begin building log cabins for winter quarters at Fort Smith, Captain Gouldin, the company commander, headed west toward Hay River with his detachment and a dozen or so D-4 and D-7 bulldozers. To teach the soldiers how to operate and maintain these unfamiliar machines, several of BPC's civilian "catskinners" and mechanics agreed to come along. Gouldin never had a chance to reconnoiter his route from the air, and path led him through muskeg forest so flat and featureless that his map was almost useless for navigation. The only landmarks of note along the way were the seven rivers his men had to cross. Elsewhere, the intervening bogs and swamps made straight-line travel for any distance impossible. After two months of miserable slogging, Gouldin's inexperienced trail-builders were only halfway to Hay River, and all but one of their civilian "helpers" had long since quit.[29]

Although building winter trails and hauling cargo north to Norman Wells were Colonel Wyman's main concerns east of the Rockies that fall, he was now spending considerable time on the west side of the Continental Divide, where CANOL 2's pipeline between Skagway and Whitehorse was beginning to take shape. Here, as General Hoge and others had already learned, his biggest problems were the limited capacities of the port of Skagway and the White Pass and Yukon Railroad.

In late August, BPC workmen began stringing 4-inch pipe for CANOL 2 along the railroad right-of-way from Skagway toward Carcross. More than 20 miles of pipe had been laid as of September 10, when several days of torrential rain began, creating hazardous conditions in the steep, narrow valley leading up to White Pass. Early on the morning of September 12, 15 miles inland from Skagway, approximately 1,000 tons of granite broke loose from a cliff high above the line and buried several hundred yards of railroad track and pipe under a small mountain of rubble.[30] Although no one was injured, this was one more setback to report to General Somervell, who had already made it unmistakably clear to every senior U.S. Army officer in northwest Canada that *any* delay angered him—no matter what the reason for it.

11

Brass Hats and Brass Bands at Fifteen Below

On August 19, 1942, after their meeting at Waterways with Colonel Wyman to review Project CANOL, Lieutenant General Somervell, the Army's top logistician, and Major General Reybold, the Chief of Engineers, landed at Fort St. John to begin a four-day inspection tour of the Alaska Highway.

As at Wyman's headquarters, Somervell wanted to see for himself what problems existed and what, if any, organizational changes were needed. Now that the highway was likely to be open all the way to Fairbanks by winter, it was time to consider putting its northern and southern sectors back under one commander. Transportation bottlenecks were another concern. Already clogged with supplies for the highway, the limited facilities in Edmonton, Skagway, and Prince Rupert now had to handle the growing logistical requirements of CANOL as well. Somervell was determined not to allow shipping delays to endanger the construction timetable of either project.

Returning to Washington, Somervell met with his staff. Colonel O'Connor's half of the highway was a "first class construction job," he told them, but he was not happy with what he had seen and heard in Whitehorse. Everything there seemed to be in short supply. Moreover, General Hoge's troops were ill-prepared for the coming winter, and lately they had run into permafrost (permanently frozen ground) near the Alaskan border, causing an unexpected slowdown.[1]

Acting with his usual decisiveness, Somervell set out to correct the deficiencies and problems his trip had uncovered. His boldest stroke came first: as of September 4, Brigadier General Hoge and Colonels O'Connor and Wyman no longer took their orders from General Reybold. Instead, their separate commands were consolidated into a new organization under Somervell's direct control. Called the Northwest Service Command, it was responsible for:

> all activities of the [U.S. Army] in the Provinces of British Columbia and Alberta and the Territories of Yukon and Mackenzie, Canada, together with the operation, supply and construction activities connected with the White Pass and Yukon Railway, and the highway from Whitehorse to Fairbanks . . . together with such base installations as may be necessary in Skagway and Fairbanks, Alaska. . . .[2]

A disinterested observer might have expected that Somervell would put General Hoge in charge of the Northwest Service Command, as a reward for his hard work during the preceding seven months. But his choice for the position (and promotion to brigadier general) was James A. O'Connor. Bill Hoge had just been fired.

Looking back on this incident in a 1974 interview with an Army historian, Hoge asserted that he lost his job in September 1942 more as a result of Somervell's egotism and vindictiveness than because of his own mistakes and shortcomings. A holder of grudges with a well-deserved reputation as a "mean son-of-a-bitch," Somervell had an old score to settle with Hoge. The bad blood between the two men originated, said Hoge, during their service together in the Memphis Engineer District in the early 1930s. Somervell left after a clash with the District Engineer, Colonel Harley Ferguson. Close friends with Ferguson, Hoge took over Somervell's job.

Ten years later came Somervell's inspection visit to chaotic, overcrowded Whitehorse, where beds rented by the hour and meals were eaten standing up for lack of table space. A man who relished the perquisites of his three-star rank and important position, Somervell expected to be met, briefed, and put up in style. O'Connor and Wyman accommodated his whims, but Hoge had no time for such "eyewash." With a road to open before winter, he had not bothered to set up an elaborate headquarters or fancy facilities for visiting VIPs. The best he could offer his guest from Washington was a bunk in his own tiny cottage and his wife's home cooking. That evidently wasn't good enough for Somervell.[3]

Nonetheless, other, more substantive factors clearly influenced Somervell's decision to relieve Hoge—no doubt including his strained relations with the PRA. In the 1974 interview, Hoge said as much.

Moreover, he also admitted that his men were not ready for winter, although he insisted that this was not his fault. Hoge claimed that because the way to Fairbanks was not originally expected to be open until mid-1943, he was promised (presumably by Sturdevant) that the troops could winter over in the States after the 1942 construction season ended. But when it became evident that the road would be usable by the late 1942, said Hoge, the higher-ups "reneged" on that promise. On August 13, only four days before Somervell arrived in Canada, Sturdevant informed Hoge by telegram that some of his troops would be needed to keep the road open through the winter and that the rest would be transferred to the Alaskan Defense Command. Sturdevant's timing covered his own backside, but not that of his former protegé. The best Hoge could come up with on such short notice was a plan to house everyone left behind to maintain the highway through the winter in heated, double-walled tents with wooden floors. Somervell was not satisfied. He wanted permanent barracks for 2,000 men and 40 to 80 officers built not only in Whitehorse, but also in Dawson Creek and Fairbanks.[4]

Another sore point was Hoge's negative reaction to Somervell's scheme to extend the Alaska Highway another 800 miles due west, all the way from Fairbanks to Nome, on the Bering Sea. Nome was also to be the last stop on Frederick Delano's pet project—the railroad he wanted Somervell to build via Route B and the Rocky Mountain Trench. The President's uncle shared Somervell's strategic vision of Nome as a major naval base and logistical bastion on the very doorstep of Asia, an American version of the Russian port of Vladivostok.

Although Generals Hoge and Buckner agreed that the well-protected facilities at Anchorage—800 miles southeast of Nome—already served that purpose and at far less cost and risk, Hoge's main objection to Somervell's plan for a road to Nome was its impracticality. He explained to Somervell that the permanently frozen ground the 18th Engineers had begun to encounter in the vicinity of the Alaskan border presented a far more difficult problem than muskeg ever had. His men had coped with muskeg by avoiding it, excavating it, or corduroying it. None of these solutions worked with permafrost, which covered many areas to great depths along the northern third of the route. With permafrost, when Colonel Paules's bulldozers followed their usual practice of stripping away the covering vegetation to let the sun dry the ground, the frozen soil melted into a cold muck instead. Hoge told Somervell that Paules was experimenting with new construction techniques to solve the problem, but he warned that further progress might be slow.[5] That was another piece of bad news that Somervell did not want to hear.

Despite the fact that Stefansson had warned the Army of the difficulties of building roads over permafrost, Somervell's ignorance of the problem was understandable. No American engineer, military or civilian, had ever actually encountered it before. That included the builders of the Richardson Highway and all of the "experts" who had so loudly touted the obstacle-free advantages of Route A over the Army's Inland Route. "Everyone talked about muskeg and everybody talked of mountains and crossing lakes and rivers," Hoge recalled, "but they never heard of permafrost, which was the worst thing we had to contend with."[6]

Somervell was not about to be dissuaded from pursuing his grand design by unforeseen problems or nay-saying subordinates. "Hoge has to go," was his verdict after returning to Washington from Whitehorse.[7] Having made this decision, Somervell applied himself to helping Hoge find another assignment. Hoge's new boss was Major General Jacob Devers, who was then at Fort Knox developing the armored forces and tactics that would spearhead the U.S. Army's sweep across France two years later.[8] In March 1945, Hoge's tanks and men were first across the Rhine, capturing the bridge at Remagen before the Germans could blow it up.

In hindsight, Hoge admitted that he had been fortunate to leave Whitehorse in September 1942. Otherwise, he said, "I would have been stuck there for maybe a year or two." But he never forgave Somervell for the circumstances of his leaving. Even in 1974, nineteen years after Somervell's death and his own retirement as the four-star commander of all U.S. Army forces in Europe, Hoge still felt bitter about it:

> He came up there. . . . He didn't know the country. . . . He didn't know what my instructions were. . . . Then he decided that I wasn't making a big enough show and spread. It didn't suit him . . . it had to be the biggest, most expensive that anybody could have. His history in the Second World War was like that. Now, I'm not depreciating Somervell because in some respects he's a great person. . . . [B]ut he was just as flatsided on that side of show and making the biggest thing and spending money than anyone I've ever known.[9]

On September 10, Hoge said goodbye to his headquarters staff in Whitehorse. Seven noncommissioned officers and enlisted men who worked there handed him a farewell note. "It has been an honor and a pleasure to serve under the direct supervision of such a capable and fair-dealing commander," they wrote. "We wish you the best of health, success and happiness in your new assignment."[10]

Hoge's sudden departure and O'Connor's elevation to oversee Somervell's burgeoning northwest empire necessitated a series of reassignments down the chain of command. On September 6, Colonel Robert Ingalls moved to Fort St. John as the new southern sector commander. Major James McCarty, newly promoted and now the highest-ranking officer left in the 35th Engineers, took Ingalls's old job.

Less than a month later, Ingalls decided he needed an experienced officer to supervise the expansion of the Dawson Creek railhead, which was fast becoming a serious bottleneck as the logistical buildup ordered by Somervell continued. Ingalls's choice for railhead commander was his old friend and former sidekick, Colonel Heath Twichell. In early October, after only eleven weeks with the 95th Engineers, Twichell turned his command over to Lieutenant Colonel Owain Hughes and headed south down the road once again.

The dust took just as long to settle around Whitehorse. By early October, Colonel Earl Paules had become the new northern sector commander. Colonel Frank Johnson, the former Commanding Officer of the 93rd Engineers, ended up with Paules's old outfit, the 18th Engineers. Finally, in this military version of musical chairs, the executive officer of the 18th, Lieutenant Colonel Walter Hodge, moved up and took over the 93rd.

For administrative purposes, both sectors now came directly under the Northwest Service Command; but to deal with Ingalls and Paules on purely operational matters, O'Connor put Colonel John Wheeler in charge of a small intermediate organization, designated as Headquarters Alcan Highway.[11]

Amid all this brass shuffling in Canada, General Sturdevant's reassignment in Washington went almost unnoticed. But if anyone in the War Department was the "father" of the Alaska Highway, it was Sturdevant. He had fleshed out the plan, selected Hoge, chosen the seven regiments, set the wheels in motion and, over the past seven months, done his best to keep them rolling smoothly. Whether he had incurred Somervell's displeasure is uncertain, but Sturdevant's transfer may have been precipitated by his friendship with Hoge and his coolness toward O'Connor—feelings that he did not bother to conceal from the latter. At any rate, on October 10, a puzzled and dismayed Sturdevant wrote Hoge that he, too, had been taken off the project: "Somebody has pulled some underground dirt which I can't put my finger on. My connection with the Alcan road ceases with the report for Sept. . . ." Henceforth he was to serve as Assistant Chief of Engineers for troop training.[12]

The shakeup precipitated by Somervell's August visit went even further. The root cause of many of the problems and delays in the northern sector was the limited hauling capacity of the antiquated, narrow-gauge White Pass and Yukon Railroad. Supplies and equipment that were urgently needed on the highway often sat in Skagway for days before reaching Whitehorse, and the tonnage being added for Project CANOL only increased the congestion.

Hoge had become friendly with the railroad's powerful owner, a shrewd Canadian named Herbert Wheeler. His advice to Hoge on local soil and weather conditions had proved helpful, and Wheeler's workmen had built the little green-painted cottage in Whitehorse for Nettie Hoge. Wheeler had long opposed any attempt to break his transportation monopoly in the Whitehorse region, and he resisted the U.S. Army's attempts to change the modus operandi of his railroad. Although Wheeler's freight handlers and train crews delivered six times more cargo to Whitehorse during August 1942 than they did in an average prewar month, they had very nearly reached the limit of their capacity. And still the backlog in Skagway grew.

Somervell's solution was simple and direct: he arranged for the U.S. Army to lease and operate the White Pass and Yukon Railroad for the duration of the war. In mid-September, Railway Engineering Unit 9646-A debarked at Skagway. Although few of the unit's GIs had ever seen such steep grades and tight curves before, most were experienced railroaders—veterans of years on the "Pennsy," the Santa Fe, or the Union Pacific. To augment Wheeler's overworked rolling stock, the unit brought in fifty boxcars, twenty flatcars, seven locomotives, and one rotary snow plow. During August, the White Pass Line had carried an average of 450 tons per day; two months later, that figure was up to 550 tons.[13]

The high-level changes in Whitehorse and Fort St. John meant little to the 'dozer operators and bridge-building crews out in the bush. Their work still went on, sixty or more hours per week. Nevertheless, as the days grew noticeably shorter and colder, scarcely a soldier among the 10,000 men working on the road was not caught up in the excitement of the race to open the way to Fairbanks before the first hard freeze. In late September 1942, attention focused on the rapidly shrinking gap just east of Watson Lake between the lead bulldozers of the 35th Engineers and those of the

340th. Whoever had a dollar in either regiment's betting pool and came closest to predicting the time and place of the linkup would win enough to pay for a glorious spree—far enough away from the highway to have all the fresh food, hot showers, clean sheets, hard liquor, and easy women he wanted—provided, of course, that the brass ever let up on the work schedule and began allowing leaves.

The long-awaited linkup between the northern and southern sectors occurred at 5:00 P.M. on September 24. It took place in the middle of a small tributary of the Liard River that has been known ever since as Contact Creek, exactly 305.1 miles west of Fort Nelson. A few minutes before five, the advance clearing crew of the 340th Engineers reached the west bank and stopped. Only the lead bulldozer kept its engine running. Above its low, rumbling idle the tired and dirty men could hear the approaching machines of the 35th Engineers, crashing through the last quarter mile of dense thicket on the opposite bank. As that noise grew louder, more members of the 340th straggled up from the rear. An equally grubby group from the 35th began assembling expectantly on their side of the creek. There was much yelling back and forth: a raucous mix of humorous profanity and boasting about which regiment had won the race to Watson Lake (the 340th had) and which outfit had built the most miles of road to get where they were now (the 35th).

The banter faded as the 35th's first bulldozer suddenly burst from the thicket. Trailing broken vines and mangled branches, it lumbered down the bank and into the shallow stream. In the cab beside the operator was the regiment's new Commanding Officer, Major McCarty. Colonel Lyons jumped aboard the 340th's lead machine as it lurched forward to meet them. The 'dozers touched blades, the two commanders shook hands, the 340th's band played, most of the onlookers got wet in the ensuing horseplay, and—when the hoopla subsided—the pioneer trail between Dawson Creek and Whitehorse was finally open.[14]

Many miles of filling and grading in both directions from Contact Creek remained to be done, but the Army knew a good public relations opportunity when it saw one. On September 22, two young soldiers, Corporal Otto H. Gronke of Chicago and Private First Class Robert Bowe of Minneapolis, loaded their sleeping bags, some gasoline cans, and a case of C-rations into a Dodge half-ton weapons carrier and left Dawson Creek with orders to get through to Whitehorse. At an average clip of 15 mph, it took them five days, and seventy-one hours of actual driving time, to cover the 1,030 miles to their destination. Despite all the hazards of a highway still under construction—steep grades, hairpin curves, boggy spots, and treacherous fords—their only unscheduled stop was to fix a flat tire. On September 27, photographers captured two grinning soldiers chatting with a Mountie in front of a dusty weapons carrier that bore a freshly painted sign, "First Truck, Dawson Creek to Whitehorse." Daily supply runs over the same route began three days later.[15]

Attention now shifted northward, to the 100-mile gap between the 18th and 97th Engineers, the last uncleared stretch on the way to Fairbanks. The border between Canada and Alaska bisected this stretch, making it an easily identifiable finish line for another interregimental competition. In recent days, however, neither the 18th nor the 97th had made enough progress to cheer about. Back in August, the 18th's lead bulldozers had begun to encounter permafrost. As Hoge had reported to Somervell, under the thin layer of moss and humus that supported the border region's shallow-rooted black spruce and shrubby undergrowth, the ground was indeed frozen solid to a depth of many feet.

Here, almost everything the Army Engineers had learned that summer about road building no longer applied. No more bulldozers five abreast, rooting up trees and pushing them aside to leave a 100-foot swath of raw earth drying in the sun. Thus exposed, permafrost quickly dissolved into a slush that was futile to excavate, impossible to drain, and incapable of drying. Trucks and 'dozers that tried to make headway by taking to the woods on either side of this aisle of mud only succeeded in widening it. In the words of the 18th Engineers' historian:

> The ground was so soft that one truck could not follow in another's tracks without bogging down. Each driver took his best shot and kept going as long as he could. Sometimes you would see a D-8 hauling a "train" of three or four trucks, dragging them through the gumbo. Our 1½-ton dumps were too light for this going and many springs and axles were broke.[16]

Clearly, the only way to construct a firm, stable roadbed over permafrost was to ensure that it never melted. But determining how best to do that took much trial and error. The solution turned out to be quite simple, although the radically different construction techniques involved were tedious and time-consuming.

To disturb the forest floor's thin soil as little as possible and thus preserve its insulating properties, the Engineers had to cut down all vegetation by hand and leave it where it fell. For the same reason, the width of the cleared swath could be little more than the shoulder-to-shoulder dimension of the finished road. The next step was to pile on extra insulation, building up the roadbed in the process. First came additional logs, laid corduroy-style, or branches and brush crushed and compacted by a team of bulldozers. Over this layer went truckloads—sometimes as many as 1,000 in a single day—of fresh earth and gravel, delivered by relays of dump trucks from the nearest streambed or borrow pit. Other bulldozers then spread and shaped this topping into an approximation of the final roadway, and graders and rollers finished the job. Snaking cross-country from horizon to horizon, the result looked like an endless dike or berm, little more than 25 feet wide at its base and 2 to 4 feet high, with a narrow dirt road on top. Building a half mile of such a road was a hard day's work for an entire Engineer regiment.[17]

The September slowdown was especially galling to the 18th Engineers, whose record-setting pace over the 150 miles from Whitehorse to Kluane Lake during June and early July had established them as the highway's undisputed road-building champs. Although it then took them until mid-August to push the road to the northwest end of Kluane Lake, Colonel Paules and his men were equally proud of this accomplishment.

Forty miles long, up to 6 miles wide, and surrounded by magnificent snowy peaks, Kluane Lake presented many of the same engineering challenges faced by the 35th Engineers at Muncho Lake—but on a far larger scale. Quicksand flats and the boulder-strewn, braided channels of Slim's River, fed by nearby Karskawalsh Glacier, blocked the 18th's path near the southern tip of the lake. While companies "E" and "F" tackled these obstacles, pontoon rafts ferried companies "A," "B," "C," and "D" to work sites farther north along the lake. Special efforts were required for the 1,000-foot Slim's River bridge and a mile of roadway that had to be blasted from the granite slopes along Kluane Lake's western shore.

Having succeeded in these tasks, the 18th Engineers had hoped for easier going beyond the lake. They had not counted on hitting permafrost. It took them six weeks of trial and error on the 32-mile stretch of wilderness south of the Donjek River to learn the best ways of dealing with it.[18]

After landing at Valdez in 3 feet of snow back in April, the 97th Engineers had also overcome more than their share of problems with frozen ground. Poorly trained (only one man in the regiment had ever operated a bulldozer before) and working with mostly worn-out equipment, the black soldiers of the 97th were characterized by Hoge many years later as being "practically useless"—an assessment that seems to have been not only racially biased but factually incorrect. In defense of Hoge's professional judgment, however, it must be noted that the 97th had only begun to hit its stride before he left the highway.

Commanded by Colonel Stephen C. Whipple, the 97th Engineers got off to a rocky start 200 miles north of Valdez at Slana. From there, it took them more than two months to build 78 miles of trail over the Mentasta Mountains to Tok in the upper Tanana River valley, where the regiment's assigned section of the Alaska Highway began. Starting north on June 7, Whipple's clearing crews immediately hit some of the toughest terrain anywhere along the highway. By June 10, the regiment had advanced exactly 1 mile. While working on the precipitous terminal moraine beyond Slana, the lead bulldozers repeatedly slipped off the narrow trail and "threw a track." Although the job of winding the heavy caterpillar tread back onto its drive sprocket was not particularly difficult on level ground, doing it on a 23-ton machine that was teetering on the edge of a crumbling slope of glacial debris called for great skill and calm nerves. Eventually, the 97th's inexperienced operators became masters at such on-the-spot repairs, but not before much precious time was lost.

Although the 97th began picking up speed in Mentasta Pass at the end of June, Colonel Whipple's progress for the month was unimpressive in comparison to that of the other six regiments. What his men had to show for twenty-three days of hard work was 20 miles of roadway located, of which only 6 miles had been completed and 9 more were under construction. Although the monthly progress report on Hoge's desk indicated just slightly better mileage figures for the 340th Engineers (20/10/10), Colonel Lyon's outfit had only started work on June 18. The other commanders all reported at least three times as much progress during June—with one regiment, Colonel Paules's 18th, way ahead of the pack: 170 miles located, 112 completed, and 43 under construction.[19]

Like the 95th Engineers under Colonel Neuman, many of the 97th's problems could be traced to its commander. In the eyes of many of his junior officers, Colonel Whipple was a fussy, plodding nitpicker who lacked rapport with his troops. Following a mid-July visit to the 97th's sector by Generals Hoge and Sturdevant, Whipple was relieved of his command. His executive officer, Lieutenant Colonel Lionel E. Robinson, a reserve officer with years of experience as a civilian contractor, took over the regiment.[20]

Coming down from the pass into the broad Tanana valley, the 97th

Engineers followed the Little Tok River, a swift and turbulent mountain stream. Many days behind schedule, Robinson made up some time by employing a clever adaptation of the leapfrog tactics used so successfully by the 18th Engineers. He simply split his regiment and used the Little Tok as a one-way "access trail" to resupply the forward companies. Careening through the woods and swamps and into the valley below went their 'dozers and graders, each pulling a trailer or log sled piled high with rations and bedding. Enough supplies for several additional weeks came floating down the Little Tok behind them, to be caught by a log boom after bobbing and bumping along over rapids and sandbars for 15 miles: fuel in half-filled drums; rations, spare parts, and miscellaneous items in lightly-loaded pontoons. By mid August the trail from Slana to Tok and the Tanana River was finally open, the last miles pushed across the river's floodplain by Company A in a single day. Behind the regiment, up in the pass, the PRA's civilian contractors were already widening and surfacing the roadbed.[21]

Although the PRA had plans to start on a 365-foot timber span across the Tanana within a few days, Colonel Robinson was in too much of a hurry to wait for a bridge. Commandeering a passing paddlewheel riverboat, the lead company commander rapidly ferried his men and equipment across the river to begin work on the pioneer trail on the north bank.[22] Less then 100 miles away, southeast up the wide, swampy valley, was the international boundary. Colonel Paules's regiment was then about the same distance from the border on the Canadian side. The race between the 18th and 97th Engineer Regiments to close the last gap on the Alaska Highway had begun.

September and October were months of increasing frustration and hardship for both regiments. They kept in touch with each other's progress by radio and compared notes on common problems, particularly on the subject of permafrost. But when winter arrived in mid-October, in the form of continuous sub-freezing temperatures, permafrost was no longer their biggest problem. "The increasing bitterness of the weather," wrote the 18th's historian, "was affecting us more every hour." He elaborated:

> Swift moving Yukon streams resisted freezing and the underside of trucks that crossed them became ice-coated. . . . After driving through water it was absolutely necessary to keep a vehicle moving, as ice would lock the wheels of a truck . . . that stood still for a few seconds (not minutes, seconds), and any attempt to move forward would snap an axle. Sometimes the . . . brakes could be smashed

free with a sledge, sometimes gallon cans of burning gas or diesel had to be set under them.

Gravel froze in solid masses in the beds of trucks and men were stationed at the end of the haul to beat it out with picks and sledgehammers. . . .

Vehicles frequently sputtered and stopped dead on the road when water froze in the gas lines. The copper lines had to be disconnected and blown out by mouth. . . .   A mouthful of sub-zero gasoline is not exactly tasty. . . .

Trucks used to snake logs through the woods when cats were not available emerged without bumpers, fenders, mufflers, or running boards.

Trucks with bent frames and beds and distorted springs moved crabwise up the road. Some trucks broke in half, were left beside the road as derelicts.

Men suffered but held up better than equipment. . . . Mechanics went nuts.[23]

With less than 75 miles of uncleared black spruce forest still separating the 18th and 97th Engineers, Colonel Paules, now the sector commander, ordered both regiments to keep going but to build nothing more elaborate than a winter trail—one like the rough-hewn pathway that had gotten the 35th Engineers to Fort Nelson the previous March. This short stretch of winter trail would be no more difficult than any other part of the highway to keep open over the winter; afterward, upgrading it to an all-weather road would be one more job for the PRA.[24]

The two regiments finally met on October 25, 1942, in a scene very much like the one that occurred at Contact Creek. Although the exact location is still the subject of some dispute, their linkup took place in the vicinity of Beaver Creek, at least 20 miles east of the border—which meant that the highway's mileage champs had been beaten in a fair race by the "practically useless" black soldiers of the 97th Engineers. Crossing the border from Alaska into Canada, members of the 97th put up a cocky sign: "Los Angeles City Limits." The proud professionals of the 18th could grumble all they liked about whose road had been built under tougher conditions or to higher standards; Robinson's troops had a palpable triumph to celebrate. There was poignant symbolism in the wire-service photograph that soon appeared in hundreds of newspapers in the United States and Canada. It showed two grimy but jubilant soldiers shaking hands atop their 'dozers. One was a black man from Philadelphia,

Corporal Refines Sims, Jr. The other man was white, Private Alfred Jalufka, from Kennedy, Texas.[25]

While the 18th and 97th Engineers labored to improve their hastily cut trail, Secretary of War Henry Stimson issued this statement on October 29:

> Trucks started to roll the entire 1671 mile length of the Alcan highway this week, carrying munitions and material to troops in Alaska. . . . The formal opening will probably take place Sunday afternoon, November 15, at the Alaskan-Canadian border.
>
> Ten thousand soldiers . . . and 2000 civilian workmen . . . completed the job in slightly over six months. They pushed forward at the rate of eight miles a day, bridged 200 streams, laid a roadway 24 feet between ditches, [and] at the highest point, between Fort Nelson and Watson Lake, reached an altitude of 4212 feet.
>
> Thousands of trucks will run all winter carrying soldiers and supplies to Alaskan posts. Plans are under way to haul strategic raw materials southward on the return trips. . . . [26]

In the rush to have this statement ready for Stimson's press conference, the subordinate who wrote it evidently did not have time to check all his facts. To be fair, the "official" mileage between Dawson Creek and Fairbanks kept dropping as the PRA's contractors continually straightened and shortened the Army's crooked pioneer trail; but the actual distance at that time was 52 miles less (1,619) than the figure announced by Stimson. Nor were his figures accurate with regard to the numbers of soldiers and civilian workmen engaged on the project. The total military workforce had grown to 11,782 by then, and the PRA's to at least 4,100.[27]

Stimson's statement contained several other inaccuracies, but these were attributable to uncertainties in Whitehorse rather than to sloppy staff work in Washington. Most notably, General O'Connor had not yet picked a site for the opening ceremony. While staging it at the Canadian-Alaskan border might have made good political sense, that particular part of the highway was the least-accessible stretch between Whitehorse and Fairbanks and consisted of nothing but a crudely bulldozed trail. What the Army needed for a backdrop was a more impressive example of the road-building prowess of the Corps of Engineers.

One of O'Connor's staff officers found the perfect location 162 miles west of Whitehorse, at a place now called Soldiers' Summit. The highest point on the roadway built by the 18th Engineers along the western shore of Kluane Lake that summer, the site commanded a breathtaking view. To the northeast, across the lake, the austere white contours of the Ruby and Nisling ranges rose a mile or more above its frozen surface. Paralleling the near shore, and towering nearly 7,000 feet above it, was the Kluane Range. Farther west, drawfing even these summits, loomed the St. Elias Mountains, where 12,000-foot peaks were so numerous that many hadn't yet been named.[28]

Having selected the site, O'Connor's staff began preparations to hold the opening ceremony on November 15, as tentatively announced by Secretary Stimson. But then, starting on November 10, a warm chinook wind swept over the southern sector of the highway for four straight days, pushing the temperature as high as 55°F and causing the 1-foot-thick ice on suddenly flooding rivers and streams to break up. Dozens of timber bridges, large and small, were battered and weakened by fast-moving floes; two gave way under the strain. First to collapse was a 148-foot span over the Smith River, 100 miles east of Watson Lake. Three days later, on November 13, despite attempts to break up the ice jam with dynamite, the mounting pressure tore a 200-foot gap in the PRA's recently completed, 2,200-foot, timber-pile Peace River bridge. Rather than hold an opening ceremony for a highway that was, in fact, closed, O'Connor postponed it. He picked a new date, November 20, ordered the damaged bridges repaired—and most likely prayed for the return of colder weather.

The Smith River structure was one of the 35th Engineers' bridges; by working round-the-clock, they rebuilt it in twenty-four hours. The Peace River bridge was harder to restore. It was not ready for traffic again until November 21. Meanwhile, General O'Connor went ahead with the opening ceremony.[29]

More than 200 guests had been invited. The Honorable Ian Mackenzie, Canada's Minister of Pensions and National Health, represented Prime Minister Mackenzie King. Other Canadian dignitaries included Dr. Charles Camsell, Northwest Territories Commissioner; Major General George R. Pearkes, Chief of the Canadian Army's Pacific Command; Major General H. N. Ganong, commanding the 8th Division; and Inspector William Grennan, head of the Royal Canadian Mounted Police in the Yukon Territory.

The senior American official attending was E. L. (Bob) Bartlett, Alaska's Secretary of State, standing in for Governor Ernest Gruening. General O'Connor was accompanied by most of his senior staff officers. The sector and regimental commanders were also invited. Finally, representing Mayor LaGuardia in his capacity as Co-

Chairman of the Permanent Joint Defense Board was Grover Whalen, former Police Commissioner and chief meeter-and-greeter of the City of New York. The usually dapper Whalen, whose political savvy, business skills, and urbane wit made him LaGuardia's man-for-all-occasions, arrived in Whitehorse looking rumpled after three days on the Greyhound Bus Line's inaugural run north from Fort St. John. General Hoge was, of course, not on the guest list.[30]

More sensitive to the care and feeding of VIPs than Hoge had been, O'Connor did his utmost to make the ceremony a memorable celebration. By the standards of the Yukon wilderness in the middle of November, the accommodations at Kluane Lake were deluxe. Stove-heated, generator-lit, and redolent of spruce planks and tar-paper, new dormitory barracks had been erected at the south end of the lake near the 1,050-foot Slim's River bridge. In the mess hall, thanks to the efforts of Army hunting parties, cooks were preparing such local delicacies as moose steaks and roast mountain sheep. Even the standard GI ration items had been "Yukonized" for the occasion. According to the menu, guests would nibble on "Fairbanks Cheese" and "Dawson Creek Crackers." Imported for the occasion, hothouse tomatoes and iceberg lettuce had become "Slim's River Salad."

With the ceremony scheduled for 9:30 A.M. on November 20, O'Connor's guests began arriving late the previous afternoon, making the bone-chilling five-hour drive out from Whitehorse in official sedans, open command cars, or Army trucks. Eventually, everyone was present and accounted for except General Pearkes and his party, whose flight from Fort St. John had been delayed by a storm over the mountains.

The evening passed in easy conversation around the barracks stoves; many people turned in early just to stay warm. When programs for the next day's festivities were passed out, one of the young black enlisted participants brought his to the senior officers' barracks and shyly asked if General O'Connor would autograph it. The general, clad only in his long johns, climbed out of his sleeping bag, put on his spectacles, and obliged—much to the amusement of his companions still awake. "That's the epitome of democracy, isn't it?" chuckled Alaska's Bob Bartlett.[31]

Around 2:00 A.M. up to the darkened barracks drove General Pearkes and his entourage, resplendent in their red-trimmed great-coats and gold braid. General O'Connor's aide, Lieutenant Richard L. Neuberger, recalled the scene:

I was awakened by a gentle padding on the lumber floor. . . . General O'Connor, in his long underwear, with his fur cap on his head and his parka thrown round his shoulders, was tip-toeing to the door. He threw it open . . . and in walked Generals Pearkes and Ganong. I lay there in my sleeping bag and struggled between comfort and duty. . . .   Could I stay in bed while [General O'Connor] welcomed our late-comers? Soon from a nearby bag another shape in long underwear emerged. It was Colonel K. B. Bush, our chief of staff. He and General O'Connor, looking like union-suit advertisements, were convoying the Canadian generals to their bunks. My conscience overcame my drowsy laziness and I got up and added my size 42 underwear to the scene. "You chaps look quite nifty in those," said . . . the aide to General Pearkes.[32]

As the sky over Kluane Lake slowly lightened next morning, the temperature stood at $-15°F$ and a dusting of tiny snowflakes fell lazily through the still air. At Soldiers' Summit, 10 miles from the Slim's River campsite, all was in readiness for the ceremony. To keep their instruments from freezing, members of the 18th Engineers' band waited inside heated tents on a knoll overlooking the road and the lake below. Some 30 feet of red, white, and blue ribbon stretched waist-high across the road, guarded by a line of Mounties standing at rigid attention in crimson tunics and high-top leather boots. Overhead, the U.S. and Canadian flags hung from freshly cut, spruce-trunk flagpoles. Several smoky bonfires crackled in the background, their plumes rising slowly into the gray overcast.

Shortly before 9:30, the convoy of army sedans and command cars arrived. The band played a medley of martial airs as the guests and participants gathered quickly around the ribbon. After the invocation, Colonel Bush made some opening remarks and took over as master of ceremonies. First came messages of congratulations from Vice President Henry Wallace, Alaska's Governor Gruening and Congressional Delegate Anthony Dimond, Secretary of War Stimson, General Somervell, Frederick Delano, Premier William Aberhart of Alberta, and Premier John Hart of British Columbia. General Pearkes brought greetings from Canada's armed forces. Each message was greeted by vigorous applause and foot-stomping—stimulated in equal measure, no doubt, by the sentiments expressed and the frigid setting.[33]

How cold it was can be judged by what happened during a slight pause midway through the ceremony. The Mounties, those paragons of stoic, disciplined endurance, suddenly "did a right turn as one man and marched with precision toward their tent. About halfway they broke ranks and ran into it, and set a record for a quick change into fur caps, buffalo coats, and mukluks."[34]

The guests of honor, Alaska's Bob Bartlett and Canada's Ian Mackenzie, spoke next. Bartlett presented O'Connor with an Alaskan flag from the Fairbanks chapter of the DAR. Mackenzie brought long-winded greetings from Prime Minister King and said of the highway: "Canada provided the soil; the United States provided the toil."

Heedless of the numbing cold, General O'Connor responded in kind. The road, he said, was a bond between the United States, Canada, and Alaska of incalculable significance for the future. He praised the courage, skill, and perseverance of the soldiers and civilians who had built it. These men, he speculated,

> would tell their children of the building of the road, and as the tales grew taller and taller, it was possible that the Alcan Highway might become an American saga ranking with the epics of Fremont and Lewis and Clark.[35]

The two honored guests jointly accepted a pair of gold-engraved scissors from Colonel Bush, who announced that President Roosevelt and Prime Minister King would each receive one of the blades. Four specially chosen American soldiers then moved forward to hold the ribbon. Representing the troops of the northern sector were the two 'dozer operators from the October 25 linkup near Beaver Creek, Corporal Sims and Private Jalufka. The southern sector sent Master Sergeant Andrew E. Doyle of Philadelphia and Corporal John T. Reilly of Detroit. Like Sims, Reilly was black.

Bartlett and Mackenzie stepped forward to cut the ribbon amidst rising cheers and the strains of "God Save the King" and the "Star-Spangled Banner." The music faded, a benediction was said, and Colonel Bush asked the spectators to clear the roadway for the first convoy through to Fairbanks. Around the bend from the south came a column of 2½-ton cargo trucks, led by the same Dodge weapons carrier which had pioneered the Dawson Creek–Whitehorse run back in September. In the cab of the Dodge, as before, were Corporal Gronke and Private Bowe. As the convoy began the twenty-four-hour, 460-mile trip to Fairbanks, the band sent them north on their lonely way with "The Maple Leaf Forever" and the "Washington Post March." By the time Gronke, Bowe, and their fellow drivers reached the bleak outwash valley beyond Kluane Lake, General O'Connor and his guests were sitting down to a feast of "moose steak à la

Donjek," "Pickhandle beans," "Karskawalsh potatoes," and "Horse Camp pudding." As they dined, the band played "Tales from the Vienna Woods" and "The Blue Danube."[36]

During the month of November alone, 1,000 trucks were dispatched north over the highway from Dawson Creek—the majority bound for destinations short of Whitehorse such as the airfields at Fort Nelson and Watson Lake and the various offshoot projects related to CANOL. Very few vehicles drove all the way through to Fairbanks. Although the road was now officially open from end to end, it was still really only an emergency supply route—particularly northwest of Whitehorse—and a very tenuous one at that.[37]

Keeping it open over the coming winter and intact through the spring breakup would tax the endurance and ingenuity of the Army Engineers; transforming whatever then remained of the original rough pioneer trail into a permanent, all-weather, two-lane highway would be no less a challenge for the PRA. The road to Alaska that opened on November 20, 1942, was not yet the highway it was to become.

PART THREE

Finishing Up

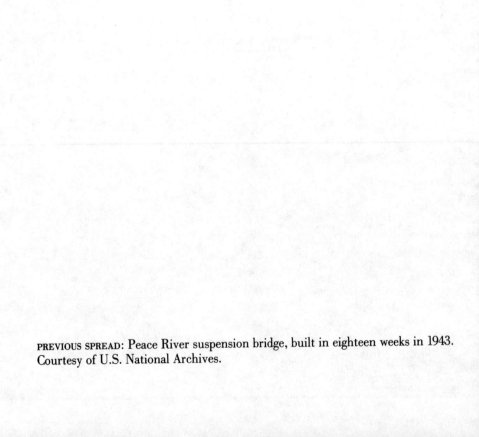

12

The Frostbite Express

The winter of 1942–1943 was one of the coldest ever recorded across much of northwest Canada and Alaska. Only once before, back in 1917, had denizens of the region seen temperatures sink so low for so many days at a time. As oldtimers well knew (and as the 35th Engineers had quickly learned the previous March), when the mercury dropped much below −30°F, metal tools turned brittle, machinery refused to operate, and the only sane thing to do was to stay indoors. The U.S. soldiers and civilians who were about to spend their first winter on the Alaska Highway and Project CANOL had been given a "cold-weather orientation," but no routine briefing could fully prepare them for the climatic realities of a region where the temperature could reach −70°F.[1]

Regardless of the frigid weather, General O'Connor's orders were explicit: keep the Alaska Highway open as a supply line; stockpile materials for repairing spring washouts and flood damage; begin work on the Whitehorse refinery and CANOL 1 pipeline; put the highway's petroleum distribution pipelines (CANOL 2, 3, and 4) into operation as soon as possible; and see that needed supplies get to Norman Wells over the winter trails of CANOL 6.[2]

If insufficient supplies got through to Norman Wells over the winter trails, Colonel Wyman intended to deliver more by air. There was only one problem with this plan: cargo planes taking off from Edmonton for Norman Wells would need to refuel at Fort Simpson on both legs of the round trip, but little aviation gasoline was stockpiled there. Moving enough fuel to Fort Simpson to support a massive emergency airlift thus meant building another winter trail, this one starting at Fort Nelson and running north through 250 miles of muskeg forest to the nearly completed airstrip at the confluence of the Liard and Mackenzie rivers. Work began at the Fort Nelson end of the Fort Simpson trail in early November. With Task Force 2600 already stretched thin, Wyman had to borrow manpower from one of the Engineer regiments then finishing up on the highway. The lucky outfit to get this new assignment was a battalion from the 35th Engineers commanded by the best man for the job, (recently promoted) Captain Mike Miletich.[3]

As if all these balls weren't enough for General O'Connor to juggle, he soon had another one thrown at him. On November 10, 1942, General Somervell ordered construction to begin on the "Haines Cutoff"—an all-weather road intended to link the port of Haines, near the head of the Inside Passage, to a point on the Alaska Highway midway between Whitehorse and Kluane Lake. This would enable ocean cargo bound for the northern half of the highway to bypass the Skagway–Whitehorse transportation bottleneck. For Somervell, such a time-saving advantage outweighed the extra cost and effort of building another 158 miles of road—50 miles of it over Chilkat Pass, a route so steep and rough that an estimated 2,225,000 cubic yards of soil and rock would have to be excavated before trucks could make the grade. Nor was Somervell deterred by reports that Army and PRA survey parties working their way through the pass were encountering swirling whiteouts and 30-foot snow drifts.[4]

Such extreme conditions were relatively rare farther inland. Just as the Army had predicted in defending its choice of the Inland Route against the criticisms of Senator Langer and others, snowfall along much of the main line of the highway was normally measured in inches, not feet. Routine plowing and sanding sufficed to keep traffic moving in most areas.

The most difficult winter problem turned out to be ice. Ice buildup occurred in cutaway areas along the highway wherever groundwater veins had been exposed. The slowly freezing seepage clogged drainage ditches and culverts and then rose inexorably to spread an ever-thickening layer over the road. Maintenance crews had to cope with hundreds of such "mini-glaciers," the largest burying half-mile stretches of the right of way under as much as 6 feet of ice.

One quick solution was to keep the iced-over stretches sanded and pretend they were the road; another was to build temporary bypass trails. Where conditions made these options impracticable, only three other ways remained to deal with the problem: blast the ice out with dynamite (difficult to do without damaging the road); chop it up with pickaxes; or melt it away with diesel-fueled hot-air blowers or steam jets. Blowers or steam jets were also essential for reopening ice-clogged culverts and keeping them open, thus preventing the buildup from starting all over again. The long-term solution—putting in larger culverts and better drainage systems—was, of course, part of the PRA's mission for the coming summer.

A different type of ice buildup occurred in the permafrost region northwest of Kluane Lake, where the swift-flowing streams tended to freeze from the bottom up. This was another peculiar sub-arctic phenomenon not mentioned in Army field manuals. As the rapidly thickening bottom ice pushed the turbulent water above it ever higher, the stream eventually flooded the surrounding countryside, where the buildup continued beneath the onward rushing flow. The Engineers were well-prepared for the damage that ice jams and fast-moving floes could do to their temporary timber spans, but they stood by, helpless and astonished, as a number of their bridges were completely enveloped by a gently rising mantle of white. Such structures had to be written off as a total loss. Buried under an icy shroud until spring, they were sure to be swept away during the breakup.

For much of the winter, ice buildup from flooded streams and groundwater seepage closed long sections of the highway from the Donjek River on the Canadian side of the border all the way to Big Delta, Alaska. Farther south, the problems tended to be more localized and easily remedied, since they resulted mainly from ice-blocked culverts. In the mountainous region between Fort Nelson and Watson Lake, more than eighty such trouble spots required constant tending.[5]

A more vexing problem, north or south, was the question of who was responsible for maintenance work on any given stretch of road. The question quickly became a sore point between the Army and the PRA. While the confusion and friction between the two organizations over this issue undoubtedly had many causes, one major contributor was the series of constantly changing Army directives issued on the subject of winter maintenance. Another was the baffling, if not downright bizarre, management style of Colonel Wyman. As the newly appointed Northwest Division Engineer, Wyman had become responsible for directing all engineering work on both CANOL and the Alaska Highway. His ostentatious new headquarters on the grounds of the Jesuit College in Edmonton reflected one aspect of

Wyman's way of doing business. His tendency to make impetuous decisions without consulting his staff revealed another.

In late July 1942, when it began to look as though there might be enough of a road finished to be worth keeping open all winter, General Sturdevant had given the task of maintenance to the PRA. Although Engineer troops were still doing much of the plowing and sanding when Wyman took over as Division Engineer on December 1, the PRA was in the process of organizing and deploying enough of its civilian contractors to comply with Sturdevant's July directive.

Wyman immediately and peremptorily countermanded that order with one of his own. Henceforth, he said, all winter maintenance would be done by soldiers. The PRA responded by sending the bulk of its civilian workforce home for the rest of the winter. But then, right after Christmas, Wyman issued a new directive splitting the job 50/50. Even as the contractors scrambled to get some of their workmen back, Wyman decided to go back to the status quo ante. By mid-January, the PRA was once more primarily responsible for winter maintenance of the highway—at least officially. In reality, however, as a result of Wyman's vacillations, the PRA's contractors were now so shorthanded that they had to rely on Army help to do the upkeep on many sections. Army-PRA relations, never cordial, sank with the temperature.[6]

Wyman's original plan to keep the highway open using only troop labor made sense as long as enough Engineer regiments were available to him. Their upkeep was a fixed expense to Uncle Sam wherever they were sent; temporarily reducing the size of the highway's civilian workforce would save the government money. Wyman's mistake was in failing to realize how overcommitted the dwindling Engineer units on the highway already were. Had members of his staff been allowed to do their normal job of anticipating, checking, and coordinating, they could have saved him much embarrassment.

Perhaps Wyman saw himself as a bold and decisive manager like Somervell, but he possessed neither his superior's ability nor his power. What the two men had most in common was ambition and a growing number of enemies. An Army Service Forces inspector, Colonel George Horowitz, scornfully described the atmosphere in Wyman's headquarters as reflecting "mental desuetude, physical paralysis, resort to processes of temporization, empiricism, mysticism, and insouciance."[7]

Given General Somervell's determination to prove the value of the Alaska Highway as a supply line for both Project CANOL and the airfields of the Northwest Staging Route, the Dawson Creek railhead was a very busy place that winter—all the more so because weather-related accidents and breakdowns, plus an occasional avalanche, had cut by half the flow of supplies reaching Whitehorse via the White Pass and Yukon Railroad.[8]

On November 13, 1942, the Dawson Creek commander, Colonel Twichell, at last had time to explain to Frances why she hadn't received a letter from him in a month. "I have been simply snowed under," he said, "and . . . have been just too fagged out to even think of writing." He continued:

> The railhead is a very small bottleneck through which is being poured all the tremendous stores needed to put the road in operation. . . . It has been a hard fight to get the material—nails, lumber, roofing paper and the like, and labor, fast enough to build warehouses for incoming goods. Usually a warehouse will be full before the roof is up. . . . Solid trainloads of trucks are arriving and must be serviced and put on the road. . . . We have been just a jump ahead of the hounds all the time, but so far we have kept our yards fairly clean, and have shoved stuff North as fast or faster than it arrived. Already we have shipped out a good part of the material needed to house the troops, mostly steel huts . . . which are really quite warm and comfortable and can be erected quickly. . . .
>
> There are a hundred new problems to be met and overcome in the operation of the road. . . . Providing shops for instance, for repairing all the thousands of trucks that will be in operation this winter, huge parts warehouses, protection against freezing for rations, and a host more. . . .
>
> Have had our first touch of winter, with the thermometer down to 20 degrees below. Work goes on unabated through this, and the increasing night. We have only about 8 hours of daylight now, and the days will be still shorter in mid-winter.[9]

The skilled labor to construct all these new facilities at Dawson Creek was provided by Colonel Lane's 341st Engineers and several of the PRA's civilian contractors. Most of the unloading and warehousing of supplies was done by black soldiers, in this case members of a battalion from Twichell's former command, the 95th Engineers. Thus, as of mid-November, with all of the 341st and half of the 95th concentrated at Dawson Creek, plus one battalion of the 35th Engineers engaged in cutting the winter trail to Fort Simpson, the only troop units fully available to Colonel Ingalls for highway maintenance in the southern sector were a battalion each from the

35th and 95th Engineer Regiments. He had no choice but to ask for help from the PRA.[10]

In the northern sector, Colonel Paules had considerably more troops available, for the moment at least. But given the terrible condition of the road between the Donjek River and Big Delta, there was already more than enough work for the PRA in his sector as well. Moreover, on January 1, 1943, the 18th and 93rd Engineers were scheduled for transfer to General Buckner's Alaskan Defense Command, which would leave only two regiments, the 97th and 340th, under Paules's control.[11]

A further complication arose when 1,700 brand-new 2½-ton cargo trucks arrived in Dawson Creek (the "solid trainloads" mentioned by Twichell) almost two months ahead of the 2,000 Quartermaster soldiers who were supposed to drive and maintain them. Since the trucks were needed at once for hauling supplies, it was necessary to levy the Engineer regiments along the highway for enough drivers and mechanics to set up a makeshift convoy system.[12]

No commander in his right mind—especially one already hard-pressed to fulfill his own primary mission—volunteers his best men in such a situation. But no faster way to ruin a fleet of new trucks could have been devised than to send them out in sub-zero weather over one of the world's most hazardous roads with inexperienced drivers at the wheel.

Not all of the thousands of accidents and breakdowns that occurred along the highway that winter could be blamed on driver error, however. The U.S. Army's ordnance experts still had a lot to learn about the design and maintenance of vehicles that could hold up under such extreme conditions. With Ingalls's cooperation, the highway's southern sector soon became a kind of cold-weather automotive test track. Twichell's office served as the data bank.

Told to compile statistics on every aspect of convoy operations—not just the usual miles driven and tons hauled—Twichell's staff began keeping track of the performance of each truck, noting such things as the number and type of breakdowns, the distance between breakdowns of the same kind, the temperature and weather conditions at the time, and the type of motor oil being used. One of the first things that became obvious from this mass of data was that the rate of most types of mechanical failure went up dramatically at temperatures below −30°F, a problem eventually alleviated by the use of specially formulated cold-weather lubricants.[13]

The data in the files at Twichell's headquarters acted as a magnet that attracted all sorts of people with an official need to know, including representatives from the major automotive and heavy-equipment manufacturers whose products were then in use along the highway. These men were the real-life counterparts of the resourceful Alexander Botts, the fictional field representative of the "Earthworm Tractor Company," whose humorous exploits were periodically chronicled by William H. Upson in the *Saturday Evening Post.* Like Botts, these men were useful to the Army as problem solvers and spare-parts expediters. Like Botts, many of them were so useful that they enjoyed the prestige, privileges, and pay of a commissioned officer while continuing to act as middlemen between the Army and their former employers. Like Botts they were even more useful to the corporations they represented. What better way was there to impress the Army with your company's desire to meet its needs, while keeping a close eye on the competition at the same time?

During his visit to the highway in the summer of 1942, William Upson almost surely encountered the Caterpillar Tractor Company's man in Dawson Creek, a Mr. Hotelling. Perhaps Upson also met C. N. Schultheis, the Studebaker Corporation's senior representative there. What follows are excerpts from a long report to the home office by Schultheis mailed on February 3, 1943. Alexander Botts might have written it.

After making sure his boss understood just exactly how cold it was in Dawson Creek, how primitive the accommodations were, how much red tape he had to put up with, and how much easier his job would be if the factory would just ship all those back-ordered parts, Schultheis got down to business:

> We have carefully and deliberately met General O'Connor; Colonels Wheeler, Soderstrom . . . and other officers who are really in command of the highway and the truck operation. We have discussed in detail [the parts shortage] as it applies to the Studebaker truck operation, which is vastly in the majority here over all other makes. [Of the 1,700 new trucks, 1,500 were Studebakers; the rest were made by G.M.C.] Frankly, Studebaker has an opportunity here to do for Studebaker, after the war, just what the old four-cylinder Dodge, in World War I, done for Dodge after that war. . . .
>
> The exact locations of individual trucks are not immediately known. . . . Some are operating locally at camp, some in highway freight hauling; perhaps 500 total [awaiting repair]; and about 500 are loaned to subcontractors [for] "Canol," who are laying a pipeline . . . ; "Catel," who are just now setting poles and stringing telephone wires along the highway, only sixty miles north of Dawson Creek. . . .

Competition is represented as follows: Gardner Lewis, G.M.C., at Fairbanks on cold operation investigation; and with plenty of money to spend he has the inside track there. . . . At Dawson Creek, the Greyhound Bus Lines have five or six men, and they are operating . . . buses over the southern 250 miles of the road. . . . The Greyhound men have the inside track [here], due mainly to an endless supply of money and liquid refreshments, which talks here because there is absolutely no other means of entertainment. . . . So with an absolute minimum expenditure for liquid refreshments, we have gained a friendly confidence of the . . . Ordnance, Quartermaster and Engineer officers, who are cooperating to keep Studebaker in the front. . . . I was offered a Captaincy, which, of course, is not good enough financially . . . nothing less than a Majority would be adequate or justified to permit one to do a job here. . . .

After several pages devoted to how much he was doing about the spare parts shortage and what more the home office could do to help, Schultheis came back to the subject of Studebaker's competitors:

Oh yes, I almost forgot to include—White Motors is represented by Mr. Fred Huber. Chrysler by Mr. Crowell. Caterpillar by Mr. Hotelling, and Cummins Diesel by Mr. Paul Phillips.

The few G.M.C. trucks appear too lightly built and the drivers say the "Jimmies" positively do not have as much power as the Studebakers have. . . . Most G.M.C. units look sorely in need of a general overhaul. . . . Practically every truck on the Highway, regardless of make, is equipped with a G.M.C. deluxe hot water heater in the cab. . . . It gets our goats to be greeted with a nice big G.M.C. nameplate every time we get into a truck built at our factory. The installation [of our heaters] at the factory would be very, very helpful. . . .

Last came a paragraph detailing Schultheis's expenses, showing how frugal he was with company money. He closed with a final reminder: "We want to do a good job here and we think we can do it if we get the much needed parts quickly."[14]

The name CATEL that Schultheis briefly mentioned in his report was short for "Canadian Telephone." The purpose of this project, at a cost of $4.3 million, was to provide reliable, multichannel telephone and teletype communication with the outside world for every Army and Air Force installation along the Alaska Highway, with a branch line north to Camp CANOL as well. In a setup much like the one devised for CANOL, civilian contractors were hired to construct the CATEL system while depending on nearby military installations for basic logistical support. Most of the line-stringing work was handled by two firms, Oman and Smith and the Miller Construction Company.[15]

Although field surveys for CATEL were begun in late October 1942, the Miller Company needed another month to assemble enough men and equipment to start setting poles and stringing wire at the Edmonton end of the 2,000-mile line to Fairbanks. The company's first goal, established with much fanfare by the U.S. Army Signal Corps, was to have the line up and working as far as Dawson Creek by December 1. Like many other Americans in northwest Canada that winter, Miller's workmen were not really prepared for the difficulties they encountered. Dynamite had to be used in place of earth augers to allow workers to set telephone poles in the solidly frozen ground—over a distance of 442 miles.

As December 1 approached, it was clear that the line would still be well south of Dawson Creek on that date. The Signal Corps project officer for CATEL, Major Ora Roberts, came to Colonel Twichell looking for help in averting an embarrassing crisis. He got it.

When Brigadier General Frank Stoner, the Assistant Chief of the Signal Corps, received a call in his Washington home at 7:45 P.M. on December 1, the senior officer at Dawson Creek was speaking on the other end. "He never suspected," Twichell later wrote, "that the last few miles of the line were laid on the bare ground, with soldiers patrolling every few hundred yards to fix breaks or shorts as they occurred."[16]

Such cooperation to keep the higher-ups unaware of things that might make them angry occurs in every organization. Soldiers have their own name for the practice: "the old Army game." Twichell was clearly no slouch at it; General O'Connor seems to have been a better player than General Hoge; and General Somervell was in a class by himself. But soldiers of any rank could play, as illustrated by another of Twichell's stories from his days at Dawson Creek.

None of the well-insulated new Quonset huts that housed the railhead's 1,500-man garrison had indoor plumbing. Since a nighttime trip to the distant row of privies could be a numbing experience at −50° or −60°F, the area closest to the barracks began to take on the appearance of a congealed open-air cesspool. Having "called this to the attention of those concerned" and observed immediate improvement, Twichell soon forgot the matter. "However," he recalled, "[sixteen] months later I was visiting old friends in the 341st in England prior to the jump off in France. Among the songs with which I was regaled was the following set to appropriate music:

We go in the snow
And cover it up
So the old man won't know.[17]

Not every mess created by the massive American presence in Dawson Creek could be overlooked easily. Late in the afternoon of February 13, 1943, an employee of the Oman and Smith Construction Company named Glen Barnhardt parked his truck at one end of a livery stable near the center of town and went to find a bite to eat before heading north to the company camp near Fort St. John. The stable was also used for storage and maintenance by CATEL's other contractor, the Miller Construction Company, and several Miller employees joined Barnhardt for supper. While the group was eating, a fire started in the stable and rapidly spread to the adjacent buildings.

Although the town firefighters were quickly reinforced by soldiers from the base and soon had the blaze contained, they had no idea what hazards they were facing until Barnhardt told them that his truck was loaded with sixty cases of dynamite. Worse yet, unbeknownst to Barnhardt, twenty cases of blasting caps were temporarily being stored at the Miller Company's end of the stable. The firemen frantically tried to warn away the crowd of onlookers, but too late. Suddenly, the caps and dynamite went off, engulfing everything within a radius of several hundred feet in a white-hot fireball and scattering burning debris and shards of glass for blocks around. Orval Couch was there:

> You didn't know which way to move because all that stuff was coming down from the sky, and if you moved to one side you might get your brains knocked out. I was standing alongside a Yankee boy and he says to me "Hey Mac, give me a hand, will ya?" I turns around and here was about four inches of white bone sticking out through the pants of his tunic. Something had hit him. It happened just that quick.[18]

Within seconds, the heart of Dawson Creek was ablaze. Townspeople and soldiers who were not injured by the initial blast battled the fire with buckets and brooms through the night and kept it from spreading beyond the business district. But in the morning all that remained of a block-square cluster of stores, restaurants, and hotels was a smoking ash heap and several forlorn, free-standing brick chimneys. Although the casualties from the blast were remarkably low, they were bad enough: 5 people killed and 164 more with assorted burns, cuts, and broken bones. With help from the U.S. Army, the downtown area was quickly rebuilt; but for many in Dawson Creek, nothing was ever again quite the same—including their feelings about the "Yankee boys."[19]

Twichell was in Dawson Creek on the night of the "great fire," but he was no longer the railhead commander. He had just taken charge of the southern sector, after having gone to Fort St. John in early January to understudy Colonel Ingalls for a month before replacing him. (As part of the phased withdrawal of Engineer units following completion of the pioneer road, command of the northern sector also changed at this time, with Colonel Russell Lyons, the 340th's Commanding Officer, taking over from Colonel Earl Paules. In this latest round of military musical chairs, Twichell's old job at Dawson Creek went to Colonel Albert Lane, Commanding Officer of the 341st Engineers.) Ingalls, who had long been suffering from a stomach ulcer and needed better food and medical care than he had been getting, was being reassigned to command Camp Ellis, a new training base in Illinois.

A kindly man despite his reputation as a hard taskmaster, Ingalls was very proud of what the 35th Engineers had achieved during his thirteen months as their commander, and his fatherly concern for the welfare of his former outfit had been no less strong since that time. The last order he ever had to give the regiment left him in anguish.

On January 24, 1943, General O'Connor sent Ingalls a message instructing him to build yet another winter trail, this one to serve as an access road for the civilian contractors who would soon begin work on the 577-mile CANOL 1 pipeline that was to bring crude oil from Norman Wells over the Mackenzie and Pelly mountains to the refinery at Whitehorse. The 35th's new mission (Miletich's battalion having just finished the 248-mile Fort Nelson–Fort Simpson winter trail) was to construct the southern half of this pipeline access road—from Johnson's Crossing on the Alaska Highway northward through a series of narrow passes, across the Pelly River, and on toward Sheldon Lake. So difficult was this terrain that an American surveyor named Kent Fuller, dispatched from Whitehorse the previous September to lay out the route, had not yet reached Sheldon Lake when the 35th Engineers received their orders. (Meanwhile, the equally rugged stretch from Norman Wells to the lake had been surveyed by a Canadian team headed by Guy Blanchet. Both Fuller and Blanchet traveled by dog sled and relied heavily on native guides.)[20]

"I was with Colonel Ingalls . . . when he received this telegram [from O'Connor]," Twichell recalled:

and remained with him until he had sent the necessary one to Major McCarty. Then he sat for some time with his head in his hands, completely sunk in despair. I shared his feelings. It was a tough job to give anybody. Particularly since he was going to the States in a few days, and so would be unable to follow the doings of his beloved "galloping canaries."[21]

With the 35th Engineers now fully engaged in constructing the access road for CANOL 1, and the 341st still working in and around Dawson Creek, the dreary job of hauling supplies and maintaining the recently completed trail to Fort Simpson fell to the black 95th Engineers. Despite spending much of their time hunkered down against the bitter cold in makeshift shelters, they managed to keep the hard-frozen pathway open except during the worst blizzards. Twichell worried less about the 95th's morale after he heard about the sign at the entrance to their base camp, halfway to Fort Simpson. "Welcome to Little Siberia," it said.[22]

The northern sector commander faced all the same problems as his counterpart at Fort St. John—and then some. The road in the vicinity of the Alaskan border was often in such bad shape that not even the 18th and 97th Engineers' own supply trucks could get through, let alone the much publicized "Fairbanks Freight" from Dawson Creek. Emergency supplies of food and fuel frequently had to be flown in or dropped by parachute to the most isolated units, sometimes in weather so bad that Army pilots could refuse to accept the mission.

When that happened, Colonel Paules turned to Les Cook, who had been General Hoge's civilian pilot on so many flights the previous summer. Already a hero to more than one company of cold and hungry soldiers, Les Cook's name passed into highway legend on the night of November 17, 1942. Two days earlier, a few miles north of the Donjek River, a soldier in Company "D" of the 29th Topographic Battalion, a surveyor working with the 18th Engineers, was stricken with appendicitis. Contacted by radio, Whitehorse promised to dispatch an evacuation plane. It never arrived. As the patient's condition worsened, the 18th's doctor sent another radio message: to save the man's life an immediate appendectomy was now necessary, but he lacked the proper instruments to perform it. A surgical team would have to fly out from Whitehorse. "The weather was bad, extremely cold, the sky overcast," said the regimental historian. This is what happened next:

A affirmative radio was received and we learned . . . that Les Cook and two Army surgeons [had] volunteered for the dangerous mission. Because of the overcast, Cook flew past the Donjek and did not know his position until he recognized the White River [35 miles beyond] through a break in the clouds [and] turned the plane south. All vehicles that could be found near the Donjek were now lined up on the sand flat in darkness, their feeble lights outlining the emergency landing place.

We had an hour or so to convert the front of [a] barracks into an operating room . . . by hanging blankets on wires. . . . The minutes dragged by as we waited for the sound of a plane. The wind howled outside driving snow flurries before it. To fly a plane up the valleys and land in the basin on that dark night seemed suicidal. At nine o'clock the plane dipped above the camp and gunned the engine as a signal. . . . The ambulance picked up the medical officers and ten minutes later they entered the "operating room" shaking snow off their clothes. An hour was spent sterilizing instruments . . . scrubbing up, donning sterile gowns. . . . A spinal block failed and the operation was performed after preparation of an ether mask. . . . The job was finished at midnight. The patient convalesced at this camp.[23]

Les Cook was awarded the Army's Legion of Merit for this gallant mercy flight, but he did not live to receive it. Less than three weeks later, he died in a crash-landing on a Whitehorse street after his engine stalled out during a routine test flight. The northern sector officers took up a collection to pay Cook's funeral expenses. With the money left over, they bought a gold watch for his son, then just an infant. On the case was this inscription:

To Leslie Rand Cook, as a token of esteem and high regard felt by officers of the United States Army for his father as a pilot and friend. December, 1942.[24]

By late December, the 18th and 93rd Regiments had been taken off the highway and were en route, via Whitehorse and Skagway, to their new assignments in Alaska. (Both units would participate in the campaign that spring to push the Japanese out of the Aleutians.) Their departure left Colonel Lyons, the new Commanding Officer for the northern sector, with only the 97th and 340th Engineers under his command. Although Colonel Wyman's most recent directive specified that the PRA was thenceforth to be primarily responsible for winter maintenance of the highway, Lyons took a flexible and pragmatic approach. His soldiers gave the PRA a hand whenever and wherever they could, as long as it didn't interfere with their other missions.

Since the black 97th Engineers were not given any other important assignments until April, road maintenance was all they did that winter. Prior to late January, however, Colonel Robinson's men were often so short of food, fuel, and warm winter clothing that their first priority was sheer survival. Living in drafty, improvised shelters spaced along 140 miles of highway from Tanacross, Alaska, to Beaver Creek near the Yukon border, the regiment was stationed too far from its supply base in Whitehorse—a 700-mile round trip, when trucks could get through.

A move to heated barracks near the airbase at Big Delta, less than 100 miles southeast of Fairbanks, did wonders for the 97th's efficiency and morale. (The regiment next moved to Livengood, 85 miles north of Fairbanks, and worked on a pioneer trail in the direction of Nome until June, when General Somervell canceled the Fairbanks-to-Nome leg of the Alaska Highway.)[25]

In March, the 340th Engineers went back into the business of road construction, when the 2nd Battalion was given the mission of building the northern half of the Haines cutoff. Starting southward into the mountains toward Haines from a point on the Alaska Highway 108 miles west of Whitehorse, the battalion's forward elements were soon isolated and all but immobilized by the spring breakup. Resupplied by air until June, they finally linked up with the PRA's Haines-based contractors on August 1 near Chilkat Pass.[26]

Meanwhile, Bechtel-Price-Callahan had completed CANOL 2, and the first tankerload of gasoline was pumped to Whitehorse from Skagway over the 4-inch pipeline on January 20, 1943. Soon thereafter, BPC's crews began extending a 2-inch distribution line toward Watson Lake (CANOL 3) and a 3-inch line toward Fairbanks (CANOL 4). It was midsummer, however, before gasoline reached Watson Lake via CANOL 3, and Fairbanks received none at all via CANOL 4 until the following winter. Work on both pipelines had to be suspended for several months during and after the spring breakup when washed-out bridges and mudslides once again made long stretches of the highway impassable.[27]

CANOL 1 also had its share of problems during the winter of 1942–1943. These began with Secretary of the Interior/Petroleum Coordinator for War Harold Ickes, who was still adamantly opposed to the project. Calling CANOL a "crack-brain scheme," he managed for several months to block the Army's attempts to acquire a small, used refinery located in Corpus Christi, Texas, for shipment to Whitehorse. When Ickes grudgingly relented under all the pressure General Somervell could muster, it was mid-November.

Transporting a dismantled refinery from Texas to the Yukon and reassembling it in Whitehorse would have been a difficult job in the best of circumstances. Rather than damage or lose some complex piece of machinery en route, it seemed more sensible to wait until the dense fog and unpredictable winter storms abated on the Inside Passage and the avalanche season on the White Pass and Yukon Line was over. CANOL 1's refinery finally began to take shape in Whitehorse in April 1943.

As for the access road for the CANOL 1 pipeline, spring found the 35th Engineers bogged down in the muskeg of the Pelly River Valley, about 100 miles north of the Alaska Highway and halfway to their goal, Sheldon Lake. Another 400 miles farther north, BPC's road builders had made even less progress toward Sheldon Lake from their starting point at Camp CANOL. The two groups were still over 200 miles apart when the 35th Engineers reached Sheldon Lake and were ordered back to the United States in July 1943. At that point, only about 200 miles of actual pipeline had been laid.[28]

Most disappointing of all were the results of CANOL 6. Of the total of 19,188 tons of cargo dispatched over the winter trails from Peace River and Fort Smith, only 5,293 tons reached Norman Wells. Another 3,567 tons—mostly fuel and food—were consumed en route, as intended, but that still left 10,328 tons of supplies cached at various points along the Mackenzie River and the Grimshaw Road, well short of their destination. At an enormous cost in effort and resources, CANOL 6 had delivered about one-third of the cargo it was supposed to. The percentage would have been even lower had Colonel Wyman not switched to trucks in midwinter and stopped using the cumbersome, slow-moving tractor-trains.

Events on the sidelines of CANOL 6 did nothing to help Wyman's standing with General Somervell—or with the men of the 388th Engineers. Isolated and all but forgotten at Fort Smith, Wansley Hill and the rest of Company "B" did survive the winter, thanks mainly to their ability to find ingenious ways to fight the numbing boredom and cold. Indeed, so frigid were their log quarters that Hill's friend George Young kept a frozen moose haunch under his bunk, now and then hacking off a slice and cooking it on the barracks stove to supplement the monotonous mess hall chow.[29]

Adding a final note of futility to the CANOL 6 operation were the figures for the Fort Nelson–Fort Simpson winter trail. Only 297 barrels of aviation gasoline were delivered to Fort Simpson before Wyman canceled his plans for an emergency airlift to Norman Wells—a move that rendered the entire trail unnecessary. After less than a month in their "Little Siberia," the 95th Engineers were glad to abandon it.[30]

What happened next was predictable. On March 25, 1943, Colonel Wyman was relieved of his duties as Northwest Division Engineer. His successor was Colonel Ludson D. Worsham, Corps of Engineers, who shortly thereafter became a brigadier general.[31]

Whether Project CANOL's benefits would ever justify all the cost and effort involved was still an open question after almost a year. By contrast, the commanders responsible for the Alaska Highway had considerably more cause for both satisfaction and hope. "Dear Folks," Twichell wrote on March 14, 1943:

> In two or three days, it will be just a year since we arrived in the North Country, and how much has happened in that short time. Looking back, the months are crowded full of accomplishment, and the memory of stirring events. Recently I flew to Whitehorse . . . over my section of the road, about 1000 miles in all. . . . It still seems impossible that in the short space of months what was an unmapped wilderness has become a civilized community. Everywhere I saw long lines of trucks, rushing north with all the supplies and food that will be needed to sustain the troops and contractors' men during the period of the break-up that is just around the corner now. Permanent bridges are under construction at the principal streams. . . . Telephone lines are going in, and new roads leading to landing fields along the way. . . .
>
> My principal responsibility now is to get up all the supplies in time, and this involves a lot of thought and planning. . . . Fortunately, we have . . . had some reasonably cold weather which we hope will continue for a few weeks yet, as with the thaw will come all the bottomless mud and swollen streams that we struggled with last spring. I shall breathe a sigh of relief when we have gotten our . . . supplies up, and can sit back and let nature take its course.
>
> Aside from this, things are fast becoming routine, as with civilian agencies taking over the construction work, and troops of other branches taking over the operation, the work of this headquarters is becoming . . . less and less important. It is possible that I may have a new assignment . . . soon. I feel that my work is about wound up, and would be happy to move on to some more exciting field.[32]

Within a month, he got his wish. And by midsummer, all of the remaining Engineer regiments that had participated in pushing the pioneer trail through to Alaska were also on their way to "more exciting fields"—some to the South Pacific, and others to England to prepare for the Normandy Invasion. After a short assignment in the States, Twichell was sent on to England.

13

MARCH 1942–OCTOBER 1943

Cut, Fill, and Straighten

Wartime military considerations and the tough professionalism of the U.S. Army Corps of Engineers brought the Alaska Highway into existence. But their rapidly bulldozed pioneer road was never intended to be more than a "rough draft" of the all-weather gravel highway subsequently built by the Public Roads administration and its consortium of American and Canadian civilian contractors. For all of its continuing problems with dust, rough spots, and washouts, the postwar highway was a much better road than it might have been. Even though the Corps of Engineers set the specifications and controlled the project, the PRA's inherent tendency to reject temporary expedients in favor of permanent solutions led to many disagreements with the Army over construction methods and standards. Moreover, the PRA won enough of these arguments to ensure that what would be left to the North American public at the end of the war was not just a hastily constructed and already deteriorating emergency supply route.

For most of its seventy-plus years of existence as an agency of the United States government, the PRA has been better known as the Bureau of Public Roads. The goal of the original bureau was to improve America's rural roads for the benefit of farmers. Although this remained a fundamental purpose of the BPR after World War I, other important functions were added as the nation became increasingly motorized: setting standards for road and bridge construction; researching improved materials and equipment; and performing

240

traffic density studies to aid in planning the national highway system. In addition, using local contractors hired for each specific project, the BPR was responsible for constructing and maintaining all roads within the national park system. By the eve of World War II, under the leadership of Thomas H. MacDonald, an experienced highway engineer and a careful and far-seeing administrator, the BPR/PRA had come to possess considerable clout.[1]

Just prior to the attack on Pearl Harbor, Congress passed the Defense Highway Act, which directed the PRA to concern itself solely with projects needed to bolster the national defense. When the War Department finally got serious about building a highway to Alaska in February 1942, the PRA was a natural choice to assist the Army Corps of Engineers. It was to be a cooperative undertaking between two powerful federal organizations.

The original agreement between the Army and the PRA regarding the highway was worked out in a series of letters in March 1942 between Commissioner MacDonald and Brigadier General Sturdevant, Assistant to the Chief of Engineers. Using the Army's pioneer road as an access trail, the PRA was to survey, locate, and lay out the route of the finished highway; prepare plans, specifications, and estimates for building it; and hire and supervise the civilian contractors needed to get the job done.

The Alaska Highway was the largest single project ever undertaken by the PRA. Many of its best engineers and management personnel were quickly diverted from less essential tasks and given new assignments related to the highway: surveying the proposed route; finding the best sites for bridge crossings, gravel pits, sawmills, and work camps; requisitioning office and storage facilities in nearby towns; and scouring the United States for unused prefabricated buildings, furnishings, tools, construction equipment, and winter clothing. Finally, they were to recruit and place under contract the fifty or more construction firms that would do the actual work.

With wartime priorities and procedures still being decided, the scramble for resources to support the national mobilization then underway was frantic. Fortunately, many of the items on the PRA's "shopping list" were still the property of two New Deal agencies that had been made superfluous by the wartime revival of the economy—the Civilian Construction Corps (CCC) and Work Projects Administration (WPA). From CCC camps in Minnesota, Montana, Washington, and Oregon came completely furnished prefabricated buildings of all types, everything from dormitory barracks and mess halls to kitchens and machine shops. In padlocked CCC and WPA warehouses, purchasing agents found thousands of other used but supposedly serviceable items, from bulldozers and road scrapers to typewriters and adding machines. North it all went, by road, rail, or ship. There was no time to weed out the junk; the prevailing policy seemed to be: "We'll sort it out at the other end, and what doesn't work can be cannibalized."[2]

Sorting it out at the other end proved to be a logistician's nightmare. During one five-week period in the spring of 1942, 600 boxcars and flatcars of PRA supplies and equipment rolled into Dawson Creek, already jammed with the Army's gear, while 200 more carloads were backed up at Prince Rupert awaiting barges for Skagway or Valdez. Spare covered warehouse space was nonexistent; with every gymnasium, movie theater, and curling rink as far away as Edmonton long since requisitioned for storage, there was no alternative but to stack materials outdoors in the mud until they could be picked up and transported to the various work sites by the contractors who needed them.[3]

By late June 1942, all of the 10,000 troops assigned to General Hoge and Colonel O'Connor had arrived and were at work on the pioneer road. The PRA's civilian work force took longer to mobilize, but in view of Commissioner MacDonald's lack of an existing organizational structure to handle a project of this magnitude, the PRA's response to the emergency was as impressive as the Army's. Back in March, MacDonald had made two key decisions that enormously simplified his organization's future operations.

First, he decided that the PRA would not negotiate directly with every small businessman interested in working on the highway. Instead, the agency selected four large firms (one of which was Canadian) to act as management contractors for specified segments of the highway, and another company to manage the transportation and housekeeping needs of the entire project. Each of these organizations was given authority to hire the smaller contractors and specialists needed for its share of the job, with the added provision that the Canadian management contractor would employ only Canadians. Together, these five firms managed the activities of forty-seven companies during the 1942 construction season and eighty-one during 1943. The total contractors' payroll for the summer months of those two years grew to 7,500 and 14,100 men, respectively.

Second, since the situation made detailed cost estimates and bids a matter of pure guesswork, MacDonald arranged for a special type of contract, under which the government would agree to pay rent on each contractor's equipment, plus the cost of his labor and supplies. On top of this would come a fixed fee (subject to renegotiation) in proportion to the size and difficulty of the project, which constituted the contractor's profit and recompense for his skills. In addition, using the scrounged-up CCC and WPA supplies, the PRA would furnish contractors with whatever prefabricated buildings and additional equipment they needed.[4]

Herbert Reese was typical of the many small contractors whose work was supervised for the PRA by the construction management firms. A native of Greenbush, Minnesota, Reese had been a mechanic, a farmer, a car salesman, and a trucker before he finally settled into road-building during the 1930s. Working all over the upper Midwest, from Wisconsin to Montana, he accepted almost any job that came his way, whether it was building 20 miles of country road or dredging a farmer's pond. He owned a small number of 'dozers, graders, and trucks, and hired by the week whatever additional workmen and machinery he needed for large jobs. In the spring of 1942, one of the five management contractors, the Okes Company of St. Paul, Minnesota, asked him and his partner, G. A. Olsen, whether they were interested in a big job in Canada. Indeed they were.[5]

By early June, Reese and Olsen had assembled more than 250 men and were among the first of the fifteen contractors under Okes to arrive in Dawson Creek. As Reese recalled it:

> We had to build our own unloading dock to receive the first 20 carloads of our equipment when it arrived. . . . The small dock . . . at the Northern Alberta Railroad yard was blocked with U.S. Army equipment. . . . We were happy to see that the Army had a D8 dozer standing by. We used ties and poles laid on top of a pile of dirt we dozed up alongside one of the flatcars. We soon had our equipment unloaded.[6]

After some trouble getting across the Peace River (a bargeload of Reese and Olsen's trucks and 'dozers broke loose, drifted miles downstream, and took several days to recover), the company set up its first camp north of Fort St. John in a muddy field near Charlie Lake. By the end of that summer, its men were widening and graveling a 20-mile stretch of road south of the Muskwa River, not far from Fort Nelson.[7]

Reese and Olsen got their 'dozer operators, truck drivers, mechanics, and cooks in the same way as all the other contractors did:

workmen not hired directly by them before they left the States were sent north by Seattle's E. W. Elliott Company, which set up a nationwide network of employment offices and filled the available vacancies from the flood of applicants attracted by advertisements offering higher pay, an interesting year's work, and a chance to travel. (These ads never said "blacks need not apply," but blacks still got the message. Even though the federal government had decreed that defense plants now had to hire them, no laws or regulations existed to require small contractors like Herbert Reese to take on black workmen, and no all-black construction firms had been invited to participate in the Alaska Highway project. The PRA's workplace was "lily-white.")

Thirty-year-old Robert Thorkelson quit his boring job in an ammunition plant in Minneapolis in August 1943 after his application to be a truck driver on the Alaska Highway was accepted. There wasn't much paperwork, he recalled, just an interview concerning his previous experience (farmer, freight handler, assembly-line worker) and some forms for an FBI background check. Within a week he found himself on a train bound for Edmonton with several hundred men much like himself. There, at the PRA's Calder Field staging base, everyone was issued a sleeping bag, given a hygiene inspection and a cold weather briefing, and then, after waiting around for several days, shipped up the line to go to work. Thorkelson was one of a dozen or so workers assigned to the firm of Metcalf-Hamilton-Kansas City Bridge, which operated out of the huge Army base at Big Delta, Alaska.

During the two weeks it took Metcalf-Hamilton's new employees to travel by train, boat, and plane to Big Delta via Prince Rupert, Skagway, and Whitehorse, they met hundreds of returning workmen, some whose contracts were up and others who had quit to escape the isolation and difficult working conditions and were now paying their own way home. "Don't go up there," many of them said, "it's a miserable place." Undeterred, Thorkelson and his traveling companions had to see for themselves. "Driving a truck on that highway was no barrel of monkeys," he later admitted, but for $1.45 an hour— more money than he'd ever made in his life—Bob Thorkelson was willing to put up with a lot of mud, mosquitos, muskeg, and ice. Besides, making the daily supply run to the various Metcalf-Hamilton work sites in all kinds of weather gave him great satisfaction. Hundreds of people were depending on him.[8]

In the rush to round up workmen for the project, many individuals were hired who had been less than candid about their backgrounds.

Here again, the policy seemed to be, "We'll sort it all out at the other end." Thorkelson, for example, lied about his previous experience as a truck driver, which was in fact nil. But it turned out that he could do the job, and that was what mattered. Recruits who tried to cover up a criminal record, however, quickly ran afoul of the FBI. Herbert Reese was badly shaken by a call from Washington telling him that his capable new office manager was a convicted embezzler. Reese instantly transferred the company's funds to another bank and "encouraged" the man to quit.[9]

Overseeing the diverse problems of this huge but scattered workforce was the PRA's own regional staff of more than 1,300 employees, headed by J. S. Bright, formerly the District Engineer in San Francisco. Bright initially tried to work out of an office in Seattle, but soon moved his headquarters to Edmonton. Even then, he often had difficulty communicating with his division officers in Fort St. John and Whitehorse, not to mention the numerous PRA branch offices that were strung along the highway or in strategic places such as Prince Rupert and Skagway. Sometimes the only way for Bright to get a message or a high-priority item through was by air. Like Hoge and O'Connor, he made good use of local bush pilots.

Despite the scale of the Alaska Highway project and the speed with which it got underway, there was nothing particularly unusual about the organizational structure or management methods employed by the PRA. That these worked so well in such a difficult environment was a tribute to the competence and perseverance of MacDonald, Bright, and their subordinates. They shared a common task with the Army Engineers, but the partnership was not always an easy one.[10]

The original agreement between the Army and the PRA envisioned the construction of two essentially separate roads, each built for a specific purpose. The Army's overriding criterion was military necessity. General Hoge had been told to connect the airfields of the Northwest Staging Route with a no-frills pioneer trail and to push an emergency supply route through to Fairbanks—all in one season, if possible. The PRA was there to support the Army, but Bright and his fellow civil engineers also had a responsibility to future users of the highway. As a result, safety and permanence were their guiding considerations.

This divergence was not only understood and accepted by both sides, it was embodied in the construction standards set forth in their original agreement. The finished highway was to have had a 36-foot-wide roadway (30 feet in mountainous terrain), surfaced to a width of 24 feet with crushed rock or gravel plus an oil or asphalt topping. This was the typical, two-lane, country road that contractors like Herbert Reese had been building all over rural America for the past twenty years. On the other hand, the Army's pioneer road was to have a maximum width of 24 feet and could dwindle to 15 feet in rugged terrain. Wherever possible, local materials were to be used to provide the road surface of the Army road; if gravel was available, fine, but it was not to be hauled in if the existing soil made a usable dirt road. A corduroy surface of logs over muskeg and marshy spots was also acceptable. Similar differences existed in the specifications for curves, grades, and sight distances. The Army's road tended to go over the hills, not around them, and 20 percent slopes were not uncommon. Suicide Hill is still a legend among old-timers along the highway. "Prepare to meet thy God," said a sign at the top.[11]

Differences such as these meant that the pioneer road tended to follow the path of least resistance with regard to speed of construction, but this in turn meant a longer, more meandering road than the route being surveyed by the PRA. Only on level, dry terrain would the two routes be likely to coincide. In rougher or wetter areas every attempt would be made to prevent major divergences, but on occasion the two routes might end up much as 5 or 10 miles apart. This, however, was a problem most often faced during the 1943 construction season. During the late summer and fall of 1942, the biggest question was whether the Army's pioneer road could be pushed to completion before winter halted all earth-moving operations. Much to their dismay, the PRA and its contractors found themselves being diverted from their work on the permanent highway to help finish the Army's road in time.

The blunt words of a directive from the Army's Chief of Engineers on August 8, 1942, almost managed to conceal what amounted to a major change in policy:

1. A recent inspection of the. . . . project discloses that Sector Commanders and. . . . [PRA] engineers are not working in the close cooperation intended. . . . It appears that two separate roads are in large measure being located . . . the resulting duplication of effort is considered a waste of Government funds and is disapproved.

2. It is desired that the pioneer road be incorporated in the permanent road to be constructed by the PRA insofar as practicable.

Commissioner MacDonald's letter that same day to J.S. Bright conveyed his acceptance of the Army's new policy but may also have betrayed his real feelings:

> In view of the magnitude of our proposed operations in the limited time available . . . our entire efforts must be concentrated upon the completion of our assigned task this season regardless of Public Road procedure and policies as followed in our regular work.[12]

Summarizing the results of this change, the PRA's year-end report for 1942 again managed a nice blend of tact and honesty:

> Under this revised program, with Engineer troops and contractors pulling together, the pioneer road was cut through in a single short season. . . .
>
> The Army [also] required assistance in building warehouses, barracks, mess halls, water and sewer systems at Dawson Creek [and elsewhere], necessitating withdrawal of . . . construction crews from other work on the project.
>
> By forbearance, patience and persistence all difficulties and obstacles were surmounted. . . . Contractors were rushed to uncompleted sections of the pioneer road . . . [but much is left] to be done to make the pioneer road usable highway for movement of freight. . . .[13]

A few simple statistics show the extent of PRA assistance on the Army's pioneer road. At the time of the official opening of the highway on November 20, 1942, truck odometer readings recorded its length as 1,619 miles. Of this total, 245 miles had been constructed by the PRA's contractors without any Army assistance, and another 979 miles consisted of Army-built pioneer road that had been widened and improved by the PRA. In other words, 75 percent of the original road was built either partly or entirely by civilians.

Moreover, as the PRA's report tactfully noted, much work remained to be done to make the Army's road a "usable highway." One example: during 1943, 133 permanent bridges were scheduled for construction to replace the Army's temporary wooden structures. Over the winter, while the PRA's purchasing agents scoured the States to find the necessary steel and concrete, its architects and draftsmen prepared plans and specifications for each new bridge.[14]

Meanwhile, as the Army and the PRA worked out their differences over who had primary responsibility for winter maintenance of the highway, contractors like Herbert Reese were caught in the middle, unsure of how many men to let go until spring. Reese played it safe, releasing only about 10 percent of his workforce prior to Christmas. He also did what he could to brighten the holidays for those who stayed on:

> We decided to have a Christmas tree but didn't know what to decorate it with. . . . We had no tinsel or tree lights so I told the men to pin their [ID] badges on the branches. That way, everyone there could get in on Christmas in the Alcan. The cooks fixed a special meal. Father Laquice came along [from Fort Nelson] and said Mass for us and stayed for dinner. [15]

January 1943 was a month of bitter cold. Broken-down equipment began to accumulate in the repair shops and sometimes, quickly trapped by the flow of freezing groundwater, along the highway as well. It was often so cold (-71°F was the record low that month near the Alaskan border; -60°F in the Fort Nelson area) that all outside work stopped. On such days, the best place to be was next to a roaring stove, but even that could be dangerous. Almost every camp—military or civilian—experienced at least one serious fire. Herbert Reese never forgot the one at his Muskwa River base that almost put him and his partner out of business:

> We had fifteen buildings, 24′ × 120′, with 45 barrel stoves going. . . . It would take about four cords of wood per day to keep the camp warm. When it got really cold, 60 below, it took up to seven cords. . . . On January 19th, in the evening when everyone was in for supper, our supply building caught fire. No one noticed it until the fire was through the roof. . . . It was 55 below. Men rushed out . . . many without coats or caps, trying to help put the fire out. We had very little water [the ice on the nearby river was four feet thick] and snow did not seem to help. [Because of the wind] fire was starting on the roofs of other buildings. . . . If it had not been for Harold Grill and Roman Witzman who thought of pushing the burning building away from the rest . . . with our D8 dozer, I am sure we could not have saved our camp. They ran the dozer up to the burning building . . . and let it go through by itself. As the cat went through . . . it also pushed supplies, etc., out. The men then caught the cat, turned it around and sent it through again. In that way we saved the camp, and some of the supplies also. [16]

Driving the highway could be as hazardous as working on it, especially if you got sleepy on an icy mountainside in the middle of the night. During the following winter, Bob Thorkelson had a close call "going down [to Whitehorse] to get oil":

> I'd been driving since seven in the morning. At two o'clock the next morning I'm . . . crossing a high mountain and I'd gone to sleep . . . with my eyes open. I went to shift gears and got it into neutral—this was a semi—and the darned thing started to slide. Well there were no brakes on that bloody thing that would hold anything. . . . So I was going backwards pretty fast [but] it didn't jackknife on me. There was a thousand foot drop over there and I jammed that thing and [finally] got it into reverse. Got it stopped. I stayed awake the next 100 miles into Whitehorse. Yeah, that's where I learned to smoke. You'd light a cigarette at the bottom; when you got to the top you'd throw it out if it was a third smoked or what because you didn't want any fire in there if you cracked [up]."[17]

Whitehorse seems to have been a magnet for every U.S. soldier and civilian working in northwest Canada or Alaska during World War II, no doubt in part because of its central location along the Alaska Highway, the Northwest Staging Route, and CANOL's pipe-line network. But the town also had a colorful past familiar to most people through the writings of Robert Service and Jack London, and it was experiencing another boom of gold-rush proportions: its population exploded from less than 700 in 1941 to over 20,000 by 1943.

For all the money in the Americans' pockets, however, this boom was tame compared to the one in 1898. Liquor was rationed and very expensive. According to Bob Thorkelson, you had to stand in line for hours to pay three times the price back home for a bottle of legal whiskey—and the U.S. Army MPs and Canadian Mounties were as hard on bootleggers as they were on prostitutes. Still, Thorkelson insisted, you could find a good time if you knew where to look, even though you might not find a bed to sleep it off in. Innkeepers filled their rooms with cots and rented each one in eight-hour shifts.

Herbert Reese had equally pleasant memories of his occasional visits to Whitehorse. Once, in 1943, he even took some of his men up to see "This Is the Army," a USO show written by Irving Berlin. One of the stars on the bill, Reese liked to recall, was a so-so Hollywood actor in uniform, Lieutenant Ronald Reagan.[18]

After May 1943, as the new construction season began, there was less time for pleasure trips to Whitehorse. Getting there was nearly impossible. All that remained of the original pioneer road in many places was an endless soggy swath through the forest, punctuated by swollen streams and the wreckage of washed-out log bridges. But such a situation had been anticipated by the PRA. The best parts of the pioneer road were to be saved and incorporated into the final highway; the rest had lasted long enough to serve its purpose and would be replaced that summer by an all-new roadbed. It did not quite work out that way.

Through June and early July, the mood along the highway was optimistic. The ground was finally dry, every contractor reported good progress, and work had begun on all of the new bridges; the spectacular Peace River suspension bridge was almost completed. Supplies were moving up the highway in quantity. Anticipating no more major problems, the Army was getting ready to transfer the few construction regiments still assigned to the project. Then it began to rain.

On July 9 and 10, more rain fell than most people in the region had seen in fifty years. Hardest hit was the area within a 200-mile radius of Fort Nelson, where twenty-four of twenty-five bridges were washed away, along with countless culverts and many thousands of cubic yards of soil and gravel. According to Herbert Reese, whose men were then hauling fill for the abutments of the 970-foot Muskwa River bridge, the river rose 34 feet overnight and took with it one of his cranes and 300 barrels of fuel. "It became necessary to dynamite the fills at the end to save the bridge," he recalled. [19]

The extensive damage had only just been repaired and additional bridging materials stockpiled at the most critical sites, when, in early August, the rains returned. This time only four bridges went out, but massive mudslides blocked several other sections of the road. By now well prepared for this sort of thing, the PRA simply diverted several contractors from less critical assignments. Within five days, traffic was moving again. The project as a whole was now several weeks behind schedule, however, and the Army had set October 31, 1943—less than three months away—as the date by which all construction along the highway was to be finished. To meet this deadline, shortcuts and compromises became necessary.

During late August and September, the Army ordered the PRA to stop working on a whole series of jobs. Most of these involved relocating sections of the route away from the original pioneer road in order to improve grades and curves or to provide greater protection against floods and mudslides. Now, to save time and money, the contractors were instructed to do the best they could to upgrade the existing trail. In addition, the Army encouraged them to use less durable materials and time-consuming construction methods. For example, bridge decking might be made of wooden planks instead of poured concrete. Similarly, wooden culverts—not steel or concrete—would suffice.

Most of these orders, particularly those halting major relocations, produced angry confrontations between the Army and the PRA. Bright and his men usually took the position that not finishing such improvements was both wasteful of resources already expended and shortsighted. But the Army's argument made equally good sense: why build a better road than the military situation warranted, particularly when other wartime construction projects now had a higher priority? More often than not, that argument prevailed; but occasionally the PRA got its way. Several relocated stretches were so near completion that Bright was able to make a convincing case that finishing them was cheaper and faster than going back to the pioneer road.[20]

Under these revised groundrules, the PRA essentially met the Army's deadline. On October 13, 1943, the Utah Construction Company closed the last major gap in the highway, the troublesome stretch of permafrost and muskeg northwest of Kluane Lake near the Alaskan border. By the end of October, all of the contractors still working on the road had ceased operations and released their men to return home. A few bridges remained unfinished, and most of these were turned back to the Army to complete. In November, Bright's Edmonton office packed up and moved to Chicago, while the field offices along the highway retained skeleton staffs to supervise the evacuation of equipment and the ragtag remnants of the contractors' forces.

Maintenance of the completed highway for the duration of the war was made the Army's responsibility, but Canadian civilians recruited from the ranks of the departing construction workers were hired to do the work. To help organize and train this maintenance force the Army retained a PRA highway engineer named Frank C. Turner. He stayed on as a maintenance consultant until Canada assumed control of its segment of the highway in April 1946. Thus, a PRA engineer was the last American to come home from the Alaska Highway when the war was over.[21]

A full accounting of the PRA's role in the construction of the Alaska Highway requires further discussion of its many bridges. Of the 133 permanent bridges of various types designed by the PRA's staff, the contractors had completed 99 by the end of October 1943. The average length of these was 340 feet, and placed end-to-end they would have had a total length of about 8½ miles. More than half were fairly short wooden trestle spans, similar in design to the Army's temporary bridges, but far sturdier. (For an example of the contrast between the PRA and Army bridges, see the first photograph of the side-by-side spans across the Sikinni Chief River in the photo section.) Of the remaining structures, a few were built of reinforced concrete, but most were of steel. The most beautiful bridge on the entire highway was the 2,130-foot Peace River suspension bridge, erected by the John A. Roebling Company, world-famous for its earlier work on the Brooklyn Bridge.

The first concern of the Roebling Company's engineers when they arrived at the Peace River site in the winter of 1943 was the condition of the ice. It had to be at least 4 feet thick to support the weight of the temporary erection tower that would be used to construct the bridge's two permanent towers, and it had to remain frozen solid until they were up. The ice was indeed thick enough to hold the erection tower, but exactly when the spring breakup would come was anybody's guess. The PRA's official report for 1943 described with some pride the outcome of Roebling's race against time:

> The erection tower was set up on the ice during the clear, cold days of early March—temperature 20 degrees below zero—skidded into position, and bridge tower erection began on March 27. During this period there were many trials and tribulations. Shipments of materials became lost en route, trucks hauling from Dawson Creek got out of control on the slippery roads, an epidemic of flu . . . broke out in camp and there was a shortage of essential workmen. The force was divided into two 10-hour shifts but work did not go on for a full 20 hours a day as men had to stop to warm numbed hands.
>
> As the first main tower began to go toward the sky in late March the sun warmed up and this was followed by rain. A situation that had been alarming became critical. Would the ice hold until the towers were up? The south . . . tower was quickly reared to full height and the erection tower was dragged across the ice into position at the north tower . . . [which was] completed on April 5. Seven hundred tons of steel had been erected . . . in 9 days of elapsed time.
>
> Then began the job of placing and adjusting the cable and erecting steelwork for the roadway. Steelwork and concrete roadway were completed on July 31 and the bridge was opened to traffic early in August. An erection job which, in a milder climate, would normally have taken eight months was accomplished in four months and one week.[22]

Although the Peace River bridge was an impressive achievement, the most massive structure on the highway was the high span across the Teslin River at Johnson's Crossing. It was one of the few bridges not completed until the 1944 construction season, because of wartime steel shortages. In most cases, the PRA got around the shortage by dismantling unused bridges in the United States and shipping them north to be reassembled on new foundations.[23] All of the PRA's timber bridges and some of its steel structures (including the Peace River bridge) have since been replaced, but the rest are still in use and still in good shape.

Of the 1,420 miles of highway across Canada to Alaska that were opened to the public after World War II, about two-thirds (970 miles) consisted of the original Army pioneer road, all of which had been substantially improved and upgraded by the PRA. Another 450 miles of the highway were new—and strictly PRA-built. Here the Army's pioneer road had served its original purpose as an access route and was abandoned thereafter. The wartime cost of the Alaska Highway came to a seemingly modest $138 million—less than $100,000 per mile.[24]

The surest way to start a heated argument among veterans of the Alaska Highway is to raise the question of who deserves more credit for this incredible achievement—the Army Engineers or the PRA and its contractors. Even General Hoge, who knew better, later belittled the help he got from the PRA. "They did send us some help," he said in 1974, "but . . . they were only backups. . . . They were always behind us, always."[25] Such partisanship misses the point. There is more than enough credit to go around.

A more difficult question to answer is whether the taxpapers got their money's worth. Certainly, in stating the cost of the Alaska Highway as $138 million, the War Department chose to be selective in its accounting. Left out of that total, for example, were the costs of paying, feeding, and equipping 10,000 Engineer soldiers for more than a year. Moreover, the expenses involved in such essential adjuncts to the highway as the Haines cutoff, improvements to the Northwest Staging Route, and CATEL's telephone lines were also omitted. So too was the entire amount spent on the biggest "extra" of all: Project CANOL. Among the critics who sought a more thorough accounting from their government for all this was the junior U.S. Senator from Missouri, Harry S. Truman.

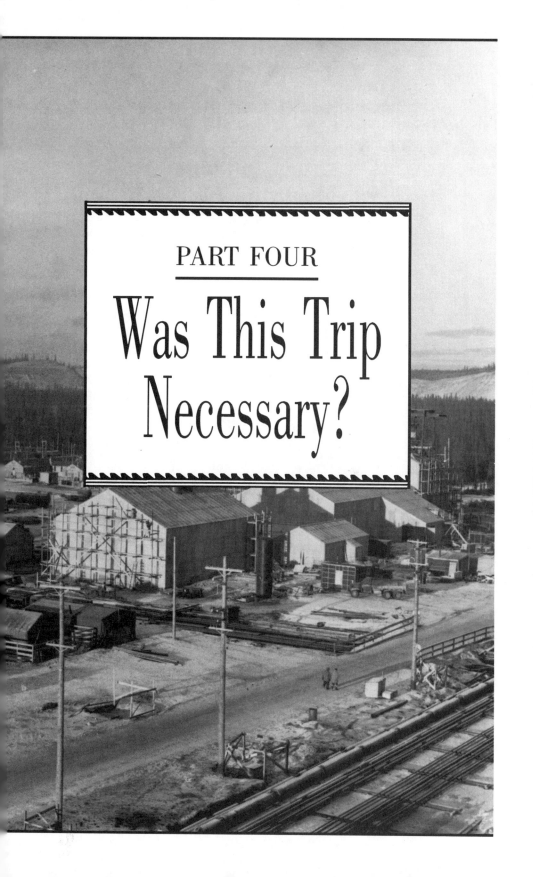

PART FOUR

Was This Trip Necessary?

14

Senator Truman Investigates

A lthough universally acknowledged as an epic feat of military logistics and engineering, the Alaska Highway has never been without its detractors. The opposition was loudest during World War II. At first critics said that the highway was in the wrong place and would take too long to build; later complaints centered on the mushrooming cost and complexity of "add-ons" such as Project CANOL. With the benefit of 20/20 hindsight, some critics even went so far as to say that the whole huge effort was of such little use that it should never have been undertaken at all.

The most dogged foe of the Army's road was Congressman Warren Magnuson of Washington State, who called the November 1942 opening ceremonies at Soldier's Summit "a fraud" and charged that the highway was still unfit for heavy traffic a year later. (Both assertions contained a sizable grain of truth.) For years, Magnuson kept introducing legislation to authorize construction of Route A—"the real Alaska Highway," as he called it. Although his postwar efforts to raise Canadian support for building Route A were met "with all the enthusiasm of a cow contemplating the Sahara Desert," according to a U.S. observer in Ottawa, Magnuson was still lobbying in Washington for the coastal route as late as 1947.[1] Other critics were almost as persistent.

The June 1942 preliminary hearing in response to Senator Langer's charges that the highway was "an engineering monstrosity, an economic absurdity and militarily insignificant" was only the first in a series of Congressional investigations sparked by continuing criticism of the project's location, purpose, scope, cost, and military value. The reports issued by two committees conducting inquiries into these questions—one in 1943 by Senator James G. Scrugham's Committee on Post Offices and Post Roads and the other in 1946 by Representative J. W. Robinson's House Committee on Roads—while critical of some details, nevertheless endorsed the enterprise as a whole. A close reading of both reports, however, shows that much of their content was lifted verbatim from self-justifying staff studies obligingly provided by the War Department.[2]

The only investigative body on Capitol Hill that consistently did its own spadework on the War Department's turf was a Senate committee under the chairmanship of Harry Truman. Compared to the findings of Senator Scrugham and Congressman Robinson, the facts unearthed by Truman's Special Committee Investigating the National Defense Program regarding the Army's brobdingnagian construction projects in northwest Canada had a much more pungent odor.

By the summer of 1943, when Senator Truman decided to look into allegations of waste and mismanagement in Project CANOL, his work in uncovering similar problems elsewhere on the home front had already propelled him to national prominence. As the man responsible for his committee's investigative agenda and the tone of its hearings, Truman had become a force to reckon with on Capitol Hill. But many in Washington had not yet learned to take him seriously.

Harry S. Truman entered the United States Senate in 1934 at the age of fifty. His hitherto unremarkable career had included overseas service as an artillery captain during World War I, failure as a haberdasher in Kansas City after the war, and twelve years as a Missouri county judge. A man of deep personal integrity, Truman nevertheless owed both his judgeship and his senate seat to the patronage of Kansas City's notorious political boss, Thomas J. Pendergast. "Boss" Pendergast once contemptuously referred to his hard-working protegé as an "office-boy," but he also seems to have valued Truman's service precisely because of his reputation for honesty.

Truman was a solid supporter of President Roosevelt's New Deal policies during his first term in the Senate, and his homespun humor and love of poker and well-aged bourbon soon made him one of its more popular members. Like any good politician, he made friends easily and worked at keeping them. Bennett Champ Clark, Missouri's senior senator, became his mentor. (Clark would later be Senator

Langer's nemesis during the 1942 preliminary hearing on the Alaska Highway.)

Truman's greatest personal and political liability was the faint scent of corruption that clung to him from his years of association with Pendergast. Opponents also liked to point out that he had failed as a businessman. And he could be a stubborn cuss, taking positions that were sure to cost him dearly later on. He broke with Roosevelt on several issues during the latter's second term and opposed on principle his plans to run a third time. Roosevelt reciprocated by withholding his support during Truman's own bid for reelection in 1940, but the man from Independence won anyway.[3] The attack on Pearl Harbor was then thirteen months away.

Harry Truman was sworn in for his second term in the Senate on January 3, 1941. Five weeks later, on February 10, with the Congress appropriating billions of dollars to speed preparations for a war Americans still hoped to avoid, he made a speech that galvanized his colleagues and changed the course of his career. Truman's reasons for giving this speech are best described in his own words:

I was concerned about charges that the huge contracts and immense purchases that resulted from these [multi-billion-dollar] appropriations were being handled through favoritism. There were rumors that some of the plants had been located on the basis of friendship. I feared that many of the safeguards usually observed in government transactions were being thrown aside and overlooked, although these safeguards would in no way have slowed up the program. I knew, too, that certain lobbyists were seeking the inside track on purchases, contracts and plant locations. There were rumors of enormous fees being paid to these gentlemen and of purchases being concentrated among a few manufacturers of supplies.

I saw cliques in labor and in capital, each greedy for gain, while small production plants by the hundreds were being pushed aside . . . by big business.

I gave a lot of thought to this situation, and when I realized that it was growing increasingly worse, I decided to take a closer look at it. I got into my automobile and started out from Washington to make a little investigation of my own. I drove thirty thousand miles in a great circle through Maryland and from there down to Florida, across to Texas, north through Oklahoma to Nebraska, and back through Wisconsin and Michigan. I visited war camps, defense plants, and other . . . projects which had some connection with the total war effort, and did not let any of them know who I was.

The trip was an eye-opener, and I came back . . . convinced that something needed to be done fast. I had seen at first hand that grounds existed for a good many of the rumors that were prevalent in Washington. . . . [4]

Impressed by Truman's personal fact-finding odyssey and startled by the enormity of the problems he had uncovered, the Senate was quick to give him the broad investigative powers he requested. Senate Resolution 71, adopted on March 1, 1941, set up a committee of seven members (five Democrats and two Republicans, with Truman as chairman) and authorized it:

to make a full and complete study of the national defense program including:

1. the types and terms of contracts awarded;
2. the methods by which contracts are awarded and contractors selected;
3. the utilization of small business;
4. the geographic distribution of contracts and the location of plants and facilities;
5. the effect of the defense program on labor and the migration of labor;
6. the performance of contracts and the accountings required of contractors;
7. benefits accruing to contractors with respect to amortization for the purposes of taxation;
8. practices of management or labor, and prices, fees and charges which interfere with or unduly increase the costs of the program;
9. such other matters as the committee deems appropriate.

To cover staff salaries and other committee expenses, however, the resolution set a budget ceiling of only $15,000—not the $25,000 Truman had asked for.[5]

Truman immediately went looking for a good lawyer to be the committee's chief counsel, "a person of tact as well as ability," he recalled, "who had common sense, who would be loyal to the objectives of the committee, and who would make a hard-hitting investigator." Assistant U.S. Attorney General Hugh Fulton, already successful in prosecuting a number of politically sensitive cases, turned out to be the perfect man for the job. Nonetheless, Truman's first impression of Fulton was anything but favorable:

He came in wearing a derby hat, a big, fat fellow with a squeaky voice. I said to myself, "Oh shucks!" However, I paid him more than half the money I had, $8,500 a year which was $500 more than he was getting.

That left only $6,500 to pay for the committee's clerical help, as well as the services of several investigators, but it was enough to get started. The first day of hearings took place on April 15, 1941.[6]

Secretary of War Henry Stimson, Navy Secretary Frank Knox, and Army Chief of Staff George Marshall were among the first week's witnesses. Each official testified at length from his own particular perspective about the problems of mobilization. Truman later said that his purpose in calling them was to accumulate "the background information necessary for intelligent consideration of the defense problem" and to establish "confidence and a working relationship with the executive branch."[7] That groundwork laid, the committee got down to business.

More than twenty carefully documented investigations over the course of the next two years earned Truman a well-deserved reputation as the "watch-dog of the war effort." Soon given more adequate funding by an appreciative Senate, the Truman Committee, as it was popularly known, scrutinized everything from mismanagement in the construction of military camps to labor unrest in the coal mines to wasteful practices in the aluminum, steel, and rubber industries. One highly publicized investigation in 1942 found evidence that the Carnegie-Illinois Steel Corporation was faking the test results of its armor plate. An even more devastating inquiry the next year uncovered proof of criminal negligence in the manufacture of defective aircraft engines at the Curtiss-Wright Corporation.

Truman's most sensational probe, if not his most important, involved the Army's motion picture division and several Hollywood moguls, most notably Daryl Zanuck of 20th Century–Fox. Zanuck, given a lieutenant colonel's commission to help produce military training films and propaganda (while continuing to draw his civilian salary of $5,000 per week), appeared to be favoring his own company with more than its share of contracts. Noting that he got more mail over the Zanuck affair than over any other investigation, Truman grumped to a friend that nobody seemed to care about the more serious aspects of the defense program.[8]

Every investigation began with Truman's learning of some specific problem affecting the war effort—whether through his own personal observations or from the expressed concerns of his colleagues (the camp construction scandal) or from tips by whistle-blowing employees (the Curtiss-Wright and Carnegie-Illinois Steel cases) or as a result of media coverage (grievances in the coal mines) or from the volume of mail he received on a particular subject (the shortage of farm machinery). Of course, the thousands of letters he received each year included a few from cranks and crackpots. For example, one loonie was indignant that the government had ignored his proposal that every U.S. soldier be equipped with a one-man airplane carrying "a few square yards of good American soil" to dump on Tokyo. Taking off in a huge formation, he asserted, this aerial armada would "bury Japan in defeat."[9]

Such missives could safely be ignored, but Truman insisted that his investigators look into all substantive leads, no matter how improbable they might seem. That policy soon put him on the trail of the super-secret Manhattan Project, which was consuming prodigious quantities of materials and money with no visible results. Puzzled by this military equivalent of a black hole, Truman went to Secretary of War Stimson for an explanation, only to be told that such secrecy was essential to the project, the success of which could well determine who won the war. On the strength of Stimson's word, Truman agreed not to probe any further.[10] He remained unaware of the existence of the atomic bomb until he became President in the spring of 1945.

The Truman Committee bore no responsibility for taking remedial or punitive action in any of the cases it investigated, nor did it usually recommend what that action should be. Truman was content to expose whatever incompetence, stupidity, or dishonesty his investigators found, confident that the wartime atmosphere and, if necessary, the glare of publicity would make it very difficult for the proper authorities not to take corrective measures. With rare exceptions (the CANOL case, for one), his assumption proved valid.

Although the threat of embarrassing exposures was no doubt his most powerful weapon, much of the credit for the rather surprising cooperation Truman got from the majority of his investigative targets was due to the way he and his people went about their work. The senator did his utmost to ensure that every inquiry be handled in an even-handed and thoroughly professional manner. There was no witch-hunt atmosphere or grandstanding for personal political gain, and there were no games played with information leaks to the newspapers. Opponents who tried to use the press to discredit the Committee's findings, however, quickly discovered that Truman was a tough counterpuncher. His threat to make public the full extent of the wrongdoing forced more than one highly placed official to drop the challenge.[11]

In investigating Project CANOL, the Truman Committee followed its usual procedures. But in this case, the outcome did not follow the normal script.

Truman was well aware of many of CANOL's problems before he decided to have his committee look into it officially. Both the Budget Bureau and the War Production Board had already expressed serious misgivings about the project, and the Budget Bureau had gone so far as to send two experts to inspect the work in progress at Norman Wells, Whitehorse, and Skagway. Their report stated that the partially completed pipeline network delivering gasoline from Skagway to points along the highway (CANOL 2, 3, and 4) was serving a useful purpose already. But because there was no longer a serious Japanese threat to Alaska or the West Coast, these men recommended that work be stopped on the Norman Wells–Whitehorse pipeline and the associated refinery (CANOL 1). Pointing out that this would save more than $50 million in fiscal 1944, the Budget Bureau diplomatically suggested to the Secretary of War on June 2, 1943, that the Joint Chiefs of Staff review CANOL 1 to determine whether it was still vital to the war effort.

Secretary Stimson's reply to the Budget Bureau, delivered by Under Secretary Robert P. Patterson on July 27, was a polite brush-off. Abandoning CANOL 1 would mean wasting the $50 million already spent, said Patterson. Besides, he concluded tersely, "Military necessity requires that the CANOL Project be completed as rapidly as possible."[12]

The War Production Board, which was responsible for the allocation of scarce materials, equipment, and manpower among competing sectors of the domestic economy, also got short shrift when it questioned the rationale for a $200 million line of communications to Alaska "which will never serve a useful purpose." Patterson's reply to this was that both the Alaska Highway and Project CANOL were being built for "strategic reasons," and thus were not within the purview of the WPB.[13] In other words, said the Army, "stay out of our business."

Truman's own investigation was an attempt to end this standoff between the Army and its critics. In view of his charter, he could hardly be told that CANOL was none of his business. Moreover, he strongly suspected that such cryptic phrases as "military necessity" and "strategic reasons" were not a valid justification in this particular case, but only a cloak.

While a team of "committee dicks," as Truman's sleuths were known, patiently went through files and interviewed various officials in Washington during August and September, a two-senator subcommittee traveled to Edmonton and Whitehorse to hold closed-door preliminary hearings. By the end of September 1943, this was the picture Truman had pieced together:

CANOL 2—the barge/pipeline system for delivering U.S. petroleum products to Whitehorse via Skagway that had more or less been forced on the Army by Interior Secretary Harold Ickes—was in operation and working as planned. So too was CANOL 3, the pipeline from Whitehorse to Watson Lake. Completion of CANOL 4 to Fairbanks, however, had been delayed because long stretches of the Alaska Highway between Kluane Lake and Big Delta were still being rebuilt by the PRA and were not yet open for through traffic. (CANOL 4 came on-line in early 1944.)

As for CANOL 1, there was very little good news. It was true that wildcat drilling in and around the Norman Wells field had recently struck enough oil to reach the hoped-for production goal of 20,000 barrels per day. But the maximum capacity of both the Whitehorse refinery and the 577-mile pipeline leading to it had been based on the original goal of 5,000 barrels per day. To handle four times that flow, the system would need bigger pipe, more powerful pumps, and a larger refinery. No such scarce and costly equipment had been ordered because the Army had no budget authorization for it—and was obviously reluctant to ask for one from Congress.

Meanwhile, since converting a barrel of crude oil into diesel fuel and low-octane gasoline was simpler and cheaper than maximizing the output of high-octane aviation fuel, determining the proportions of various petroleum products the refinery should produce became a hotly contested bureaucratic issue. The battle over the optimum mix to satisfy the most customers at the least cost went on and on, causing repeated design changes and construction delays. The refinery's completion date had already been pushed back to December 1943 from the original (and unrealistic) target of October 1942; now Bechtel-Price-Callahan was looking at a further delay, perhaps until summer 1944.

The pipeline-laying crews working on CANOL 1 were also behind schedule at both ends of the newly opened trail to Norman Wells. Their problems could be summed up under three headings: bad weather, rough terrain, and soggy muskeg. The best they could hope for was to link up north of Sheldon Lake and finish the last weld sometime during the coming winter.

CANOL's 12,000-man workforce was now entirely civilian, except for the dozen or so detachments of flight-strip personnel and Signal Corps technicians scattered down the length of the Mackenzie River and the 400 officers and men who staffed the plush Edmonton headquarters of Colonel Wyman's successor as Northwest Division Engineer, General Ludson D. Worsham. Task Force 2600 had stayed long enough to put its boats and barges back into operation before turning the job of delivering the remaining cargo for Norman Wells over to Marine Operators, a private company set up specifically for that purpose. CANOL's three battalions, like the regiments on the Alaska Highway, were all on their way back to the States for refresher training and new assignments. (Wansley Hill and his buddies in the 388th Engineers were scheduled for deployment to Europe.)

Compared to the crude, drafty log huts that had housed most of CANOL's troops over the winter, the accommodations provided for the project's civilian workers were positively luxurious: heated barracks and dayrooms, comfortable cots, much better chow. Bechtel-Price-Callahan, CANOL's largest employer, had its major base in Edmonton, plus another sprawling complex of comfortably furnished offices and barracks outside Whitehorse and a self-contained mini-city at Camp CANOL, across the Mackenzie River from Norman Wells. To compensate for the harsh climate and isolation, CANOL's workers earned 10 to 25 percent more per hour than they had made in the States—in addition to generous overtime, which could double a man's paycheck. Yet, despite all this, and the fair warning given to prospective employees by BPC's "THIS IS NO PICNIC" signs, the annual turnover rate in the workforce exceeded 100 percent. The extra money it cost to recruit and transport so many replacements—not to mention the time lost breaking in new men on the job—was a small scandal in itself.

The terms of the cost-plus-fixed-fee contracts so hastily negotiated with CANOL's various contractors during the summer and fall of 1942 constituted another scandal. Essentially, there was no risk for anyone involved except the United States. Truman's investigators were especially critical of the cost-free opportunity the government accorded Imperial Oil to develop, expand, and modernize the facilities of its own field. They also felt that the arrangement with the Canadian government for the postwar disposition of CANOL's assets needlessly slighted U.S. strategic interests regarding future access to the oil at Norman Wells.

As of September 1943, the various components of CANOL had cost American taxpayers more than $65 million (not counting, of course, the expense of maintaining Task Force 2600, which came out of funds for the upkeep of the Army as a whole). Both the Budget Bureau and the Army estimated that it would take at least another $54 million to finish the project, most of it earmarked for CANOL 1's pipeline and refinery. But not until mid-1944, at the earliest, would the refinery produce the first drop of gasoline.

In the meantime, CANOL 2's barge/pipeline system had proved entirely adequate for supplying the petroleum needs of the Alaska Highway and the Northwest Staging Route. Moreover, as one of Truman's staffers calculated, if Alaska's fuel needs dramatically increased, a single medium-size oil tanker could deliver more gasoline to Skagway in seven round trips than the finished refinery could produce in a year. And, even if several tankers were sunk, the cost of building them was a mere $5 million apiece—far less than what the Army planned to spend on CANOL 1.[14]

Miles H. Knowles, assigned by the War Department to accompany Truman's two colleagues on their travels around Project CANOL, heard what they heard and saw what they saw. On his return to Washington in late September, Knowles reported his observations to Julius H. Amberg, Legal Assistant to the Secretary of War. CANOL 1, said Knowles, was "indefensible."[15] That was not a welcome message. Amberg's job became to figure out how to defend the indefensible.

In October 1943, the Joint Chiefs of Staff finally agreed to the longstanding request of CANOL's critics for a review of the project. A committee of lower-ranking officers actually conducted this review, which made extensive use of documents and testimony favorable to CANOL, including a memorandum supplied by General Somervell which was misleading in several respects. This document stated that an "intensive study" of the Norman Wells field had been conducted prior to the initiation of the project; it also used a highly questionable statistical analysis to show that CANOL would be cost-effective. Only one of CANOL's many critics, Harold Ickes, was permitted to send a spokesman before the Committee presented its recommendation to the Joint Chiefs: completion of the project was "necessary to the war effort." On October 26, without further examination of the supporting evidence, the Joint Chiefs adopted this recommendation as their own.[16]

The authority and prestige of the Joint Chiefs were now clearly behind Project CANOL, making it more difficult for Truman to press his investigation. He had never questioned the right of the defense establishment to define what was of strategic importance and/or vital for national security, and his committee had scrupulously avoided second-guessing the brass on questions of military strategy or tactics. But he also knew enough about CANOL to realize that the phrase "necessary to the war effort" was another cloak. On November 22, 1943, the Truman Committee began public hearings to put the facts about CANOL on the public record.

The first important witness to appear was the Under Secretary of War, Robert Patterson. With Julius Amberg seated beside him, Patterson began his testimony with a statement:

> The War Department is proud of CANOL. . . . CANOL was a bold undertaking. The results so far have surpassed our hopes. We are confident that even greater success lies ahead. . . . We uncovered a rich continental resource of oil, far beyond the original target of 3,000 barrels a day. Twenty thousand barrels a day is now assured. . . . That is a major oil field in anybody's language.

Patterson's air of confidence slowly evaporated under the heat of questioning. Senator Harley M. Kilgore took him up on his assertion that *any* local source of oil was valuable for the defense of Alaska. Kilgore first pointed out that the refinery was expected to convert 3,000 barrels of crude oil per day into no more than 479 barrels of aviation gasoline, plus about 1,500 barrels of lower-octane products. He then asked Patterson an obvious question:

> SENATOR KILGORE: "I am wondering really how much of an aid that [small amount of] aviation gasoline would be to the strategy of defending Alaska with an all-out defense."
>
> MR. PATTERSON: "Any supply you could get at the source— What are you laughing at Mr. Fulton?"
>
> MR. FULTON [the Committee's Chief Counsel]: "No matter."
>
> MR. PATTERSON: "You have been laughing all through this. I haven't seen the humor in it yet."
>
> MR. FULTON: "I have been laughing at the concept that any supply, no matter what it was, would be valuable, without regard to the cost in man-hours and materials together."[17]

In the end, the only defense Patterson had left was that CANOL had been declared "necessary" by the Joint Chiefs of Staff.

A large part of the Army's justification for CANOL rested on two assertions: first, that the Navy could not guarantee safe passage for oil tankers to Alaska; and second, that the Air Corps wanted a secure local source of aviation fuel for planes using the Northwest Staging Route. Both assertions proved shaky.

As for the danger from Japanese submarines in the Gulf of Alaska, Navy officials not only characterized an occasional tanker sinking as no threat to Alaska's oil supplies, they denied having been asked about the problem by the Army. Although this was true in connection with CANOL, General Marshall had raised the same issue with Admiral King when the Alaska Highway was being planned. On that occasion, King's answer had been equivocal.

The committee next called Major General St. Clair Streett, the senior Air Force officer present at the April 1942 War Department meeting at which the military potential of oil from Norman Wells was first seriously discussed. General Streett was asked what his contribution had been to that discussion. Streett's answer was that he had offered his opinion as an aviator that oil from Norman Wells would be a "godsend" for the airfields of the Northwest Staging Route. But he also conceded that there had been absolutely no discussion at the meeting of the costs involved or of the pros and cons of the Norman Wells project as against other sources of fuel.[18]

Soon it was the turn of Dean James H. Graham, Somervell's dollar-a-year consultant on transportation and logistics, to face Senator Truman and his colleagues. Graham had sent the one-page memorandum to Somervell recommending that Project CANOL be undertaken and completed, ready for operation, by October 1, 1942. The Committee wanted the record to show how casually the two men had set CANOL's wheels in motion. Graham was an easy target. His testimony clearly showed that his recommendations to Somervell had been made

> without a survey of the route of the projected pipeline and with no knowledge of the conditions to be met there . . . without considering the number of pumping stations . . . and the most advantageous size of the pipeline . . . without considering the possible alternative locations of the refinery; without considering the costs and difficulties inherent in transporting the materials and men and maintaining them at the project; and without considering possible alternative methods of obtaining oil products for the ALCAN Highway.[19]

As a classic example of bureaucratic arrogance and stupidity, here was a modern version of the "Great Reindeer Fiasco" of 1898, only on a vastly larger and more expensive scale.

When Dean Graham departed, the stage was finally set for the committee to question General Somervell. Truman was confident of the outcome of the confrontation, but he was not really looking for headlines or scapegoats. His main purpose here, as in all his previous investigations, was to stop waste and inefficiency in the prosecution of the war effort.

On December 2, he offered Somervell and the War Department a face-saving way out of the impending showdown. Truman did this by urging Secretary of War Stimson, Secretary of the Navy Knox, Petroleum Administrator for War Ickes, and Chairman Nelson of the War Production Board to meet and decide what to do about CANOL. The four men gathered in Stimson's office on December 7. Knox, Ickes, and Nelson all agreed that work on the Norman Wells–Whitehorse pipeline and refinery should be stopped at once, which would at least save the $30 million that remained unspent from CANOL's current budget. Stimson, backing Somervell all the way, refused to give in. He sent Truman a letter explaining his reasons: only $10 million could be saved by stopping now, not $30 million; and the $100 million already spent would then be thrown away. In addition, the oil field at Norman Wells was much larger than originally believed and thus of greater strategic value. Lastly, since the Joint Chiefs thought CANOL was necessary, it should be continued.[20]

General Somervell appeared before the Committee on December 20, sleek and suave as ever. Though his prepared remarks were ably presented with accompanying charts and statistics, they amounted to a rehash of the contents of Stimson's recent letter to Truman. Then, trying to show how near to completion the Norman Wells–Whitehorse pipeline was, Somervell resorted to "the old Army Game": "It was alleged that oil would not flow through the pipes," he said firmly. "We can dismiss all those fears . . . because we are pumping oil through the line now." But his listeners already knew that the 100-mile gap in the northern third of the line could not possibly be closed for another two months. Senator Homer Ferguson, seconded by Hugh Fulton, called his bluff:

> SENATOR FERGUSON: "General, what part of the line are you pumping oil through?"
> GENERAL SOMERVELL: "From Norman Wells. We started to fill the line on the 18th of December, and it is now 29 miles from Norman Wells. . . . In other words, the thing is all but

finished. The oil is actually flowing through the line from the wells toward the refinery."

MR. FULTON: "What would be the purpose of that, General Somervell?"

GEN. SOMERVELL: "Of what?"

MR. FULTON: "Of sending oil from Norman Wells 25 or 30 miles toward Whitehorse."

GEN. SOMERVELL: "It is going to go all the way to Whitehorse, It will be 81 miles on Christmas Day, and it will keep on going until it gets to Whitehorse, where it will be put in the refinery, and get refined." . . .

MR. FULTON: "When will the line be finished and the first drops of oil reach Whitehorse?"

GEN. SOMERVELL: "Would you mind if I finished the statement?"

MR. FULTON: "No; but I couldn't understand. Why put oil in a pipeline that wouldn't be finished for many months?"

GEN. SOMERVELL: "That isn't true. The line will be finished before many months. . . . You must remember that you have to fill the line before you can take anything out of the opposite end."

MR. FULTON: "Oh, yes. But you have to keep pumping it while it is in the line in order to keep it from settling down [and clogging the line with paraffin], don't you?"

GEN. SOMERVELL: "Oh, absolutely; if you want anything to come out the other end." . . .

MR. FULTON: "In other words, you will pump it back and forth."

GEN. SOMERVELL: "No, no."

MR. FULTON: "You can't get it to Whitehorse until March."

GEN. SOMERVELL: "We are testing the line, as I told you . . . and the oil will be pumped through there . . . to the refinery for refining purposes early in May."[21]

Although the senators allowed General Somervell the benefit of the doubt as to CANOL's potential value in the uncertain days of early 1942, they kept trying to get him to admit that it made no sense to continue the project into 1944, in view of the vastly improved strategic situation in the Pacific. Senator Ball almost cornered him:

SENATOR BALL: General, I understood you to say . . . that if in April 1942, you had realized that this would not be in operation, production, until the spring of 1944, you probably would not have approved it.

GEN. SOMERVELL: That is correct, Senator.

No doubt anticipating Ball's trap, Somervell launched a counterattack. "It is a reckless man indeed who questions the strategy that has pulled us up and is going to lead us to victory," he blustered. "We had just as well have got off Tarawa after killing the first squad of Japs as to get out of [CANOL] now."[22] The analogy did not impress the senators.

Senator Truman had been content to let others do most of the questioning, but it was he who had the last word with Somervell. Although the general conceded that the U.S. Navy was not consulted about CANOL in the spring of 1942, he implied that its top brass were now in favor of the project. He reminded Truman that the Chief of Naval Operations, Admiral King, as a member of the Joint Chiefs of Staff, had recently agreed that CANOL was "necessary to the war effort." Truman easily trumped Somervell's King: "The Secretary of the Navy, however, has the other opinion," he shot back. "This meeting will stand adjourned."[23]

Over the Christmas recess, every official who had appeared before the committee was given a transcript of his testimony and asked to check it for accuracy; Secretary Stimson got a draft of the Truman Committee's findings to look over. An advance copy of the final report also went to President Roosevelt. Thus there were no surprises when Senator Truman released his report on Project CANOL on January 8, 1944. Among its conclusions were these:

- General Somervell had approved the project with inadequate technical information about the field at Norman Wells; with no estimate of costs; with a date of completion that "was on its face impossible of accomplishment"; and with "no consideration of possible alternative methods of obtaining the same or greater supplies of oil."
- Qualified experts had repeatedly warned the Army of the project's "unsoundness and excessive cost." While there might have been "some slight excuse" for Somervell's initial decision in view of the war situation at the time, his insistence on continuing with the project in the face of these warnings was "inexcusable."
- The project failed in its original purpose of quickly providing a

local source of oil to help with the defense of Alaska. Instead, "it was a drain on our resources in 1942 and 1943."

As for continuing the project into 1944, the Committee left it up to the War Department:

> *The Committee is definitely of the opinion that the CANOL project should not have have been undertaken, and that it should have been abandoned when the difficulties were called to the attention of the War Department* [italics in the original]. . . . However, this project has been so largely completed that only a small amount, proportionately, could be saved by abandoning it now. The committee therefore believes that the decision as to whether it should be abandoned now should be made by the War Department.[24]

Despite the Committee's focus on the hasty planning and casual decision-making that contributed to CANOL's enormous cost and meager results, it was clear that the senators felt the same way about the Alaska Highway: "If the CANOL and ALCAN Highway projects could be reviewed from their inception," said the report, "the Committee would be of the opinion that the entire Alaska Highway project should be examined most carefully for the purpose of ascertaining whether it should be constructed."

The only positive paragraph was the last:

> The Committee acknowledges the work done by the soldiers and workmen engaged on the CANOL project. They have undergone the rigors of climate and separation from their homes. . . . They were admonished at the time of their employment . . . that "this is no picnic," and despite almost insufferable conditions, the work . . . was pressed and, in many instances, miracles were accomplished under the stress of necessity. The Nation owes them its thanks for their labor.[25]

Adopting the argument that to cancel CANOL would now cost more than to complete it, the War Department went ahead with the project. The first crude oil from Norman Wells reached the White-horse refinery on April 16, 1944, but several months passed before the refinery itself went into operation—and even then it could only produce diesel oil. The plant was not ready to make 100-octane aviation fuel until that October. Less than a year later, on April 5, 1945, the refinery was shut down. Its total output during the previous nine months had been 23,417 barrels of aviation gasoline, 31,370

ABOVE: Linkup between the 35th and 340th Engineers at Contact Creek, September 1942. Courtesy of Chief of Engineers, Office of History. LEFT: Permafrost—deep ice under a thin layer of soil. Courtesy of U.S. National Archives.

ABOVE: The 18th Engineers encounter permafrost, September 1942. Courtesy of Yukon Archives, MacBride Museum Collection.

OPPOSITE, TOP: Convoy to Whitehorse near Stone Mountain, October 1942. Courtesy of Chief of Engineers, Office of History.

BOTTOM: First truck, Dawson Creek to Whitehorse, September 1942. Courtesy of Chief of Engineers, Office of History.

ABOVE: Bulldozer pulling trucks through permafrost, near Pickhandle Lake. Courtesy of U.S. National Archives.
BELOW: The right way to build on permafrost, near Alaskan-Canadian border. Courtesy of U.S. National Archives.

ABOVE: The Slim's River
Bridge, built by the 18th
Engineers, July 1942. Courtesy
of U.S. National Archives.
RIGHT: Ice floes threatening the
Peace River Bridge, November
1942. Author's collection.
BELOW: The 18th Engineers
drilling and blasting a road to
Soldier's Summit, July 1942.
Courtesy of Chief of Engineers,
Office of History.

The 97th Engineers cutting trail over permafrost, September 1942. Courtesy Walter E. Mason.

Link-up of the 18th and 97th Engineers, opening the Pioneer Road, October 1942. Courtesy of Chief of Engineers, Office of History.

Ribbon cutting at Soldier's Summit, November 20, 1942. Courtesy of Chief of Engineers, Office of History.

Royal Canadian Mounted Police Honor Guard for opening ceremony, Soldier's Summit, November 20, 1942. Courtesy of Chief of Engineers, Office of History.

First truck to Fairbanks after opening ceremony. Courtesy of Chief of Engineers, Office of History.

TOP: The highway south of Kluane Lake, winter 1943.
Courtesy of University of Alaska (Fairbanks) Archives.
ABOVE: Digging out after an avalanche on the White
Pass and Yukon Railroad line, winter 1943. Courtesy
of Chief of Engineers, Office of History.
RIGHT: The White Pass and Yukon Railroad line, winter
1943. Courtesy of Chief of Engineers, Office of History.

LEFT: Dawson Creek after the fire, February 1943. Courtesy of South Peace Historical Society. BELOW: "The Army's road tended to go over the hills, not around them." Courtesy of Chief of Engineers, Office of History.

ABOVE: Delivering pipe for CANOL I pipeline. Courtesy of Chief of Engineers, Office of History.
LEFT: Welding the CANOL I pipeline. Courtesy of Chief of Engineers, Office of History.

Christmas 1943 at a
PRA Camp. Courtesy of
Yukon Archives,
Waddington Collection.

Workmen, Utah Construc-
tion Company, October
1943. Courtesy of
University of Alaska
(Fairbanks) Archives,
George Smith Collection.

Mess hall, Utah
Construction Company,
1943. Courtesy of
University of Alaska
(Fairbanks) Archives,
George Smith Collection.

Government liquor store, Whitehorse, 1943. Courtesy of Yukon Archives, U.S. Army Collection.

Main Street, Whitehorse, Yukon Territory. Courtesy of South Peace Historical Society.

Irving Berlin's *This Is the Army* with Lieutenant Ronald Reagan, Whitehorse, 1943. Courtesy of Yukon Archives, Waddington Collection.

RIGHT: What all the fuss was about—
the pipeline in Dodo Canyon, not far
from Camp CANOL. Courtesy of
U.S. National Archives.
BELOW: The CANOL Road in the
Mackenzie Mountains. Courtesy of
U.S. National Archives.

The author with the remains of a flagpole at Soldier's Summit. Courtesy of Mark Singley.

The Aishihik River Bridge, built in 1904, restored by the 18th Engineers in 1942, and again by the Yukon government in 1987. Courtesy of Mark Singley.

The CANOL pipeline suspension bridge at Ross River. Courtesy of Mark Singley.

ABOVE: The original Watson Lake signpost. RIGHT: The "signpost forest" today. Courtesy of South Peace Historical Society. Inset courtesy of Mark Singley.

barrels of motor gasoline and 256,358 barrels of diesel oil. This result was accomplished at a cost of $134 million, exclusive of the Army's overhead for Task Force 2600 and General Worsham's headquarters.

After the war, the refinery was sold by the U.S. government to the Imperial Oil Company for $1 million and dismantled. With the exception of CANOL 2's pipeline, which was purchased by the White Pass and Yukon Line to pump petroleum products from Skagway to Whitehorse (and is still in use), the rest of the pipeline network was sold off for scrap. These sales further reduced the net cost of CANOL by another $700,000; but that was it. The pro-rata cost to U.S. taxpayers of each gallon of gasoline from CANOL 1 was $7.72—while the wartime price per (U.S.) gallon at civilian gas stations in Whitehorse was 29 cents.[26]

Aside from being made to look like a fool by the Truman Committee, General Somervell suffered no immediate damage from the CANOL investigation. In fact, as the commander of Army Service Forces, he was soon awarded his fourth star in recognition of his role in organizing the logistics of victory. Against the backdrop of his immense contribution to the successful campaigns in Europe and the Pacific, the CANOL fiasco seemed a minor aberration, proof that he was not infallible.

But why such a capable man had approved such a risky project against the advice of trusted subordinates like Generals Robins and Clay puzzled many people. Knowing his boss's impatient energy, Clay gave a generous explanation: "The first year of the war almost drove him crazy. . . . I think that's why we had the Alcan Highway and a number of other projects: he just had to do something." Even more puzzling was Somervell's stubborn refusal to pull the plug on CANOL 1 long after its critics had documented a convincing case for doing so. Here, less generously, the most likely explanation is that his ego and pride led him astray. Perhaps he took too seriously the motto he coined for the Army Service Forces: "The difficult we do immediately. The impossible takes a little longer."

Thus, Somervell had seriously embarrassed the Roosevelt administration and damaged the Army's credibility. On the strength of his affirmation of the need for CANOL, War Secretary Stimson and the Joint Chiefs of Staff had gone way out on a limb with him. Truman gave them all several chances to climb back down as he was sawing away. Washington insiders had long speculated that Somervell would be General Marshall's successor as Army Chief of Staff; many thought that he even had presidential aspirations. Such talk stopped after the

CANOL hearings. Somervell retired from active duty in 1946, collecting board chairmanships and honorary degrees until he died in 1955.[27]

After the CANOL hearings, Truman's star rose higher than ever. During the months leading up to the Democratic National Convention in July 1944, the Truman Committee continued with its hearings on a variety of problems: shoddy workmanship in certain shipyards, questionable practices in the chemical and publishing industries, and profiteering at the government's expense by Florida real-estate tycoons. At the same time, Truman found himself increasingly in demand as a speaker at Democratic fund raisers and gatherings of the party faithful, which naturally heightened his visibility and speculation about his future political intentions. There was increasing talk of his being an ideal running mate for Roosevelt. But to everyone who asked, Truman's answer was the same: "I am not interested in the Vice-Presidency."

Truman's biographers make much of the fact that he never used the work of his committee for personal political advantage and that, despite his rising fame, he never sought his party's nomination as Roosevelt's running mate. In this regard, two actions by Truman in early 1944 are of considerable interest. The first was his graceful fence-mending with senior War Department officials who may have felt roughly treated by his committee, particularly during the bruising CANOL hearings. The second was the method he used to publicly affirm his personal loyalty to the President and to remind him of the Truman Committee's great service to his administration. Neither action could have been construed as an overture toward the Vice-Presidency. But both had the effect of increasing his chances of being put on the ticket.

Truman's peace offering to the top echelon at the War Department was a masterpiece of political subtlety. A lifelong student of history, he was especially fascinated by the American Civil War. Its most important lesson for him in directing the work of his committee was what it taught about how *not* to investigate the conduct of a war. "Many congressional committees," he wrote in his *Memoirs*, ". . . have been guilty of departing from their original purposes and jurisdiction." He continued:

> The most outstanding example of misdirected investigation occurred during the Civil War when the Committee on the Conduct of the War attempted to direct military operations in the field. . . . The Committee . . . abused witnesses unmercifully. In reading [its] reports . . . I was made ashamed of the Congress. . . .
>
> The special committee [the Truman Committee] never discussed military strategy, although we took testimony from many generals and admirals. The military policy of the United States was entrusted to the

President and the Joint Chiefs of Staff and not to any congressional committee.[28]

To make sure that the men entrusted with the military policy of the United States understood and appreciated the great contrast between the Truman Committee's methods and those of its Civil War predecessor, Senator Truman arranged a little history lesson for them. The occasion was a black-tie dinner given by Truman in the Federal Room of Washington's Statler Hotel on March 20, 1944. Invited, with their wives, were Secretary of War Henry Stimson and Secretary of the Navy Frank Knox; their Under Secretaries, Robert Patterson and James Forrestal; Army Chief of Staff George Marshall and Chief of Naval Operations Ernest King; and Truman's committee colleagues. The guest of honor was the distinguished historian of the Civil War, Douglas Southall Freeman, Robert E. Lee's biographer, who gave a vivid after-dinner account of the blatant attempts by the Committee on the Conduct of the War to wrest control of the war effort from President Lincoln, a bitterly partisan campaign that began shortly after the first Union defeats in 1861 and ended only with the South's capitulation. The black-tie affair was a pleasant social occasion and a gracious gesture toward reconciliation, but these were quite possibly not its only purposes.[29]

Truman's election-year fence-mending with FDR was less subtle. In a series of well-publicized speeches around the country between February and May, he expressed confidence in the administration's management of the war effort, warned against partisan criticism of Roosevelt's leadership in the continuing crisis, and called for his reelection. Said the *New York Times* of one of these speeches:

> Mr. Truman's statement, which had the effect of giving a stamp of approval to the nation's war leaders and war program from a source which commands considerable respect, is an important boost for President Roosevelt's nomination and for his chances with the electorate next November.[30]

Up until then the Truman Committee had received much praise for its consistently nonpartisan approach to its responsibilities. That Truman himself was now trading on the good reputation of his committee for political purposes led its two Republican members, Senators Homer Ferguson and Joseph H. Ball, to cry foul.[31] But no uproar resulted. Far greater partisan abuses, as Truman the armchair historian well knew, were as traditionally American as the Fourth of July.

Despite the supportive tenor of his speeches, however, Truman remained just another face in the Washington crowd as far as President Roosevelt was concerned. The two men had never been close. Despite being a loyal Democrat on most issues, Truman had, after all, opposed Roosevelt's decision to run for a third term. And although the President may have appreciated Truman's ability to focus criticism on serious problems in the management of the war effort without impugning him personally, Truman as his fourth-term running mate was not a possibility he had previously considered.

Roosevelt had let it be known that he was perfectly happy to run again with his current Vice-President, Henry A. Wallace, whose popularity was strongest in the Midwest and with the Democratic Left. On the other hand, Wallace was detested by many of the more conservative king-makers in the Democratic party; and after three strenuous terms, President Roosevelt's health was visibly failing. His inner circle of advisors was confident of his reelection, but they worried whether he could survive another term. Whoever was nominated to run with Roosevelt was thus very likely to succeed him in office.

As convention time approached, several insiders, led by Robert E. Hannegan and Edwin W. Pauley—the Chairman and Treasurer, respectively, of the Democratic National Committee—embarked on a "conspiracy" (as they called it themselves) to convince Roosevelt that Henry Wallace was a political liability. Truman was near the top of their list of acceptable Vice-Presidential candidates, but both men took him at his word that he was not interested. Instead they subtly worked to turn the President against his current Vice-President. They succeeded.

But while Roosevelt gradually lost his enthusiasm for Wallace, he could not be pinned down as to a replacement. When pressed, he affirmed that Truman was acceptable to him, but on other occasions he expressed a preference for Supreme Court Justice William O. Douglas or Director of War Mobilization James F. Byrnes—among others. In typical fashion, Roosevelt was keeping his options open until the last moment.[32]

The backroom political machinations that took place at the Democratic National Convention and resulted in Harry S. Truman's nomination for the Vice-Presidency of the United States on July 21, 1944, are not easily summarized. Nor, for this story, do they need to be. Suffice it to say that what made Truman a serious contender that day was his outstanding three-year performance as Chairman of the Special Committee Investigating the National Defense Program. Among the other factors that clinched the nomination for him—whether he planned it that way or not—was undoubtedly his consummate skill at fence-mending in the aftermath of the CANOL investigation.

15

ALSIB: Warplanes for Russia

F ew, if any, of the Alaska Highway's wartime critics were aviators. Thanks to the highway, the Northwest Staging Route became the least hazardous of the three main airways used by the U.S. military during World War II to fly to Alaska and points beyond. Prior to late 1943, however, the Staging Route was anything but a milk run.

For a while, the U.S. Army Air Force saw more advantage in developing the so-called "Low-level Route," which would have incorporated the chain of landing strips along the Athabasca, Slave, and Mackenzie rivers that were built to service Project CANOL. Beyond Norman Wells this route followed the Mackenzie for another 300 miles and then swung west into the Yukon River valley over the same low pass (the Rat–Bell portage) where Emily Craig and her Klondike-bound companions had barely survived the winter of 1898.[1]

As Vilhjalmur Stefansson never tired of pointing out, the Mackenzie and Yukon river valleys not only lay along the great circle route connecting the North American heartland with Asia, they also skirted the "high-granite country" between Edmonton and Fairbanks. Nevertheless, as Project CANOL's problems mounted and the opening of the Alaska Highway increased the safety and efficiency of the Northwest Staging Route, the Air Force lost all interest in the Mackenzie–Yukon airway. This was one more disappointment for Stefansson.

The other alternative to the Northwest Staging Route was the coastal airway pioneered prior to World War II by Billy Mitchell's "World Cruisers" and Pan American's "Clipperships." Most of these

277

sea-level airfields nestled against towering peaks and were subject to all of the notorious weather hazards of the Inside Passage and the Gulf of Alaska. Pilots hated this route—with good reason. It, too, declined in military importance after 1943.

On the other hand, air traffic over the Northwest Staging Route increased steadily throughout the war. With the highway finally open all the way to Fairbanks, pilots taking off from Edmonton had few worries about finding fuel, repair parts, a hot meal, or a clean cot at any of seven major bases on the two-day, 2,000-mile flight. These same bases were also equipped with radio homing beacons and other modern navigational devices; but given what the northern lights and local magnetic anomalies could do to the signals such instruments emitted, the most reliable aid to navigation—when visibility was good—was the highway itself. If an in-flight emergency precluded reaching one of the major bases, pilots could put down on one of more than a dozen roadside landing strips with minimal facilities that were conveniently located at intervals between them. And as a last resort, a pilot in really serious trouble could almost always find a level stretch of gravel road straight enough to land on.

The increasing air traffic to Fairbanks had little to do with combat operations against the Japanese—at least after the successful conclusion of the Aleutian Campaign. (Although the Northwest Staging Route played a crucial role in the airpower buildup for the campaign, the 12,000 troops who stormed ashore on Attu on May 11, 1943, were transported and supplied by ships from the west coast, not by trucks over the Alaska Highway.) By mid-1943, U.S. strategy had evolved into a massive two-pronged offensive toward Japan via the Central and South Pacific. That made Alaska, despite Billy Mitchell's predictions, a military backwater once again. But General Mitchell had been correct in a broader sense about Alaska's future importance as a strategic crossroads. Starting in September 1942, Ladd Field in Fairbanks became the crossroads airfield on the Alaskan/Siberian (ALSIB) Ferry Route.

Under the terms of the Lend-Lease Program with Russia, fighters and bombers from U.S. factories were brought north to Ladd Field; and from there they were flown by Soviet pilots over the Bering Strait and on across Siberia to bases within striking distance of Hitler's armies at the gates of Moscow and Leningrad. In the three years of ALSIB's existence, the Soviet Union received 7,926 Lend-Lease aircraft at Ladd Field. Only 129 of those planes left Fairbanks during 1942, however, the first flight—ten A-20 light attack bombers—taking off on September 29.[2]

ALSIB started slowly for several reasons. The first had to do with some tough U.S.–Soviet negotiations over where the American pilots would turn over their planes to Soviet flyers. To maximize the number of aircraft reaching the Eastern Front in combat-ready condition, the United States wanted the transfer to take place as close to the fighting front as possible—which was a polite way of saying that the American pilots and mechanics were more careful and better trained than their Russian counterparts. It also meant that every airbase on the Soviet side of the ALSIB route would need a contingent of U.S. military person- nel—ground crews, tower operators, weather forecasters, and the like—all of them, in Soviet eyes, potential spies. In addition, Stalin may have feared that allowing U.S. military aircraft to use Siberian bases that also happened to be within striking distance of Japan might tempt the United States to launch a raid from (or provoke a Japanese preemptive attack on) Soviet territory. Either possibility would plunge the Soviet Union into a disastrous two-front war. At any rate, despite Stalin's desperate need for more Lend-Lease aircraft in the summer of 1942 (some, but not enough, were getting through on ships to Murmansk or being flown by way of South America–Africa–Iran), he refused to allow any ALSIB flights until the United States agreed to let the transfer point be on American soil.[3]

A host of lesser problems soon cropped up in Fairbanks: a shortage of interpreters (fewer Americans spoke Russian than vice versa); Russian insistence that every plane be in mechanically perfect condi- tion; the lack of critical spare parts and winterization equipment. One by one these glitches were overcome, and the number of planes that changed hands each month slowly began to increase.[4]

But the still-primitive conditions at the more remote airfields of the Northwest Staging Route remained the most serious bottleneck during ALSIB's first twelve months. Although every major base had at least one usable runway by the fall of 1942, it took at least another year to equip places such as Fort Nelson, Watson Lake, and Northway with sufficient all-weather navigational aids, auxiliary runways, and maintenance facilities to handle the ever-increasing traffic with a margin of safety. Some of this delay could be blamed on the fact that long stretches of the Alaska Highway remained closed for one reason or another (ice, floods, rebuilding by the PRA) during most of 1943. Until October of that year, for example, all the heavy equipment and supplies needed to upgrade the base at Northway had to be flown in.[5]

At the Staging Route airfields within Canada, however, labor disputes, politics, and Canadian pride were the chief obstacles to faster progress. Many Canadians complained that using U.S. Army

Engineers and/or American civilians to construct these projects was robbing Canadians of jobs. Canada's labor unions and contractors said to Ottawa, in effect: "The Americans are doing most of the construction on their highway, so let us build the airfields." Having already decided that Canada's long-term aviation needs—and not the momentary (and possibly exaggerated) military requirements of the United States— should determine the extent and layout of the permanent facilities at each field, Ottawa welcomed this demand from the private sector. The Canadian government repeatedly pointed to domestic political pressures in resisting Washington's demands to let the United States take over and upgrade the bases that lay on Canadian soil.

It was a losing battle, however. Rising American impatience with Ottawa's red tape, with the hidebound methods of Canadian contractors, and with the leisurely pace of their unionized workforce forced Canada into a series of compromises—all in the name of "military necessity." By 1944, most of the construction work being done on the Northwest Staging Route was proceeding under American control. (Although Canada ultimately picked up most of the nearly $120 million tab for building the Staging Route and its auxiliary landing strips, as of 1943 Ottawa had spent only about $25 million on its own construction program for the Staging Route; after the war it reimbursed the United States for the balance of the work, minus $14 million for "items of non-permanent value.")[6]

All of these factors had an impact on the capacity and efficiency

ALSIB TOTALS, BY YEAR

Year	Number of Planes Delivered
1942 (4 months)	129
1943	2,497
1944	3,156
1945 (8 months)	2,144
TOTAL	7,926*

ALSIB TOTALS, BY TYPE OF AIRCRAFT

FIGHTERS			BOMBERS		CARGO	OTHER
P-39	P-40	P-63	A-20	B-25	C-47	
2,618	48	2,397	1,363	732	710	58

*An additional 6,092 Lend-Lease aircraft were delivered to the Soviet Union via all other routes.

of the Northwest Staging Route. Although Lend-Lease aircraft bound for the Soviet Union were by no means the only planes headed north from Edmonton, they did constitute a growing percentage of the military traffic as the war progressed. The figures given in the accompanying tables tell the bottom line of the ALSIB story.[7]

But the real story of ALSIB is in the experiences of the people who flew all those planes. Every airplane sent to the Soviet Union via Fairbanks and Nome was flown by at least three different pilots: one who picked it up from a factory somewhere in the United States and delivered it to the ALSIB staging base at Great Falls, Montana; another who flew it the 2,500 miles from there to Ladd Field; and a third, who took it another 7,000 miles across Russia to the Eastern Front.

The last leg of the trip was unquestionably the most hazardous; there was no equivalent of the Alaska Highway linking the chain of primitive airstrips across the desolate mountains and steppes of Siberia. That fact, however, did little to dampen the enthusiasm of the Soviet pilots chosen by their government to bring back planes from Fairbanks. Combat veterans all, they viewed the chance to get away from front-line flying for a few weeks as both an honor and a reward. The honor was in being trusted enough to represent the Soviet Union abroad; the reward was in being allowed a brief R&R in Fairbanks, with enough U.S. dollars for a shopping spree (the money usually went for lingerie, soap, cosmetics, perfume, watches, and jewelry) and an evening or two on the town. Most of these men flew only one ALSIB mission before returning to combat. But Squadron Commander Peter Gamov repeatedly flew back to Fairbanks. A much-decorated bomber pilot, his wartime assignment was to lead groups of fighters across to the Eastern Front; he made the round trip several hundred times. (With his wife, Elena Makarova, a wartime interpreter at Ladd, Peter Gamov returned to Fairbanks in 1991 for a reunion of American and Russian ALSIB pilots.)[8]

Like Gamov, pilots assigned to one of the Ferry Groups of the U.S. Army Air Force Air Transport Command had the job of delivering airplanes. Four Ferry Groups handled all deliveries within the continental United States, whether the planes were to go from the factory to a flight training center or to a staging base for shipment overseas—or simply from one airfield to another. Thus, when a factory responsible for making one of the six main types of aircraft that were being sent to the Soviet Union had a shipment of planes ready, the mission of flying them to Great Falls normally went to the Ferry Group nearest that factory: the 2nd Ferry Group at Wilmington,

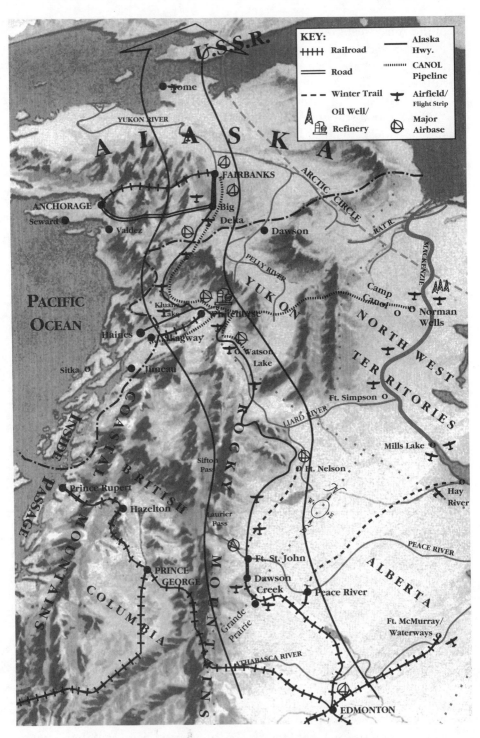

THE NORTHWEST STAGING ROUTE

Delaware; the 3rd at Romulus, Michigan; the 5th at Dallas, Texas; or the 6th at Long Beach, California.[9] At each group headquarters, however, deciding who would fly a particular mission was a little more complicated.

To be assigned a ferry mission, a pilot had to be both "available"— that is, rested and physically able to fly—and "checked out" or qualified on the particular type of aircraft being delivered. How the chain of command chose to interpret these two provisos quickly became an important issue for the female pilots the Air Force reluctantly began to accept for training in late 1942. During the next two years, more than 1,000 of these women went through an intensive military flight training program and won their wings as WASPs— Women Airforce Service Pilots. Most WASPs were assigned to one of the four domestic Ferry Groups of the Air Transport Command, although some later ended up in the Air Training Command towing target sleeves for anti-aircraft gunners to shoot at. Wherever a WASP found herself assigned, patronizing male superior officers usually invoked supposed gender differences to limit her assignments and opportunities.

Not long out of college, Virginia (Ginny) Hill, Celia Hunter, and fifty-eight other young women arrived in Houston, Texas, to form WASP Class 43-2, on December 11, 1942. Although everyone in the group already had at least 200 hours of flying time and a commercial pilot's license, seventeen women would "wash out" during the next five and one-half months of high-pressure training. The classes covered everything from drills on marching and saluting to lessons in Morse Code, night instrument flying, and cross-country navigation. Basic flying instruction in the Vultee BT-15 "Valiant" (better known, because of its invigorating ride, as the "Vultee Vibrator") was followed by many hours of advanced training in the North American AT-6—the "Awful-Terrible 6." New silver wings came on graduation day, May 28, 1943.[10] Celia Hunter drew the 2nd Ferry Group in Delaware as her new assignment; Ginny Hill joined the 6th Group in California.

As Ginny Hill recalls it, the rank and position of the women pilots in the 6th Group were ambiguous. Even though WASPs wore a uniform of sorts (khaki slacks and blouse), they were technically not in the military at all, but Civil Service employees. Still, they could use the PX and the Officers' Club and were subject to the same Air Force rules and regulations as their male counterparts, all of whom were commissioned officers.

Then there was the question of the WASPs "availability" for ferry missions. For safety's sake, no pilot could fly more than a certain number of hours per month, but in the Air Transport Command there was a double standard. As the 6th Group's operations officer delicately explained to Ginny and her cohorts, it was unfair to expect them to fly on "those days." He also implied that premenstrual tension might adversely affect their piloting skills. He therefore instructed them to keep him apprised of the dates of their menstrual periods so he could keep a chart showing who was able to fly on any given day. As for their delivering anything but training planes and other lightweight aircraft, that was out of the question. Women, they were told, lacked the strength and coordination needed to fly fighter planes, let alone large bombers—notwithstanding that the bigger planes had hydraulically assisted controls.

Under the twin pressures of female indignation and pilot short-ages, these arbitrary rules began to crumble. In the 6th Group, for example, the WASPs informed the operations officer that their biological rhythms were none of his or anyone else's business. Soon, the various Group Commanders were surprised to discover that women were quite capable of flying heavier and faster aircraft.

Late in 1943 the 6th Group began receiving limited quotas for WASPs to take transition training at the Pursuit Plane School in Palm Springs. By mid-1944, Ginny Hill and her friends were fully checked out and routinely ferrying the "hot" fighter planes of the day: Lockheed P-38 "Lightnings," Bell P-39 "Aircobras" and P-63 "Kingcobras," Curtiss P-40 "Warhawks," Republic P-47 "Thunder-bolts," and North American P-51 "Mustangs." As with the Vultee "Vibrator," each make had two nicknames—one given it by some Air Force publicity flack, the other what the pilots actually called it. Ginny Hill sprinkled her conversations with references to the "Bell Booby Trap" (P-39), the "Curtiss Novelty Company" (P-40), and (her favorite to fly) the "Peter-Dash-Flash" or "Spam Can" (P-51). Her friend Celia Hunter flew a lot of "Jugs," or P-47s.

Every ferry mission Ginny Hill flew followed essentially the same sequence: pick up a plane at Point A (or B or C . . .); fly it to Point X (or Y or Z); go to the nearest commercial airport for a flight back to Long Beach; and then stand by to do it all over again. There was no room for luggage in the cockpit of a fighter plane, so the WASPs traveled light. Ginny Hill carried everything she needed, even a party dress, in one overnight case stowed neatly in the plane's ammunition compartment. Returning to California, she learned to ignore the angry reactions of the traveling businessmen and minor government bureaucrats bumped from their hard-to-obtain airline seats by her Class 2 travel priority. Among the many ferry missions Ginny Hill flew during 1943–1944 were a number of flights in Lend-Lease P-39s to the ALSIB staging field outside Great Falls, Montana. There, at the Air Force's East Base (now Malmstrom Air Force Base), she turned her aircraft over to the all-male 7th Ferry Group, who winterized them, painted on the red star insignia of the Soviet Union, and flew them north to Fairbanks.[11]

Because of the hazards of the 2,500-mile flight from Great Falls, as well as the rather unsophisticated radio and navigational equipment of that era's fighter planes, single-engine aircraft being ferried over the Northwest Staging Route were supposed to travel in formation and be accompanied by a "mother ship"—usually a twin-engine C-47 transport or A-20 light bomber. In addition to possessing better electronic gear, every mother ship also carried spare parts for its "flock" and, frequently, various other kinds of Lend-Lease cargo and supplies for the Soviet Union as well. Rare was the C-47 or A-20 that landed in Fairbanks with its formation of fighters intact, however. Delayed by any of a thousand possible mechanical and weather problems, the stragglers came limping into Ladd Field hours, days, or sometimes weeks later.

Air Force Lieutenant Gordon Leenerts flew more than forty missions to Fairbanks during 1942–1943, returning to Great Falls after each delivery with a dozen or more other ferry pilots aboard an Army-chartered Northwest Airlines C-46. Like fighter pilots of every nationality, Leenerts and his friends were a cocky bunch. "I started flying in the winter of '42 which was a very severe winter," he recalled:

> Sometimes we'd go down very low on the highway . . . and play chicken with the truck drivers. . . . At first they'd stop the trucks and jump out because they were afraid. Then they'd start throwing rocks at us, and that forced us up to at least the height of [a] building.

Once, landing in a blizzard at Watson Lake, Leenerts misjudged the runway:

> Came in so hard, I buckled the landing gear and bent the prop. They couldn't fly in parts with the base socked in . . . took a while to fix my plane. But things could've been a lot worse. A USO troop was stranded there, too, so we had entertainment every night: magicians, jugglers, and a lady accordion player. . . .

As for the Russian pilots he met at Fairbanks, said Leenerts, "It appeared to me that they had instructions not to mingle too closely with us. They weren't unfriendly, but it just seemed that every time we'd make friendly overtures, they'd back away."[12]

The language barrier was one obvious explanation for the Russians' standoffish behavior, but the real problem was their deeply ingrained suspicion of foreigners—a mistrust that unfortunately aroused the same paranoid tendencies among some of their American hosts. The monthly Army intelligence reports forwarded to Washington summarizing the activities of Soviet military personnel and alleged "Soviet sympathizers" in the Fairbanks area during World War II consistently attributed motives of espionage and subversion to the members of both groups.

Nevertheless, both sides sometimes managed to overcome their mutual suspicions and have a good time together, usually with more than a little help from the obligatory vodka toasts to Russian-American friendship. For the senior officers and visiting VIPs of both nationalities, these occasions most often took the form of a formal banquet or reception; the junior officers and NCOs much preferred informal parties and dances. Even forty-five years later, Ginny Hill still smiled when she talked about dancing the night away with a Russian liaison officer at Great Falls.[13]

It was hard for most Americans not to admire these self-assured veterans of the Eastern Front. At Ladd, one Soviet pilot, disregarding instructions from the tower, landed his P-40 on a taxiway and then wove erratically in and out through a line of parked planes before cutting his engine. As he climbed out of the cockpit, a young American operations officer ran up and began to chew him out. The Russian cut him off with "I got eight Nazi planes. How many you got?" Most Soviet pilots were similarly casual about preflight inspections. Instead of following a careful checklist, they simply climbed into their planes, gunned the engine once or twice, and then took off. Yet they clearly knew their business. Recalled an American instructor pilot:

> A young fighter pilot with a girl interpreter came over to my P-40 for a check. The Russian climbed into the cockpit, the girl got on one wing and I got on the other. He asked me only four questions and then took off. The first thing he wanted to know was, "How do you start it?" I told the girl, she told him and he said, "Da" . . . Then he asked for the maximum pressure and RPM for takeoff. His next question, "How do you keep the oil temperature and coolant up?" Finally, he wanted to know how to operate the radio. Then he took the plane up for a test run, and he could fly it too.[14]

Even without the special hazards on each leg of the ALSIB run and the cavalier attitude toward safety by many Soviet pilots, some crashes and fatalities would have been inevitable in an operation of this magnitude. According to John H. Cloe, a U.S. Air Force historian who has written about ALSIB, an overall loss rate of 5 percent—one aircraft in twenty—would have been considered acceptable. In fact, only one in every sixty Lend-Lease aircraft crashed on the way north to Fairbanks, less than half of them (63) after leaving Great Falls. Along the Staging Route, most of the pilots bailed out close enough to the highway to walk to safety or be found by search parties; only fifteen members of the 7th Group lost their lives on the ALSIB run.

For their part, the Soviets (who also used mother ships to escort their fighter formations) claimed that 499 out of every 500 aircraft that left Fairbanks reached the Eastern Front. That figure is highly suspect, however—even allowing for the fact that the hard-nosed Soviet inspectors at Ladd Field never accepted any plane not in absolutely perfect mechanical condition. What is known for certain about Soviet losses is that thirteen Russian aviators died on U.S. soil and were buried at Fort Richardson, just outside Fairbanks. According to a recent article in a Siberian newspaper, another 112 died in crashes en route to the front. [15]

In some respects, ALSIB may have worked too well. It provided a conduit not only for nearly 8,000 Lend-Lease airplanes, but for many other items on the Soviet Union's wartime "shopping list." Some things had no conceivable military value (13,328 sets of false teeth, for example); others were of such importance that they had to be obtained by espionage. Only the recipients in Moscow knew what was in the hundreds of black suitcases, sealed under diplomatic immunity and shipped in batches of fifty through Great Falls by the Russian embassy in Washington, but an American Army major claimed after the war to have opened several on his own initiative and found various highly classified U.S. military and diplomatic documents not meant for foreign eyes. It has also been alleged (though never proved) that ALSIB was one of the channels for stolen U.S. atomic secrets. [16]

Finally, ALSIB provided a quick and relatively safe way for high-ranking officials to travel back and forth between Washington and Moscow. Vice-President Henry Wallace, Soviet Foreign Minister Vyacheslav Molotov, and Ambassador Andrei Gromyko were among the many VIPs who repeatedly used the route. Most were given a code name for security reasons. Molotov's alias was "Mr. Brown"; he is said to have been so fearful of being gunned down or poisoned en route that he habitually traveled with a pistol and a piece of sausage in his briefcase.[17]

In assessing the wartime relationship of ALSIB and the Northwest Staging Route to the Alaska Highway, it is impossible not to recognize the element of truth in the April 1942 statement by Alaska's Governor Ernest Gruening that "What appears to be sought by the Army is not a highway at all but a kind of leading string for the young flyers."

But in weighing the combined contribution of the Northwest Staging Route and the Alaska Highway to the outcome of World War II, another quote seems appropriate: "Never in the history of aviation," said Air Force General Henry H. Arnold in 1943, "has a road been so important to airmen."[18] To that, even the grim-faced Ambassador Gromyko (later dubbed "Mr. Nyet" for his veto record at the U.N.) could no doubt say a grudging "Da!"

16

1942–1945

Canadians and the
"Army of Occupation"

Whitehorse residents who remember World War II like to tell a story that still rings true. Telephone calls to the Northwest Service Command headquarters, they claim, were often answered by a cheerful voice saying, "Army of Occupation. What office are you calling?"

That anonymous "Yankee boy" doubtless meant only to amuse. Americans stationed in the Canadian Northwest used the phrase jokingly.[1] But the local people, acutely aware of the massive U.S. military presence throughout the region, very likely saw less humor in the situation than did their allies. Many Canadians still have ambivalent feelings on the subject. In fact, two Canadian scholars, Kenneth S. Coates and William R. Morrison, have published a book, *The Alaska Highway in World War II: The U.S. Army of Occupation in Canada's Northwest*, that scrutinizes the mixed blessings conferred by the wartime activities of the U.S. Army.[2]

Visitors from the United States who encounter this touchy ambivalence among their northern neighbors are often puzzled by it, all the more so if they know anything about the roads, airfields, and telephone lines—not to mention the piles of surplus equipment and millions of dollars in paycheck money—left behind by U.S. servicemen and civilians.

Why such seeming ingratitude? And what was so offensive to Canadians about the telephone manners of that cheerful GI? The answers can be found in the intertwined history of the United States and Canada, neighbors who have evolved along separate pathways ever since the American Revolution.

This is not the place for an extended essay on how Canadians and Americans have seen each other over the past 200 years. Besides, Seymour Martin Lipset has already written the book the subject deserves. Aptly titled *Continental Divide*,[3] it offers a convincingly argued thesis and a useful historical framework for any discussion of Canadian–American relations.

Lipset's thesis is that the Canadians (including Loyalist emigrés from the rebellious colonies), having supported the losing side in the Revolutionary War, had good reason to dislike and fear the newly independent nation on their southern border. Not only was its rambunctious individualism subversive of their conservative political and social order, but its greater military power and obvious interest in territorial expansion posed threats to their continued existence as a separate political entity. Despite two centuries of peaceful coexistence, Canada's own (more gradual) transition from colony to sovereign nation, and the bonding effects of mass communications and commerce, Lipset asserts, much that divided the two countries in 1783 divides them still.[4] Beneath the normally placid surface of U.S.–Canadian relations lurk long-held Canadian grudges and fears that are quickly aroused by certain kinds of American behavior.

For example, Canadians resent the frequent U.S. assumption that they are just like people in the States—or want to be. It also rankles them when U.S. politicians take their support in international affairs for granted. Pointed reminders of the United States' greater wealth and power are, not surprisingly, another sore point. At bottom lies the unavoidable awareness of U.S. power that underlies the old Canadian fear of being swallowed up. From the Canadian perspective, that threat did not end with the signing of the Anglo-American Articles of Peace in 1783. The possibility that the victorious Union Army might be deployed for a cross-border land grab after the Civil War gave impetus to the formation of the Canadian Confederation in 1867.[5] In this context, Canadians could easily have interpreted the U.S. purchase of Alaska that same year as part of a larger plan. Small wonder, then, that some of Prime Minister Mackenzie King's advisors saw the danger of an eventual U.S. takeover of northwest Canada in the various proposals for a highway to Alaska that were being discussed just prior to World War II.

Thus, in 1942, when Canada reluctantly agreed to the Alaska Highway and CANOL under the pressure of wartime necessity, these projects were bound to give new life to the old animosities. And true to form, most Americans displayed almost complete obliviousness to Canadian sensitivities. A seemingly trivial story about an American GI's thoughtless way of answering the telephone thus touches a sore place on the national psyche.

For the purposes of this book, a brief summary will suffice to draw together and highlight the most significant Canadian experiences with the U.S. "Army of Occupation."

First, at the governmental level, Washington consistently took for granted Ottawa's acquiescence in its plans for the Alaska Highway and Project CANOL. Preparations for both were well underway before Canada's permission for either of them was sought; thereafter, the Americans often began work on one or another phase of the highway and pipeline program without waiting for Ottawa's approval— and, in some instances, without even asking for it. The underlying assumption in the U.S. War Department during the early stages of the war seems to have been that it had carte blanche in northwest Canada.

Preoccupied with overseas military matters, Mackenzie King and his cabinet went along with the highway and pipeline projects for the sake of the larger goals of the alliance, but King's top diplomatic advisors felt rather strongly that the entire U.S. construction program was neither necessary nor in their country's best interests. As their internal memoranda show, they resented Canada's being maneuvered into acquiescence.

By early 1943, a growing number of senior officials in Ottawa had an uneasy feeling that Canada was losing control over the western third of its territory. How could they reverse the trend without embarrassing the government at home or provoking a crisis with the United States? Their solution was unorthodox, but it worked. They persuaded Malcolm MacDonald, the British High Commissioner to Canada and a close personal friend of Prime Minister King, to make an informal visit to inspect CANOL and the Alaska Highway in March 1943. Alarmed by what he had seen and heard, MacDonald spent an evening with King immediately upon his return; two days later he also briefed the cabinet.[6] His subsequent written report said in part:

> It is perhaps easy to overstate the danger of so much initiative and decision belonging to our American allies. Admittedly it is highly important [for] . . . the vigorous prosecution of the war that these roads and routes should be built forthwith, and they will in any case be of immense value to Canada after the war. But it is surely

unfortunate that the Canadian authorities have little real say as to, for example, the exact placing of these airfields, and the exact route of these roads, on Canadian soil. The Americans decide these according to what they consider American interests. Responsible American officers will tell you frankly in confidence that in addition to building works to be of value in this war, they are designing these works also to be of particular value for (a) commercial transport and aviation after the war and (b) waging war against the Russians in the next world crisis. . . .

The Canadian counterparts of the Americans who swarm through the country are conspicuous by their absence. The inhabitants of those regions are beginning to say that it seems that the Americans are more awake to the importance of the Canadian North-west than are the Canadian authorities. This state of affairs tends to play into the hands of those Western Canadians who are inclined to assert that the West receives little sympathy and help from Eastern Canada and that its destiny lies in incorporation with the United States of America. [7]

MacDonald's recommendation was that Canada appoint a special commissioner for the area, invested with sufficient authority and given enough staff to supervise and control the activities of the Americans. His attention now focused on the problem, Mackenzie King acted promptly. On May 20, 1943, Major General W. W. Foster was sent to Edmonton with the mission of reasserting Canada's sovereignty in its own Northwest.

Prior to General Foster's arrival, the Americans had been accustomed to dealing with two capable but powerless liaison officers, Leonard E. Drummond and C. K. LeCapelain, both of whom reported to the Department of Mines and Resources in Ottawa. From Edmonton, Drummond had the thankless task of keeping track of CANOL's bewildering proliferation; LeCapelain traveled endlessly up and down the Alaska Highway reporting on local conditions and the progress of construction. Neither man had authority to tell the Americans what they could or couldn't do.

General Foster's initial attempts to take control of the situation met resistance. When he tried to find out what was going on at Norman Wells, for example, U.S. officials blandly told him they could not divulge secret information. Eventually, however, Foster accomplished what he had been sent to do. He soon won the cooperation and respect of Generals O'Connor and Worsham, who appreciated both his fair-mindedness and his power to make quick decisions. The United States government's embarrassment over the CANOL fiasco also strengthened Foster's hand; after the Truman Committee hearings, the War Department lost its taste for wheeling and dealing in northwest Canada.[8]

Of all of Canada's citizens, the ones most profoundly affected by the presence and activities of the "Army of Occupation" were the native peoples who lived in the vicinity of the Alaska Highway. Many of the changes they experienced were not improvements, but not all of the blame for that can be put on the Americans—certainly not the mixed results of several ill-conceived social welfare programs begun after 1945 such as relocation programs and housing projects. Still, the highway did extend Ottawa's reach into once-remote villages and bring in the well-meaning social workers, just as it had earlier brought in even more disruptive influences—in particular, the white man's diseases.

"Until the advent of this new era," wrote C. K. LeCapelain after visiting the native settlements of Teslin and Lower Post in July 1943, "the[se] Indians . . . have been almost completely isolated from contacts with white people and have had the least opportunity of creating an immunity to white people's diseases." He continued:

> Consequently they have been distressingly affected by the new contacts. No doubt a contributing factor has been the fact that to a considerable extent the adult males have abandoned their normal nomadic pursuits and have accepted work on various construction projects. . . .
>
> The band of Teslin suffered epidemics of measles and whooping cough, which in some cases developed into pneumonia last year, and now are plagued with an epidemic of meningitis and have suffered three deaths so far. . . . The bands at Lower Post were devastated last spring with an epidemic of influenza which caused 15 deaths among a total population of about 150. . . . There is no doubt in my mind that if events are allowed to drift along . . . the Indian bands at Teslin and Lower Post will become completely decimated within the next four years.[9]

By contrast, the natives who lived in and around the settlements along the Mackenzie River and near such towns as Whitehorse had become relatively well immunized from most of these diseases by regular contacts with whites over the years. Even so, the sheer variety of germs brought in by the hordes of strangers temporarily in their midst took its toll on these people as well. The skimpy statistics that exist indicate that many more deaths than births occurred among the region's native peoples in 1942 and 1943, a trend not decisively reversed until 1947.[10]

Another acute vulnerability of the natives was to alcohol. Although it had long been illegal for them to buy or make alcoholic beverages, it was always possible to find whites willing to sell them liquor—or trade it for sexual favors. What changed for the worse during World War II was the number of whites in the region who had booze to sell or trade. The incidence of alcoholism and of alcohol-related crimes among the native population went up sharply and has remained a problem ever since.[11]

One aspect of life for the northwest natives that did not change as decisively during the war years as is often thought was how they made their living. Although more jobs, money, and consumer goods came in with the highway than anyone in the region had ever seen before, far fewer natives than whites benefited from this fact. Most contractors preferred to hire only whites; those who did hire native men usually gave them menial work at minimum pay and then shrugged off their drifting away as "typical of Indians."[12]

But the average native was already making a living by trapping or fishing and had little interest in trading the natural cycles of that existence for a life bound by mechanistic rules and work schedules. Some, like Charlie MacDonald, preferred to pick up extra money by acting as guides.

Long before MacDonald was hired by the 35th Engineers in June 1942, he had spent his summers guiding hunting parties through the region between Fort Nelson and Watson Lake. His main source of income, however, continued to be the pelts of the animals he trapped. MacDonald was thus no stranger to the white man's cash economy or to store-bought goods; but living close to the land as he did, he was no slave to them either. He worked for whites because it suited him, not because he had to. For him, the U.S. Army regiments and their highway were a curiosity and perhaps an annoyance—but little more. His ability to support his family depended far less on their largesse than on the price being paid for furs at the nearest trading post and on his skills as a woodsman. That equation has long since changed for MacDonald's children and their families.[13]

Indisputably, the main beneficiaries of the work done by the "Army of Occupation" were the white residents along the corridor of the Alaska Highway; and yet they, too, had grounds for resentment as well as gratitude. Two of the more appalling side effects of the overwhelming U.S. presence were the overcrowding and sanitation problems at places like Dawson Creek and Whitehorse and the thousands of square miles of forest destroyed by carelessly discarded cigarette butts. One wartime observer called Whitehorse "an open sewer." In Dawson Creek, anti-American feelings ran high in the aftermath of the dynamite explosion and fire that leveled the town's business center; the town council subsequently resigned in disagreement over how hard to press the United States for restitution. Had protecting the environment been the issue then that it is today, the Americans would have had even more to answer for. As it was, nobody made much fuss about the forest fires or the leaks in CANOL's pipelines.[14] After all, there was a war on.

Another source of resentment was the contrast between the casual affluence of the Americans and the thrifty habits of their Canadian hosts. American and Canadian workmen doing the same job on adjacent sections of the highway were paid according to wage rates set by their respective governments, and Ottawa's rates were much lower than Washington's. Then there was the wastefulness of the "Yanks." Living a patch-up and make-do existence, the locals could scarcely believe how much they shamefully squandered. A Yukon trapper named Norman Harlin recalled:

We missed too many meals in the bush, livin' on bannock and moose meat, to ever waste anything. . . .

On the CANOL line, when we were surveyin' it, they brought a reefer of meat up there, whole reefer, probably twenty tons, and the medics—their refrigerating plant had gone on the hog—and the medics opened it up and took a look at it, and the meat . . . on top had started to lose the frost. It hadn't thawed much. The frost had gone off . . . and they took a look at it and: "Dump 'er!"

Twenty ton! Mostly big, choice pork loins and sides o' choice beef. And they dumped 'er.[15]

The amount of waste got even worse in 1945, when the Americans began to pull out. They did make a conscientious effort to round up and ship home the thousands of pieces of heavy equipment that were still running or economically repairable, but anything that cost more than its "book value" to send back was simply abandoned or destroyed.[16] Earl Bartlett was serving as an electrical repairman with the Canadian Army at Fort Nelson when the Americans left:

And there was all of this stuff. They just drove away and left it. One warehouse had four or five lighting plants in it. . . . And [there was] a great mass of new electrical parts and equipment just stored in there. No inventory. No shopkeeper. I don't even know whether there was a lock on the door. They just moved out of the camp and left the whole shebang there. . . . One friend of mine . . . was at the dump where a lot of very valuable clothing . . . was being put on

the bonfire . . . eiderdown sleeping bags that are now worth something like eighty or ninety dollars. A truck had just brought a
truckload and thrown it on there and went back for another load, and
a guard was . . . walking up and down and a rifle over his back,
and this fellow . . . said to the guard, "what would happen if I went
down there and rolled off a couple of those sleeping bags into the bush
there?" He said, "I could use them." Well the guard says, "Just don't
let me see you do it, that's all."[17]

Thousands of such stories have entered into the lore of the Alaska
Highway. Anyone who lives along it can tell you a dozen or more.

On the positive side, there are just as many stories about the
kindness and generosity of the GI's. Many hospitals and orphanages
in northwest Canada were adopted for the duration by nearby
American units. The benefits included everything from regular
donations of food and medical supplies to festive parties at Christmas
and other holidays. More than one institution got new beds and office
furniture, courtesy of Uncle Sam's leaky supply system. Under the
embroidered altar cloth at St. Phillip's Anglican Mission in the
village of Teslin, Yukon Territory, stenciled in black on the side of
the simple wooden portable altar are the initials "U.S." that identify
it as having once been issued to an Army chaplain.

The rector's wife at St. Phillip's, Audrey Proctor Aylard, was born
in Dawson Creek before World War II. She has pleasant childhood
memories of wandering through the nearby army camp with her young
brothers, of being gently teased by the soldiers, and of coming home
with her pockets full of chewing gum and candy. Mrs. Aylard says her
mother had no reason to fear for her children's safety; the only
scolding she ever gave them for these outings was, "You'll spoil your
supper!"

But Mrs. Aylard also remembers her mother's anger at the
Americans on at least one occasion. In the summer of 1942, the
people of Dawson Creek put on a potluck supper and variety show to
welcome their visitors and to thank them for the highway they were
building. The evening was a great success—until a U.S. Army major
got up and made a speech in which he grandly assured his hosts that
they would all be American citizens after the war.[18]

Gratitude for the gift of the highway; resentment at the arrogance,
insensitivity, and wastefulness of many of its builders: forty years
later, in 1982, I encountered those same mixed feelings in another
room full of Canadians and Americans brought together by the
Alaska Highway. The occasion was a two-day symposium sponsored

by Fort St. John's Northern Lights College to commemorate the highway's fortieth anniversary. Scholars and writers from both nations read papers on various aspects of the highway's history. My contribution was an early draft of this book's chapter on the PRA. A special attraction was Richard Finnie's classic motion picture about the building of the highway, a documentary shot for the U.S. Army and one of the first ever filmed in color. The hall was crowded with a mixture of local history buffs and former members of the 35th and 341st Engineer Regiments, the veterans visiting Fort St. John for their fortieth reunion.

The second half of the symposium, devoted to papers by Canadians on such subjects as "U.S. Military Involvement in the Canadian Northwest" and "The Alaska Highway in Canada–United States Relations" turned out to be a session of U.S.-bashing. Most of the Army veterans in the audience disappeared after the first coffee break, but the locals stuck it out. Late in the day, after yet another presentation on the sins of Canada's wartime "occupiers," a man stood up in the back of the room and spoke:

> I've heard a lot of this talk from you people. You're typical of the intellectuals and bureaucrats from Ottawa who don't give a damn about western Canada. You never have. Let me tell you, if it hadn't been for the Americans we never would have had the Alaska Highway. Out here we think it's been a godsend—no thanks to the likes of you![19]

Epilogue

PREVIOUS SPREAD: The old highway...and the new. Courtesy of Mark Singley.

17

North Down
Memory Lane

H ow's the highway up ahead?" is a pointless question at roadside stopping places on the U.S. Interstate System. What else can be said about all those perfectly engineered miles of concrete except, "Excellent road, but borrrring"?

Along the Alaska Highway, the question is a surefire conversation starter. In August 1991 at Tok, Alaska, on my fifth trip through in the last eleven years, I ask it of Paul Smith, a husky former longshoreman and longtime proprietor of the Golden Snowshoe Motel and Gift Shop.

"That depends," Smith says, "on what you were expecting. There's at least forty-eight different answers." Stealing a glance at my brother-in-law's Volkswagen camper van and its New Jersey plates, he explains: "People from Florida or Texas in their air-conditioned Cadillacs, up here the first time, in a hurry to get to Fairbanks, they bitch 'cause they can't go seventy-five and there aren't any McDonald's. I usually tell 'em they should turn around and head home if they don't have six weeks to enjoy the trip."

When he learns that I'm writing a "then and now" book about the Alaska Highway, he has more to say about how the road surprises people. "Lots of folks seem disappointed at how few wild animals they see. But if I were a moose or a bear," he chuckles, "I sure as hell wouldn't be standing alongside the right of way. Not with all this traffic." Shaking his head, he adds, "And you wouldn't believe how many people ask me 'where are the igloos?'"

Paul Smith looks around. It is 82°F and sunny this afternoon, and we are standing outside his gift shop next to a planting bed containing gigantic ornamental cabbages and some of the most spectacularly flourishing petunias, pansies, and marigolds I have ever seen. "On the other hand," he smiles, circling back to my topic, "people come in here who last drove the ALCAN in the '50s or '60s—or even worked on it during the war—and they remember the dust and the blowouts and how the flying gravel ruined their windshields and they can't believe how good a road it's become. Them I agree with." He first drove the Alaska Highway in 1956, coming north in a borrowed pickup truck to look for work and a quieter place to raise a family than Oakland, California.

My first trip up the highway was also in a borrowed pickup truck. It began on August 1, 1980, one day after I'd retired from twenty-four years in the Army. With no immediate job prospects, I thought it might be fun to try to complete an unfinished manuscript that I'd recently inherited from my father—an account of his wartime experiences on the Alaska Highway. And so, with Tom Melcher, the whip-smart sixteen-year-old son of a good friend as my "research assistant," I set out for Fairbanks from Newport, Rhode Island, in a rust-pocked Chevy "Luv."

Two months, 9,000 miles, and fifty interviews later I was back in Rhode Island, awed by what I had seen and heard—but discouraged about turning my father's manuscript into a book. I doubted that I could do justice to the sweep of the story or the majesty of its setting. In any case, his part in it, while significant, was just one thread in a historical tapestry far larger and more complex than I had imagined. I played around with various outlines but nothing seemed right. After several months, I put it all aside and began a second career as a college professor.

I had been too easily discouraged back then. Now, here I was in August 1991, with this book almost finished, heading for Fairbanks once more and asking "How's the highway?" of people like Paul Smith along the way.

My traveling companion this time was my brother-in-law, Mark Singley, who caught the Alaska Highway bug from the Twichell family long ago. Mark is a retired professor of agricultural engineering who knows more about soils, rocks, vegetation, and things mechanical than I ever will. He is also an expert photographer and owns a camper van. We had made a deal: I would provide a narrated tour of the highway: "Around the next bend we'll come to Contact Creek, where the 35th and 340th Engineers linked up in September

1942 . . .”; he would take pictures and help me understand the engineering problems those men faced. We also agreed to share expenses and take turns with the driving and cooking.

We had rendezvoused in Seattle on August 1, traveled by ferry up the Inside Passage to Skagway, and now, having used the Haines Cutoff to reach the Alaska Highway at Haines Junction, were driving north toward Fairbanks. Tok is on the way. From Fairbanks, we planned to drive back down the entire length of the highway, stopping at Whitehorse, Watson Lake, Fort Nelson, and Dawson Creek before heading home. I needed to visit several places that I had written about but never seen and to plug a few holes in my research, but our schedule was loose enough to accommodate a fair number of spur-of-the-moment detours. Most of all, the trip was to be an exploration of memories.

What follows are some verbal snapshots—a more or less chrono-logical series of impressions and reflections from our one-month odyssey. (Readers looking for practical help in planning their own trip should purchase the latest edition of the *Milepost* from the Alaska Northwest Publishing Company of Anchorage.)

I wanted to travel the length of the Inside Passage to get a sense of what the voyage must have been like back in 1942, so Mark and I booked passage to Skagway from Bellingham, Washington, 80 miles north of Seattle, on the MV *Columbia*, the flagship of the Alaska Marine Highway ferry system. Unless you fly in, these ferries are still the only way to get to most of the isolated communities of the Alaskan Panhandle. Even though we already knew we were going to be sleeping in the passenger lounge (all the private cabins had sold out six months in advance, and our van was "off limits" down in the hold), our seventy-eight hours on the *Columbia* were a lot more like time spent on a wartime troopship than either of us had bargained for.

Four hundred more people were on board than the ship had bunks for, and the seats in the main passenger lounge didn't recline, which put a premium on out-of-the-way patches of carpeted deck where you could roll out a sleeping bag. Some hardy souls pitched tents outside on the open deck. Vaguely explained "mechanical troubles" delayed our sailing by six hours; after that the published schedule was a joke. The ventilation system worked only while we were underway, the overtaxed restrooms grew grungy, and the cafeteria food, though plentiful, was indifferent in quality and overpriced. The whole experience was like being trapped in a crowded bus terminal for three days. I think I now understand how those thousands of

Engineer soldiers and civilian workmen must have felt when their ships finally docked.

One compensation for our discomfort was the wonderful diversity of our fellow "steerage" passengers: college students with bikes and backpacks, octogenarians on a last adventure, traveling salesmen making the rounds, native families visiting relatives up the coast, military personnel going to new assignments, thirty-somethings changing jobs, aging flower children going nowhere in particular. The amiable man in the next seat had been a big-league baseball pitcher until he hurt his arm; now he was a salmon fisherman with a native wife and two lively boys. People respected each other's privacy, but they also seemed delighted to pass the time in conversation.

Best of all was the beauty of the glacier-carved fjords and steeply forested slopes all around us, even when we could barely glimpse their somber gradeur through the rain squalls—or only sense it behind the swirling sea fog. Several times, pilot whales swam alongside the ship. In the Wrangell Narrows, there seemed to be a nesting eagle in every tenth tree, and sea otters looked up from their play as we glided past. Travel brochures call the 1,500-mile route of the Alaska Marine Highway "the world's most scenic cruise." No argument there.

We docked in Skagway at 5:45 A.M., with the sun barely touching the surrounding peaks and the town just waking up. Broadway Street still looks about the same as I remember it from old photographs and my visit in 1980: board sidewalks and restored gold-rush-era saloons and shops, all gussied up and waiting for the next wave of tourists. Three more boatloads were in town by midmorning.

Skagway's harbor has changed a lot. In 1942 it had a single wooden pier (subsequently enlarged by the U.S. Army), and the usual method of handling incoming supply barges was to beach them and wait until low tide to unload them. Now, to accommodate all the gleaming white "Love Boats," there are several steel piers as well. The newest addition to the waterfront is a huge black shed— a state-of-the-environmental-art facility for transferring to waiting ships the lead-zinc-silver ore concentrates brought down from the Faro Mine, deep in the Yukon interior. In the old days, only the narrow-gauge White Pass and Yukon Railroad could have delivered that ore to Skagway, but now a good highway runs over the pass, and trucks can do the job. The railroad no longer carries any freight between Skagway and Whitehorse; its only function is to give tourists a thrill by hauling them to the top of the pass and back in time for shipboard cocktails.

Although the transportation monopoly of Herb Wheeler, General Hoge's friend and benefactor, is long gone, the White Pass Line is still managed by a shrewd businessman. Its current CEO is a portly former U.S. Army officer named Marvin Taylor, who came to Skagway in 1942 with the Transportation Corps outfit sent in by General Somervell to run the railroad for the duration. Taylor stuck around after the war and now sits in Wheeler's old chair. Later in the trip, when I visited his office in Whitehorse, he proudly showed me a beautifully detailed model of one of the company's large new container ships. Asked what happened to the CANOL 2 pipeline from Skagway to Whitehorse, he puffed on his cigar and said with a smile, "We bought it for a song from Uncle Sam back in 1962. We've kept it up. Everybody in the area still gets their gasoline and fuel oil from us."

Skagway is less than an hour's ferry ride from Haines, where we camp overnight before setting off for Fairbanks. Built in 1943 to bypass the Skagway–Whitehorse transportation bottleneck, the 158 miles of the Haines Cutoff are a dramatic introduction to the scenic splendors ahead. For the first 30 miles, the road runs through a towering spruce forest along the glacier-fed Chilkat River, whose banks and placid braided channels are littered with such a jumble of giant boulders and deadfall that it is easy to picture the violent spring torrents that deposited them. Just as the road begins its ascent into the St. Elias Mountains, we pass from Alaska into Canada, our one-minute stop at Canadian customs seemingly only a formality. After a few routine questions, the friendly but sharp-eyed customs official waves us through.

Another pleasant surprise: the road on the Canadian side of the border is now two lanes of blacktop all the way. In 1980, only the stretches of the Haines Cutoff and Alaska Highway that lay in U.S. territory were paved (though they still had lots of teeth-jarring potholes); thirteen years before that, when Mark last drove this way on a camping trip with his family, the entire length of the highway was gravel and not in much better shape than it was in 1945.

The 20-mile climb from the border over the backbone of the St. Elias Range is so gradual that I can't believe we're up very high. In fact, we're not. According to our map, the floor of the wind-swept valley connecting the Three Guardsmen and Chilkat passes is only about 3,500 feet above sea level. In milder climates, trees grow at much higher elevations, but not here. Even though we are in our shirtsleeves on this brilliant August morning, I remember the accounts of the surveyors who struggled in snow drifts and whiteouts looking for the best route through here in the winter of 1942–1943. I also recall the PRA's calculations as to how many millions of cubic yards of soil and rock would have to be moved before trucks could make this grade.

The engineering logic that went into building this road makes its present location seem somehow inevitable, but that is an illusion. Someone else might have put it farther up the slope, or even in the next valley. Whoever said "Geography plus time equals destiny" coined a memorable aphorism but left no room for choice or chance. Most probably, the Haines Cutoff would never have been built if General Somervell hadn't been so hard-nosed. And geography certainly favored Route A—not the Army's Inland Route.

We head down into the vast region of mountains and lakes drained by the Yukon and its tributaries, stopping for lunch at Haines Junction. The town looks and feels comfortably familiar to us: same language, same kinds of houses and cars, same products on the store shelves. No wonder many Americans take Canadians for granted—at least in the English-speaking parts of Canada. Only when we convert some U.S. currency does it begin to sink in that we are in a foreign country. Filling up the tank with $2.00-per-gallon Canadian gasoline drives the point home.

By midafternoon, we reach the southwest end of Kluane Lake, where the road is cut into the base of a cliff. A sign at an overlook identifies this spot as Soldier's Summit, the location of the 1942 opening ceremony. I have long suspected that the actual site is farther up the mountain, but have never before had time to look for it. Above us, through the ragged stands of spruce, we can see a faint horizontal scar that might be a road. We park the camper and start climbing.

Soon we are standing on the lower end of a trail that slopes up and around the face of the mountain far above the present highway. But is this the original road? Parts of it look as though a bulldozer has been here recently. We follow the pathway for several hundred yards until we come to a level area overlooking the lake. "I think this is the spot," I shout to Mark, but he is skeptical. "It doesn't feel like the place you've described in your book," he says. "Let's keep going."

Sure enough, around the next bend is another, larger area with an even more spectacular view. Proof that this is the real Soldier's Summit lies before us: the two spruce-trunk flag poles that appear in the photographs of the ceremony are still there, now toppled, 40 feet apart and rotting on the ground.

We drive on and stop for the night a few miles down the lake at a beautifully laid-out campsite. In the quiet of a long summer evening, with the sun and the mountains at my back and 100 square miles of crystal-clear lake lapping on the pebbled beach, I sit on a piece of driftwood and revise my description of the opening ceremony.

We're on the road early the next morning, destination Tok, Alaska, 240 miles closer to Fairbanks. Not far north of Kluane Lake we come upon a roadside cairn—a memorial to Lieutenant Ronald R. Small of the 18th Engineers, who died here in August 1942, when his jeep overturned on a soft shoulder. Although weeds surround the lieutenant's monument, someone has recently placed a bunch of wildflowers on it.

Mark asks how many men were killed during the building of the highway, and I have to admit that I don't know the exact number. I've seen several different totals in various documents, but the Army and the PRA kept separate records, and neither organization listed any deaths in their reports that were not clearly construction-related. Thus, in December 1942, when Les Cook and his two flight mechanics crashed on a test-flight between missions for the Army, their deaths were not counted as part of the highway's toll. Lord knows what the total would come to if all the ambiguous cases like Cook's were added in, but my estimate for soldiers and civilians killed while working on the highway is about thirty—almost half of them in one accident, when a pontoon raft overturned in a storm on Charlie Lake. As for fatalities attributable to Project CANOL, my guess is less than a dozen. Not many, all things considered. Mark agrees. Touched by the wildflower bouquet, we drive on.

Soon we've crossed the Donjek, another glacier-fed river strewn with boulders and deadfall, and are starting up the stretch of highway that almost broke the spirit of the 18th Engineers. From this point all the way to the border, 90 miles farther on, there is no way to avoid the permafrost and muskeg. On bad days along this stretch, the 18th barely advanced a few hundred yards, only to watch as their laboriously built-up roadbed sank back into the surrounding quagmire. From the thousands of cracks and sags in the present macadam surface, it is jarringly evident that fifty years of construction experience still haven't fully solved the problem of how to build a stable roadbed over permafrost. We later learned from Carl Molby, a retired state highway engineer who lives in Tok, that a similar two-lane stretch on the U.S. side of the border has been rebuilt four times since 1959—most recently at a cost of $1 million per mile.

Mark and I look up Paul Smith when we get to Tok. (A contact in Fairbanks has suggested him as someone who knows how the highway has changed over the years.) Busy with customers, Smith says he'll be glad to talk in the morning. That leaves us with time to kill before we camp for the night. I suggest that we take a 140-mile side-trip from Tok over the Mentasta Pass to Slana and back, to look over the route bulldozed by the black 97th Engineers in the summer of 1942. Off we head into the mountains, retracing their path. The highway is now so well engineered and easy to drive that I have to remind myself of their travails as they passed this way.

Next morning, after a pleasant two hours spent talking to Paul Smith, Mark and I are back on the road to Fairbanks. For 80 miles or so the blacktop runs straight and wide between the Tanana River on the right and the snow-clad Alaska Range on the left, but as we approach Delta Junction the mountains gradually recede to the horizon and the highway narrows almost to its 1943 dimensions. Beyond Delta Junction the road widens again, but the sinkholes in the pavement demand more of the driver's attention than the magnificent vistas of the river valley. About 15 miles outside Fairbanks, at North Pole, Alaska, a giant roadside Santa Claus marks a kind of time-warp boundary of commercial development. Around the next bend is a shopping mall; then the road divides and becomes a four-lane freeway. Wendy's, McDonald's, and Burger King are not far ahead.

We spend four days in Fairbanks, two of them interviewing people, another at the University of Alaska Archives to see what's new in its Alaska Highway holdings since I was last here (a lot), and the fourth being tourists.

Mark couldn't come this far without visiting the University's Ag School, so on our tourist day we wander through an acre of flowers and vegetables even more eye-popping than those in Paul Smith's planting beds. Nearby is an experimental farm whose pastures contain not cattle and pigs, but musk oxen, caribou, and reindeer (almost certainly descendants of the survivors of the Great Reindeer Fiasco of 1898). We get an impromptu tour from a staff member who tells us that caribou and reindeer are closely related and capable of interbreeding. The offspring? "Why, caradeer or reinibou," he laughs, "take your pick." We end the day by strolling the midway of the Tanana Valley Agricultural Fair. Where else can you ride a ferris wheel while munching on a mooseburger?

Among the people responsible for making our stay in Fairbanks so memorable is Ginny Hill Wood, World War II ferry pilot. I had already interviewed Mrs. Wood once, back in 1985, but now I need to ask more questions. Mark and I drive out to her log home, tucked into a wooded hillside a few miles from Fairbanks, and find her weeding the vegetable garden. Brushing her hands on well-patched dungarees, she invites us in for tea. Her longtime friend and fellow ferry pilot, Celia Hunter, joins us. After the two women have gone over their wartime experiences for my benefit, the conversation turns to their years of charter flying in Alaska and, finally, to their most recent adventures. Celia Hunter has recently returned from a kayak trip down a Siberian river with a group of young Russians; Ginny Wood talks about the fun she has each summer guiding parties into the remote reaches of Alaska's Brooks Range, well above the Arctic Circle.

As I sit listening, it occurs to me that almost all the "old-timers" I've interviewed for this book—particularly those living in the north country—have two things in common: remarkably good memories and a strong determination to live in and for the present.

Two other Fairbanks residents who fit this description are Kay Kennedy and Randy Acord. Prior to our arrival I had contacted Susan Kemp, the statewide coordinator for the Alaska Highway's Fiftieth Anniversary Celebration, to ask for help in locating people with stories to tell about their experiences on the ALCAN or the Northwest Staging Route. Randy Acord, an Air Force cold-weather test pilot at Ladd Field from 1943 to 1946, was waiting for me in Ms. Kemp's office when I walked in. Kay Kennedy, a retired freelance journalist with a special interest in Alaskan aviation, asked me over to her tiny, cluttered apartment in the Fairbanks Pioneers' Home. Both interviews were unforgettable experiences, not only because of what Randy Acord and Kay Kennedy know—each has an encyclopedic knowledge of the history of Alaskan aviation—but because of who they are.

Kay Kennedy is now 86 and suffers from glaucoma and cataracts. Yet at 82 she received the annual "Woman of Achievement" award from the National Federation of Press Women. More recently, she has organized her personal and professional papers and donated them to the University of Alaska at Fairbanks, where the boxes take up 22 linear feet of archival shelf space. Currently, between interruptions from people like me, she is collaborating with a younger writer to finish a project she began long ago, a book about Alaska's aviation pioneers. Frank Barr will be in the chapter on bush pilots.

Randy Acord belongs to the postwar generation of Alaskan flyers, but he also deserves a chapter in somebody's book. Recently nominated by the U.S. Air Force to receive an award for "outstanding contributions to American Aviation," he spends most of his time these days raising funds and collecting artifacts to establish a permanent air museum at AlaskaLand, the year-round cultural exhibit center in Fairbanks. Meanwhile, until his dream comes true, Randy Acord's garage and back yard are chock-a-block with pieces of Alaska's aviation history—everything from photos of famous people and events to engines, propellers, and several flyable aircraft of unusual design. He's always looking for more. The mythical Fountain of Youth was supposed to have been somewhere in Florida; perhaps it is really in Alaska.

Susan Kemp has one more name for me as Mark and I get ready to leave Fairbanks. It seems that her late father, Sam Kelly, was a cat-skinner on Project CANOL, and Mrs. Kelly has some photographs and stories of his adventures on the winter trail to Norman Wells. Would I mind, Susan asks shyly, stopping at Kelly's Motel in Delta Junction to interview her mother on my way south?

Chaddie Kelly is expecting us when we reach Delta Junction. Unfortunately, the snapshots she has are small and out of focus— nothing I can use in the book. We come away, however, with a good story about Sam Kelly, who drove the lead bulldozer ahead of the first tractor-train of supplies to reach Norman Wells in the winter of 1943. As Sam pulled into camp there after spending six weeks breaking trail in sub-zero misery all the way from Mills Lake, a cargo plane was taxiing to take off from the adjacent flight strip. He ran for it. A buddy yelled after him, "Sam, come back. You don't even know where that plane's going!" Sam's over-the-shoulder answer was, "I don't give a damn where, as long as it's out of here!"

Chuckling, we climb back in the van and head for Tok. Having come up this stretch only a week ago, we now pay less attention to the scenery and more to the highway. The first thing I notice is that almost all the old wooden mileposts are gone, either rotted away or perhaps stolen for souvenirs. These were originally installed by the Army at 1-mile intervals, giving the exact distance from that spot to Mile 0 at Dawson Creek. Old-timers still refer to places as if the markers were still there, but word of a "washout at milepost 1202" (translation: Beaver Creek has flooded again) would be meaningless to today's average motorist. In Canada, the government has installed small metal kilometer markers, but nobody refers to Beaver Creek as "kilometer 1934.4."

Mark and I invent some simple ways to while away the passing miles. One is to count the number of vehicles we see on the road in a ten-minute period. Except on the busier stretches between Fairbanks and Delta Junction, around Whitehorse, and from Fort Nelson to Dawson Creek, the count in mid-August 1991 is rarely more than twelve.

Another game is to look for evidence of the original gravel road weaving back and forth across the line of the present highway. In most places there is no longer any obvious sign of the old road, but occasionally we can glimpse it—particularly where a cut made by today's more powerful earth-moving machines goes straight through a hill and the old trail goes around it. A good place to see the effects of improved road-building technology since 1943 is near milepost 1276 (one of the few markers still left). There, a deep modern cut has shortened the nearby original trail by several hundred feet. My guess is that only about 20 percent of the present road still follows the 1943 grade and alignment; Mark's estimate is less than 10 percent. I doubt whether anybody really knows.

A variant on "Where's the old road?" involves searching near the abutments of today's bridges for the remains of wooden pilings, indicating where the Army's bridges were. This game soon gets old, but I can vouch for the pilings under half-a-dozen structures, including the Tanana River bridge near Tok and the Muskwa River bridge at Fort Nelson.

There are also remnants of the wartime highway in less obvious places, but finding them can be a challenge. Walter Mason, a lieutenant with the 97th Engineers, has told me that the ruins of eight cabins built by his platoon as shelter from the terrible cold in December 1942 can be found at Beaver Creek. Mark and I search there for an hour, stumbling around in the woods through ankle-deep moss, with no luck. (Later, on the telephone, Mason tells me I was looking on the wrong side of the creek.)

One of the few relics of the old highway preserved on its original site is the Aishihik River Bridge, 20 miles past Haines Junction on our way south. The bridge, an odd-looking log-arch structure, actually predates the Alaska Highway by forty years, having been built during the Gold Rush to help fortune-seekers heading up-country from Whitehorse. The 18th Engineers merely reinforced it in 1942, no doubt grateful for one less construction job that summer. Downstream stands its all-steel replacement, the angles of its superstructure mimicking the shape of the original bridge. On a high bluff overlooking both bridges and the mountains beyond is a native burial ground, where a split-rail fence encloses a handful of corpse-sized wooden houses, empty now but still kept up. A barely discernible pathway leads up to the site from the river and merges with a nearby stretch of the Army's old trail. Something I wrote long before I ever stood on this lovely spot comes to mind: "Following the easiest contours of the land, a footpath broadens with increasing use . . . and eventually becomes a thoroughfare. Paving and grading do not make such a highway; they only confirm its existence."

Two hours later we are in Whitehorse. The town has grown back to its wartime population of 20,000 but, this time around, with an adequate sewer system and a modicum of urban planning. The first order of business is to look up my contact here, Ken Spotswood. Ken handles public relations for the Yukon Anniversaries Commission, the Yukon government's equivalent of Susan Kemp's organization in Fairbanks. He has kindly taken the time to locate some people I need to interview and, to my surprise, has set me up to be interviewed by both a local newspaper reporter and a radio talk-show host. I also need to spend time at the Yukon Archives. After three fruitful days, Mark and I are off again.

We have decided to take another side-trip, leaving the main route 80 miles southeast of Whitehorse and driving up the old CANOL road to Ross River, about one-third of the 500-mile distance to Norman Wells. I'd like to go farther, but we don't have time; besides, the 200 miles of road beyond the Yukon border are in such bad shape that only hikers are allowed to proceed—and only in the summertime. Even the trip to Ross River is not to be undertaken casually. As we turn off the Alaska Highway onto the dusty CANOL road, a sign warns: "No Services Between This Point and Ross River."

We have entered another time-warp. The gravel road ahead looks exactly the way the Alaska Highway must have looked fifty years ago: not only no services, but no settlements. Nothing but rank upon rank of mountains marching away into the purple distance. We encounter just five vehicles on the five-hour drive. The road is surprisingly well maintained and is wide enough in most places for cars to pass, but for 20 of the last 30 miles into Ross River it is cut into the wall of a very deep gorge. Although heights don't usually bother me, the combination of a 12-foot roadbed with crumbling edges, no guardrails, and an 800-foot drop into the rapids below does funny things to my sweat glands and pulse rate. Now I understand why the 35th Engineers had such trouble opening this trail in 1943.

We are glad to get to Ross River, even though its attractions are limited: a scruffy motel, a general store and gas station, two missions (one Roman Catholic, the other Anglican), a regional school, the RCMP detachment, and perhaps 100 houses, the newest of which are pastel split levels that look like transplants from some Midwestern suburb.

For me, the town's main point of interest is a 400-foot suspension bridge across the Pelly River, one of the few surviving monuments to "Somervell's Folly." The bridge was not built for motor vehicles (there's a ferry for that), but to carry the 4-inch CANOL 1 pipeline on its way through here to Whitehorse. The pipeline has long since been cut up and sold for scrap, but the bridge still stands, its catwalk slightly askew. Pedestrians and bikers can use it if they don't care to ride the ferry, but the cables that hold up the walkway are showing their age. Two young German cyclists, wearing dayglow outfits and carrying high-tech camping gear, hail the ferry from the north bank and come across. I ask if they've seen any abandoned equipment up ahead, old Army trucks and such. "Ja, a lot," says one. "Maybe 100 along the road."

Although this is as close as we get to Norman Wells, I know from a 1985 CBC program that General Somervell's ambitious plan to pump 20,000 barrels per day of crude oil from the Norman Wells field has finally been realized—not, of course, for the benefit of the U.S. military, but for the stockholders of Imperial Oil and Exxon Corporation. As Somervell already knew back in 1943, much of the field lies under the bed of the Mackenzie River; so in 1983, Exxon's engineers and technicians simply built six large artificial islands in the middle of it and tapped into the pool. A 12-inch pipeline now carries the crude to transfer terminals in northern Alberta. Like General Mitchell, General Somervell was decades ahead of his time.

A postscript to the CANOL story: Camp CANOL, abandoned in 1945 and slowly rusting and rotting across the river from Norman Wells, was finally razed in 1977 as an environmental hazard and eyesore by the Canadian government. Evicted in the process was the camp's last occupant, an indignant prospector, who had set up comfortable housekeeping in an insulated, walk-in meat locker.

Back on the Alaska Highway after camping overnight near Ross River, Mark and I head next for the native village of Teslin, where I hope to fill in one more blank: the identity of the priest at Lower Post who put Captain Eschbach up for the night in August 1942. Ken Spotswood, my contact in Whitehorse, has suggested that Audrey Aylard, the wife of Teslin's Anglican rector, might be of help.

Mrs. Aylard doesn't know who the priest at Lower Post was, but she does have vivid memories of her childhood in Dawson Creek in the early years of World War II. Father Aylard, for his part, is anxious to show us his "Army surplus" altar. They generously send us on our way with fresh carrots from their garden and a frozen moose steak to cook for supper. Such experiences keep happening: in looking for one thing, we find something better. When we stop in Teslin's George Johnston Museum on our way out of town, it happens again.

The local people are justly proud of their museum, a handsome showplace for native artifacts and a fitting monument to the innovative and influential man for whom it is named. George Johnston ran the local general store for many years; he was also a skilled photographer who developed and printed his own pictures. Long before the Alaska Highway came through here, he bought an automobile in Whitehorse, shipped it home on a barge, and built 3 miles of road to drive it on. Each winter the car, painted white, became a mobile wolf-hunting blind for Johnston and his friends. This and many other chapters of Teslin's history are captured in his photographs, which Mark and I are admiring when we become aware that someone else is, too: a well-dressed native man in his fifties, who is showing off the museum to a visitor. Mark starts up a conversation. The man turns out to be George Johnston's nephew, Sam Johnston. A chance encounter becomes an interview.

"What do the people of Teslin think about the highway and how it has changed their lives?" I ask Johnston.

"Some of the elders blame it, and the white man, for the bad things that have happened here," he says, referring to the wartime epidemics and the perennial problem of alcoholism. "But the highway was inevitable. And blaming the white man doesn't help much. We have to take responsibility for our own lives." He speaks hopefully about a recovery program created specifically for native alcoholics. He also emphasizes that the disease afflicts a great many north country whites as well.

Our serendipitous conversation in the museum turns up another valuable bit of information. From the beginning of this expedition, Mark and I have been hoping to locate some descendants of Charlie MacDonald, the 35th Engineers' native guide, to find out what became of him after the war. Asked about Charlie MacDonald by Mark, Johnston beams. "Charlie's been dead awhile," he says, "but his brother's family lives in Watson Lake. I'd ask there." Watson Lake, 170 miles away over the Continental Divide, happens to be our next destination. As we leave, I ask Johnston for his address, in case

I have further questions. He hands me his card. It reads: "Sam Johnston, Speaker of the Yukon General Assembly."

Most of the road to Watson Lake is wide and straight except the middle third, which the Yukon government and Sam Johnston haven't gotten around to fixing up yet. Crossing the line of the Continental Divide is a bit of a disappointment. A sign marks the spot, but the elevation is only about 3,000 feet and the scenery (what we can see of it through the rain and low-lying clouds) is not particularly dramatic. I want it to be impressive, not only because of the geographic significance of the Divide, but also because this seemingly obvious route through the barrier of the Rockies wasn't even on the map until Les Cook and General Hoge found it in 1942.

Six miles west of Watson Lake we pass the entrance to the Cassiar Highway and a sign saying "Hazelton, Britsh Columbia: 815 km./570 mi." An approximation of the southern half of the long-proposed Route A, the Cassiar Highway was completed more than twenty years ago, but much of it is still unpaved. (As for Route B, the southern half of the Rocky Mountain Trench is now Williston Lake, formed in the mid-1960s behind a massive hydroelectric dam on the Peace River west of Fort St. John.)

It is still overcast and misting when we pull into Watson Lake. While I check at the Visitors' Information Center to see if any natives named MacDonald still live hereabouts, Mark stays outside to take pictures of Watson Lake's famous "Signpost Forest." This got its start fifty years ago when a whimsical GI put up a road sign giving the mileage to Tokyo, New York, Chicago, and several points in between. More than 15,000 signs have since been added, put up by tourists from all over the world. "Peoria City Limits" says one; *Wilkommen in Berlin* says another. It is great fun to look for the most distant or oddly named hometown.

At the Visitors' Center I've learned that John MacDonald, Charlie MacDonald's nephew, works as a firefighter at the Watson Lake Airport. John takes us home to meet his family. His sister Linda happens to be visiting from Whitehorse. Their mother, a mixed-race woman who is the daughter of Frank Watson, the founder of Watson Lake, says hello and quickly disappears, but John and Linda seem pleased that an outsider is interested in their uncle and the rest of the MacDonald clan. From them, we learn a lot of new information about Charlie MacDonald. Unlike his brother Peter, who went to work at the airport early in the war, Charlie stayed in the mountains and stuck to trapping and guiding until his death in 1975. John and Linda are convinced that he would have died wealthy if unscrupulous whites hadn't staked a claim to the best part of his trapping territory and cheated him out of his share in a silver mine. Linda also tells me that Charlie's wife Nellie was the sister of his first wife, who died before the war. Nobody seems to know exactly how many children he had, but the consensus is four by each wife. I ask if any of the eight are still alive and where we can find them. The answer, hesitantly given, is Muncho Lake, scene of the demolition exploits of Mike Miletich of the 35th Engineers.

The reason for John and Linda MacDonald's reluctance to talk about their Muncho Lake cousins becomes apparent when we arrive there the next day. By pure luck, two of Charlie's children, a man and a woman of indeterminate age, are hanging around the gas station where we stop to fill up. Both speak no English and seem mentally retarded, although they eventually light up when they understand that we are interested in their father. According to Jack Guiness, the station proprietor, who claims to know a lot of Charlie MacDonald lore, another of Charlie's sons carries on his guiding business, but inbreeding has done the damage we see grinning before us.

Mark and I are struck by the contrast between Charlie's life and Peter's—and what it has meant for their children. One man chose to adapt as little as possible to the changes brought by the highway; the other made his peace with them long ago. For all their painful ambivalence about being "assimilated," John and Linda MacDonald surely face brighter possibilities than their cousins up in the hills.

As we head toward Fort Nelson, the drizzle intensifies and fog obscures some of the highway's most spectacular scenery. We might as well be driving through a murky, winding tunnel. To lighten the mood, we talk about all the amusing things we have recently heard. Mark had asked Jack Guiness about the huge logs chained to the bank where the narrow roadbed runs along the cliffs at the southeast end of Muncho Lake. Mark's educated guess was that the logs probably kept ice floes from grinding away the shoulders of the road, but Guiness's deadpan explanation of their purpose was: "They keep the fish from jumping out and damaging your car. We used to fix a lot of broken windshields here." The twinkle in his eye gave him away.

Some of the other highway "whoppers" in circulation are a bit more plausible than Jack Guiness's jumping fish. For example, another gas station owner solemnly assured us that the road was built with such crazy twists and turns to make it difficult for Japanese fighter planes to strafe the convoys. I'm not sure whether he actually believed this or was just pulling the legs of a couple of tourists. Not wanting to spoil his fun in either case, I didn't point out that one of the Army's best arguments for the Inland Route was that it put the highway beyond the range of Japanese planes—or that the real reason the road zigged and zagged was to avoid patches of muskeg and permafrost. In any case, this particular tall tale really tickles Mark. Every time we careen around a sharp bend in the road, he shouts something like "Look out for the Zero!" or "Ha! Missed us again, you sons of Nippon!" Getting punchier by the mile, we pass Summit Lake and leave the Rocky Mountains behind.

Fort Nelson is bigger and more prosperous looking than I had remembered, but it is still a small frontier town, despite the restaurants, bars, and gas stations that line the highway. We stop just long enough to visit the local museum and look up a Roman Catholic priest, Father Poullet, who, it turns out, had the mission in Lower Post fifty years ago. I had expected the priest in Captain Eschbach's story to be dead by now, but here he is at 79, still active in his calling. It soon develops that he too knows a lot about Charlie MacDonald, having officiated at his wedding, baptized his children, and buried him. Before we leave I can't resist showing Father Poullet my account of Eschbach's reconnaissance with MacDonald and their stopover at the mission at Lower Post. The priest reads it slowly, smiling and nodding in agreement until he comes to the last few sentences. "No," he says firmly, "this part about my selling dried fish so I could buy medicine for the Indians is not correct. The government gave me medicines to treat them with." I fall asleep that night trying to think of a way to use both versions of the story.

After a soggy week, we awake next morning to sunny skies and warmer weather. This will be our last day on the Alaska Highway, so we dawdle, stopping at all the places my father wrote about to explore and take pictures. Mark is especially fascinated by the old PRA bridge at the Sikinni Chief River, now closed to traffic but still standing. We look for the remains of the 95th Engineers' bridge beside it, but find nothing.

The rolling landscape gradually changes as we head south from Fort Nelson. At first the view from the highway is mostly of spruce forest and muskeg bogs; then comes a long stretch stripped and scarred by loggers and studded with hundreds of natural gas wells; finally, near the Peace River and Fort St. John, cattle farms and fields of grain predominate. All of the towns on this end of the highway have obviously benefited from the boom in natural gas and petrochemicals, but Fort St. John has grown the most. I barely recognize its business district from my visit just nine years ago.

We buy our first paper in two weeks and learn that a coup has been attempted in the Soviet Union and that a hurricane has recently struck the East Coast. Even though people who live up here get their news via TV satellite, nobody we've talked to in the last few days has mentioned either event. They seem to have happened on a different planet.

Last stop before heading home: Dawson Creek, Mile 0 of the Alaska Highway. Farming is still the mainstay of the local economy, but tourism is clearly becoming increasingly important. The railroad station where General Hoge and his party arrived on a chilly February morning in 1942 to begin their reconnaissance to Fort Nelson has been moved. Enlarged and converted into a museum and information center about the highway, it now stands next to one of the five grain elevators that once towered over the business district. The other four have been torn down and replaced by more efficient structures at the edge of town. The elevator that remains no longer holds grain; painted red to match the nearby station, it houses an art gallery.

In Dawson Creek, of all the places we've visited on this trip, it is easiest to see how the Alaska Highway has changed over the last fifty years: built in haste and fear in the darkest days of World War II, it has become both a tourist attraction in its own right and the gateway to a realm of incredible variety and beauty. But Paul Smith is right. If you can't spare the time to savor the marvel of the highway, why bother to come?

A SALUTE

To see what the years have brought to places like Fort Nelson, Watson Lake, Teslin, and Tok, you will always be able to visit them—thanks to the Alaska Highway. Not so the thousands of soldiers and civilians who helped plan and build it. Fewer are left every year. I honor them all, with a final salute for the men in this story:

Vilhjalmur Stefansson, the controversial Arctic explorer and publicist, eventually found a niche in academe at Dartmouth College, which established a repository for his huge collection of Arctic literature after World War II and made him head of its Northern Studies Program. Well into his eighties, Stefansson continued to write, lecture, and consult on the subject he knew best. Claiming, with some justification, that his Route D proposal had been bastardized, to the end of his life he stubbornly maintained the superiority of his original concept over the Army's Inland Route.

Major General **Simon Bolivar Buckner**, charged with responsibility for the defense of Alaska until 1944, was then promoted to three-star rank and given a command in the Pacific Theater of Operations. He was killed in action during the invasion of Okinawa on June 13, 1945.

Brigadier General **Clarence L. Sturdevant**, War Department shepherd of the Alaska Highway project, remained deskbound in the Chief of Engineers' Office until 1944, when he, like Buckner, was rewarded with a command assignment in the South Pacific. He retired as a Major General in 1946 and raised chickens on a farm near Washington, D.C., until the twin advances of suburbia and old age caught up with him.

Brigadier General **William M. Hoge**, the first commander on the Alaska Highway, went on to lead an armored division across Europe, winning honors for his courage and audacity at the Battle of the Bulge and the Remagen bridgehead. He rose to four-star rank after World War II and was Commander in Chief of the U.S. Army in Europe at the time of his retirement in 1955. He later called his work on the Alaska Highway "the toughest job, the one you couldn't see a solution to . . ."

Colonel **Robert D. Ingalls**, Commanding Officer of the 35th Engineer Regiment and later in charge of the Alaska Highway's southern sector, subsequently commanded the Engineer Training Center at Camp Ellis, Illinois. Ingalls tried his best to make good Engineers of the men sent to Ellis, many of whom were in the lower mental and physical categories, the draft having earlier skimmed off the cream. When his tough methods resulted in a rise in training injuries and AWOLs, complaints reached General Somervell's office. Though staunchly defended by his immediate superiors, Ingalls was transferred to another assignment in May 1944. He retired in 1945 and began a second career. Despite his stomach ulcer and a developing heart condition, he taught mathematics and mechanical engineering at the University of Alabama for eighteen years.

Brigadier General **James A. O'Connor** commanded the highway's southern sector until General Somervell selected him over Hoge to head the Northwest Service Command. O'Connor remained on the Alaska Highway until 1944, when he became the Chief Engineer of the China-Burma-India Command. That job was followed by a year as Division Engineer in Boston, before his retirement at the age of 61 in 1946.

Master Sergeant **Wansley W. Hill**, First Sergeant of Company "B," 388th Engineer Regiment, served with that outfit until the end of World War II. After leaving Project CANOL in late 1943, Hill and the 388th went through five months of retraining in the States and then shipped out for England to participate in the Normandy Invasion. Discharged in 1945, he married his fiancée of four years, finished college under the GI Bill, and went to work as a post office clerk. Wansley Hill is now fully retired after twenty-five years with the Postal Service and eight more as the part owner of a travel agency. He lives with his wife in Yeadon, Pennsylvania.

Colonel **Heath Twichell**, successively the Executive Officer of the 35th Engineers, Commanding Officer of the 95th Engineers, Officer in Charge of the Dawson Creek Railhead, and Southern Sector Commander, left Canada in May 1943. He remained on active duty for twelve more years, serving in the United States, Europe, and Japan. Stymied in his hopes for a second career as a civil engineer by the lack of jobs for a man his age, he turned instead to writing his memoirs. These were well begun when a prolonged series of small strokes and heart attacks gradually paralyzed his powers of speech and movement. He died in 1973.

Now the story he started to write is finished.

ACKNOWLEDGMENTS

Although the inspiration and the single most important source for *Northwest Epic* has been my father's account of his experiences building the Alaska Highway, I could never have written this book without the encouragement and support of my sister, Ruth Twichell Cochrane. Her unwavering belief in the importance of the story has kept me at the task. I have many others to thank as well.

For their generous assistance during my periodic research trips to Washington, D.C., I am particularly beholden to John Greenwood and Hannah Zeidlik of the U.S. Army Center of Military History and to Martin Gordon, a historian for the Corps of Engineers. Tom Melcher was an enormously helpful research assistant and a delightful traveling companion during my first trip up the highway in 1980. I am also indebted to the staffs of the U.S. and Canadian National Archives, the Yukon Archives, the Franklin D. Roosevelt and Harry S. Truman Libraries, the Baker Library (Stefansson Papers) at Dartmouth College and the Alaska and Polar Regions Department of the University of Alaska's Rasmuson Library in Fairbanks.

The chore of converting my rough drafts and frequent revisions into a polished manuscript has been handled with dependable efficiency by Susan Wilson. I managed to wear out a good many of her word-processor ribbons, but never her patience and sense of humor.

Susanna Sturgis, Patty Blakesley, Hope Waingrow, and George Mills—good writers and good friends all—have read and critiqued every chapter. Whatever turgid prose remains is no fault of theirs.

Steven Gray, my incredibly thorough copy editor, was even more relentless in his criticism than they, finding more logical inconsistencies in my narrative and gaps in my research than I care to admit.

All of the perspective maps were produced by Carolee R. Paul of Seahorse Pre-Press, who worked extra hours and stretched the limits of her computer-graphics system to give me what I wanted. The other maps are the work of Howell Brewer, a professional cartographer, who painstakingly re-drew an old PRA map to my specifications.

I am also grateful to my agent, Audrey Adler Wolf, for her willingness to gamble on a book about a gravel road. In Robert Weil she found me just the right senior editor, a man with a penchant for "road books" and a reputation for doing well by his authors. I could not have asked for a more persistent and effective advocate at St. Martin's Press than Bob.

Finally, thanks are due to my wife, Gwen, for her help and advice in most of the above categories—and in other ways beyond counting. Her gifts are rare indeed.

—Heath Twichell
Oak Bluffs, Massachusetts
January 1992

NOTES

ABBREVIATIONS USED IN
NOTES AND BIBLIOGRAPHY

AGO: Office of the Adjutant General, U.S. Army.

AOG: Association of Graduates, United States Military Academy, West Point, New York.

ASF: U.S. Army Service Forces (Successor to SOS).

BC: British Columbia

CD: Control Division (ASF agency responsible for reports and statistics).

CG: Commanding General.

CMH: U.S. Army Center of Military History, Historical Research Collection, Washington, D.C.

GPO: U.S. Government Printing Office.

NA: U.S. National Archives.

NAC: National Archives of Canada.

OCE: Office of the Chief of Engineers, U.S. Army.

OHCE: Office of History, Historical Research Collection, U.S. Army Corps of Engineers, Fort Belvoir, Virginia.

PRA: Public Roads Administration.

RG: Record Group.

SOS: U.S. Army Services of Supply.

SPHS: South Peace Historical Society, Dawson Creek, British Columbia.

UAKF: University of Alaska at Fairbanks.

USMA: United States Military Academy.

YA: Yukon Archives, Whitehorse, Yukon.

CHAPTER 1

1. Vilhjalmur Stefansson, *Northwest to Fortune: The Search of Western Man for a Commercially Practical Route to the Far East* (New York: Duell, Sloan & Pearce, 1958), pp. 101–2.

2. Ibid., pp. 106–34, 156–69; J. E. Rea, "Sir Alexander Mackenzie," *Encyclopedia of World Biography* 7 (New York: McGraw-Hill, 1973), pp. 70–74.

3. Robert England, "British Columbia," *Encyclopedia Americana*, Int'l ed. 4 (Danbury, CT: Grolier, 1982), pp. 568, 572.

4. Lawrence J. Burpee, "A Road to Alaska," *Canadian Geographical Journal* 21(5) (Nov. 1940): pp. 260–61; Stefansson, *Northwest to Fortune*, pp. 244–84.

5. John Sherman Long, *McCord of Alaska: Statesman for the Last Frontier* (Cleveland: Dillon/Liederback, 1975), p. 23.

6. Alfred Hulse Brooks, *Blazing Alaska's Trails*, 2d ed. (Fairbanks: University of Alaska Press, 1973), pp. 343–46.

7. Philip H. Godsell, *The Romance of the Alaska Highway* (Toronto: Ryerson Press, 1944), p. 44; Brendan Kennelly, "Moodie . . . And the Country He Travelled," *Alaska Highway News: Compendium Issue* (Agricultural Section No. 2, Jan. 4, 1945): 4–5.

8. Stefansson, *Northwest to Fortune*, pp. 172–76, 191–95, 222–35.

9. Ibid., pp. 235–37. Emily Craig Romig, *A Pioneer Woman in Alaska* (Caldwell, ID: Caxton Printers, 1948), pp. 76–106. The quote is from p. 81.

10. Vilhjalmur Stefansson, *Discovery: The Autobiography of Vilhjalmur Stefansson* (New York: McGraw-Hill, 1964), pp. 7–16, 25–90.

11. Ibid., pp. 101–44.

12. Ibid., pp. 144–248; Leslie H. Neatsby, *Conquest of the Last Frontier* (Athens, OH: Ohio University Press, 1961), p. 408. Richard J. Diubaldo's *Stefansson and the Canadian Arctic* (Montreal: McGill-Queen's University Press, 1978) offers a more objective account of the explorer's Arctic exploits than does Stefansson's *Discovery*. Most of Stefansson's claims and predictions are no longer controversial, but the "blond Eskimo" mystery remains unsolved. To this day, no one knows whether their European ancestors were eleventh-century Vikings or shipwrecked sailors from some eighteenth- or nineteenth-century Arctic expedition. Opinion also remains divided on the benefits of a raw-meat diet, but the issue is moot for most cultures but the Inuit.

13. U.S. Alaska Road Commission, "The Proposed Pacific Yukon Highway" (Juneau: Feb. 1, 1931), pp. 20–24; British Columbia–Yukon–Alaska Highway Commission, "Report of Proposed Highway Through British Columbia and the Yukon Territory to Alaska" (Ottawa: Aug. 1941), pp. 7–10. Both reports are housed in the Archives of the UAKF.

14. Richard Morenus, *Alaska Sourdough: The Story of Slim Williams* (New York: Rand McNally, 1956), pp. 241–49.

15. Ibid., pp. 250–74; *Chicago Tribune*, Sept. 17, 1933, pp. 10, 17.

16. Alaska International Highway Commission, "Report to the President," 76th Congress, 3d Session, House Document No. 711 (Washington: GPO, 1940), pp. 5–10.

17. David Remley, "The Latent Fear: Canadian–American Relations and Early Proposals for a Highway to Alaska," in *The Alaska Highway: Papers of the 40th Anniversary Symposium*, Kenneth Coates, ed. (Vancouver, BC: University of British Columbia Press, 1985), p. 1–7.

18. Alaska International Highway Commission, "Report," pp. 10–27; "The Alaska Highway," Control Division Report compiled for the CG, ASF (May 1945), p. 3 [hereafter cited as CD/HWY Report]. Report is located in Alaska Highway Files, OHCE.

19. Burpee, "A Road to Alaska," pp. 257–60; Laurent Cyr, "A 201-day Cycling Journey Down the 'Alaska Highway,'" undated clipping from *Yukon News* in the Alaska Highway Collection, YA.

20. Godsell, *Romance of the Alaska Highway*, pp. 99–107; "It's an Ill Wind That Blows . . . ," *Alaska Highway News: Compendium Issue* (Transportation Section, Jan. 5, 1945): p. 6; Bedaux's obituary, *New York Times*, Feb. 20, 1944, p. 1; *Grand Rapids Herald*, Feb. 20, 1944, p. 1; Diary entry is from "A Diary of the Bedaux Expedition," excerpt from the diary of F. C. Swannel, in the Alaska Highway Collection of the Dawson Creek Public Library, Dawson Creek, BC.

21. Ibid.

22. Stefansson papers, H. L. Halvorson to V. Stefansson, Dec. 26, 1941, Alaska Highway

Folder, 1941; CD/HWY Report, Exhibits Section, p. 110. Stefansson's papers are in the Baker Library at Dartmouth College.

23. Stefansson, *Discovery*, pp. 315–16, 327–29; CD/HWY Report, Exhibits Section, pp. 17, 38–39, 116. There is considerable confusion among my sources as to the labels given these various routes. Halvorson's Route C proposal was so lightly regarded by some authorities that they ignored it and gave the "C" designation to Stefansson's proposal instead. This, in turn, led to more confusion when the U.S. Army came up with its own route (see chapter 3), known to most as the "Inland Route," but called by others "Route D"—or "Route X." I have adopted the majority usage.

CHAPTER 2

1. Stefansson, *Northwest to Fortune*, pp. 333–36.
2. James L. Cole, "Mitchell, William," *Dictionary of American Biography* 11, Supp. 2 (New York: Charles Scribner's Sons, 1958), pp. 460–62; John H. Cloe, *Top Cover for America: The Air Force in Alaska, 1920–1983* (Missoula, MT: Pictorial Histories Publishing, 1984), p. 1.
3. Ibid., pp. 2–5, 8–10.
4. Robert B. Holtz, "Aviation," *Encyclopedia Americana*, Int'l ed. 2 (Danbury, CT: Grolier, 1982), pp. 864–66; Cole, "Mitchell," pp. 460–62.
5. Holtz, "Aviation," pp. 866–69; National Resources Planning Board, Alaska Regional Planning Office, "Post-Defense Economic Development in Alaska" (Washington, Oct. 1941). The NRPB report is located in CMH.
6. Archie Satterfield, *Alaska Bush Pilots in the Float Country* (Seattle: Superior Publishing, 1969), pp. 96, 118–26.
7. Ibid., pp. 84–92; Dermott Cole, *Frank Barr: Bush Pilot in Alaska and the Yukon* (Edmonds, WA: Northwest Publishing, 1986), pp. 1–8.
8. Ronald A. Keith, *Bush Pilot with a Briefcase: The Happy-Go-Lucky Story of Grant McConachie* (Don Mills, Ont.: General Publishing, 1972), pp. 24–30, 43–47.
9. Ibid., pp. 48–66, 78–99.
10. Ibid., pp. 100–09, 166–76.
11. Ibid., pp. 186–93, 208–12; Dorothy and Al Chappell and Lodema George interviews, Fort Nelson, BC, Aug. 18, 1980.
12. Vic Johnson interview, Watson Lake, Yukon, Aug. 20, 1980. The McConachie–Johnson dialogue is from Keith, *Bush Pilot with a Briefcase*, pp. 220–21.
13. Ibid., pp. 177–85.
14. Ibid., pp. 226–27; Cecil Pickell and Cora Ventress interviews, Fort St. John, BC, Aug. 15–16, 1980.
15. J. A. Wilson, "Northwest Passage by Air," *Canadian Geographical Journal* 26 (Mar. 1943), pp. 107–29.
16. Charles P. Stacy, *Arms, Men and Governments: The War Policies of Canada, 1939–1945* (Ottawa: Queen's Printer for Canada, 1970), pp. 336–39; Stanley W. Dziuban, *U.S. Army in World War II: Military Relations Between the United States and Canada, 1939–1945* (Washington, D.C.: GPO, 1959), pp. 22–28.
17. Thomas Kessner, *Fiorello H. LaGuardia and the Making of Modern New York* (New York: McGraw-Hill, 1989), pp. 48–56, 336–38, 417–19.
18. Ibid., p. 484; Stacy, *Arms, Men and Governments*, p. 343.
19. Ibid., p. 347; Dziuban, *U.S. Army in WWII, Military Relations, U.S. and Canada*, p. 201.
20. Ibid., pp. 201–2; "Saga of Fort Nelson Trail, 1941," *Alaska Highway News: Compendium Issue* (Transportation Section, Jan. 4, 1945): 4–5.
21. Slim Byrnes, "Trails North" (unpublished MS in Fort St. John Public Library), p. 9.
22. Dziuban, *U.S. Army in WWII, Military Relations, U.S. and Canada*, p. 202; Edwin R.

Carr, "Great Falls to Nome: The Inland Air Route to Alaska, 1940–1945," unpublished Ph.D. dissertation (University of Minnesota, 1946), pp. 13, 18, 20–22.

23. Stetson Conn and Byron Fairchild, *U.S. Army in World War II: The Framework of Hemisphere Defense* (Washington, DC: GPO, 1960), pp. 373–75, 383–86, 389; Dziuban, *U.S. Army in WWII, Military Relations, U.S. and Canada*, pp. 202–5; Stacy, *Arms, Men and Governments*, p. 380.

24. U.S. Army, Western Defense Command, "History of the Western Defense Command, 17 Mar. 1941–30 Sept. 1945" 1(2), pp. 1–3. Location: CMH.

25. Ibid., pp. 3–8, Annex C, p. 2.

26. Ibid., p. 3.

27. U.S. Army Alaskan Department, "Official History of the Alaskan Department, June 1940–June 1944," ch. 1, p. 1. Location: CMH.

28. Western Defense Command, "History," pp. 8–9, Annex D, p. 4.

CHAPTER 3

1. Heath Twichell, Sr., papers, "Pearl Harbor: The Way It Was" (unpublished MS by Helen Twichell Stermer), pp. 4–11. Location of Twichell Papers: in author's possession until Dec. 31, 1992; thereafter: OHCE.

2. CD/HWY Report, p. 7 and Exhibits Section, pp. 95–99; T. Dodson Stamps and Vincent J. Esposito, eds., *A Military History of World War II*, Vol. I, *Operations in the European Theater* (West Point, NY: USMA, 1953), pp. 298, 303; Joseph Bykofsky and Harold Larson, *U.S. Army in World War II: The Transportation Corps: Operations Overseas* (Washington, DC: GPO, 1957), p. 32.

3. Dziuban, *U.S. Army in WWII, Military Relations, U.S. and Canada*, pp. 202–3; Western Defense Command, "History," p. 9.

4. CD/HWY Report, p. 8 and Exhibits Section, p. 59.

5. Ibid., pp. 14–16 and Exhibits Section, pp. 110, 148–49; Bykofsky and Larson, *U.S. Army in WWII, Transportation Corps*, p. 32.

6. CD/HWY Report, Exhibits Section, pp. 38–55, 110–14, 128–32.

7. Ibid., Exhibits Section, pp. 59, 111, 167–71.

8. Ibid., Exhibits Section, pp. 62–64. The 340th and 341st Engineers (and the 93rd, 95th, and 97th Engineers—see chapter 5) were designated as "general service" (GS) regiments in contrast to the 18th and 35th Engineers, whose designation as "combat" regiments was reflected in their somewhat different Table of Organization and Equipment (TO&E). The difference between the capabilities of these two types of units was relevant in a combat zone, but not on the Alaska Highway. Another minor quirk of Army nomenclature that I have ignored to avoid confusion: building *pontoon* bridges was the missioin of *ponton* companies and battalions.

9. Ibid., pp. 8A, 8B.

10. Ibid., pp. 8B, 8C, 20.

11. "William Morris Hoge," obituary, *Assembly* (published by the AOG, USMA) (June 1981): 124–25; "Clarence Lynn Sturdevant," obituary, *Assembly* (Winter 1959): 89; additional biographical information on both men from AOG files, USMA.

12. Ibid.; transcript of interview with General Hoge conducted by Lieutenant Colonel George Robertson, Jan. 14–15 and Apr. 15–17, 1974, tape 2, p. 1 [hereafter cited as Hoge interview]. Location: CMH.

13. Ibid., p. 15. Until the decision to build the highway was made public on March 5, 1942, official documents on the evolving plan were classified "Secret."

14. Heath Twichell, Sr., "An Engineer's Story," ch. 2. Unpublished MS. Location: in author's possession until December 31, 1992; thereafter, OHCE. (Because this MS contains up to three different versions of each chapter, each with different—or no—pagination, citations by page number would only create confusion.) John T. Greenwood, "General Bill Hoge and the Alaska Highway," in Coates, ed., *The Alaska*

Highways Symposium, pp. 40–41; C. F. Capes, "Report on Reconnaissance Inspection Trip on Proposed International Highway to Alaska," Mar. 6, 1942 (copy), pp. 1–2. Location: YA.

15. Keith, *Bush Pilot with a Briefcase*, pp. 238–39.

16. Stefansson papers, clipping from *Ottawa Journal*, Feb. 20, 1942, n.p., in Richard S. Finnie folder (Jan.–Mar. 1942).

17. Stefansson papers, transcript of proceedings, "Alaska Highway, Hearing Before a Subcommittee of the Committee on Foreign Relations on Senate Resolution 253, June 1, 1942," pp. 22–23 [hereafter cited as "1942 Alaska Hwy Hearings"].

18. Twichell papers, extract of letter from Col. Ingalls to Mrs. Ingalls, Feb. 20, 1942; Capes, "Report on Reconnaissance," pp. 2–3.

19. Ibid., pp. 3–9; Twichell papers, extracts of letters, Col. Ingalls to Mrs. Ingalls, Feb. 26, 28, 1942.

20. *Peace River Block News*, Feb. 26, 1942, p. 1.

21. *Los Angeles Times*, Feb. 16, 1942, p. 1; Feb. 18, p. 1; Feb. 20, p. 2; Feb. 24, p. 1; Feb. 25, p. 4; Feb. 26, p. 1; Feb. 27, p. 1.

22. Ibid., Mar. 3, 1942, p. 9; Mar. 7, p. 6; *Boston Globe*, Mar. 3, p. 13; Mar. 5, p. 10; Mar. 7, p. 1; Mar. 10, p. 1.

23. H. L. Keenlyside to N. A. Robertson, memorandum, Mar. 3, 1942, NAC, RG 24, vol. 2742, File 463–40, vol. 2.

24. F. H. LaGuardia to F. D. Roosevelt, Feb. 27, 1942, Roosevelt Papers, F.D.R. Library, Hyde Park, NY, OF 1566, Folder: Pacific-Alaska Hwy, 1942.

25. Marginal notes on Keenlyside memo, note 23.

26. CD/HWY Report, Exhibits Section, pp. 177–78.

27. *Boston Globe*, Mar. 6, 1942, p. 1.

28. Ibid., Mar. 7, p. 1; Twichell papers, copy of statement.

CHAPTER 4

1. 35th Engineers, "Regimental History, 15 July 1941–27 Feb. 1943," NA, RG 407, AGO, Entry 427, WWII Operations Reports, Box 19534 [hereafter cited as 35th Engrs, "History"]; Twichell, "Engineer's Story," ch. 1.

2. 35th Engrs, "History"; Leo Kozul interview, Fort St. John, BC, June 18, 1982. Mr. Kozul was a member of Co. "B," 35th Engrs.

3. Forrest C. Pogue, *George C. Marshall: Ordeal and Hope: 1939–1942* (New York: Viking Press, 1966), pp. 46–79; Mark S. Watson, *U.S. Army in World War II: Prewar Plans and Preparations* (Washington, DC: GPO, 1950), pp. 237–40.

4. 35th Engrs, "History"; Twichell, "Engineer's Story," ch. 1.

5. Pogue, *George C. Marshall*, p. 163.

6. Ibid., pp. 89–96, 162–65.

7. Robert Ingalls (son of Col. Ingalls), telephone interview, Oct. 20, 1990; 35th Engrs, "History"; Twichell, "Engineer's Story," chs. 1, 4 (words to song).

8. Twichell papers, H.T. to F.M.T., Mar. 4, 1942.

9. Twichell papers, copy of menu.

10. Kozul interview.

11. Twichell papers, A. C. Welling to H.T., Aug. 15, 1967.

12. Harold W. Richardson, "Alcan—America's Glory Road: Part II—Supply, Equipment and Camps," *Engineering News Record* (Dec. 31, 1942): 38.

13. Twichell papers, A.C.W. to H.T., Aug. 15, 1967; Twichell, "Engineer's Story," ch. 2; Kozul interview.

14. Ibid.

15. Ibid.; *Peace River Block News*, Mar. 12, 1942, p. 1.

16. 35th Engrs, "History"; Twichell papers, H.T. to "My Dears," Apr. 3, 1942.

17. Ibid.

18. Ibid.; A.C.W. to H.T., Aug. 15, 1967; Twichell, "Engineer's Story," ch. 2.
19. Ibid., Twichell papers, H.T. to "My Dears," Apr. 3, 1942.
20. Ibid.; A.C.W. to H.T., Aug. 15, 1967; 35th Engrs, "History"; Twichell, "Engineer's Story," ch. 2.
21. Ibid.; Twichell papers, H.T. to "My Dears," Apr. 3, 1942.
22. Ibid., A.C.W. to H.T., Aug. 15, 1967; Twichell, "Engineer's Story," ch. 2; 35th Engrs, "History."
23. Twichell papers, memorandum from Welling to Hoge, Mar. 27, 1942.
24. Twichell papers, A. M. Eschbach to H.T., Oct. 31, 1967.
25. Twichell papers, memorandum from Welling to Hoge, Mar. 27, 1942; Twichell, "Engineer's Story," ch. 2.
26. *Ibid.*
27. Ibid.; Twichell papers, H.T. to "My Dears," Apr. 3, 1942; Paul Symbol (Ingalls's adjutant) to H.T., Aug. 7, 1967.
28. Twichell, "Engineer's Story," ch. 2; Twichell papers, transcript of interview with Mike Miletich conducted by Ruth Twichell Cochrane at Fort Belvoir, Virginia, Aug. 1967, p. 6; Report of Signal Det. B, 843d Signal Bn, Mar.–Apr. 1942, NA, RG 338, U.S. Army Commands, Box 3, File 314.7: Military Histories.
29. Blanche D. Coll, Jean E. Keith, and Herbert H. Rosenthal, *U.S. Army in World War II: The Corps of Engineers: Troops and Equipment* (Washington, DC: GPO, 1958), p. 299.
30. Richardson, "Alcan—America's Glory Road: Part III—Construction Tactics," *Engineering News Record* (Jan. 14, 1943): 132.
31. Twichell papers, H.T. to "My Dears," Apr. 3, 1942.
32. Twichell papers, Miletich interview, p. 7.

CHAPTER 5

1. CD/HWY Report, Exhibits Section, p. 159.
2. Ibid., pp. 157–58.
3. Ibid., pp. 168–69.
4. Ibid., p. 170.
5. Copy of telegram, Riggs to Roosevelt, Mar. 6, 1942, in NA, RG 165, War Department General Staff, Box 1633, OPD File 611: Alaska.
6. *New York Times*, Mar. 9, 1942, p. 1.
7. CD/HWY Report, Exhibits Section, pp. 160–61.
8. See, e.g., *Los Angeles Times*, Mar. 7, 1942, p. 6, and *Seattle Post-Intelligencer*, p. 3, same date; also *Portland Oregonian*, Mar. 9, 1942, p. 4.
9. *Boston Globe*, Mar. 12, 1942, pp. 1, 28.
10. *New York Times*, Mar. 14, p. 32.
11. *Los Angeles Times*, Mar. 8, 1942, p. 4; *Seattle Post-Intelligencer*, Mar. 14, 1942, p. 8; *Boston Globe*, "Editorial and News Feature Section," Mar. 15, 1942, p. 5.
12. *Seattle Post-Intelligencer*, Mar. 14, 1942, pp. 1, 5.
13. *Alaska Weekly* (Apr. 10, 1942): 1.
14. CD/HWY Report, Exhibits Section, pp. 172–75.
15. Quote is from *ibid.*, p. 171; the best and most recent biography of Ickes is by T. H. Watkins, *Righteous Pilgrim: The Life and Times of Harold L. Ickes, 1874–1952* (New York: Henry Holt, 1990).
16. The best and most recent biography of Stimson is by Godfrey Hodgson, *The Colonel: The Life and Wars of Henry Stimson, 1867–1950* (New York: Alfred A. Knopf, 1990).
17. CD/HWY Report, Exhibits Section, p. 176.
18. Ulysses Lee, *U.S. Army in World War II: The Employment of Negro Troops* (Washington, DC: GPO, 1966), pp. 88–104, 128–29. Mayor's quote is from p. 104; for a discussion

of some implications of the cultural bias inherent in the Army's standardized tests, and an example of the effect of equipment disparities on morale, see ch. 7 of this book.

19. A. Russell Buchanan, *Black Americans in World War II* (Santa Barbara, CA: ABC-Clio, 1977), pp. 89–90; Lee, *U.S. Army in WWII: Negro Troops*, p. 617. That the African nation of Liberia was averse to having black U.S. soldiers on its soil seems surprising, but in this case, at least, the objections had nothing to do with race. Liberia's leaders feared that social unrest would result from the contrast between the wages of their impoverished citizens and those of the average black GI.

20. Ibid., pp. 438–39; CD/HWY Report, Exhibits Section, p. 241. The Chief of Engineers' Mar. 14, 1942, recommendation to add the 93rd and 97th regiments to Hoge's command was approved in the War Department on March 27. This paperwork is in NA, RG 165, War Department General Staff, Box 1633. The 95th Engineers were added on April 6, 1942. See NA, RG 77, OCE, Box 15/20, Accession 72A3173, Folder 50–28.

21. Hoge obituary, *Assembly* (June 1981): 124–25.

22. CD/HWY Report, Exhibits Section, p. 173.

23. Stefansson papers, S. Williams to V.S., Sept. 14, 1940, Alaska Hwy. Folder, 1940; the Stefansson–Halvorson correspondence cited is in same folder.

24. Ibid., Richard Finnie Folder, 1942, R.F. to V.S., Feb. 13, 1942.

25. Ibid., R.F. to V.S., Feb. 17, 1942.

26. Ibid., R.F. to V.S., Apr. 11, 12, 17, 20 and May 5, 1942.

27. Ibid., V.S. to F.A. Delano, Apr. 8, 1942.

28. Roosevelt papers, F.A.D. to F.D.R., Apr. 13, 1942.

29. David H. Bennett, "Langer, William," *Dictionary of American Biography*, Supp. 6 (New York: Charles Scribners' Sons, 1980), pp. 360–62; for Halvorson's hopes to replace Langer, see H.H. to V.S., Dec. 26, 1941, in Stefansson papers. Whatever the truth about the charges against Langer in 1940–41, he remained popular with North Dakota voters. He was still a U.S. Senator when he died in 1959.

30. William Langer, speech before the U.S. Senate, in *Congressional Record*, May 21, 1942, pp. 4569–71.

31. Stefansson papers, transcript of 1942 Alaska Hwy Hearings, pp. 6–35.

32. CD/HWY Report, Exhibits Section, "Report of Subcommittee of Foreign Relations Committee Having Under Consideration Senate Resolution 253, June 17, 1942" (extract), pp. 123–24.

33. Charles S. Lecky, "The CANOL Project and the Alaska Highway, 1942–1944," report compiled under the direction of the Northwest Division Engineer, 1944, p. 53 [hereafter cited as NW Div. Report]. Location: OHCE.

CHAPTER 6

1. Twichell papers, Miletich interview, p. 8; H.T. to "Dear Ones," May 3, 1942; Twichell, "Engineer's Story," ch. 2.

2. Ibid., ch. 3.

3. Ibid.

4. Ibid.

5. W. H. Curwen, "Report of Reconnaissance, Ft. Nelson, BC to Watson Lake, YT, Apr. 14, 1942" (copy), pp. 1–8. Location: YA. Twichell, "Engineer's Story," ch. 3 (also source of dialogue).

6. Ibid.

7. Ibid.; Twichell papers, A. C. Welling to H.T., Aug. 15, 1967; W. M. Hoge to C. L. Sturdevant, May 3, 1942, in NA, RG 77, OCE, Box 14/20, Accession 72A3173, Folder: Alaska Hwy.—General; U.S. Army, HQ Whitehorse Sector, "History of the Whitehorse Sector of the ALCAN Highway, 10 June 1943," pp. 3–5. [hereafter cited as Whitehorse Sector History]. Location: OHCE.

8. Stanley L. Jackson, "Stringing Wire Toward Tokyo: A Brief History of the Alaska

Military Highway," U.S. Army Signal Corps Historical Monograph in CMH files, pp. 7–10 [hereafter cited as Jackson, "Stringing Wire"].

9. Theodore A. Huntley and R. E. Royall, *Construction of the Alaska Highway* (Washington, DC: PRA, 1945), p. 102.

10. Greenwood, "General Hoge and the Alaska Highway," in Coates, ed., *The Alaska Highway Symposium*, p. 43.

11. Ibid.

12. David Remley, *Crooked Road: The Story of the Alaska Highway* (New York: McGraw-Hill, 1976), p. 106.

13. Hoge interview, tape 2, p. 31.

14. Whitehorse Sector History, pp. 7–11.

15. Ibid., pp. 5–7; 18th Engineers, "General Orders, 1942," NA, RG 407, AGO, Entry 427, WWII Operations Reports, Box 19523 [hereafter cited as 18th Engrs, "G.O."]; Ken Rust, "History of the 18th Engineers (Combat) in the Yukon Territory," pp. 5–25 [hereafter cited as Rust, "18th Engrs History"]. Location: OHCE.

16. 93rd Engineers, "Regimental History, Jan. 1, 1938–Jan. 1, 1943," and 340th Engineers, "Regimental History, Mar. 5, 1942–Apr. 30, 1944," both in NA, RG 407, AGO, Entry 427, WWII Operations Reports, Boxes 19549 and 19579 [hereafter cited as 93d Engrs, "History" and 340th Engrs, "History," respectively].

17. Fenton B. Whiting, *Grit, Grief and Gold: A True Narrative of an Alaskan Pathfinder* (Seattle: Peacock Publishing, 1933) pp. 55–65; Ralph H. Browne, "Men of the High Iron," unpublished MS in Archives of UAKF, pp. 1–3; V. I. Hahn (Supt. WP&YRR) to W. P. Wilson (CO, RR Det.), Feb. 5, 1943, in NA, RG 336, Chief of Transportation, Box 310.

18. Whitehorse Sector History, pp. 5–6; 93d and 340th Engrs, "Histories."

19. Remley, *Crooked Road*, p. 82; Whitehorse Sector History, pp. 11–13.

20. Ibid., pp. 7, 9; 93d and 340th Engrs, "Histories."

21. Walter Mason interview, Lexington, Virginia, Apr. 13, 1991. Mr. Mason was a lieutenant in the 97th Engineers; Whitehorse Sector History, pp. 6–7, 10–12.

22. Ibid., pp. 11–12.

23. 341st Engineers, "Regimental History, Mar. 6, 1942–July 29, 1943," NA, RG 407, AGO Entry 427, WWII Operations Reports, Box 19580 [hereafter cited as 341st Engrs, "History"]; Twichell, "Engineer's Story," ch. 8; *The Long Trail: 341st Engineers on the Alaska Military Highway, 1942–1943* (Charlotte, NC: Herald Press, no date). Preface and pp. 1–2.

24. Ibid.

25. Twichell, "Engineer's Story," ch. 4; Twichell papers, A. M. Eschbach to H.T., Oct. 31, 1967 (maps attached).

26. Ibid.

27. 35th Engrs, "History"; Twichell, Engineer's Story," chs. 5–7.

28. Ibid., ch. 5.

29. Twichell papers, A. M. Eschbach to H.T., Oct. 31, 1967.

30. Twichell, "Engineer's Story," chs. 2, 4.

31. *Edmonton Journal*, Aug. 15, 1942.

CHAPTER 7

1. 95th Engineers, "Regimental History," 15 Apr. 1941–Dec. 1946", NA, RG 407, AGO Entry 427, WWII Operations Reports, Box 19553, [hereafter cited as 95th Engrs, "History"]; Twichell, "Engineer's Story," ch. 4.

2. Ibid., ch. 8; 341st Engrs, "History"; 95th Engrs, "History."

3. Lee, *U.S. Army in WWII: Negro Troops*, p. 45.

4. Ibid., pp. 27–50; "James Alexander O'Connor," obituary, *Assembly* (Apr. 1953): 49–50.

5. Morris J. MacGregor, *Integration of the Armed Forces, 1940–1965* (Washington: GPO, 1981), pp. 6–7; Bernard C. Nalty and Morris J. MacGregor, eds., *Blacks in the Military: Essential Documents* (Wilmington, DE: Scholarly Resources, 1981), p. 89.

6. Ibid., pp. 82–84; Lee, *U.S. Army in WWII: Negro Troops*, pp. 5–20.

7. Nalty and MacGregor, *Blacks in the Military*, pp. 84–85.

8. Lee, *U.S. Army in WWII: Negro Troops*, pp. 35–49.

9. MacGregor, *Integration of the Armed Forces*, pp. 56–57, 231–33, 428–34.

10. Lee, *U.S. Army in WWII: Negro Troops*, p. 244.

11. Ibid., pp. 241-45.

12. Ibid.

13. Ibid., pp. 107–10, 191–93.

14. MacGregor, *Integration of the Armed Forces*, pp. 10–14.

15. Nalty and MacGregor, *Blacks in the Military*, pp. 105–6.

16. Ibid., p. 108.

17. Ibid., p. 109.

18. Lee, *U.S. Army in WWII: Negro Troops*, pp. 79–80.

19. Ibid.; Benjamin O. Davis, Jr., *Benjamin O. Davis, Jr., American: An Autobiography* (Washington: Smithsonian Institution Press, 1991), pp. 1–6, 67.

20. Phillip McGuire, *Taps for a Jim Crow Army: Letters from Black Soldiers in World War II* (Santa Barbara, CA: ABC-Clio, 1983), Introduction, pp. xxxv–xxxvi.

21. Buchanan, *Black Americans in WWII*, pp. 15–27.

22. Lee, *U.S. Army in WWII: Negro Troops*, pp. 141–42.

23. Ibid., pp. 145–50, 157–74.

24. Ibid., p. 88.

25. Ibid., p. 268.

26. Charles Gardner interview, Hempstead, NY, Dec. 11, 1990.

27. Lee, *U.S. Army in WWII: Negro Troops*, pp. 186–87.

28. Ibid., p. 183.

29. Ibid., p. 235.

30. Wansley Hill interview, Yeadon, PA, Apr. 7, 1991.

31. George Owens, response to author's questionnaire, July 27, 1990.

32. S. B. Buckner to C. L. Sturdevant, Apr. 20, 1942, in NA, RG 77, OCE, Box 14/20, Accession 72A3173, File: Correspondence, Alaska Hwy.

33. Hoge interview, tape 2, p. 21.

34. Huntley and Royall, *Construction of the Alaska Highway*, pp. 9, 59–61, 145–46.

35. 93d Engrs, "History"; 95th Engrs, "History"; Whitehorse Sector Report, p. 9.

36. Godsell, *Romance of the Alaska Highway*, p. 161. Godsell's version of this story, with its "minstrel show" dialect, has the flavor of a racist joke.

CHAPTER 8

1. Hill interview.

2. "Historical Record of Task Force 2600," NA, RG 338, U.S. Army Commands, Box 30, pp. 10–11 [hereafter cited as TF2600 History]; brief histories of the component units of TF2600 (89th and 90th Heavy Ponton Bns & 388th Engineer Regt) are in NA, RG 407, AGO, Entry 427, WWII Operations Reports, Box 18635 [hereafter cited as 89th Engr Bn, 90th Engr Bn, 388th Engr Regt, "Histories"]; NW Div. Report, pp. 37–41, 44.

3. ASF, CD, "Report on CANOL Project, 1 June 1945," pp. 1–3 [hereafter cited as CD/CANOL Report]. Location: OHCE.

4. Ibid., pp. 36–40; NW Div. Report, p. 25.

5. CD/CANOL Report, p. 33.

6. Vilhjalmur Stefansson, "The American Far North," *Foreign Affairs* 17 (3) (April, 1939): 508–23; CD/CANOL Report, pp. 37–38.

7. Ibid., pp. 39–40.
8. Ibid., p. 40; governors' telegrams are in Roosevelt papers, OF1566, Box 2.
9. CD/CANOL Report, pp. 34–35, 43.
10. Ibid.
11. Ibid., pp. 38–39.
12. Ibid., p. 43.
13. Ibid., pp. 43–44.
14. Ibid., pp. 44–46.
15. Ibid.
16. Ibid.
17. Ibid.
18. Jean E. Smith, *Lucius D. Clay: An American Life* (New York: Henry Holt, 1990), p. 115; for General Robins's initial objections to CANOL, see CD/CANOL Report, p. 46 and NW Div. Report, p. 28.
19. Ibid., pp. 28–31; CD/CANOL Report, pp. 53–58, 80.
20. Ibid., pp. 54–58; NW Div. Report, pp. 35–36.
21. Price Day, "No Red Tape Fetters Army's Good Provider," *Baltimore Sun Sunday Magazine*, Mar. 5, 1944, p. 1; Charles J. V. Murphy, "Somervell of the S.O.S.," *Life* (Mar. 8, 1943), pp. 91–92; "Brehon Burke Somervell," obituary, *Assembly* (Oct. 1955): p. 65; James E. Hewes, Jr., "Somervell, Brehon Burke," *Dictionary of American Biography* Supplement 5 (New York: Charles Scribner's Sons, 1977), pp. 642–44.
22. Ibid. Murphy, "Somervell of the S.O.S.," pp. 91–92. Stefansson, *Discovery*, pp. 321–26.
23. Richard M. Leighton and Robert W. Coakley, *U.S. Army in World War II: Global Logistics and Strategy, 1940–1943* (Washington, DC: GPO, 1955), pp. 219–27; Smith, *Lucius D. Clay*, pp. 108–12.
24. Murphy, "Somervell of the S.O.S.," pp. 84–85.
25. Smith, *Lucius D. Clay*, p. 112.
26. Ibid., pp. 112–16; Day, "No Red Tape," p. 1; telephone interview with John Ohl, Mesa, Arizona, on Jan. 29, 1992. Dr. Ohl is preparing a biography of General Somervell, scheduled for publication in 1993. The details of General Somervell's treatment of General Olmstead are in George R. Thompson, Dixie R. Harris, Pauline M. Oakes, and Dulaney Terrett, *U.S. Army in World War II, The Signal Corps: The Test* Washington: GPO, 1957), 560–63. General Marshall was willing to allow Olmstead a face-saving assignment, but not Somervell.
27. Memorandum from Somervell to Reybold, Mar. 25, 1942, in NA, RG 336, Chief of Transportation, Box 51, "Alaska" File.
28. CD/CANOL Report, pp. 80–81; Stacy, *Arms, Men and Governments*, pp. 384–85.
29. NW Div. Report, p. 37; CD/CANOL Report, pp. 53–54, 81.
30. Ibid., pp. 63–64.
31. Ibid.
32. Ibid., pp. 61–62.
33. Dziuban, *U.S. Army in WWII, Military Relations, U.S. and Canada*, p. 141.
34. CD/CANOL Report, pp. 58, 61–62; NW Div. Report, pp. 34–35.
35. Ibid., pp. 62–64; CD/CANOL Report, p. 68.
36. Ibid.; NW Div. Report, pp. 64–67.
37. TF2600 History, pp. 5–8, 11–25; NW Div. Report, pp. 44–48, 60–62; L. E. Laurion, "Reconnaissance Report, June 18, 1942," HQS 89th Engr Bn, in NA, RG 407, AGO, Entry 427, WWII Operations Reports, Box 18635.
38. Richard Finnie, *CANOL: The Sub-Arctic Pipeline and Refinery Project Constructed by Bechtel-Price-Callahan for the Corps of Engineers, U.S. Army, 1942–1944* (San Francisco: Ryder and Ingram, 1945), p. 5.

CHAPTER 9

1. Twichell papers, A. M. Eschbach to H.T., Oct. 31, 1967.
2. Ibid.
3. Ibid.; Fr. Pierre Poullet interview, Ft. Nelson, BC, Aug. 21, 1991. For Fr. Poullet's version of this conversation, see ch. 17.
4. 35th Engrs, "History."
5. Twichell, "Engineer's Story," chs. 5, 6; the description of the road-building sequence is from Twichell papers, H.T. to "Dear Folks," May 19, 1942; Richardson, "ALCAN— Part III: Construction Tactics," *Engineering News Record* (Jan. 14, 1943): 63–67.
6. Richardson, "ALCAN—Part I: Strategy and Location," *Engineering News Record* (Dec. 12, 1942): 83–85; see the series of monthly Operations Reports to the Chief of Engineers from each Sector HQS, Apr.–Dec. 1942, in NA, RG 77, OCE, Box 16/20, Accession 72A3173. Mileage figures are from July reports.
7. Huntley and Royall, *Construction of Alaska Hwy*, pp. 3, 159.
8. Ibid., p. 127.
9. Jackson, "Stringing Wire," pp. 7–10.
10. "Fiasco to Alaska," *Pic* (Aug. 18, 1942): pp. 7–8.
11. Richard Olsenius, "Alaska Highway: Wilderness Escape Route," *National Geographic* 180(5) (November, 1991): 78; Collection of press clippings, Aug.–Dec. 1944, in OHCE Files, WWII Theaters of Operation, X, Box 2, Folder 6: "Lend-Lease via Alaska."
12. "Northwest Passage," *Time* (Aug. 31, 1942): p. 80.
13. Somervell attempted to banish all military dependents from the NWSC area as of December 15, 1942, but the policy met with so many protests and requests for exception that it was delayed and eventually watered down. See NA, RG 338, U.S. Army Commands, NWSC, Box 1, File 092.
14. "Northwest Passage," *Time* (Aug. 31, 1942): p. 79.
15. Ibid.; Gardner interview; Twichell papers, H.T. to "Dear Ones," June 3, 1942.
16. Photos of "Eleanor" and "Franklin" in *The Long Trail*, n.p.
17. Gardner interview; 35th Engrs, "History"; Twichell papers, H.T. to "Dear Ones," May 3, 1942.
18. Froelich Rainey, "Alaskan Highway an Engineering Epic," *National Geographic* (Feb. 1943): pp. 161–62; on gambling, see the excerpt from censored mail of a soldier in the 93rd Engrs, located in NA, RG 77, OCE, Box 15/20 Accession 72A3173, Folder 50–26.
19. CD/HWY Report, pp. 20–21.
20. 95th Engrs, "History"; Twichell, "Engineer's Story," ch. 8; Twichell papers, Folder: 95th Engrs—Misc.; Rainey, "Alaskan Highway," p. 157.
21. McGuire, *Taps for Jim Crow Army*, pp. 118-19.
22. Excerpts from censored mail of officers and men of the 95th Engrs are in the same location cited in note 18. All military personnel were briefed on the rationale for censorship and what kind of information was prohibited in personal letters.
23. Twichell, "Engineer's Story," chs. 4, 8 (two versions of the story); Twichell papers, Folder: 95th Engrs.
24. Twichell papers, H.T. to "Dear Ones," July 26, 1942.
25. Twichell, "Engineer's Story," chs. 4, 8.
26. Ibid.
27. Ibid.
28. Twichell papers, Folder: 95th Engrs.
29. Ibid., copy of Weekly Operations Report, July 26–Aug. 1, 1942.
30. Twichell, "Engineer's Story," chs. 4, 9 (two versions of story).
31. Ibid.
32. Twichell papers, W. H. Upson to R. T. Cochrane, Apr. 15, 1967; W. H. Upson, "Give Us More Rope," *Saturday Evening Post* (Dec. 12, 1942): pp. 18, 68–73. Another

Upson story featuring the same cast of characters, "Alexander Botts Will Fix Everything," appeared in the April 8, 1944, issue of the *Post*.

33. Twichell, "Engineer's Story," ch. 4.
34. Twichell papers, H.T. to "Dear Folks," Aug. 29, 1942.
35. Twichell, "Engineer's Story," ch. 4; 341st Engrs, "History"; 35th Engrs, "History."
36. Ibid.; Twichell, "Engineer's Story," ch. 4; Twichell papers, H.T. to "Dear Folks," Aug. 29, 1942.
37. Ibid.; Twichell, "Engineer's Story," chs. 6, 7.
38. *The Long Trail*, "C" Company History; Huntley and Royall, *Construction of Alaska Hwy.*, p. 31.
39. Twichell papers, H.T. to "Dear Folks," Aug. 29, 1942.

CHAPTER 10

1. Hill interview; NW Div. Report, p. 79.
2. Ibid., p. 71; TF2600 History, pp. 19–21.
3. Ibid., pp. 20, 24; Hill interview.
4. TF2600 History, p. 29; NW Div. Report, pp. 69.
5. Ibid., p. 80.
6. Ibid.; NW Div. Report, p. 35; Hill interview.
7. Ibid.; George Young interview, Yeadon, PA, Apr. 7, 1991.
8. Hill and Young interviews.
9. NW Div. Report, pp. 67–68; TF2600 History, pp. 30–31.
10. Ibid., p. 31; Finnie, *CANOL*, pp. 28–29, 132.
11. NW Div. Report, pp. 60–62, 69, 78; TF2600 Report, p. 25.
12. Ibid., pp. 19–20; Finnie, *CANOL*, pp. 19–27.
13. NW Div. Report, pp. 68, 70; TF2600 Report, pp. 23–24, 28.
14. Ibid., pp. 26, 29–33; CD/CANOL Report, p. 71; NW Div. Report, pp. 60–61, 75–76.
15. Ibid., pp. 62, 69–70, 72; Patricia S. Barry, *The CANOL Project: An Adventure of the U.S. War Department in Canada's Northwest* (Edmonton, Alberta: Atlas Book Bindery, 1985), limited ed., pp. 109, 121. Ms. Barry's thesis, supported largely by circumstantial evidence, is that Project CANOL was a thinly disguised cover for postwar U.S. commercial penetration of Canada. That U.S. corporations hoped to use CANOL for such purposes is obvious, but that the U.S. War Department intentionally aided and abetted such plans is unlikely—and unproved by Ms. Barry. Her work is nevertheless a valuable source of information about CANOL in the context of Canadian political and social history.
16. NW Div. Report, pp. 69–70; TF2600 History, pp. 37–38; CD/CANOL Report, pp. 71, 83; Carr, "Great Falls to Nome," p. 68.
17. Ibid., p. 69.
18. Ibid.
19. Ibid., pp. 75–76.
20. Ibid., pp. 76–77.
21. Ibid., pp. 77–78; NW Div. Report, pp. 100–2.
22. CD/CANOL Report, p. 83. Production of 20,000 bpd in the Norman Wells area would have required significantly increasing the capacity of the CANOL 1 pipeline and refinery. Adopting a "wait and see" position on the outcome of the wildcatting, the Army proceeded with its original plans for these facilities.
23. Ibid., p. 89.
24. Stefansson papers, V.S. to A.F., Sept. 4, 1942.
25. Ibid., R.F. to V.S., Sept. 29, 1942.
26. Ibid.
27. CD/CANOL Report, p. 83; NW Div. Report, pp. 102, 104, 106–7.
28. TF2600 History, pp. 43–44, 46.

29. Ibid.; NW Div. Report, pp. 113–18.
30. Ibid., pp. 80–81, 99.

CHAPTER 11

1. Minutes of Staff meeting, HQ SOS, Aug. 24, 1942, in NA, RG 336, Chief of Transportation, Box 51, File: "ALCAN Hwy" [hereafter cited as Minutes, HQ SOS, Aug. 24, 1942].
2. NW Div. Report, p. 83.
3. Hoge interview, tape 2, p. 29; tape 3, pp. 5–6.
4. Ibid., tape 3, pp. 3–4; telegram, Sturdevant to Hoge, Aug. 13, 1942, in NA, RG 77, OCE, Box 14/20, Accession 72A3173, File: "Alaska Hwy.—General."
5. Hoge interview, tape 2, p. 32; tape 3, pp. 2–3.
6. Ibid., tape 3, pp. 1–2.
7. Minutes, HQ SOS, Aug. 24, 1942; Greenwood, "General Hoge and the Alaska Highway," in Coates, ed., *The Alaska Highway Symposium*, pp. 50–51.
8. Ibid., Hoge interview, tape 2, p. 38.
9. Ibid., tape 3, pp. 5–6, 12.
10. Note in Hoge papers, copies of which are in OHCE files. Originals are in Command and General Staff School Library, Ft. Leavenworth, Kansas.
11. NW Div. Report, p. 83; Whitehorse Sector History, p. 15; 35th Engrs, "History"; Twichell, "Engineer's Story," ch. 5.
12. C.L.S. to W.M.H., Oct. 10, 1942, in OHCE copies of Hoge papers. For Sturdevant's coolness toward O'Connor, see the series of memos and letters during June–July, 1942, in NA, RG 77, OCE, Boxes 14/20 and 15/20, Accession 72A3173, especially C.L.S. to J.A.O., June 4, 1942, and July 29, 1942.
13. Hoge interview, tape 3, pp. 2–4; Browne, pp. 2–4; V. I. Hahn to W. P. Wilson, Feb. 5, 1943, in NA, RG 336, Chief of Transportation, Box 310.
14. 35th Engrs, 340th Engrs, "Histories"; Kozul interview.
15. NW Div. Report, pp. 92–93.
16. Whitehorse Sector History, pp. 8, 11; Rust, "18th Engrs History," p. 61.
17. Ibid., pp. 66–71; Richardson, "ALCAN—Part III," p. 135.
18. Rust, "18th Engrs History," pp. 57–65.
19. Richardson, "ALCAN—Part III," p. 134; NW Div. Report, p. 54; Mason interview.
20. Ibid.
21. Ibid.; Richardson, "ALCAN—Part III," p. 134; Huntley and Royall, *Construction of Alaska Hwy*, pp. 23–24.
22. Mason interview.
23. Rust, "18th Engrs History," pp. 77–78.
24. Ibid., pp. 75–76; Huntley and Royall. *Construction of Alaska Hwy*, pp. 24–25.
25. Mason interview; Jerome F. Sheldon, "This Is the Silver Anniversary Year for the Alaska Highway," *Alaska Sportsman* (Sept. 1967): pp. 22–23; Twichell papers, clipping from *Washington Post*, Nov. 5, 1942. Every official account of the linkup gives its location as Beaver Creek, but it is also a matter of record that, by October 25, the lead bulldozers of the 97th Engineers had reached the Snag River, 10 miles farther inside Canada. An explanation that reconciles these facts is that the two regiments' lines of advance intersected at an angle rather than meeting head-on, with the 18th Engineers' lead 'dozer encountering the flank of the 97th's work column. This possibility is consistent with a description of the linkup in a letter from Col. Paules to Gen. Sturdevant on Dec. 10, 1942, in Hoge's papers at OHCE.
26. Ibid., War Dept. press release, Oct. 29, 1942.
27. Huntley and Royall, *Construction of Alaska Hwy*, p. 12; memorandum, subject: Monthly Report of Operations, Nov., 1942, from Chief of Engineers to CG, SOS, Dec.

29, 1942, in NA, RG 77, OCE, Box 16/20, Accession 72A3173, File: Alaska Hwy. Progress Reports.

28. Richard L. Neuberger (Gen. O'Connor's aide) to Anthony J. Dimond (Alaska's Congressional Delegate), Nov. 29, 1942, in OHCE Files, WWII Theaters of Operation, X, Box 6, Folder 6: "Articles and Press Releases."

29. Memo, OCE to CG, SOS, Dec. 29, 1942; 35th Engrs, "History"; Huntley and Royall, *Construction of Alaska Hwy*, p. 26.

30. R. L. Neuberger to A. J. Dimond, Nov. 29, 1942; Memo, OCE to CG, SOS, Dec. 29, 1942.

31. Neuberger to Dimond, Nov. 29, 1942.

32. Ibid.

33. *New York Times*, Nov. 22, 1942, p. 1; *Whitehorse Star*, Nov. 20, p. 1.

34. Sheldon, "Silver Anniversary Year," p. 24.

35. *Whitehorse Star*, Nov. 20, 1942, p. 1; *New York Times*, Nov. 22, 1942, p. 1.

36. Ibid.; Neuberger to Dimond, Nov. 29, 1942; Twichell papers, copy of program w/menu.

37. Memo, OCE to CG, SOS, Dec. 29, 1942.

CHAPTER 12

1. Huntley and Royall, *Construction of Alaska Hwy*, p. 30; Twichell, "Engineer's Story," ch. 11.

2. CD/CANOL Report, pp. 78–80; NW Div. Report, pp. 109, 126.

3. Ibid., pp. 97, 138; Twichell, "Engineer's Story," ch. 6; 35th Engrs, "History."

4. NW Div. Report, p. 94; Twichell papers, NW Div. press release, "The Haines Cutoff," 9/13/43; Huntley and Royall, *Construction of Alaska Hwy*, p. 27. The possibility of building the cutoff had been under discussion and investigation since April 1942.

5. Ibid., pp. 27–30; A. C. Clark, "Alaska Highway—Problems in Roadway Design," *Western Construction News* (Mar. 1943) pp. 108–8.

6. Huntley and Royall, *Construction of Alaska Hwy*, p. 29.

7. "The Alaska Highway, An Interim Report from the Committee on Roads," 79th Congress, 2d Session, House Report No. 1705, p. 304.

8. V. I. Hahn to W. P. Wilson, Feb. 5, 1943, in NA, RG 336, Chief of Transportation, Box 310; Huntley and Royall, *Construction of Alaska Hwy*, pp. 28–30.

9. Twichell papers, H.T. to F.M.T., Nov. 13, 1942.

10. Twichell, "Engineer's Story," ch. 11.

11. Whitehorse Sector History, pp. 18–19.

12. Twichell, "Engineer's Story," chs. 11, 12.

13. Ibid.; Twichell papers, H.T. to "Dear Folks," Feb. 14, 1943.

14. C. N. Schultheis to R. E. Cole, Feb. 3, 1943, in NA, RG 338, U.S. Army Commands, Box 8, File 611: "Alaska Highway."

15. Jackson, "Stringing Wire," pp. 10, 80.

16. Ibid., pp. 20–23; Twichell papers, Folder: "CATEL & D.C. Fire."

17. Twichell, "Engineer's Story," ch. 11.

18. Orval Couch interviews, Whitehorse, Yukon, Aug. 24, 1980, and Aug. 17, 1991; the quote is from "Mayhem, Morons and a Mobile Machine Shop" by Ken Spottswood in *Yukon Anniversaries Newsletter* (Mar. 22, 1991): 4. Couch was a civilian mechanic employed by the U.S. Army.

19. Ibid.; NW Div. Report, pp. 147–50; Art Webb, Fred Johns, and Sid Cooper interviews, Dawson Creek, BC, Aug. 13–14, 1980.

20. NW Div. Report, pp. 123–24; a long narrative account of Blanchet's reconnaissance by George Blondin, one of his native guides, is given in Barry, *The CANOL Project*, pp. 434–55; Twichell, "Engineer's Story," ch. 12.

21. Ibid.

22. Ibid.; Twichell papers, Folder: "95th Engrs."

23. Rust, "18th Engrs History," p. 50.
24. Ibid., p. 51.
25. Mason interview.
26. 340th Engrs, "History"; NW Div. Report, pp. 163–64, 188.
27. CD/CANOL Report, pp. 97, 119.
28. Ibid., pp. 72–74, 79, 98–100; 35th Engrs. "History."
29. Hill, Young interviews.
30. Ibid; Twichell papers, Folder: "95th Engrs."
31. NW Div. Report, p. 147; CD/CANOL Report, pp. 160–61.
32. Twichell papers, H.T. to "Dear Folks," Mar. 14, 1943.

CHAPTER 13

1. "Preliminary Inventory for Records of the Bureau of Public Roads," National Archives, RG 30, Bureau of Public Roads, pp. 4–7. This finding aid contains an excellent short history of the BPR.
2. Ibid.; Huntley and Royall, *Construction of Alaska Hwy*, pp. 3–4; Frank Turner interview, Arlington, Virginia, May 26, 1982, Mr. Turner, a highway engineer, began his service with the BPR in 1929; he was assigned to the Alaska Highway project from 1942 to 1946.
3. Ibid.; Huntley and Royall, *Construction of Alaska Hwy*, p. 4.
4. Ibid., pp. 10–12, 33, 77.
5. Herbert R. Reese, *Seventy Years Down the Road* (Hawley, MN: Hawley Herald, 1973), pp. 17–31, 38–50, 61.
6. Ibid., pp. 62, 70.
7. Ibid., pp. 64, 70, 73.
8. Robert Thorkelson interview, Hayden Lake, Idaho, Sept. 11, 1980.
9. Ibid.; Reese, *Seventy Years*, pp. 71–72.
10. Huntley and Royall, *Construction of Alaska Hwy*, p. 79.
11. Ibid., pp. 7–10, 14; Reese, *Seventy Years*, p. 62.
12. Huntley and Royall, *Construction of Alaska Hwy*, pp. 127–30.
13. Ibid., p. 14.
14. Ibid., pp. 9, 59–67.
15. Reese, *Seventy Years*, pp. 63, 80.
16. Ibid., pp. 76–77.
17. Thorkelson interview.
18. Ibid.; Reese, *Seventy Years*, p. 63.
19. Ibid., p. 67; Huntley and Royall, *Construction of Alaska Hwy*, pp. 35–40.
20. Ibid., pp. 41–45.
21. Ibid., pp. 46–47. According to Orval Couch, a roving mechanic on the highway, Turner's responsibilities included keeping the FBI informed of criminal and subversive activities at U.S. installations in northwest Canada.
22. Huntley and Royall, *Construction of Alaska Hwy*, pp. 60–61, 66.
23. Ibid., pp. 61–67. Water erosion around the base of one tower caused the collapse of the Peace River suspension bridge in 1957. Its replacement is a safer, cantilevered steel truss design.
24. "The Alaska Highway," House Report 1705, Mar. 13, 1946, p. 26.
25. Hoge interview, tape 4, pp. 51–52.

CHAPTER 14

1. Warren G. Magnuson, "Gross Waste in Building Alaska Highway," *Seattle Post-Intelligencer*, May 9, 1944; for the "cow" quote, see the February 18, 1946, report of the U.S. Naval Attaché in Ottawa in NA, RG48, Dept. of Interior, Box 3675.

2. "The Alaska Highway," House Report 1705, Mar. 13, 1946, reproduces the entire Exhibits Section of CD/HWY Report; Senator Scrugham's Report No. 548, "The Alaska Highway," 78th Congress, 1st Session, Nov. 29, 1943, is essentially a narrative history based on Army documents.

3. Jonathan Daniels, *The Man of Independence* (New York: J. B. Lippincott, 1950), pp. 216–21; Harry S. Truman, *Memoirs*, vol. 1, *Year of Decisions* (Garden City, N.Y.: Doubleday, 1955), pp. 140–63.

4. Ibid., p. 165.

5. Donald H. Riddle, *The Truman Committee: A Study in Congressional Responsibility* (New Brunswick, N.J.: Rutgers University Press, 1964), p. 15.

6. Ibid., pp. 22–23; Truman, *Memoirs*, pp. 166–67.

7. Ibid., pp. 168–69.

8. Roger E. Willson, "The Truman Committee," unpublished Ph.D. dissertation (Harvard University, 1966), pp. 393–401.

9. Riddle, *The Truman Committee*, p. 38.

10. Ibid., p. 37.

11. Ibid., p. 25; Willson, "The Truman Committee," pp. 401–4, 411–12.

12. Riddle, *The Truman Committee*, pp. 108–9.

13. Ibid., pp. 110–11.

14. Ibid.; CD/CANOL Report, pp. 90–107.

15. Riddle, *The Truman Committee*, pp. 111–12.

16. Ibid., pp. 112–13; CD/CANOL Report, pp. 107–8.

17. Riddle, *The Truman Committee*, p. 114.

18. U.S. Senate Special Committee Investigating the National Defense Program, 78th Congress, 1st Session, Report No. 10, Part 14: *The CANOL Project* (Washington: GPO, 1944), p. 23 [hereafter cited as Truman Committee *Report*].

19. Ibid., p. 3.

20. Riddle, *The Truman Committee*, p. 113.

21. U.S. Senate Special Committee Investigating the National Defense Program, 78th Congress, 1st Session, Report No. 11, Part 22: *Hearings: The CANOL Project* (Washington, DC: GPO, 1944), pp. 9663–72 [hereafter cited as Truman Committee *Hearings*].

22. "Somervell Justifies Canol," clipping from *New York Times*, Dec. 21, 1943, in NA, RG 253, Petroleum Administrator for War, Box 4708, File 717: CANOL Project.

23. Truman Committee *Hearings*, pp. 9716–17.

24. Truman Committee *Report*, p. 7.

25. Ibid., pp. 30–31.

26. Riddle, *The Truman Committee*, pp 117–19.

27. Smith, *Lucius D. Clay*, pp. 161–62; Somervell's obituary in *Assembly* (Oct. 1955): 65.

28. Truman, *Memoirs*, pp. 188–89.

29. Invitations and correspondence pertaining to this affair are in Truman's papers at the Harry S. Truman Library in Independence, Missouri: H.S.T. Senate and Vice-Presidential Papers, Box 170, Folder: Aug. 1943–Apr. 1944.

30. Willson, "The Truman Committee," p. 424.

31. Ibid., p. 425; press clipping, "How Bosses and F.D.R. Put Truman Over," *Washington Times Herald*, July 25, 1944, in Truman papers, Democratic National Committee, Box 126, Democratic National Convention, 1944, Folder: 1.

32. Edwin W. Pauley, "Why Truman Is President," unpublished MS in Truman papers, White House Confidential File, Box 30, File: "The President"; Truman, *Memoirs*, pp. 190, 193.

CHAPTER 15

1. Dziuban, *U.S. Army in WWII, Military Relations, U.S. and Canada*, pp. 213–15; Stacy, *Arms, Men and Governments*, p. 381.
2. Cloe, *Top Cover for America*, pp. 149–50; taped interview (#H-83-1) with Leslie Spoonts (LTC, USAF, Ret.), by J. H. Cloe, July 9, 1982, in Oral History Collection, Archives, UAKF.
3. Carr, "Great Falls to Nome," pp. 56–65; Randy Acord interview, Fairbanks, Alaska, Aug. 13, 1991. The Soviet Union did not declare war on Japan until August 8, 1945, three months after Germany unconditionally surrendered to the Allies, and two days after the atomic bomb was dropped on Hiroshima.
4. Ibid., Carr, "Great Falls to Nome," pp. 66–68; "ALSIB," *North Star Magazine* (Nov. 1944): pp. 1–6 (published by U.S. Air Force Air Transport Command, Alaskan Division), in OHCE Files, X: WWII Theaters of Operation, Box 2, Folder 6.
5. Carr, "Great Falls to Nome," pp. 71–78, 106–26.
6. Ibid., pp. 126–36; Dziuban, *U.S. Army in WWII, Military Relations, U.S. and Canada*, pp. 205–15; Stacy, *Arms, Men and Governments*, pp. 380–81; Eric Bramley, "Canada Gets Ready-Made System of Bases," *American Aviation* (Sept. 1, 1944): 17–18.
7. Dziuban, *U.S. Army in WWII, Military Relations, U.S. and Canada*, p. 216. In 1942 to 1943, of the 3,087 aircraft delivered to Fairbanks, 2,639 (83 percent) went to the Russians and 449 (17 percent) were kept in Alaska for U.S. use. By 1944, 95 percent of the deliveries went to the Russians.
8. Cloe, *Top Cover for America*, 150–51; Ken Spottswood, "Lend Lease Pilots Reunite in Fairbanks," *Yukon Anniversaries Commission Newsletter* (June 29, 1990): 1, 3; Acord interview.
9. Kay G. Chaffey, "Women Airforce Service Pilots, WWII, WASP Class 43-W-2: History" (privately printed, copy in possession of Celia Hunter, Fairbanks, Alaska).
10. Ibid.; Ginny Hill Wood interview, June 20, 1985; G. H. Wood and Celia Hunter interview, Fairbanks, Alaska, Aug. 12, 1991; also taped interview (H-84-36a&b) with Mrs. Wood in Oral History Collection of University of Alaska, Fairbanks.
11. Ibid.; Jeffrey P. Rhodes, "What They *Really* Called Them," *Air Force Magazine* (Sept. 1990): pp. 68–72.
12. Spottswood, "Pilots Played Chicken with Truck Drivers," *Yukon Anniversaries Commission Newsletter* (June 29, 1990): p. 2; Gordon Leenerts telephone interview, Jan. 6, 1992.
13. G. H. Wood interview. For Army Intelligence reports on the activities of Soviet airmen and their American "sympathizers" in the Fairbanks area, see NA, RG 407, AGO, Entry 427, WWII Operations Reports, Box 6.
14. Cloe, *Top Cover for America*, p. 153.
15. Ibid., p. 154; Telephone interview with Brynes Ellender, Billings, Montana, March 29, 1992. Mr. Ellender, a former pilot in the 7th Ferry Group and its unofficial historian, is writing a history of the group. Ivan Negenblya, article in *Yakutin Youth* quoted in *Yukon Anniversaries Commission Newsletter* (Oct. 26, 1990): p. 3. The author has been unable to find statistics on U.S. fatalities on the ALSIB run.
16. Stan Cohen, *The Forgotten War: A Pictorial History of World War II in Alaska and Northwestern Canada* (Missoula, MT: Pictorial Histories Publishing, 1981), p. 46; Cloe, *Top Cover for America*, p. 154.
17. Ibid.; Acord interview.
18. From statement of General Arnold quoted in *Edmonton Bulletin*, May 26, 1943.

CHAPTER 16

1. Curtis R. Nordman, "The Army of Occupation: Malcolm MacDonald and U.S. Military Involvement in the Canadian Northwest," in Coates, ed., *The Alaska Highway*

Symposium, pp. 83, 98; Laurent Cyr, Charlie Benson, and Dean Elston interviews, Whitehorse, Yukon, Aug. 22, 24–25, 1980.

2. Norman, OK: University of Oklahoma Press, 1992.
3. Full title: *Continental Divide: The Values and Institutions of the United States and Canada* (New York: Routledge, 1990).
4. Ibid., pp. 1–8.
5. Ibid., p. 43.
6. Nordman, "Army of Occupation," in Coates, ed., *The Alaska Highway Symposium*, pp. 86–87.
7. Ibid., pp. 97–98.
8. Richard J. Diubaldo, "The Alaska Highway in Canada–United States Relations," in Coates, ed., *The Alaska Highway Symposium*, pp. 104–6.
9. C. K. LeCapelain to R. A. Gibson, July 17, 1943, in Yukon Archives, YRG 1, Series 1, Vol. 9, File; 149b, Part J.
10. Ken Coates, "The Alaska Highway and the Indians of the Southern Yukon," in Coates, ed., *The Alaska Highway Symposium*, pp. 157–61.
11. Ibid., pp. 162–65; Sam Johnston, interview, Teslin, Yukon, Aug. 18, 1991.
12. Julie Cruikshank, "The Gravel Magnet," in Coates, ed., *The Alaska Highway Symposium*, pp. 178–80.
13. John and Linda MacDonald and Russell and Louise Novodvorsji interviews, Watson Lake, Yukon, Aug. 20, 1991.
14. Barry, *The CANOL Project*, pp. 341–43.
15. Remley, *Crooked Road*, pp. 177–78.
16. CD/HWY Report, pp. 46–49.
17. Remley, *Crooked Road*, p. 179.
18. Audry Aylard interview, Teslin, Yukon, Aug. 16, 1991.
19. John Greenwood, a U.S. Army historian attending the symposium, also recalls this indignant outburst.

BIBLIOGRAPHY

A. PRIMARY SOURCES

1. GOVERNMENT RECORDS AND DOCUMENT COLLECTIONS

Canada National Archives. Record Group 2: Records of the Privy Council.
———. Record Group 24: Records of the Ministry of National Defence.
———. Record Group 25: Records of the Ministry of External Affairs.
———. Record Group 36: Records of the Special Commissioner for Defence Projects in Northwest Canada.
United States Army. Center of Military History, Washington, D.C.: Alaska, Alaska Highway, and CANOL materials in CMH Historical Research Collection.
———. Chief of Engineers, Office of History, Fort Belvoir, Va.: Alaska, Alaska Highway, and CANOL materials in OHCE Historical Research Collection.
United States National Archives. Papers of Franklin Delano Roosevelt: FDR Library, Hyde Park, N.Y.
———. Papers of Harry S. Truman: HST Library, Independence, Mo.
———. Record Group 30: Records of the Bureau of Public Roads.
———. Record Group 48: Records of the Interior Department, Office of the Secretary.
———. Record Group 77: Records of the War Department, Office of the Chief of Engineers.
———. Record Group 92: Records of the War Department, Office of the Quartermaster General.
———. Record Group 107: Records of the War Department, Office of the Secretary of War.
———. Record Group 111: Records of the War Department, Office of the Chief Signal Officer.
———. Record Group 112: Records of the War Department, Office of the Surgeon General.
———. Record Group 126: Records of the Interior Department, Office of Territories.
———. Record Group 160: Records of the War Department, Headquarters, Army Service Forces.
———. Record Group 165: Records of the War Department, War Department General Staff.

————. Record Group 253: Records of the Petroleum Administrator for War.

————. Record Group 336: Records of the War Department, Office of the Chief of Transportation.

————. Record Group 338: Records of the War Department, U.S. Army Commands.

————. Record Group 407: Records of the War Department, Adjutant General's Office, World War II Operations Reports.

Yukon Territorial Archives. Yukon Record Group 1.

2. PUBLISHED PUBLIC DOCUMENTS

British Columbia–Yukon–Alaska Highway Commission. *Report on Proposed Highway Through British Columbia and the Yukon Territory to Alaska.* Ottawa: King's Printer for Canada, 1941.

Congressional Record. Washington, DC: GPO.

Huntley, Theodore A., and R. E. Royall. *Construction of the Alaska Highway.* Washington, DC: Public Roads Administration, 1945.

United States-Alaska Road Commission. *The Proposed Pacific Yukon Highway.* Juneau, AK: U.S.-Alaska Road Commission, February 1, 1931.

United States House of Representatives. *76th Congress, 3d Session, House Document No. 711: Report of the Alaskan International Highway Commission to the President.* Washington, DC: GPO, 1940.

————. *Committee on Roads, 79th Congress, 2d Session, Report No. 1705: The Alaska Highway.* Washington DC: GPO, 1946.

United States Senate. *Committee on Post Offices and Post Roads, 78th Congress, 1st Session, Report No. 548: The Alaska Highway.* Washington, DC: GPO, 1943.

————. *Hearing Before a Subcommittee of the Committee on Foreign Relations, 77th Congress, 3d Session, on S. Res. 253, a Resolution Providing for an Investigation as to the Location of the Alaska Highway.* Washington, DC: GPO, 1942.

————. *Hearings Before a Special Committee Investigating the National Defense Program, 78th Congress, 1st Session, Report No. 11, Part 22: The CANOL Project.* Washington, DC: GPO, 1944.

————. *Special Committee Investigating the National Defense Program, 78th Congress, 1st Session, Report No. 10, Part 14: The CANOL Project.* Washington, DC: GPO, 1944.

3. BOOKS

Atwood, George H. *Along the Alcan.* New York: Pageant Press, 1960.

Christy, Jim. *Rough Road to the North: Travels Along the Alaska Highway.* Garden City, NY: Doubleday, 1980.

Davis, Benjamin O., Jr. *Benjamin O. Davis, Jr., American: An Autobiography.* Washington, DC: Smithsonian Institution Press, 1991.

Hull, Cordell. *The Memoirs of Cordell Hull.* New York: Macmillan, 1948.

Ickes, Harold L. *The Autobiography of a Curmudgeon.* New York: Reynal and Hitchcock, 1943.

Lindbergh, Anne Morrow. *North to the Orient.* New York: Harcourt, Brace, 1935.

The Long Trail: 341st Engineers on the Alaska Military Highway, 1942–1943. Charlotte, NC: Herald Press.

McGuire, Phillip, ed. *Taps for a Jim Crow Army: Letters from Black Soldiers in World War II.* Santa Barbara, CA: ABC-Clio, 1983.

Nalty, Bernard C., and Morris J. MacGregor, eds. *Blacks in the Military: Essential Documents.* Wilmington, DE: Scholarly Resources, 1981.

Reese, Herbert R. *Seventy Years Down the Road.* Hawley, MN: Hawley Herald, 1973.

Romig, Emily Craig. *A Pioneer Woman in Alaska.* Caldwell, ID: Caxton Printers, 1948.

Stefansson, Vilhjalmur. *Discovery: The Autobiography of Vilhjalmur Stefansson.* New York: McGraw-Hill, 1964.

Stimson, Henry L., and McGeorge Bundy. *On Active Service in Peace and War.* New York: Harper & Row, 1947.

Strong, F. S., Jr. *What's It All About?: Thoughts from the Nineties.* Privately published, 1985.

Truman, Harry S. *Memoirs.* Vol. 1, *Year of Decisions.* Garden City, NY: Doubleday, 1955.

4. UNPUBLISHED PERSONAL PAPERS, CORRESPONDENCE, AND MANUSCRIPTS

Byrnes, Slim. "Trails North." Public Library, Fort St. John, BC.

Calverly, Dorothea. "The Rails Bring Life to a Pioneer Village." School District Resource Center, Public Library, Dawson Creek, BC.

Dimond, Anthony. Papers. Rasmuson Library, UAKF.

Hoge, William M. Papers. Command and General Staff College Library, Fort Leavenworth, KS. (OHCE has copies.)

Pauley, Edwin W. "Why Truman Is President." Truman papers. Harry S. Truman Library, Independence, Mo.

Stefansson, Vilhjalmur. Papers. Baker Library, Dartmouth College, Hanover, NH.

Stermer, Helen Twichell. "Pearl Harbor: The Way It Was." Twichell papers. (See below.)

Twichell, Heath, Sr. "An Engineer's Story." In author's possession until 12/31/92; thereafter, in OHCE.

————. Papers. In author's possession until 12/31/92; thereafter, in OHCE.

5. CORRESPONDENCE AND/OR INTERVIEWS *RE* THE ALASKA HIGHWAY

a. *Between the Author and the Following:*

Randall Acord, Fairbanks, Alaska.
Robert Auld, Fort St. John, British Columbia.
Audrey Proctor Aylard, Teslin, Yukon.
Bob Beatty, Fort St. John, British Columbia.
Charlie Benson, Whitehorse, Yukon.
Bruce Boynton, Skagway, Alaska.
Eddie Broadhagen, Watson Lake, Yukon.
Earl Brown, Fort Nelson, British Columbia.
Charlie Burnham, Skagway, Alaska.
Gordon Caller, Dawson Creek, British Columbia.
Dorothea Calverly, Dawson Creek, British Columbia.
Al and Dorothy Chappell, Fort Nelson, British Columbia.
Melville Clark, Fort St. John, British Columbia.
Sid Cooper, Dawson Creek, British Columbia.
Orval Couch, Whitehorse, Yukon.
John Cox, Fort St. John, British Columbia.
Laurent Cyr, Whitehorse, Yukon.
Byrnes Ellender, Billings, Montana
Dean Elston, Whitehorse, Yukon.
Molly Galbreath, Mentasta, Alaska.
Fr. Gallart, Skagway, Alaska.
Charles Gardner, Hempstead, New York.
Andrew Gayak, Fairbanks, Alaska.
Lodema George, Fort Nelson, British Columbia.
Jack Guiness, Muncho Lake, British Columbia.
Ed Hanousek, Skagway, Alaska.
Wansley Hill, Yeadon, Pennsylvania.
Celia Hunter, Fairbanks, Alaska.
Robert Ingalls (son of Col. Ingalls), Reno, Nevada.
Thomas Ingalls (son of Col. Ingalls), Burlington, North Carolina.
Fred Johns, Dawson Creek, British Columbia.
Vic Johnson, Watson Lake, Yukon.

Sam Johnston, Teslin, Yukon.
Chaddie Kelly, Delta Junction, Alaska.
Kay Kennedy, Fairbanks, Alaska.
Leo Kozul, Fort St. John, British Columbia.
Gordon Leenerts, San Bernardino, California.
Reginald Lucas, Fort St. John, British Columbia.
Jack MacDonald, Whitehorse, Yukon.
John and Linda MacDonald, Watson Lake, Yukon.
Walter Mason, Lexington, Virginia.
Malcolm Moe, Skagway, Alaska.
Burt Moffatt, Dawson Creek, British Columbia.
Carl Molby, Tok, Alaska.
Carl Mulvihill, Skagway, Alaska.
Louise and Russ Novodvorsji, Watson Lake, Yukon.
John Ohl, Mesa, Arizona.
George Owens, Jackson, Mississippi.
Cecil Pickell, Fort St. John, British Columbia.
Ralph Pomeroy, Fort St. John, British Columbia.
Fr. Pierre Poullet, Fort Nelson, British Columbia.
George Rapuzzi, Skagway, Alaska.
Day Roberts, Dawson Creek, British Columbia.
Paul Smith, Tok, Alaska.
Ken Spotswood, Whitehorse, Yukon.
Marvin Taylor, Whitehorse, Yukon.
Ralph Thomson, Dawson Creek, British Columbia.
Robert Thorkelson, Hayden Lake, Idaho.
Frank Turner, Arlington, Virginia.
Lloyd Vandergrift, Dawson Creek, British Columbia.
Cora Ventress, Fort St. John, British Columbia.
Art Webb, Dawson Creek, British Columbia.
Ginny Hill Wood, Fairbanks, Alaska.
Al Wright, Whitehorse, Yukon.
Walter Wright, Dawson Creek, British Columbia.
b. *By Other Interviewers:*
William M. Hoge. Interviewed by Lieutenant Colonel George Robertson on Jan. 14–15 and Apr. 15–17, 1974, under the auspices of the Senior Officer Debriefing Program, U.S. Army Military History Research Collection, Carlisle Barracks, Pennsylvania. (Copy of transcript is in CMH.)
Mike Miletich. Interviewed by Ruth Twichell Cochrane at Fort Belvoir, Virginia, in August 1967. Tape and transcript in Twichell papers.
Leslie Spoonts and Ginny Hill Wood. Tapes in Oral History Collection, Alaska and Polar Regions Department, UAKF.

6. MAPS AND GUIDE BOOKS

"Alaska Highway." *Mundy's Pocket Map of Northwest Canada and Part of Alaska.* Edmonton, Alta.: C. G. Mundy Map, 1943.
Canada and United States, 1:1,000,000, ONC Sheets C-9, 10; D-10, 11, 12. Edition 5. St. Louis: Defense Mapping Agency, 1985.
Cole, Terrence. *Ghosts of the Gold Rush: A Walking Tour of Fairbanks.* Fairbanks: Tanana-Yukon Historical Society,
The Milepost: All-the-North Travel Guide. Anchorage: Alaska Northwest Publishing, 1991. (Updated yearly.)
Peace River Alaska Highway Tourist Association. *Travel Guide.* Kalispell, MT: Northwest Publishing, 1982.

Yukon Government. *The All About Yukon Book*. Whitehorse: Ministry of Tourism and Economic Development, 1980.

7. PHOTOGRAPHIC SOURCES

Canada National Archives.
Couch, Orval. Whitehorse, Yukon.
Rasmuson Library, UAKF.
Singley, Mark. Belle Mead, New Jersey.
South Peace Historical Society, Dawson Creek, British Columbia.
Stefansson papers.
Twichell papers.
United States National Archives.
United States Army, OHCE.

B. SECONDARY SOURCES

1. REFERENCE WORKS

Dictionary of American Biography. New York: Charles Scribner's Sons.
Encyclopedia Americana. Danbury, CT: Grolier.
Encyclopedia of World Biography. New York: McGraw-Hill.
Langer, William L., ed. *Encyclopedia of World History*. Boston: Houghton Mifflin, 1962.
Morison, Samuel Eliot. *Oxford History of the American People*. New York: Oxford University Press, 1965.
Morris, Richard B., ed. *Encyclopedia of American History*. New York: Harper & Row, 1961.

2. OTHER BOOKS

Barry, Patricia S. *The CANOL Project: An Adventure of the U.S. War Department in Canada's Northwest*. Limited ed. Edmonton, Alta.: Atlas Book Bindery, 1985.
Borg, Dorothy, and Shumpei Okamoto, eds. *Pearl Harbor as History: Japanese-American Relations, 1931–1941*. New York: Columbia University Press, 1973.
Brooks, Alfred Hulse. *Blazing Alaska's Trails*. 2d ed. Fairbanks: University of Alaska Press, 1973
Buchanan, A. Russell. *Black Americans in World War II*. Santa Barbara, CA: ABC-Clio, 1977.
Bykofsky, Joseph, and Harold Larson. *United States Army in World War II, The Technical Services: The Transportation Corps: Operations Overseas*. Washington, DC: GPO, 1957.
Cloe, John Haile. *Top Cover for America: The Air Force in Alaska, 1920–1983*. Missoula, MT: Pictorial Histories Publishing, 1984.
Coates, Kenneth S., ed. *The Alaska Highway: Papers of the 40th Anniversary Symposium*. Vancouver: University of British Columbia Press, 1985.
Coates, Kenneth S., and William R. Morrison. *The Alaska Highway in World War II: The U.S. Army of Occupation in Canada's Northwest*. Norman, OK: University of Oklahoma Press, 1992.
Cohen, Stan. *The Trail of '42: A Pictorial History of the Alaska Highway*. Missoula, MT: Pictorial Histories Publishing, 1979.
————. *The Forgotten War: A Pictorial History of World War II in Alaska and Northwestern Canada*. Missoula, MT: Pictorial Histories Publishing, 1981.
Cole, Dermot. *Frank Barr: Bush Pilot in Alaska and the Yukon*. Edmonds, WA: Northwest Publishing, 1986.
Coll, Blanche D., Jean E. Keith, and Herbert H. Rosenthal. *United States Army in World War II, The Technical Services: The Corps of Engineers: Troops and Equipment*. Washington, DC: GPO, 1958.

Conn, Stetson, and Byron Fairchild. *United States Army in World War II, The Western Hemisphere: The Framework of Hemisphere Defense.* Washington, DC: GPO, 1960.

Current, Richard N. *Secretary Stimson: A Study in Statecraft.* New Brunswick, NJ: Rutgers University Press, 1954.

Daniels, Jonathan. *The Man of Independence.* New York: J. B. Lippincott, 1950.

Davies, Marguerite, and Cora A. Ventress. *Fort St. John Pioneer Profiles.* Fort St. John, BC: Fort St. John Centennial Committee, 1971.

Davies, Marguerite, Edith Kyllo, and Cora A. Ventress. *The Peacemakers of North Peace.* Fort St. John, BC: Davies, Ventress & Kyllo, Publishers, 1973.

Diubaldo, Richard. *Stefansson and the Canadian Arctic.* Montreal: McGill-Queen's University Press, 1978.

Dod, Karl C. *United States Army in World War II, The Technical Services: The Corps of Engineers in the War Against Japan.* Washington, DC: GPO, 1966.

Dziuban, Stanley W. *United States Army in World War II, Special Studies: Military Relations Between the United States and Canada, 1939–1945.* Washington, DC: GPO, 1959.

Ellis, Frank H. *Canada's Flying Heritage.* Toronto: University of Toronto Press, 1954.

Finnie, Richard. *CANOL: The Sub-Arctic Pipeline and Refinery Project Constructed by Bechtel-Price-Callahan for the Corps of Engineers, United States Army, 1942–1944.* San Francisco: Ryder and Ingram, 1945.

Franklin, John Hope, and August Meier, eds. *Black Leaders of the Twentieth Century.* Chicago: University of Illinois Press, 1982.

Godsell, Philip H. *Pilots of the Purple Twilight.* Toronto: Ryerson Press, 1955.

———. *The Romance of the Alaska Highway.* Toronto: Ryerson Press, 1944.

Hodgson, Godfrey. *The Colonel: The Life and Wars of Henry Stimson, 1867–1950.* New York: Alfred A. Knopf, 1990.

Ingram, Robert L. *The Bechtel Story.* San Francisco, 1968.

Keil, Sally VanWagenen. *Those Wonderful Women and Their Flying Machines: The Unknown Heroines of World War II.* New York: Rawson, Wade Publishers, 1979.

Keith, Ronald A. *Bush Pilot with a Briefcase: The Happy-Go-Lucky Story of Grant McConachie.* Don Mills, Ont.: General Publishing, 1972.

Kessner, Thomas. *Fiorello H. LaGuardia and the Making of Modern New York.* New York: McGraw-Hill, 1989.

Kirwan, L. P. *A History of Polar Exploration.* New York: W. W. Norton, 1960.

Lee, Ulysses. *United States Army in World War II, Special Studies: The Employment of Negro Troops.* Washington, DC: GPO, 1966.

Leighton, Richard M., and Robert W. Coakley. *United States Army in World War II, The War Department: Global Logistics and Strategy, 1940–1943.* Washington, DC: GPO, 1955.

Lipset, Seymour Martin. *Continental Divide: The Values and Institutions of the United States and Canada.* New York: Routledge, 1990.

Long, John Sherman. *McCord of Alaska: Statesman for the Last Frontier.* Cleveland: Dillon, Liederbach, 1975.

McGinniss, Joe. *Going to Extremes.* New York: Alfred A. Knopf, 1980.

MacGregor, Morris J. *Integration of the Armed Forces, 1940–1965.* Washington, DC: GPO, 1981.

McPhee, John. *Coming into the Country.* New York: Farrar, Straus & Giroux, 1976.

Menzies, Don. *The Alaska Highway: A Saga of the North.* Edmonton, Alta.: Douglas Printing, 1943.

Michener, James A. *The Journey.* Toronto: McClelland and Stewart, 1989.

Minter, Roy. *White Pass: Gateway to the Klondike.* Toronto: McClelland and Stewart, 1987.

Morenus, Richard. *Alaska Sourdough: The Story of Slim Williams.* New York: Rand McNally, 1956.

Neatsby, Leslie H. *Conquest of the Last Frontier.* Athens, OH: Ohio University Press, 1961.

Pogue, Forrest C. *George C. Marshall: Ordeal and Hope, 1939–1942.* New York: Viking Press, 1966.

Prange, Gordon W. *At Dawn We Slept: The Untold Story of Pearl Harbor*. New York: Penguin Books, 1981.

Remley, David A. *Crooked Road: The Story of the Alaska Highway*. New York: McGraw-Hill, 1976.

Riddle, Donald H. *The Truman Committee: A Study in Congressional Responsibility*. New Brunswick, NJ: Rutgers University Press, 1964.

Satterfield, Archie. *Alaska Bush Pilots in the Float Country*. Seattle: Superior Publishing, 1969.

Smith, Jean Edward. *Lucius D. Clay: An American Life*. New York: Henry Holt, 1990.

Stacey, Charles P. *Arms, Men and Governments: The War Policies of Canada, 1939–1945*. Ottawa: Queen's Printer for Canada, 1970.

Stamps, T. Dodson, and Vincent J. Esposito, eds. *A Military History of World War II*. Vol. I, *Operations in the European Theater*. West Point, NY: United States Military Academy, 1953.

Stefansson, Vilhjalmur. *Northwest to Fortune: The Search of Western Man for a Commercially Practical Route to the Far East*. New York: Duell, Sloan & Pearce, 1958.

ten Broek, Jacobus, Edward Barnhart and Floyd Matson. *Prejudice, War and the Constitution: Causes and Consequences of the Evacuation of the Japanese Americans in World War II*. Berkeley, CA: University of California Press, 1954.

Thompson, George R., Dixie R. Harris, Pauline M. Oakes, and Dulaney Terrett. *United States Army in World War II, The Technical Services: The Signal Corps: The Test*. Washington: GPO, 1957.

Watkins, T. H. *Righteous Pilgrim: The Life and Times of Harold L. Ickes, 1874–1952*. New York: Henry Holt, 1990.

Watson, Mark Skinner. *United States Army in World War II, Chief of Staff: Prewar Plans and Preparations*. Washington, DC: GPO, 1950.

Whiting, Fenton Blakemore. *Grit, Grief and Gold: A True Narrative of an Alaska Pathfinder*. Seattle, WA: Peacock Publishing, 1933.

Wohlstetter, Roberta. *Pearl Harbor: Warning and Decision*. Stanford, CA: Stanford University Press, 1962.

3. NEWSPAPERS, MAGAZINES AND TECHNICAL JOURNALS

Air Force Magazine
Alaska Highway News
Alaska Life
Alaska Sportsman
Alaska Weekly
American Aviation
American Mercury
Assembly
Audubon Magazine
Baltimore Sun
Boston Globe
Boston Herald
Canadian Geographical Journal
Canadian Surveyor
Chicago Tribune
Civil Engineering
Collier's
Contractors and Engineers Monthly
Edmonton Bulletin
Edmonton Journal
Engineering News Record
Fairbanks Daily News Miner

Foreign Affairs
Fortune
Geographical Review
Grand Rapids Herald
Highway Magazine
Infantry Journal
Liberty
Life
Los Angeles Times
Maclean's
Military Engineer
National Geographic
Nation's Business
New York Times
New York Tribune
Northern Engineer
Ottawa Journal
Peace River Block News
Pic
Portland Oregonian
Roads and Streets
San Francisco Chronicle

Saturday Evening Post
Seattle Post-Intelligencer
Tacoma Evening News
Time
Vancouver Sun
Washington Post
Washington Star
Washington Times Herald

Western Construction News
Whitehorse Star
World Petroleum
Yank
Yukon Anniversaries Commission News-letter
Yukon News

4. UNPUBLISHED MATERIALS

Brown, Ralph. "Men of the High Iron." In UAKF.

Carr, Edwin R. "Great Falls to Nome: The Inland Air Route to Alaska." Ph.D. dissertation, University of Minnesota, 1946.

Jackson, Stanley L. "Stringing Wire Toward Tokyo: A Brief History of the Alaska Military Highway Telephone Line." U.S. Army Signal Corps Historical Monograph, Project E-1. In CMH.

Lecky, Charles S. "The CANOL Project and the Alaska Highway." Report compiled under the direction of the Northwest Division Engineer, 1944. In OHCE.

Palfreyman, W. C. "History of the Whitehorse Sector of the ALCAN Highway." 10 June 1943. In OHCE.

Robbins, Rebecca. "Canadian-American Cooperation in World War II: Communications with Alaska." Paper submitted for course in American Diplomatic History at Georgetown University. Spring 1978. In CMH.

Rust, Ken. "History of the 18th Engineers (Combat) in the Yukon Territory." In OHCE.

Selby, Robert H. "Earthmovers in World War II: R. G. LeTourneau and His Machines." Ph.D. dissertation, Case Western Reserve University, 1970. In OHCE.

United States National Resources Planning Board, Alaska Regional Planning Office. "Post-Defense Economic Development in Alaska." October 1941. In CMH.

United States Army. Alaskan Department. "Official History of the Alaskan Department, June 1940–June 1944." In CMH.

United States Department of State, Division of Research and Reports. "Report on War Aid Furnished by the United States to the U.S.S.R.," November 28, 1945. In CMH.

————. Service Forces. "The Alaska Highway." Control Division Report compiled for the Commanding General of Army Service Forces, May 1945. In OHCE.

————. Service Forces. "Report on CANOL Project." Control Division Report compiled for the Commanding General of Army Service Forces, 1 June 1945. In OHCE.

————. Western Defense Command. "History of the Western Defense Command, 17 March 1941–30 September 1945." In CMH.

Willson, Roger E. "The Truman Committee." Ph.D. dissertation, Harvard University, 1966.

INDEX

ABOUT THE AUTHOR

Heath Twichell grew up during World War II in State College, Pennsylvania, while his father was helping to build the Alaska Highway. Like his father, he chose a military career, graduating from West Point as an infantry lieutenant in 1956.

Many of Twichell's assignments took him where history was being made. In 1958, as a member of the 101st Airborne Division, he helped protect black students as they integrated Little Rock's Central High School; in 1968, he was stationed near Saigon with the 1st Infantry Division during the pivotal Tet offensive; four years later, he was again in Vietnam, this time as an advisor to a South Vietnamese regiment guarding the DMZ, when the North Vietnamese army opened the final phase of the Vietnam war by attacking in force across that line.

The Army also gave Twichell the opportunity to become a teacher. After receiving an MA in modern European history from American University in 1964, he spent three years as an instructor at West Point. In 1970 he returned to American University to finish his Ph.D. His dissertation, a biography of Major General Henry T. Allen, a distinguished figure of the World War I era, won the Allan Nevins prize in American history and was published by Rutgers

University Press in 1974. Graduating from the U.S. Naval War College in 1977, he stayed on to become a faculty member, teaching history, political science, and international relations to senior military and civilian officials.

Following his retirement from active duty in 1980, Twichell organized and became the first director of the graduate program in international relations at Salve Regina University in Newport, Rhode Island. He resigned from that position in 1988 to write this book.